GLOBAL LEGAL PLURALISM

We live in a world of legal pluralism, where a single act or actor is potentially regulated by multiple legal or quasi-legal regimes imposed by state, substate, transnational, supranational, and nonstate communities. Navigating these spheres of complex overlapping legal authority is inevitably confusing, and we cannot expect territorial borders to solve all the problems that arise because legal norms inevitably flow across such borders. At the same time, trying to create one universal set of legal rules is also often unsuccessful because the sheer variety of human communities and interests thwarts such efforts.

Instead, we need an alternative jurisprudence, one that seeks to create or preserve spaces for productive interaction among multiple overlapping legal systems by developing procedural mechanisms, institutions, and practices that aim to manage, without eliminating, the legal pluralism we see around us. Such mechanisms, institutions, and practices can help mediate conflicts, and we may find that the added norms, viewpoints, and participants that are included actually produce better decision making, better adherence to those decisions by participants and non-participants alike, and ultimately better real-world outcomes. *Global Legal Pluralism* provides a broad synthesis across a variety of legal doctrines and academic disciplines and offers a novel conceptualization of law and globalization.

Paul Schiff Berman is Dean and Robert Kramer Research Professor of Law at The George Washington University Law School. Before arriving at George Washington, he was Dean and Foundation Professor of Law at the Sandra Day O'Connor College of Law at Arizona State University. He has also served as the Jesse Root Professor of Law at the University of Connecticut School of Law and as a Visiting Professor and Visiting Research Scholar at Princeton University in the Program in Law and Public Affairs. Berman has published two edited collections, authored a pioneering casebook on cyberlaw, and written more than 25 scholarly articles and book chapters. He has also served on the Organizing Committee of the Association for the Study of Law, Culture, and the Humanities.

Global Legal Pluralism

A JURISPRUDENCE OF LAW BEYOND BORDERS

Paul Schiff Berman

The George Washington University Law School

CAMBRIDGE
UNIVERSITY PRESS

CAMBRIDGE UNIVERSITY PRESS
Cambridge, New York, Melbourne, Madrid, Cape Town,
Singapore, São Paulo, Delhi, Mexico City

Cambridge University Press
32 Avenue of the Americas, New York, NY 10013-2473, USA

www.cambridge.org
Information on this title: www.cambridge.org/9780521769822

First published 2012
Reprinted 2012

A catalog record for this publication is available from the British Library.

Library of Congress Cataloging in Publication Data

Berman, Paul Schiff.
Global legal pluralism : a jurisprudence of law beyond borders / Paul Schiff Berman.
p. cm.
Includes index.
ISBN 978-0-521-76982-2 (hardback)
1. Legal polycentricity. 2. Globalization and law. I. Title.
K236.B47 2012
340.9–dc23 2011030488

ISBN 978-0-521-76982-2 Hardback

To my parents, Ellyn and Benjamin, whose support has been unconditional, no matter the path I have taken.

To my wife, Laura, whose radiant spirit piles loveliness upon loveliness.

To my son, Julien, whose talents are plural and whose reach is global.

Contents

Acknowledgments

This book has, alas, been in gestation for more than a decade, with work on it delayed by the birth of our son, two deanships, four academic moves (including two of the transcontinental sort), and a host of other intervening events. As a result, the number of people and institutions that have supported and contributed to the finished product is quite large, and reconstructing a truly comprehensive list is daunting and likely doomed to failures of omission. Nevertheless, I have been part of so many supportive academic communities, and so many generous colleagues have offered advice along the way, that it would be churlish not at least to try to acknowledge the many debts I owe.

First, I have benefited greatly from my time at four different academic institutions while writing this book: the University of Connecticut School of Law, the Princeton University Program in Law and Public Affairs, the Sandra Day O'Connor College of Law at Arizona State University, and The George Washington University Law School. At each location, I received important research support as well as significant wisdom from colleagues, wisdom that in all cases has altered the shape of the finished product.

Second, I have presented parts of the arguments contained here at conferences, workshops, and other academic gatherings over the past decade, including, at the beginning, a trial run of the article that became *The Globalization of Jurisdiction* at the Yale/Stanford Junior Faculty Forum at Yale Law School, and later including presentations and workshops at American University, Amherst College, Boston College, UCLA, Columbia University, Duke University, University of Exeter, Georgetown University, University of Georgia, Goethe University in Frankfurt, Harvard Law School's Berkman Center on Internet and Society, Hofstra University, Humboldt University in Berlin, University of Missouri, Kyoonpook National University in Korea, University College of London,University of Montreal, Notre Dame University, University of Oregon, University of Pennsylvania, Princeton University, Temple University, University of Texas, University of Tulsa, University of Utah, Washington & Lee University, Willamette University, and two subsequent return visits to Yale. I am grateful to participants at those gatherings for probing questions, further examples, and useful insights.

Third, I must name individually the many colleagues who have gone beyond simply the norm of academic discourse to read drafts, make comments, provide advice, answer questions, or offer suggestions. These individuals include David Abraham, Robert Ahdieh, T. Alexander Aleinikoff, Kenneth Anderson, Rachel Barkow, Timothy W. Bartley, Lofty Becker, Patricia L. Bellia, Bethany Berger, Phillip Blumberg, Dan Bodansky, Mary Anne Case, Kamari Maxine Clarke, Sarah H. Cleveland, Anne Dailey, Anthony D'Amato, Meg deGuzman, Anuj Desai, Laura A. Dickinson, Graeme Dinwoodie, Mark Drumbl, Jeff Dunoff, Christine Haight Farley, David Fontana, Katherine Franke, Marc Galanter, Kate Gordon, Robert W. Gordon, Jacob Hacker, Hendrik Hartog, Helen Hershkoff, Rhoda Howard-Hassman, Dan Hunter, Vicki Jackson, Mark W. Janis, Jonathan Kahn, Stan Katz, Lisa Kloppenberg, Harold Hongju Koh, Stephen Kotkin, Janet Koven Levit, Peter Lindseth, David Luban, Stewart Macaulay, Chibli Mallat, Jamie Mayerfield, Peggy McGuiness, Sally Engle Merry, Naomi Mezey, Ralf Michaels, Russell Miller, Andrew Moravcsik, Ved Nanda, Noah Novagrodsky, Diane Orentlicher, Leonard Orland, Mark Osiel, Hari Osofsky, Jeremy Paul, Deborah N. Pearlstein, Mark Pollack, Richard Pomp, David G. Post, Catherine Powell, Margaret Jane Radin, Balakrishnan Rajagopal, Jaya Ramji-Nogales, Michael Reisman, Judith Resnik, Ellen Rigsby, Lawrence Rosen, Mark Rosen, Richard J. Ross,

Ted Ruger, Austin Sarat, Kim Lane Schepple, David Schneiderman, Vicki Schultz, Gregory Shaffer, Peter Siegelman, Kathryn Sikkink, Linda Silberman, Susan Silbey, Anne-Marie Slaughter, Avi Soifer, Clyde Spillinger, Peter Spiro, Allan Stein, Catherine T. Struve, Colin Tait, Brian Z. Tamanaha, Gunther Teubner, David R. Tillinghast, Cora True-Frost, Wibren van der Burg, Carlos Vazquez, Leti Volpp, Kay B. Warren, Carol Weisbrod, Siegfried Wiessner, Steven Wilf, and Andrew Willard.

Three scholarly debts in particular I must underline: Kay Warren, for first introducing me to the powerful lens that cultural anthropology offers to understand the world; Carol Weisbrod, for an offhand comment that became the genesis for this book (something along the lines of "You keep talking about when communities are allowed to assert jurisdiction, but communities don't ask you or anyone else for permission to assert jurisdiction; they simply do so."); and Laura Dickinson, my wife, who has read every word of my work for the past fourteen years, offering both love and insight all along the way.

Fourth, a wide variety of student research assistants have, over the years, helped me in developing what has become the final manuscript. These assistants include Shannon Bratt, Brad Burns, Rita Bustos, Marilee Corr, Kyle Cramer, Ronald Crawley, Emily Dean, Monica Debiak, Lynn Fountain, Dave Gaetano, Sarah Gessner, Joshua Horton, Jennifer Montgomery, Lorene Park, Jeffrey Pease, Dorothy Puzio, Michelle Querijiero, Alllison Rohrer, Nina Robertson, Marianne Sadowski, Monika Silva, Shuyuan Tang, Ashley Williams, Heather Wood, and Lily Yan. Special thanks are owed to James Kite and William Knight for extraordinary work on the final manuscript.

Fifth, as befits a work in gestation over a long period, I have tried out elements of the argument contained herein in my prior published work. Accordingly, this book includes excerpts from:

Conflict of Laws and the Legal Negotiation of Difference, in *Law and the Stranger* (Austin D. Sarat, Martha Umphrey, & Lawrence Douglas, eds., 2010)

Towards a Jurisprudence of Hybridity, 2010 *Utah L. Rev.* 11

The New Legal Pluralism, 5 *Ann. Rev. of L. & Social Sciences* 225 (2009)

Federalism and International Law through the Lens of Legal Pluralism, 73 *Missouri L. Rev.* 1149 (2009)

Global Legal Pluralism, 80 *S. Cal. L. Rev.* 1155 (2007)

A Pluralist Approach to International Law, 32 *Yale J. Int'l L.* 301 (2007)

Seeing beyond the Limits of International Law, 84 *Tex. L. Rev.* 1265 (2006) (reviewing *The Limits of International Law*, by Jack L. Goldsmith and Eric A. Posner)

From International Law to Law and Globalization, 43 *Colum. J. Transnational L.* 485 (2005)

Conflict of Laws, Globalization, and Cosmopolitan Pluralism, 51 *Wayne L. Rev.* 1105 (2005)

Towards a Cosmopolitan Vision of Conflict of Laws: Redefining Governmental Interests in a Global Era, 153 *U. Pa. L. Rev.* 1819 (2005) and

The Globalization of Jurisdiction, 151 *U. Pa. L. Rev.* 311 (2002)

Finally, I note that no creation is truly the work of one person. Victor Hugo, in describing the great cathedrals of Europe, pointed out that in all cases time is the true architect and the community is the builder. This book arises from a particular moment in time and a particular intellectual community, and I am grateful to be able to add these thoughts to an ongoing conversation that never ends. I feel privileged to be part of the dialogue.

Part I MAPPING A HYBRID WORLD

1 Introduction

WE LIVE IN A WORLD OF MULTIPLE OVERLAPPING normative communities. For example, I am typing these words in a house in Massachusetts, although I am a resident of Maryland, who works in Washington, DC. Thus, Massachusetts state law may govern some of my activities, while Maryland law or DC law may be relevant to other aspects of my life. And in Massachusetts, Maryland, and DC I am also located within a variety of political sub-divisions, such as towns, cities, counties, wards, neighborhood districts, water regions, and so on, each of which may have normative authority over me. Federal law governs many aspects of my life as well, from the speed limits on the interstate highways to certain environmental standards affecting the air and water, to the individual liberties the U.S. Constitution protects. International law may be the source of additional rights or protections, ranging from standards for trade, technology, and the use of satellites to the frameworks for regulating the environment, consumer product labeling, and the conduct of war. And certainly if I travel abroad or surf Internet sites based overseas or enter into contracts with foreign entities I will run up against international and transnational legal norms.

But these governmental normative communities are just the tip of the iceberg. Nonstate communities may also impose significant normative force. For example, if I think someone is violating the copyright of this book, I may use international arbitration sanctioned by the World

Intellectual Property Organization, a nongovernmental entity. If Web searches for my book do not place my Web page high enough on the list, I may need to challenge Google's search indexing protocols. And I am governed (or at least strongly influenced) by tenure rules at my university, religious rules of my faith (if I am a believer), American Bar Association rules regarding the conduct of law school classrooms, the metrics used by *US News & World Report* when it ranks law schools, and simply the practices and customs of the academic community of which I am a part. And on and on.

This book seeks to grapple with the complexities of law in a world where a single act or actor is potentially regulated by multiple legal or quasi-legal regimes. Law often operates based on a convenient fiction that nation-states exist in autonomous, territorially distinct spheres and that activities therefore fall under the legal jurisdiction of only one regime at a time. Thus, traditional legal rules have tied jurisdiction to territory: a state could exercise complete authority within its territorial borders and no authority beyond it. In the twentieth century, such rules were loosened, but territorial location remained the principal touchstone for assigning legal authority. Accordingly, if one could spatially ground a dispute, one could most likely determine the legal rule that would apply.

But consider such a system in today's world. Should the U.S. government be able to sidestep the U.S. Constitution when it houses prisoners in "offshore" detention facilities in Guantánamo Bay or elsewhere around the world? Should spatially distant corporations that create serious local harms be able to escape local legal regulation simply because they are not physically located in the jurisdiction? When the U.S. government seeks to shut down the computer of a hacker located in Russia, does the virus transmitted constitute an act of war or a violation of Russia's sovereignty? Does it make sense to think that satellite transmissions, online interactions, and complex financial transactions have any territorial locus at all? How can we best understand the complex relationships among international, regional, national, and subnational legal systems?

And in a world where nonstate actors such as industry standard-setting bodies, nongovernmental organizations, religious institutions, ethnic groups, terrorist networks, and others exert significant normative pull, can we build a sufficiently capacious understanding of the very idea of jurisdiction to address the incredible array of overlapping authorities that are our daily reality?

Thus, a simple model that looks only to territorial delineations among official state-based legal systems is now simply untenable (if it was ever useful to begin with). Thankfully, debates about globalization have moved beyond the polarizing question of whether the nation-state is dying or not. But one does not need to believe in the death of the nation-state to recognize both that physical location can no longer be the sole criterion for conceptualizing legal authority and that nation-states must work within a framework of multiple overlapping jurisdictional assertions by state, international, and even nonstate communities. Each of these types of overlapping jurisdictional assertions creates a potentially hybrid legal space that is not easily eliminated.

With regard to conflicts between and among states, the growth of global communications technologies, the rise of multinational corporate entities with no significant territorial center of gravity, and the mobility of capital and people across borders mean that many jurisdictions will feel effects of activities around the globe, leading inevitably to multiple assertions of legal authority over the same act, without regard to territorial location. For example, in 2000 a French court asserted jurisdiction over the U.S.-based web portal Yahoo! because French users could download Nazi memorabilia and Holocaust denial material via Yahoo!'s auction sites, in violation of French law.[1] Yahoo! argued in response that the French assertion of jurisdiction was impermissibly extraterritorial in scope because Yahoo!, as a U.S. corporation transmitting material

[1] Tribunal de grande instance (TGI) [ordinary court of original jurisdiction] Paris, May 22, 2000, Ordonnance de référé, *UEJF et Licra c/ Yahoo! Inc. et Yahoo France*, *available at* http://www.juriscom.net/txt/jurisfr/cti/tgiparis20000522.htm.

uploaded in the United States, was protected by the First Amendment of the U.S. Constitution.[2] Yet, the extraterritoriality charge runs in both directions. If France is *not* able to block the access of French citizens to proscribed material, then the United States will effectively be imposing First Amendment norms on the entire world. And whatever the solution to this problem might be, a territorial analysis will not help because the relevant transaction is both "in" France and not "in" France simultaneously. Cross-border environmental,[3] trade,[4] intellectual property,[5] and tax regulation[6] raise similar issues.

The problem of multiple states' asserting jurisdiction over the same activity is just the beginning, however, because nation-states must also often share legal authority with one or more international and regional courts, tribunals, or regulatory entities. Indeed, the Project on International Courts and Tribunals has identified approximately 125 international institutions, all issuing decisions that have some effect on state legal authority,[7] though those decisions are sometimes deemed binding, sometimes merely persuasive, and often fall somewhere between the two. For example, under the North American Free Trade Agreement (NAFTA) and other similar agreements, special panels can pass judgment

[2] *Id.*

[3] *See, e.g.*, *Transboundary Harm* in *International Law: Lessons from the Trail Smelter Arbitration* (Rebecca M. Bratspies & Russell A. Miller eds., 2006); Philippe Sands, Turtles and Torturers: The Transformation of International Law, *33 N.Y.U. J. Int'l L. & Pol.* 527 (2001).

[4] *See, e.g.*, Richard W. Parker, The Use and Abuse of Trade Leverage to Protect the Global Commons: What We Can Learn from the Tuna-Dolphin Conflict, 12 *Geo. Int'l Envtl. L. Rev.* 1 (1999).

[5] *See, e.g.*, *Barcelona.com, Inc. v. Excelentisimo Ayuntamiento de Barcelona,* 330 F.3d 617 (4th Cir. 2003); *GlobalSantaFe Corp. v. GlobalSantaFe.com,* 250 F. Supp. 2d 610 (E.D. Va. 2003); Graeme B. Dinwoodie, A New Copyright Order: Why National Courts Should Create Global Norms, 149 *U. Pa. L. Rev.* 469 (2000).

[6] *See, e.g.*, Paul Schiff Berman, The Globalization of Jurisdiction, 151 *U. Pa. L. Rev.* 311, 334–7 (2002).

[7] *See* Project on International Courts and Tribunals, The International Judiciary in Context (2004), *available at* http://www.pict-pcti.org/publications/synoptic_chart/Synop_C4.pdf.

on whether domestic legal proceedings have provided fair process.[8] And though the panels cannot directly review or overturn local rulings, they can levy fines against the federal government signatories of the agreement, thereby undermining the impact of the local judgment.[9] Thus, now that a NAFTA tribunal has ruled that the conduct of a Mississippi trial against a Canadian corporation "was so flawed that it constituted a miscarriage of justice amounting to manifest injustice as that expression is understood in international law,"[10] it is an open question as to how Mississippi courts will rule in future cases involving foreign defendants.[11] Meanwhile, in the realm of human rights, we have seen criminal defendants convicted in state courts in the United States proceed (through their governments) to the International Court of Justice (ICJ) to argue that they were denied the right to contact their consulate, as required by treaty.[12] Again, although the ICJ judgments are technically unenforceable in the United States, at least one state court followed the ICJ's command anyway.[13] Meanwhile, outside these more formal adjudicative processes, there are many powerful transnational networks of governmental regulators setting a kind of international policy as a de facto matter over much of the global financial system, among other areas.[14]

Finally, nonstate legal (or quasi-legal) norms add to this pluralism of authority. Given increased migration and global communication, it is not

[8] *See* North American Free Trade Agreement, U.S.-Can.-Mex., Dec. 7–17, 1992, art. 1135, 32 I.L.M. 605, 646.

[9] *Id.*

[10] *Loewen Group, Inc. v. United States*, ICSID (W. Bank) Case No. ARB(AF)/98/3 (June 26, 2003) (Final Merits Award), reprinted in 42 I.L.M. 811 (2003), *also available at* http://naftaclaims.com/Disputes/USA/Loewen/LoewenFinalAward.pdf. Publicly released documents on all NAFTA disputes are *available at* http://www.naftalaw.org.

[11] *See generally* Robert B. Ahdieh, Between Dialogue and Decree: International Review of National Courts, 79 *N.Y.U. L. Rev.* 2029 (2004) (discussing case).

[12] *See Case Concerning Avena and Other Mexican Nationals* (Mex. v. U.S.), 2004 I.C.J. 12.

[13] *See Torres v. State*, No. PCD-04–442, 2004 WL 3711623 (Okla. Crim. App. May 13, 2004) (granting stay of execution and remanding case for evidentiary hearing).

[14] *See, e.g.*, David Zaring, Rulemaking and Adjudication in International Law, 46 *Colum. J. Transnat'l L.* 563 (2008); David Zaring, Informal Procedure, Hard and Soft, in International Administration, 5 *Chi. J. Int'l L.* 547 (2005).

surprising that people feel ties to, and act on the basis of affiliations with, multiple communities in addition to their territorial ones. Such communities may be ethnic, religious, or epistemic; transnational, subnational, or international; and the norms asserted by such communities frequently challenge territorially based authority. Indeed, canon law and other religious community norms have long operated in significant overlap with state law. And in the Middle East and elsewhere, conflicts between a personal law tied to religion and a territorial law tied to the nation-state continue to pose constitutional and other challenges.[15] Bonds of ethnicity can also create significant normative communities. For example, some commentators advocate regimes that give ethnic minorities limited autonomy within larger nation-states.[16] Transnationally, when members of an ethnic diaspora purchase securities issued by their "home" country, one might argue that, regardless of where, territorially, the bonds are purchased, the transactions should be governed by the law of the "homeland."[17] Finally, we see communities of transnational bankers and accountants developing their own regulatory regimes governing trade finance[18] or accounting standards,[19] as well as the use of modern forms of lex mercatoria[20] to

[15] *See, e.g.*, Chibli Mallat, On the Specificity of Middle Eastern Constitutionalism, 38 *Case W. Res. J. Int'l L.* 13, 47–55 (2006).

[16] *See, e.g.*, Henry J. Steiner, Ideals and Counter-Ideals in the Struggle over Autonomy Regimes for Minorities, 66 *Notre Dame L. Rev.* 1539, 1541–2 (1991) (identifying three different types of autonomy regimes for ethnic minorities).

[17] *See* Anupam Chander, Diaspora Bonds, 76 *N.Y.U. L. Rev.* 1005, 1060–74 (2001) (describing debt instruments offered by the Indian government to raise capital principally from its diaspora).

[18] *See* Janet Koven Levit, A Bottom-Up Approach to International Lawmaking: The Tale of Three Trade Finance Instruments, 30 *Yale J. Int'l L.* 125 (2005).

[19] For example, the International Accounting Standards Board is an independent, not-for-profit organization that seeks "to develop a single set of high quality, understandable, enforceable and globally accepted international financial reporting standards." IFRS Foundation, About the IFRS Foundation and the IASB, *available at* http://www.ifrs.org/The+organisation/IASCF+and+IASB.htm.

[20] *See, e.g.*, Clayton P. Gillette, The Law Merchant in the Modern Age: Institutional Design and International Usages Under the CISG, 5 *Chi. J. Int'l L.* 157, 159 (2004) (noting that the Convention "explicitly incorporates trade usages into contracts that it governs, permits usages to trump conflicting [Convention] provisions, and authorizes courts to

govern business relations.[21] Such nonstate legal systems often influence (or are incorporated in) state or international regimes.[22]

These spheres of complex overlapping legal authority are, not surprisingly, sites of conflict and confusion. In response to this hybrid reality, communities might seek to "solve" such conflicts either by reimposing the primacy of territorially based (and often nation-state-based) authority or by seeking universal harmonization. Thus, on the one hand, communities may try to seal themselves off from outside influence, either by retreating from the rest of the world and becoming more insular (as many religious groups seek to do), by building walls either literal or regulatory to protect the community from outsiders, by taking measures to limit outside influence (U.S. legislation seeking to discipline judges for citing foreign or international law is but one prominent example), or by falling back on territorially based jurisdiction or choice-of-law rules. At the other extreme, we see calls for harmonization of norms, more treaties, the construction of international governing bodies, and the creation of "world law."

interpret and complete contracts by reference to usages"). *But see* Celia Wasserstein Fassberg, Lex Mercatoria – Hoist with Its Own Petard? 5 *Chi. J. Int'l L.* 67 (2004) (arguing that the modern revival of lex mercatoria departs significantly from the historical conception).

[21] *See, e.g.*, Amitai Aviram, A Paradox of Spontaneous Formation: The Evolution of Private Legal Systems, 22 *Yale L. & Pol'y Rev.* 1 (2004) (using game theory to argue that the existence of preexisting networks enhances a private legal system's ability to enforce norms); Lisa Bernstein, Opting Out of the Legal System: Extralegal Contractual Relations in the Diamond Industry, 21 *J. Legal Stud.* 115 (1992) (discussing the system of "private lawmaking" in the New York Diamond Dealers Club); Lisa Bernstein, Private Commercial Law in the Cotton Industry: Creating Cooperation Through Rules, Norms, and Institutions, 99 *Mich. L. Rev.* 1724 (2001) (describing the nonstate legal system used to govern commercial transactions in the cotton industry); Eric A. Feldman, The Tuna Court: Law and Norms in the World's Premier Fish Market, 94 *Cal. L. Rev.* 313 (2006) (discussing a "Tuna Court" in Japan that adjudicates disputes about sale prices in a tuna market).

[22] *See, e.g.*, Levit, *supra* note 18, at 165 (describing ways in which formal lawmaking institutions such as the World Trade Organization have, over time, appropriated nonstate trade finance norms into their official legal instruments). *See generally* Carol Weisbrod, Fusion Folk: A Comment on Law and Music, 20 *Cardozo L. Rev.* 1439 (1999) (using the incorporation of folk music into "high culture" classical compositions as a metaphor for understanding the relationship between state and nonstate law).

I argue that we should be wary of pinning our hopes on legal regimes that rely either on reimposing sovereigntist[23] territorial insularity or on striving for universals. Not only are such strategies sometimes normatively undesirable, but more fundamentally they simply will not be successful in many circumstances. As I will address in more detail, the influence and application of foreign norms or foreign decision-making bodies may be useful and productive, but in any event they are inevitable and cannot be willed away by fiat.

Therefore, I suggest an alternative response to legal hybridity: *we might deliberately seek to create or preserve spaces for productive interaction among multiple, overlapping legal systems by developing procedural mechanisms, institutions, and practices that aim to manage, without eliminating, the legal pluralism we see around us*. Such mechanisms, institutions, and practices can help mediate conflicts by recognizing that multiple communities may legitimately wish to assert their norms over a given act or actor, by seeking ways of reconciling competing norms, and by deferring to alternative approaches if possible. And even when a decision maker cannot defer to an alternative norm (because some assertions of norms are repressive, violent, and/or profoundly illiberal), procedures for managing pluralism can at least require an explanation of why deference is impossible.

The excruciatingly difficult case-by-case questions concerning how much to defer to another normative community and how much to impose the norms of one's own community are probably impossible to answer definitively. The crucial antecedent point, however, is that although people may never reach agreement on norms, they may at least acquiesce in procedural mechanisms, institutions, or practices that take pluralism seriously, rather than ignoring it through assertions of territorially based power or dissolving it through universalist imperatives. Processes for managing pluralism seek to preserve spaces of opportunity for contestation

[23] I borrow the term "sovereigntist" from Peter Spiro, The New Sovereigntists: American Exceptionalism and Its False Prophets, *Foreign Affairs* 9–15 (Nov./Dec. 2000).

and local variation. Accordingly, a focus on hybridity may at times be both normatively preferable and more practical precisely because agreement on substantive norms is so difficult. And again, the claim is only that the independent values of pluralism should always be factored into the analysis, not that they should never be trumped by other considerations.

Of course, even if pluralist institutions and processes better reflect the complexity of the world around us, that is not necessarily a reason to adopt them. Yet, we may find that the added norms, viewpoints, and participants produce better decision making, better adherence to those decisions by participants and nonparticipants alike, and ultimately better real-world outcomes. And while this may not always be so, the essential point is that in the design of procedures, institutions, and discursive practices these possible benefits need to be considered.

This alternative jurisprudence I propose is fundamentally both *cosmopolitan* and *pluralist*. Thus, I should take a moment at the outset to explain what I mean by both terms. This is particularly important because in political and scholarly discourse these terms are often subject to varying uses, meanings, and connotations.

By cosmopolitan, I mean to invoke a framework recognizing that we are all fundamentally members of multiple communities, both local and global, territorial and epistemic. Unfortunately, many conflate cosmopolitanism with universalism.[24] Yet cosmopolitanism does not require a belief in a single global welfare or even a single universal set of governing norms; nor does it necessarily require that global welfare trump state or local welfare. Instead, cosmopolitanism is a useful trope for conceptualizing the current period of interaction across territorial borders precisely

[24] *See, e.g.*, Viet D. Dinh, Nationalism in the Age of Terror, 56 *Fla. L. Rev.* 867, 879 (2004) ("Rather than aspiring to *universal cosmopolitanism*, statelessness may well foster reversion to a selfish individualism.") (emphasis added); *see also* Bruce Ackerman, Rooted Cosmopolitanism, 104 *Ethics* 516, 534 (1994) ("If I were a European right now, I hope I would have the guts to stand up for rootless cosmopolitanism: forget this nationalistic claptrap, and let us build a world worthy of free and equal human beings."); Anupam Chander, Diaspora Bonds, 76 *N.Y.U. L. Rev.* 1005, 1046 (2001) ("The cosmopolitan model ... dissolves the multirootedness of diasporas into a global identity.").

because it recognizes that people have multiple affiliations, extending from the local to the global (and many nonterritorial affiliations as well). Thus, cosmopolitanism is emphatically not a model of international citizenship in the sense of international harmonization and standardization, but is instead a recognition of multiple refracted differences where people acknowledge links with the "other" without demanding either assimilation or ostracism.

Pluralism goes even further and recognizes that our conception of law must include more than just officially sanctioned governmental edicts or formal court documents. As discussed previously, many different non-state communities assert various forms of jurisdiction and impose all kinds of normative demands. Moreover, people often feel themselves to be bound by such entities, regardless of the formal status of those entities. Indeed, legal pluralists have long noted that law does not reside solely in the coercive commands of a sovereign power.[25] Rather, law is constantly

[25] *See, e.g.*, Sally Falk Moore, Legal Systems of the World: An Introductory Guide to Classifications, Typological Interpretations, and Bibliographical Resources, in *Law and the Social Sciences* 11, 15 (Leon Lipson & Stanton Wheeler eds., 1986) ("[N]ot all the phenomena related to law and not all that are lawlike have their source in government."). For further discussions of legal pluralism, *see* Keebet von Benda-Beckmann, Transnational Dimensions of Legal Pluralism, in *Begegnung und Konflikt: eine kulturanthropologische Bestandsaufnahme* 33, 33–48 (2001); Boaventura de Sousa Santos, *Toward a New Legal Common Sense: Law, Globalization, and Emancipation* (William Twinning & Christopher McCrudden eds., 2d ed., 2002); *Law and Globalization from Below: Towards a Cosmopolitan Legality* (Boaventura de Sousa Santos & César A. Rodríguez-Garavito eds., 2005); Gunther Teubner, 'Global Bukowina': Legal Pluralism in the World Society, in *Global Law Without a State* 3–28 (Gunther Teubner ed., 1997); Carol Weisbrod, *Emblems of Pluralism: Cultural Differences and the State* (2002); Franz von Benda-Beckmann, Who's Afraid of Legal Pluralism? 47 *J. Legal Pluralism & Unofficial L.* 37 (2002); David M. Engel, Legal Pluralism in an American Community: Perspectives on a Civil Trial Court, 5 *Am. B. Found. Res. J.* 425 (1980); Marc Galanter, Justice in Many Rooms: Courts, Private Ordering, and Indigenous Law, 19 *J. Legal Pluralism* 1, 28–34 (1981); John Griffiths, What Is Legal Pluralism? 24 *J. Legal Pluralism & Unofficial L.* 1 (1986); Sally Engle Merry, Legal Pluralism, 22 *Law & Soc'y Rev.* 869, 870 (1988) [hereinafter Merry, Legal Pluralism]; Sally Falk Moore, Law and Social Change: The Semi-Autonomous Social Field as an Appropriate Subject of Study, 7 *Law. & Soc'y Rev.* 719 (1973) [hereinafter Moore, The Semi-Autonomous Social Field]; Balakrishnan Rajagopal, The Role of Law in Counter-hegemonic Globalization

constructed through the contest of these various norm-generating communities.[26] Thus, although "official" norms articulated by sovereign entities obviously count as "law," such official assertions of prescriptive or adjudicatory jurisdiction are only some of the many ways in which normative commitments arise.

Moreover, legal pluralists have sought to document hybrid legal spaces, where more than one legal, or quasi-legal, regime occupies the same social field.[27] Historically, such sites were most prominently associated either with colonialism – where the legal system imposed by empire was layered on top of indigenous legal systems[28] – or the study of religion – where, as noted previously, canon law and other spiritual codes have often existed in an uneasy relationship with the state legal system.[29]

and Global Legal Pluralism: Lessons from the Narmada Valley Struggle in India, 18 *Leiden J. Int'l L.* 345 (2005) (U.K.); Brian Z. Tamanaha, A Non-Essentialist Version of Legal Pluralism, 27 *J.L. & Soc'y* 296 (2000); Sally Engle Merry, *International Law and Sociolegal Scholarship: Toward a Spatial Global Legal Pluralism* (Studies in Law, Politics, & Society, Vol. 41 Austin Sarat ed., 2007).

[26] *See* Robert Cover, Foreword: Nomos and Narrative, The Supreme Court 1982 Term, 97 *Harv. L. Rev.* 4, 43 (1983) [hereinafter Cover, Nomos and Narrative] ("The position that only the state creates law ... confuses the status of interpretation with the status of political domination."); *see also* Robert Cover, The Folktales of Justice: Tales of Jurisdiction, in *Narrative, Violence, and the Law: The Essays of Robert Cover* 173, 176 (Martha Minow, Michael Ryan, & Austin Sarat eds., 1992)("[A]ll collective behavior entailing systematic understandings of our commitments to future worlds [can lay] equal claim to the word 'law.'") (alterations in original); Perry Dane, The Maps of Sovereignty: A Meditation, 12 *Cardozo L. Rev.* 959, 963–4 (1991) ("This Article belongs to a body of legal scholarship that refuses to limit the domain of law to the law of the state.").

[27] *See* Moore, The Semi-Autonomous Social Field, *supra* note 25, at 720.

[28] *See, e.g.*, Leopold Pospisil, Modern and Traditional Administration of Justice in New Guinea, 19 *J. Legal Pluralism* 93 (1981).

[29] *See, e.g.*, Carol Weisbrod, *The Boundaries of Utopia* (1980) (examining the contractual underpinnings of four nineteenth-century American religious utopian communities: the Shakers, the Harmony Society, Oneida, and Zoar). As Marc Galanter has observed, the field of church and state is the "locus classicus of thinking about the multiplicity of normative orders." Galanter, *supra* note 25, at 28; *see also* Carol Weisbrod, Family, Church and State: An Essay on Constitutionalism and Religious Authority, 26 *J. Fam. L.* 741 (1988) (analyzing church-state relations in the United States from a pluralist perspective).

Legal pluralists explored the myriad ways that overlapping legal systems interact with each other and observed that the very existence of multiple systems can at times create openings for contestation, resistance, and creative adaptation.[30]

In this book, I apply a cosmopolitan pluralist framework to the global arena and argue that this framework is essential if we are to more comprehensively conceptualize a world of hybrid legal spaces. This approach, I realize, is unlikely to be fully satisfying either to committed nation-state sovereigntists or to committed universalists. Indeed, these poles in some ways echo those that Martii Koskenniemi famously identified as the irreconcilable positions inherent in all international legal argument.[31] Thus, sovereigntists will object to the idea that nation-states should ever take into account international, transnational, or nonstate norms.[32] Universalists, for their part, will chafe at the idea that international norms should ever be subordinated to local practices that may be less liberal or less rights-protecting. And even hard-line pluralists will complain that a view focusing on how official actors respond to hybridity is overly state-centric.

All I can say to such objections is that if a perspective displeases everyone to some extent, it is, for that very reason, also likely to be a perspective that manages hybridity in the only way possible: by forging provisional compromises that fully satisfy no one but may at least generate grudging acquiescence. And, in a world of multiple norms, such provisional compromises may ultimately be the best we can do. In any event, the central argument of this book is that hybridity is a reality we cannot escape, and a pure sovereigntist or universalist position will often be unsustainable as a practical matter. Thus, cosmopolitan pluralism offers

[30] *See, e.g.*, Merry, Legal Pluralism, *supra* note 25, at 878 (noting room for resistance and autonomy within plural systems).

[31] *See* Martii Koskenniemi, *From Apology to Utopia: The Structure of International Legal Argument* (1989) (rev. ed. 2006). I am grateful to Duncan Hollis for identifying key points of contact between my argument and Koskenniemi's.

[32] In part, this objection is grounded in concerns about loss of democratic accountability and legitimacy. I address some of these concerns in Chapter 3.

both a more accurate descriptive account of the world we live in and a potentially useful alternative approach to the design of procedural mechanisms, institutions, and discursive practices.

Of course, one thing that a cosmopolitan pluralist approach will *not* do is provide an authoritative metric for determining which norms should prevail in this messy hybrid world. Nor does it definitively answer the question of who gets to decide. Indeed, pluralism fundamentally challenges both positivist and natural rights–based assumptions that there can ever be a single answer to such questions. For example, as pluralists have documented in the colonial context, the state's efforts to squelch a nonstate community are likely only to be partial,[33] and so the state's assertion of its own trumping authority is not the end of the debate, but only one gambit in an ongoing normative discourse that has no final resolution. Likewise, there is no external position from which one could make a definitive statement as to who is authorized to make decisions in any given case. Rather, a statement of authority is itself inevitably open to contest. Power disparities matter, of course, and those who wield coercive force may be able to silence competing voices for a time. But even that sort of temporary silencing is rarely the end of the story either. Thus, instead of the unitary answers assumed by both universalism and sovereigntist territorialism, cosmopolitan pluralism provides a "jurisgenerative" model[34] that focuses on the creative interventions made by various communities drawing on a variety of normative sources in ongoing political, rhetorical, and legal iterations.[35]

[33] *See, e.g.*, Lauren Benton, Making Order out of Trouble: Jurisdictional Politics in the Spanish Colonial Borderlands, 26 *Law & Soc. Inquiry* 373, 375–6 (2001) (describing jurisdictional politics in seventeenth-century New Mexico and observing that, while "the crown made aggressive claims that royal authority and state law superseded other legal authorities," in reality "[j]urisdictional disputes became not just commonplace but a defining feature of the legal order").

[34] *See* Cover, Nomos and Narrative, *supra* note 26, at 11–15.

[35] *Cf.* Seyla Benhabib, *Another Cosmopolitanism* 49 (Robert Post, ed., 2006) 49 (2006) ("Whereas natural right philosophies assume that the principles that undergird democratic politics are impervious to transformative acts of popular collective will, and

Certainly individual communities may decide that their norms should trump those of others or that their norms are authoritative. So, for example, a liberal democratic state might decide that certain illiberal community practices are so beyond the pale that they cannot be countenanced, and therefore the state may invoke its authority to stifle those practices. But a cosmopolitan pluralist approach recognizes that such statements of normative commitment and authority are themselves subject to dispute. Accordingly, instead of clinging to the vain hope that unitary claims to authoritative law can ever be definitive, cosmopolitan pluralism recognizes the inevitability (if not always the desirability) of hybridity. Cosmopolitan pluralism is thus not a framework that dictates particular substantive outcomes. It observes that various actors pursue norms, and it studies the interplay, but it does not propose a hierarchy of substantive norms and values.

Nevertheless, while it does not offer *substantive* norms, a cosmopolitan pluralist approach may favor *procedural* mechanisms, institutions, and practices that provide opportunities for plural voices. Such procedures can potentially help to channel (or even tame) normative conflict to some degree by bringing multiple actors together into a shared social space. In addition, including multiple voices may lead to better substantive outcomes because such multiplicity provides the possibility for creative alternatives that might otherwise not be heard. This cosmopolitan pluralist commitment can, of course, have strong normative implications because it asks decision makers and institutional designers at least to consider the independent value of pluralism. For example, as discussed in more detail later, we might favor a hybrid domestic-international tribunal over either a fully domestic or a fully international one because it includes a more diverse range of actors, or we might favor complementarity or subsidiarity regimes because they encourage dialogue among

whereas legal positivism identifies democratic legitimacy with the correctly generated legal norms of a sovereign legislature, jurisgenerative politics is a model that permits us to think of creative interventions that mediate between universal norms and the will of democratic majorities.").

multiple jurisdictions, and so on. And we might prefer conflict of law frameworks that recognize the reality of hybridity rather than arbitrarily choosing a single governing legal regime to resolve problems implicating multiple communities. In any event, cosmopolitan pluralism questions whether a single world public order of the sort often contemplated by both nation-state sovereigntists and international law triumphalists is achievable, even assuming it were desirable.

At the same time, mechanisms, institutions, and practices of the sort discussed in this book require actors at least to be willing to take part in a common set of discursive forms. This is not as idealistic as it may at first appear. As Jeremy Waldron has argued, "[t]he difficulties of inter-cultural or religious-secular dialogue are often exaggerated when we talk about the incommensurability of cultural frameworks and the impossibility of conversation without a common conceptual scheme. In fact conversation between members of different cultural and religious communities is seldom a dialogue of the deaf."[36] Nevertheless, it is certainly true that some normative systems deny even this limited goal of mutual dialogue. Such systems would (correctly) recognize the liberal bias within the vision of procedural pluralism I explore here,[37] and they may reject the vision on that basis. For example, while abortion rights and antiabortion activists could, despite their differences, be said to share a willingness to engage in a common practice of constitutional adjudication, those bombing abortion clinics are not similarly willing, and accordingly there may not be any way to accommodate such actors even within a more pluralist framework. Likewise, communities that refuse to allow even the participation of particular subgroups, such as women or minorities, may be difficult to include within the cosmopolitan pluralist vision I have in mind. Of course, these

[36] Jeremy Waldron, Public Reason and "Justification" in the Courtroom, 1 *J.L. Phil. & Culture* 107, 112 (2007).

[37] This is not to say that the vision of pluralism I explore should be taken as synonymous with liberalism, though they share many attributes. Pluralism arguably assigns an independent value to dialogue among communities and an importance to community affiliation that is absent from (or at least less central to) liberal theory.

groups are undeniably important forces to recognize and take account of as a descriptive matter. But from a normative perspective, an embrace of a cosmopolitan pluralist jurisprudence need not commit one to a worldview free from judgment, where all positions are equivalently embraced. Thus, I argue not necessarily for undifferentiated inclusion, but for a set of procedural mechanisms, institutions, and practices that are more likely to expand the range of voices heard or considered, thereby creating more opportunities to forge a common social space than either sovereigntist territorialism or universalism.[38] In that sense, the vision I pursue here is at least partly indebted to the proceduralist vision of Jürgen Habermas[39] and can perhaps be embraced or criticized on similar grounds.

Chapter 2 begins by providing several illustrative examples of jurisdictional hybridity, where multiple legal norms of international, state, substate, and nonstate entities may overlap. I also introduce literature on legal pluralism and argue that pluralism provides a helpful framework for understanding a hybrid world where normative assertions of multiple entities – both state and nonstate – compete for primacy.

Chapters 3 and 4 then consider the two most common responses we see in the legal arena to the sort of hybridity described in Chapter 2: sovereigntist territorialism and universalism. While each of these approaches may sometimes be deemed necessary and may sometimes be useful in addressing overlapping norms, I argue that they have serious shortcomings. First, as a normative matter both sovereigntist territorialism and universalism retreat from the potential benefits of cosmopolitan pluralism by limiting the range of norms considered and the range of voices at the table. This may be a problem in and of itself because entertaining plural points of view within a procedural or institutional structure may carry independent benefits of inclusion, diversity, creativity,

[38] This focus on jurisgenerative structure, rather than on the necessary inclusion of, or deference to, all points of view, may differentiate legal pluralism as I use it here from multiculturalism.

[39] *See generally* Jürgen Habermas, *Between Facts and Norms: Contributions to a Discourse Theory of Law and Democracy* (trans. William Rehg, 1996).

and dialogue that go beyond the outcome reached. And, of course, the outcome reached may also ultimately be more creative and more effective because of the diversity of input. Second, even if one is dubious about the normative case for cosmopolitan pluralism, I argue that, as a descriptive matter, neither sovereigntist territorialism nor universalism will actually be a fully effective response to a world of legal assertions beyond borders, and therefore a broader and more flexible framework will often be necessary simply to cope with the messy reality of law on the ground.

Chapters 5 and 6 lay out the core principles that undergird a cosmopolitan pluralist approach and then describe a variety of procedural mechanisms, institutional designs, and discursive practices already at play in the world that take such an approach. Although each of these examples can be subjected to criticism on a variety of grounds, they do at least attempt to build structures that seek to manage, without eliminating, pluralism.

Finally, Chapters 7 through 9 address the knotty doctrines known in the United States as conflict of laws, though sometimes referred to elsewhere as private international law. These doctrines attempt to negotiate the interaction of communities by delineating jurisdictional boundaries, determining which communities' norms should apply to multicommunity disputes, and analyzing the circumstances under which one community might enforce the judgment reached by another community. As such, these doctrines are potentially fundamental areas for employing a cosmopolitan pluralist frame to the legal negotiation of difference. Yet, too often conflict of laws is relegated to a technocratic process of trying to forge rules that will clarify boundaries and render only one community or one set of norms legitimate or dominant. I argue instead that these doctrines should engage interdisciplinary scholars of law and globalization and that they offer a potential site for creative thinking about the interaction of norms. And, although as noted previously my aim throughout the book is to suggest a conceptual approach not to provide doctrinal answers, I do offer a few illustrative examples of how each of these conflicts doctrines might be affected by a cosmopolitan pluralist framework.

One final potential criticism of the book should perhaps be addressed at the outset. In the oft-discussed scholarly divide between "lumpers" and "splitters,"[40] I am clearly a "lumper." That is, I offer here a highly synthetic account that draws ties among a wide variety of different doctrines and lumps together a variety of different scholarly positions into broader categories. As such, I can rightly be criticized for eliding potentially important distinctions and grouping together phenomena or perspectives that are quite different from each other. For example, I treat sovereigntist territorialism as a single perspective, even though it represents a wide variety of positions, some of which focus more on nation-state sovereignty, while others focus more on territorial approaches to conflict of laws, and so on. Yet, despite some obvious problems, I believe lumping nevertheless serves valuable purposes. By grouping together categories of thought and legal doctrines that are traditionally treated as distinct, we may be able to recognize broader patterns, make connections, and identify innovations that might otherwise have been opaque. Most importantly, while splitting is particularly useful for exploring fine distinctions with precision once a paradigm has been established, lumping can help foster the creative imaginings that make new paradigms possible. In any event, while both approaches are valuable and necessary, this book is dedicated to sparking broad-based creative thinking about a world of law beyond borders and therefore lumps concepts together, with all the advantages and disadvantages such an approach entails.

True to that lumping spirit, the book seeks to engage scholars from a wide variety of fields, including those in anthropology, sociology, cultural studies, international relations, and critical geography, as well as legal scholars studying Internet law, international business, trade and finance,

[40] *See* George Gaylord Simpson, The Principles of Classification and a Classification of Mammals, 85 *Bulletin of the American Museum of Natural History* 1, 23, (1945) ("Splitters [see] very small units .... Lumpers [see] only large units ....") (alterations in original).

public international law, and conflict of laws. I also hope to contribute to ongoing debates about the efficacy of international law, changing structures of sovereignty, and cosmopolitan theory. I argue that rational choice understandings of how international law works or pure theory debates about sovereignty are limited because they focus too heavily on coercive power, thereby deemphasizing the role of rhetorical persuasion, informal articulations of legal norms, changes in legal consciousness, and networks of affiliation that may not possess literal enforcement power. Accordingly, my invocation of "law beyond borders" refers not only to the assertion of norms across territorial borders, but also the fact that legal articulations often function "beyond" the supposed conceptual borders between law on the one hand and political rhetoric on the other.[41] And if, as discussed previously, cosmopolitanism is defined not as universalism but as an acknowledgment of multiple affiliation and a call for conversation across difference, then this book also explores law as a crucial potential site for cosmopolitan dialogue.

In all of this discussion, I emphasize a cultural analysis of law, which argues that law both reflects and constructs social reality. This is, of course, not the only way of understanding how law operates. For example, one might think law is simply about constructing simple, easily defined rules that promote efficiency and predictability, regardless of how they reflect social reality. Yet, even if such an impulse is part of the web of rationales underlying legal rules, I believe it does not capture the rich reality of how law operates in relation to social life. Indeed, a simple formalist rule that fails to accord with social reality and lived experience tends to be replaced over time, first by what are known as legal fictions and then by new legal norms. For example, as discussed in more detail in Chapter 3, very clear, simple nineteenth-century jurisdictional rules that depended on physical presence in a territorial location could not cope with the changed social reality wrought by advances in transportation

[41] *See* Koskenniemi, *supra* note 31, at 69 ("Before any meaningful attempt at reform ... the idea of legal objectivity – and with it the conventional distinction between law, politics and morality (justice) needs to be rethought.").

and communications technologies and the resulting shifts in how corporations and governments operated and how people increasingly lived their lives. Accordingly, those jurisdictional rules were altered, first, through somewhat strained judicially created notions of what constitutes "presence" in a location and then by a completely new legal regime for conceptualizing jurisdiction that shifted the focus away from simple physical presence. Thus, I start from the premise that social reality matters in legal discussions and that a more culturally based analytical framework should at least be an important part of our discussions of how to conceptualize law and globalization.

Ultimately, by studying the many local settings in which the norms of multiple communities – geographical, ethnic, national, and epistemic – become operative, scholars can gain a far more nuanced understanding of the international and transnational legal terrain. This is a world in which claims to coercive power, abstract notions of legitimacy, and arguments about legal authority are only part of an ongoing conversation, not the final determining factors. It is a world where "jurisgenerative" practices proliferate, creating opportunities for contestation and creative adaptation.[42] And though we may not like all the norms being articulated at any given moment, it will do no good to ignore them or insist on their lack of authority. In a hybrid world, law is an ongoing process of articulation, adaptation, rearticulation, absorption, resistance, deployment, and on and on. It is a process that never ends, and scholars and policy makers would do well to study the multiplicity and engage in the conversation, rather than impose a top-down framework that cannot help but distort the astonishing variety on the ground.

[42] *See id.* at 556, 596–9 (embracing international legal discourse as a space for "open political conflict and constant institutional revision").

2 A World of Legal Conflicts

ACROSS A VARIETY OF DOCTRINAL AREAS WE SEE normative overlap among international, state, and nonstate entities. This overlap includes instances when two different communities wish to assert jurisdiction to adjudicate a dispute as well as instances when a decision maker in one place is asked to apply the norms of a different community – what is sometimes called jurisdiction to prescribe or (especially in the Anglo-American system) choice of law.

This chapter begins by offering several illustrative examples of these multiple forms of jurisdictional hybridity. And though these are just a very few of the many examples I could have chosen, the sheer range of them suggests that such overlapping relationships among different normative communities are a permanent (and perhaps growing) part of the legal landscape. Accordingly, as will be discussed in subsequent chapters, it will likely be impossible to ignore these hybrid legal spaces or seek to eliminate them by imposition of a single governing norm or a single governing body. Instead, it will be necessary to seek ways of managing, without eliminating, such plural interactions.

Having gestured to this widespread jurisdictional hybridity, I conclude the chapter by arguing that those seeking to understand the multifaceted role of law in an era of globalization[1] must take seriously the

[1] Of course, the idea of an "era of globalization" is contested. Indeed, the vast debates concerning globalization's meaning, its importance, and even its existence could fill

insights of scholars who focus on legal pluralism. Indeed, I suggest that the pluralism literature could help in developing a more comprehensive framework for conceptualizing the clash of normative communities in

many volumes. For purposes of this book, I do not attempt to articulate a single definition because part of the premise of law and globalization is that multiple definitions and meanings for globalization will be salient for different populations. *See, e.g.*, Boaventura de Sousa Santos, Oppositional Postmodernism and Globalizations, 23 *Law & Soc. Inquiry* 121, 135 (1998) ("There is strictly no single entity called globalization. There are, rather, globalizations, and we should use the term only in the plural."). Thus, I use the term to refer generally to the intensification of global interconnectedness, in which capital, people, commodities, images, and ideologies move across distance and physical boundaries with increasing speed and frequency. *See, e.g.*, Anthony Giddens, *Runaway World: How Globalization Is Reshaping Our Lives* 6–19 (2003) (pointing to the increased level of trade, finance, and capital flows and describing the effects of the weakening hold of older nation-states); Saskia Sassen, *Globalization and Its Discontents* (1998) (analyzing globalization and its economic, political, and cultural effects on the world). Indeed, I am content to acknowledge that the existence of many different visions of globalization is a fundamental part of globalization itself.

Even some who acknowledge globalization nevertheless question whether globalization is really a new phenomenon. Certainly, interrelations among multiple populations across territorial boundaries have existed for centuries. For example, some argue that the pre-1914 era was in fact the high-water mark for economic interdependence, although there is also evidence that the post-1989 era surpasses that period. *See* Miles Kahler & David A. Lake, Globalization and Governance, in *Governance in a Global Economy: Political Authority in Transition* 11–15 (Miles Kahler & David A. Lake, eds., 2003). Again, I do not think such arguments need detain us. First, it seems clear that something is going on, given the pervasiveness of the ideology of market capitalism; the speed of commodity, capital, and personal movement; the ubiquity of global media; and so on. Whether such developments are truly new (or greater than ever before) seems less important than understanding the consequences of the phenomena. Second, I see the term "globalization" as also signifying the attitude about the world that tends to come into being as a result of frequent use of the term itself. Indeed, in a certain sense it does not really matter whether, as an empirical matter, the world is more or less "globalized" than it used to be. More important is the fact that people – whether governmental actors, corporations, scholars, or general citizens – think and act as if the world is more interconnected and treat globalization as a real phenomenon. In addition, there is at least some evidence that global "scripts" are exerting a broad impact at least in the officially sanctioned discourse of governmental bureaucrats. *See, e.g.*, John W. Meyer et al., World Society and the Nation-State, 103 *Am. J. Soc.* 144, 145 (1997) ("Worldwide models define and legitimate agendas for local action, shaping the structures and policies of nation-states and other national and local actors in virtually all of the domains of rationalized social life...."). For further discussion of "the problematics of globalization," *see* Paul Schiff Berman, From International Law to Law and Globalization, 43 *Colum. J. Transnat'l L.* 485, 551–5 (2005).

the modern world. Using pluralism, we can conceive of a legal system as both autonomous and permeable; outside norms (both state and nonstate) affect the system but do not dominate it fully. Thus, the pluralist framework captures a dialectical and iterative interplay that we see among normative communities in the international system, an interplay that rigidly territorialist or positivist visions of legal authority do not address.

Examples of Jurisdictional Hybridity

It would clearly be impossible to map every instance of jurisdictional overlap that exists in today's world. There are simply too many cases where multiple normative communities may assert dominion over, or seek to have their norms imposed on, a single act or actor. Of course, this sort of intermingling of normative systems is not a new phenomenon, and legal pluralists have for many years studied church-state relations, the interaction of colonial and indigenous legal systems, and so on. Likewise international law has long been interested in areas of overlapping or ill-defined jurisdictional authority. Yet, in a globally interconnected world it is not surprising to see even more instances of this sort of legal hybridity. This section therefore provides just a few illustrative examples, many of which we will return to later in the book. Such examples include conflicts involving the overlapping normative assertions of multiple nation-states, conflicts between nation-state authority and international norms and tribunals, conflicts between nation-state and substate authority in a federal system, and conflicts between state and nonstate normative communities. Each type of conflict will be discussed in turn.

Two problems with these examples (and indeed the book as a whole) must be acknowledged from the outset, however. First, while the thrust of this book is to decenter (though not to dismiss) the nation-state, most of my examples include nation-state authority as at least one of the relevant decision-making entities. Thus, one might think that methodological statism infects even my efforts to move away from state-centered frames.[2] This is, in some sense, inevitable in a work that attempts to survey legal doctrines and political mechanisms, many of which remain creatures of the nation-state, at least most of the time. And, as a practical matter, though we could certainly find pluralist mechanisms being used in a variety of nonstate community interactions, there can be no doubt that it is easier to find and document such examples in more official state-based formal contexts. After all, those are the institutions and mechanisms about which there are more likely to be written decisions, scholarly analyses, statutory references, and so on. Nevertheless, although the bias toward more formal institutions will be evident, I continue to believe the framework developed here can be applied far beyond conventional nation-state courts, legislatures, tribunals, and administrative bodies.

Second, and relatedly, many of the examples in this chapter and throughout the book involve courts or other quasi-judicial bodies. This again is largely the result of the practical availability of concrete examples, which are easier to find in written case determinations. Yet, the problem with this bias is both that one tends to forget the variety of pluralist interactions that take place outside the judicial context and, worse, that we come to think of pluralist interactions as a series of discrete one-off transactions rather than an ongoing iterative process among different epistemic communities, both judicial in character and not. Such an ongoing iterative model undoubtedly more accurately reflects the sorts of pluralist interactions I have in mind.

Despite these limitations, I believe that the examples surveyed in this chapter do at least provide a sense of the types of ongoing interactions we need to recognize. And in any event, even if these examples are only the beginning of the analysis, they at least suggest the widespread legal pluralism that is our day-to-day reality, both within and without the court system and within and without the nation-state.

[2] I gratefully acknowledge Peter Spiro for raising this important concern.

State Versus State Conflicts of Norms

In a world where the effects of activity in one place can easily be felt in a territorially distant location, we should expect conflicts, as multiple nation-states seek to assert jurisdiction over the same act or actor. Such conflicts have often arisen in the past two decades, as the terms "cyberspace" and "globalization" have become buzzwords of a new generation. And it is probably not surprising that the two words have entered the lexicon simultaneously. From its beginning, the Internet heralded a new world order of both interconnection and decentralization,[3] while the word "globalization" conjured for many the specter of increasing transnational and supranational governance as well as the growing mobility of persons and capital across geographical boundaries.[4] Thus, both terms have reflected a perception that territorial borders might no longer be as significant as they once were.[5]

[3] *See, e.g.*, Deirdre M. Curtin, *Postnational Democracy: The European Union in Search of a Political Philosophy* 4 (1997) ("Just think of how global computer-based communications cut across territorial borders, creating a new realm of human activity and undermining the feasibility – and legitimacy – of applying laws based on geographic boundaries to this new sphere.").

[4] *See, e.g.*, Michael Edwards, *Future Positive: International Co-Operation in the 21st Century* 5–6 (1999) ("Globalisation challenges the authority of nation states and international institutions to influence events, while the scale of private flows of capital, technology, information and ideas makes official transfers look increasingly marginal."); Arjun Appadurai, Disjuncture and Difference in the Global Cultural Economy, in *Modernity at Large: Cultural Dimensions of Globalization* 27, 27–29 (1996) ("[T]oday's world involves interactions of a new order and intensity.... [W]ith the advent of the steamship, the automobile, the airplane, the camera, the computer and the telephone, we have entered into an altogether new condition of neighborliness, even with those most distant from ourselves.").

[5] *See, e.g.*, Mathew Horsman & Andrew Marshall, *After the Nation-State: Citizens, Tribalism and the New World Disorder*, at ix (1994) ("The traditional nation-state, the fruit of centuries of political, social and economic evolution, is under threat."); George J. Demko & William B. Wood, Introduction: International Relations Through the Prism of Geography, in *Reordering the World: Geopolitical Perspectives on the Twenty-First Century* 3, 10 (George J. Demko & William B. Wood eds., 1994) ("Once sacrosanct, the concept of a state's sovereignty – the immutability of its international boundaries – is now under serious threat."); Seyla Benhabib, *Strange*

On the other hand, nation-state governments have been quick to reassert themselves. For example, there was a heady moment circa 1995 when it seemed as if the rise of cyberspace might cause us to jettison nation-state boundaries altogether. Most famously, David Johnson and David Post argued that cyberspace could not legitimately be governed by territorially based sovereigns and that the online world should create its own legal jurisdiction (or multiple jurisdictions).[6] Predictably, nation-states pushed in the opposite direction, passing a slew of laws purporting to regulate almost every conceivable online activity, from gambling[7] to chat rooms[8] to auction sites,[9] and seeking to enforce territorially based

Multiplicities: Democracy and Identity in a Global Era: Lecture 1, at 33 (on file with author) ("In the era of globalization, the integrative powers of the nation-state ... are challenged.").

[6] David R. Johnson & David Post, Law and Borders – the Rise of Law in Cyberspace, 48 *Stan. L. Rev.* 1367 (1996); *see also, e.g.*, David Post, Governing Cyberspace, 43 *Wayne L. Rev.* 155, 165–71 (1996) (arguing that cyberspace should be governed through decentralized processes whereby network access providers decide which rules to impose and individual users choose which online communities to join).

[7] *E.g.*, Interactive Gambling Act, 2001, pts. 2 & 2A (Austl.) (prohibiting online gambling services to customers in Australia and other designated countries), *available at* http://www.comlaw.gov.au/Details/C2005C00372; *see also Humphrey ex rel. Minnesota v. Granite Gate Resorts, Inc.*, 568 N.W.2d 715, 721 (Minn. Ct. App. 1997) (asserting personal jurisdiction over nonresident corporation and its principal for deceptive trade practices, false advertising, and consumer fraud in connection with an Internet gambling site); *Vacco ex rel. People v. World Interactive Gaming Corp.*, 714 N.Y.S.2d 844, 851–54 (N.Y. Sup. Ct. 1999) (enforcing state and federal laws to ban foreign corporation, its Antiguan subsidiary, and their principals, officers, and directors from operating or offering gambling over the Internet).

[8] *E.g.*, 47 U.S.C. § 254(l)(1)(A)(ii) (2001) (requiring schools and libraries to adopt and implement policies to ensure the safety and security of minors when using chat rooms); *Nev. Rev. Stat.* § 176A.413 (2001) (restricting ownership and use of online chatrooms by people previously convicted of cyberstalking).

[9] *E.g.*, *Ind. Code* §§ 26–2-8–101 to -302 (2001) (containing the Uniform Electronic Transactions Act, which facilitates the use of online auction sites by giving legal effect to electronic signatures and contracts); *N.C. Gen. Stat.* §§ 66–311 to -330 (2001) (same); Tribunal de grande instance (TGI) [ordinary court of original jurisdiction] Paris, May 22, 2000, Ordonnance de référé, *UEJF et Licra c/ Yahoo! Inc. et Yahoo France*, *available at* http://www.juriscom.net/txt/jurisfr/cti/tgiparis20000522.htm (enjoining Yahoo.com from permitting French users access to Nazi memorabilia via Yahoo!'s auction sites).

rules regarding trademarks,[10] contractual relations,[11] privacy norms,[12] "indecent" content,[13] and crime,[14] among others.

Yet these assertions of national authority have raised many of the legal conundrums regarding nation-state sovereignty, territorial borders,

[10] *E.g.*, Anticybersquatting Consumer Protection Act, Pub. L. No. 106–113, 113 Stat. 1501 (1999) (codified as amended in scattered sections of 15, 16, and 28 U.S.C.) (providing for the "registration and protection of trademarks used in commerce"); Rachel Ross, China Demands Jurisdiction over Domain Names in Chinese, *Toronto Star*, Nov. 13, 2000, LEXIS, Tstar File (reporting that China is seeking to ensure that it controls the distribution and administration of all Chinese-character domain names).

[11] *E.g.*, Electronic Transactions Act, 1999 (Austl.) (creating a regulatory regime intended to support and encourage business and consumer confidence in the use of electronic commerce), *available at* http://www.ag.gov.au/www/agd/agd.nsf/Page/e-commerce_Australiaslegalframeworkforelectroniccommerce; *Unif. Computer Info. Transactions Act*, 7 U.L.A. 200 (2002) (providing a model uniform state law to govern online contracts), *available at* http://www.law.upenn.edu/bll/ulc/ucita/cita10st.doc.

[12] *E.g.*, Electronic Communications Privacy Act, 18 U.S.C. § 2701(a)(1) (2000) (prohibiting unauthorized access to a "facility through which an electronic communication service is provided"); Data Protection Act, 1998, c. 29 (Eng.) (requiring technical and organizational measures against unauthorized or unlawful processing of personal data and against accidental loss of, destruction of, or damage to personal data), *available at* http://www.legislation.gov.uk/ukpga/1998/29/contents.

[13] *See, e.g.*, 18 U.S.C. § 2252A (2000) (prohibiting the receipt or distribution of sexually explicit photos of minors by any means including by computer); *Reno v. ACLU*, 521 U.S. 844, 885 (1997) (striking down, on First Amendment grounds, provisions of the Communications Decency Act, 47 U.S.C. § 223 (Supp. II 1996), that criminalized certain content transmitted via online communication); *ACLU v. Reno*, 217 F.3d 162, 181 (3d Cir. 2000) (affirming, on First Amendment grounds, preliminary injunction preventing the enforcement of the Child Online Protection Act, 47 U.S.C. § 231 (Supp. IV 1998), which also criminalized certain content sent via online communication), *vacated sub nom. Ashcroft v. ACLU*, 122 S. Ct. 1700 (2002); *Regina v. Pecciarich*, [1995] O.R.3d 748 (Prov. Ct.) (Can.) (holding that the distribution of child pornography by uploading photos to an electronic bulletin board was in violation of criminal statutes).

[14] *E.g.*, Computer Fraud and Abuse Act, 18 U.S.C. § 1030 (2000) (applying federal law to newly discovered forms of computer abuse and providing civil remedies for certain types of computer crimes); Regulation of Investigatory Powers Act, 2000, c. 23 (Eng.) (defining criminal penalties for interception of traffic on all postal and telecommunications networks and any action that may cause the content of a message to become known to people other than the sender or intended recipient); *see also Am. Online, Inc. v. LCGM, Inc.*, 46 F. Supp. 2d 444, 446, 448 (E.D. Va. 1998) (holding that defendants who harvested e-mail addresses of America On-Line members using an extractor program and then used those addresses to send unauthorized bulk e-mail advertising their pornographic Web sites were in violation of federal and state statutes).

and legal jurisdiction that Johnson and Post predicted.[15] For example, if a person posts content online that is legal where it was posted but is illegal in some place where it is viewed, can that person be subject to suit in the far-off location? Is online activity sufficient to make one "present" in a jurisdiction for tax purposes? Is a patchwork of national copyright laws feasible given the ability to transfer digital information around the globe instantaneously? How might national rules regarding the investigation and definition of criminal activity complicate efforts to combat international computer crime? Should the law of trademarks, which historically has permitted two firms to retain the same name as long as they operated in different geographical areas, be expanded to provide an international cause of action regarding the ownership of an easily identifiable domain name? And, if so, should such a system be enforced by national courts (and in which country) or by an international body (and how should such a body be constituted)? And on and on.

I have already mentioned the famous *Yahoo!* case, in which two different countries, France and the United States, claimed jurisdiction over Yahoo! concerning Nazi memorabilia and Holocaust denial material that was illegal in France (where it was downloaded) but protected by the First Amendment in the United States (where it was uploaded). This is not an isolated case. Shortly after the French court ruling, Italy's highest court, in an appeal of an online defamation case, ruled that Italian courts can assert jurisdiction over foreign-based Websites and shut them down if they do not abide by Italian law.[16] The court determined, as in the *Yahoo!* case, that Italian courts have jurisdiction both when an act or omission has actually been committed on Italian territory and when simply the effects or consequences of an act are felt in Italy. Likewise, Germany's second-highest court ruled that an Australian Website owner – whose

[15] *See* Johnson & Post, *supra* note 6, at 1371–76 (suggesting that the unique nature of cyberspace, particularly the absence of any physical location, creates regulatory and jurisdictional problems for governments).

[16] Rachel Donadio, Larger Threat Is Seen in Google Case, *N.Y. Times*, Feb. 25, 2010, at A1.

Website questioning the Holocaust is illegal in Germany but not in Australia – could be jailed for violating German speech laws.[17] The High Court of Australia similarly ruled that Australian courts could assert jurisdiction over an American publisher for publishing on its Website an article allegedly defaming an Australian citizen,[18] and the Court of Appeal of England and Wales ruled that allegedly defamatory materials posted on a U.S.-based Website were nevertheless "published" for purposes of a libel action in the jurisdiction where they were downloaded.[19] More recently, a Milan court found three senior Google executives criminally liable for material uploaded by third parties despite the fact that such material would not have created such liability under U.S. law.[20] Finally, as will be discussed later in this book, decisions in many Internet domain trademark cases are being decided based on U.S. law despite the fact that the person or entity registering the domain name had minimal or no connection with the United States.[21]

The Internet cases are only one instantiation of legal norms being applied across borders from one nation-state to another. Consider environmental harms, which often ignore territorial boundaries. In *Pakootas v. Teck Cominco Metals, Ltd.,* only one of many possible examples, the State of Washington and members of an Indian tribe sued a Canadian mining company seeking to apply U.S. environmental laws to pollution

[17] *See* Steve Kettman, German Hate Law: No Denying It, *Wired*, Dec. 15, 2000, *available at* http://www.wired.com/politics/law/news/2000/12/40669#ixzz0jTf5lnLh.

[18] *See Dow Jones& Co., Inc. v. Gutnick*, [2002] HCA 56 (Austl.).

[19] *See Lewis v. King*, [2004] EWCA Civ 1329 (Eng.); *see also Richardson v. Schwarzenegger*, [2004] EWHC 2422 (QB) (Eng.) (relying on Lewis to assert jurisdiction over a libel suit arising from an article in the *Los Angeles Times* that was available online); *Bangoura v. Washington Post*, 235 *D.L.R.* (4th) 564 (Ontario Super. Ct. Justice 2004) (asserting jurisdiction over a libel suit concerning materials on a U.S.-based Website accessible in Canada).

[20] Karin Ratzer & Teresa Basile, Milan Court Finds Google Executives Criminally Liable: Why the Ruling is Controversial (May 14, 2010), http://www.jdsupra.com/post/documentViewer.aspx?fid=869cd51b-a823-4b80-bd3f-911225fde211.

[21] *See, e.g.*, *Barcelona.com, Inc. v. Excelentisimo Ayuntamiento de Barcelona*, 330 F.3d 617 (4th Cir. 2003); *GlobalSantaFe Corp. v. GlobalSantaFe.com*, 250 F. Supp. 2d 610 (E.D. Va. 2003).

emitted in Canada but causing harm downstream in the United States.[22] Likewise, given the impact of commercial transactions across territorial borders, we should not be surprised to see transnational normative assertions in realms as diverse as antitrust,[23] securities regulation,[24] intellectual property, corporate law and governance,[25] bankruptcy, tax,[26] criminal laws,[27] civil rights statutes,[28] labor standards,[29] and so on.

Finally, international human rights norms can also be applied transnationally, from one country to another. The most celebrated such case was the effort of Spanish judge Juan Garzón to arrest and try former

[22] *Pakootas v. Teck Cominco Metals, Ltd.*, 452 F.3d 1066, 1077–79 (9th Cir. 2005) (holding that the imposition of liability under U.S. law on a Canadian corporation was not extraterritorial even though the company's release of pollutants occurred entirely within Canada). For a discussion of the case, *see, e.g.*, Shi-Ling Shu & Austen L. Parrish, Litigating Canada-U.S. Transboundary Harm: International Environmental Lawmaking and the Threat of Extraterritorial Reciprocity, 48 *Va. J. Int'l L.* 1 (2007).

[23] Joseph P. Griffin, Extraterritoriality in U.S. and EU Antitrust Enforcement, 67 *Antitrust L.J.* 159, 159 (1999) ("Extraterritorial enforcement of antitrust and competition laws has become routine in both the United States and the European Union.").

[24] Stephen J. Choi & Andrew T. Guzman, The Dangerous Extraterritoriality of American Securities Laws, 17 *Nw. J. Int'l L. & Bus.* 207 (1996); Stephen J. Choi & Andrew T. Guzman, Portable Reciprocity: Rethinking the International Reach of Securities Regulation, 71 *S. Cal. L. Rev* 903 (1998); Margaret V. Sachs, The International Reach of Rule 10b-5: The Myth of Congressional Silence, 28 *Colum. J. Transnat'l L.* 677 (1990).

[25] Detlev F. Vagts, Extraterritoriality and the Corporate Governance Law, 97 *Am. J. Int'l L.* 289, 289–94 (2003) (describing the extraterritorial application of the Sarbanes-Oxley Act).

[26] Ruth Mason, U.S. Tax Treaty Policy and The European Court of Justice, 59 *Tax L. Rev.* 65 (2005).

[27] Anthony J. Colangelo, Constitutional Limits on Extraterritorial Jurisdiction: Terrorism and the Intersection of National and International Law, 48 *Harv. Int'l L.J.* 121, 127 (2007).

[28] Ved P. Nanda & David K. Pansius, *Litigation of International Disputes in U.S. Courts* § 8:1 (2d ed. 2008).

[29] *See Spector v. Norwegian Cruise Line Ltd.*, 545 U.S. 119, 129–30 (2005) (extending the Americans with Disabilities Act of 1990 to encompass foreign-flag vessels in U.S. waters); *Jose v. M/V Fir Grove,* 801 *F. Supp.* 358, 373 (*D. Or.* 1992) (finding that Congress intended the wage provisions of the U.S. Shipping Act to apply to foreign seamen); *see also* Symeon C. Symeonides, Cruising in American Waters: Spector, Maritime Conflicts, and Choice of Law, 37 *J. Mar. L. & Com.* 491, 503–10 (2006) (discussing the extraterritoriality issues raised by the Court's decision in *Spector,* 545 U.S. 119).

Chilean ruler Augusto Pinochet in October 1998 for acts of genocide, hostage taking, and torture while Pinochet was Chile's head of state.[30] Although Pinochet claimed immunity, the British House of Lords ruled that Pinochet (who was in England at the time) had no entitlement to immunity for the crimes of which he was accused.[31] Pinochet was not ultimately extradited to Spain, but the transnational assertion of jurisdiction did spark efforts to try Pinochet in Chile itself. Likewise, in August 2003 Judge Garzón sought extradition from Argentina of dozens of Argentines for human rights abuses committed under the Argentine military government in the 1970s.[32] In addition, Garzón successfully extradited from Mexico a former Argentine navy lieutenant who was accused of murdering hundreds of people.[33]

[30] *See* Provisional Arrest Warrant by Nicholas Evans, Metropolitan Magistrate, Bow Street Magistrates' Court, London, England for Augusto Pinochet Ugarte (Oct. 16, 1998), in *The Pinochet Papers* 61 (Reed Brody & Michael Ratner eds., 2000) (asserting Spanish jurisdiction over Augusto Pinochet Ugarte). Although the House of Lords, in its final decision, ultimately determined that the International Convention Against Torture (rather than general principles of universal jurisdiction) provided its source of jurisdiction, *Regina v. Bow St. Metro.* Stipendiary Magistrate (No. 3), 1 A.C. 147, 189 (H.L. 1999), the convention itself can be seen as codifying the principles of universal jurisdiction; *see id.* at 201 ("[I]f the states with the most obvious jurisdiction ... do not seek to extradite, the state where the alleged torturer is found must prosecute or, apparently, extradite to another country, i.e. there is universal jurisdiction....").

[31] *Bow St. Metro. Stipendiary Magistrate*, 1 A.C. at 205. For the various Spanish and English court documents in the *Pinochet* case, *see generally The Pinochet Papers*, *supra* note 30. For further discussion of the case, *see generally The Pinochet Case: A Legal and Constitutional Analysis* (Diana Woodhouse ed., 2000); J. Craig Barker, The Future of Former Head of State Immunity After *Ex Parte Pinochet*, 48 *Int'l & Comp. L.Q.* 937 (1999); Andrea Bianchi, Immunity Versus Human Rights: The Pinochet Case, 10 *Eur. J. Int'l L.* 237 (1999); Michael Byers, Decisions of British Courts During 1999 Involving Questions of Public or Private International Law, 70 *Brit. Y.B. Int'l L.* 277, 277–95 (2000); Michael Byers, The Law and Politics of the Pinochet Case, 10 *Duke J. Int'l & Comp. L.* 415 (2000); Christine M. Chinkin, International Decision, United Kingdom House of Lords: *Regina v. Bow Street Stipendiary Magistrate, Ex Parte Pinochet Ugarte* (No. 3), 93 *Am. J. Int'l L.* 703 (1999); Hazel Fox, The Pinochet Case No. 3, 48 *Int'l & Comp. L.Q.* 687 (1999); Colin Warbrick, Extradition Law Aspects of *Pinochet* 3, 48 *Int'l & Comp. L.Q.* 958 (1999).

[32] *See* Larry Rohter, Argentine Congress Likely to Void "Dirty War" Amnesties, *N.Y. Times*, Aug. 21, 2003, at A3 (recounting Garzón's extradition request).

[33] Emma Daly, Spanish Judge Sends Argentine to Prison on Genocide Charge, *N.Y. Times*, June 30, 2003, at A3 ("In an unusual act of international judicial cooperation, and a

In the United States, aliens can bring human rights suits against foreign and U.S. governments and officials under the Alien Tort Statute (ATS),[34] which grants original subject matter jurisdiction over "any civil action by an alien for a tort only, committed in violation of the law of nations or a treaty of the United States."[35] Enacted as part of the Judiciary Act of 1789, this statute permits federal courts to hear suits by aliens alleging torture and various other offenses committed by officials of foreign governments.[36] ATS suits have been brought for genocide, war crimes, summary execution, disappearance, prolonged arbitrary detention, and cruel, inhuman, or degrading treatment,[37] and though the U.S. Supreme Court has cut back the scope of the statute somewhat, it has affirmed the basic principle that such suits are cognizable in federal courts.[38] The Torture Victim Protection Act of 1991 (TVPA)[39] reinforces and expands the ATS by defining specific causes of action for torture and summary execution and by permitting U.S. citizens as well as aliens to bring suit.[40] Successful suits have been brought under these statutes against various members of the Guatemalan military,[41] the estate of former Philippine

victory for the Spanish judge Baltasar Garzón, Mexico's Supreme Court ruled this month that the former officer, Ricardo Miguel Cavallo, could be extradited to Spain for crimes reportedly committed in a third country, Argentina.").

[34] 28 U.S.C. § 1350 (2006).

[35] *Id.*

[36] *Filartiga v. Pena-Irala*, 630 F.2d 876, 887 (2d Cir. 1980).

[37] *See* Beth Stephens & Michael Ratner, *International Human Rights Litigation in U.S. Courts* 343–48 (1996) (summarizing ATS cases); *see also* William Glaberson, U.S. Courts Become Arbiters of Global Rights and Wrongs, *N.Y. Times*, June 21, 2001, at A1 (discussing "the growing use of the American legal system to judge rights and wrongs all over the globe").

[38] *See Sosa v. Alvarez-Machain*, 542 U.S. 692, 725 (2004) ([A]ny claim based on the present-day law of nations [should] rest on a norm of international character accepted by the civilized world and defined with a specifity comparable to the features of the 18th-century paradigms [from when the Alien Tort Statute was enacted].

[39] Pub. L. No. 102–256, 106 Stat. 73 (1992).

[40] *Id.*

[41] *See Xuncax v. Gramajo*, 886 F. Supp. 162, 179 (D. Mass. 1995) (holding that the alien plaintiffs could establish subject matter jurisdiction and a federal private cause of action for tortious violations of international law under the ATS).

leader Ferdinand Marcos,[42] and Serbian leader Radovan Karadžić.[43] Although all of these are civil cases, and many of the monetary judgments issued may never actually be paid, the suits have strong symbolic and emotional value to the victims – they may deter potential defendants from entering U.S. territory, and they reinforce the principle of universal, or at least transnational, jurisdiction.[44]

International human rights suits against former and current governmental officials have been brought in courts outside the United States as well, even beyond the Garzón cases described earlier. For example, Hissene Habré, former leader of Chad, was indicted in Belgium for human rights abuses committed during his rule. This prosecution put pressure on the government of Senegal, where Habré lived in exile, and in 2008 the National Assembly of Senegal voted to amend the constitution to clear the way for Habré to be prosecuted there. Thus, we can see that even in cases where transnational prosecutions do not go forward, they can have real impact on the ground.

Finally, although some might not consider it truly transnational, in multiethnic regions with multiple legal systems – such as Kosovo or Cyprus – we may see the need for courts to interact even when the different ethnic groups do not actually recognize each other's autonomy. And, as with the other examples earlier, delineating spheres of authority based on geographical borders cannot capture the reality of how law actually operates.

State Versus International Conflicts of Norms

As noted in the Introduction, there are now well over a hundred international tribunals of various sorts operating around the world. The

[42] *See Hilao v. Estate of Marcos*, 103 F.3d 789, 791–92 (9th Cir. 1996) (approving the district court's assertion of federal jurisdiction under the ATS).

[43] *See Kadic v. Karadžić*, 70 F.3d 232, 241–44 (2d Cir. 1995) (finding subject matter jurisdiction exists under the ATS to bring claims of genocide, war crimes, and torture against the Bosnian-Serb leader).

[44] *See* Stephens & Ratner, *supra* note 37, at 234–38 (emphasizing the substantial nonmonetary impact of ATS and TVPA claims).

jurisdictional assertions of these tribunals inevitably create interactions with nation-state legal authority. Some – such as the World Trade Organization – are designed principally as forums for state-to-state adjudication, whereas others – such as the international courts established to try those accused of gross abuses in the former Yugoslavia and in Rwanda – adjudicate individual cases. In all instances, however, these tribunals offer an additional set of norms that may compete with those of state communities.

Perhaps the most controversial international tribunal in operation is the International Criminal Court (ICC), which came into being in 2002 after sixty countries ratified the international statute governing its creation. While the idea of international criminal justice sounds expansive, the court's jurisdiction is limited by the principle of complementarity, under which the ICC can only take cases if the local jurisdiction of the defendant is "unwilling or unable to prosecute." As of this writing, prosecutorial activity has commenced with regard to potential crimes in Uganda, the Democratic Republic of Congo, the Central African Republic, Sudan, and Kenya.

Another prominent tribunal, the International Court of Justice (ICJ), wades into disputes among nation-states, though its rulings may have impact on various entities within a nation-state. One well-known example – already touched upon in the Introduction and discussed in more detail later – concerns the role of the court in adjudicating the Vienna Convention on Consular Relations, an international agreement that, among other things, requires a signatory state to provide consular notification if it arrests a foreign national. The idea is that when foreign citizens are arrested, those citizens should be able to consult their own consulate in order to get help with their defense. Because many states within the United States were not providing such notification, Mexico brought a suit against the United States before the ICJ, which in turn ordered courts in the United States to conduct hearings to determine whether those convicted without receiving such consular assistance should be retried. This ICJ judgment unleashed years of wrangling over the degree to which states within the United States should be deemed bound by the ruling. Similar questions arise with regard to tribunals formed under regional agreements, such as the North American Free Trade Agreement. As noted in the Introduction, special panels created under such agreements can pass judgment on whether domestic legal proceedings have provided fair process.

In these examples, we see that the international forums can provide a source of alternative norms that people then use as leverage in their local settings. This can happen through a variety of processes. Thus, we may see cases brought internationally – as in the ICJ and NAFTA examples – or a case may be brought domestically but explicitly reference international norms. Indeed, there are numerous examples of communities invoking international or regional human rights regimes to pressure their own courts or government to institute reforms, and some of these will be discussed later in the book.

Sometimes the overlap between the international and the national can actually be incorporated in formal judicial bodies themselves. For example, after atrocities in Kosovo, East Timor, Sierra Leone, and Cambodia, hybrid courts were established to try those accused of committing abuses. These courts combined international and local prosecutors and judges in an effort to make the courts more integrated within their societies while still insulating them from claims of factional bias.

Finally, there is, of course, the European Union, which has probably gone the furthest in attempting to integrate nation-states within a larger international polity. And Europe's two most significant judicial bodies, the European Court of Justice and the European Court of Human Rights, have therefore become central players in the complicated dance between European norms and the customs, laws, and court rulings of member states.

Nation-State Versus Substate Conflicts of Norms

In federal systems such as the United States of America, yet more jurisdictional complexity is added because regional entities – states or provinces – also assert normative authority that may overlap with and compete with that of the national government. Indeed, the tensions of federalism have been one of the most enduring facets of American political life since the founding of the country. In recent years, these federalism tensions have tended to arise most frequently in relation to three major issues: environmental regulation, foreign affairs, and immigration.

With regard to environmental regulation, many states responded to sluggish federal environmental enforcement by the Environmental Protection Agency (EPA) during the George W. Bush administration by taking a proactive stance. For example, in *Massachusetts v. EPA*, twelve states, three cities, a U.S. territory, and thirteen nongovernmental organizations successfully sued to force the EPA to pursue regulation of greenhouse gases under the federal Clean Air Act (or at least provide a better justification for not doing so).[45] Similarly, the State of California in 2003 adopted statewide emissions standards for vehicles that were stricter than the then-prevailing federal requirements,[46] and many other states subsequently signed on to the more forceful California rules.[47] The EPA attempted to block these efforts,[48] with then-EPA administrator Stephen Johnson explaining that it was important to have uniform national standards, "not a confusing patchwork of state rules."[49] Nevertheless, the states responded by pursuing litigation[50] and congressional

[45] *Massachusetts v. EPA*, 549 U.S. 497 (2007).

[46] Cal. Health & Safety Code § 43018.5 (West 2004).

[47] Micheline Maynard, EPA Denies California Emission's Waiver, *N.Y. Times*, Dec. 19, 2007, *available at* http://www.nytimes.com/2007/12/19/washington/20epa-web.html.

[48] *Id.* As discussed in more detail in Chapter 6, section 209(b) of the federal Clean Air Act permitted California to seek a waiver from federal preemption. *See* Clean Air Act § 209(b), 42 U.S.C. § 7543(b) (2006). The EPA denied this waiver request. *See* Letter from Stephen L. Johnson, Adm'r, U.S. Envtl. Prot. Agency, to Arnold Schwarzenegger, Governor of Cal. (Dec. 19, 2007), *available at* http://ag.ca.gov/cms_ attachments/press/pdfs/n1514_epa-letter.pdf.

[49] Maynard, *supra* note 47.

[50] For examples of efforts to reverse the denial in courts, *see Petition for Review of Decision of the U.S. EPA, California v. EPA*, No. 08–70011 (9th Cir. Jan. 2, 2008), http://ag.ca.gov/cms_attachments/press/pdfs/n1514_epapetition-1.pdf; *Motion for Leave to Intervene as Petitioners, California ex rel. Brown v. EPA*, No. 08–70011 (9th Cir. Jan. 31, 2008), *available at* http://www.iowa.gov/government/ag/latest_ news/releases/

action,[51] and ultimately the Obama administration embraced the California standards.[52] Thus, we see the dynamic relationship among these lawmaking entities creating an iterative process of interaction, contestation, and change.

Turning to foreign affairs, the U.S. Supreme Court has sought to impose a doctrine of foreign affairs preemption to block efforts by states to weigh in on policy judgments that might have some impact beyond the borders of the country.[53] For example, in *Crosby v. National Foreign Trade Council*, the Court prohibited Massachusetts from disinvesting in Burma to protest the use in that country of forced labor to produce export merchandise.[54] According to the Court, the state law interfered

feb_2008/EPA_regulation.pdf; *Complaint for Injunctive Relief Under the Freedom of Information Act, California v. EPA*, No. 08–00735 (N.D. Cal. Jan. 31, 2008), http://ag.ca.gov/globalwarming/pdf/EPA_FOIA_ complaint.pdf; *Protective Petition for Review, California v. EPA*, No. 08–1178 (D.C. Cir. May 5, 2008), *available at* http://www.cleancarscampaign.org/web-content/legal/docs/petition_08–1178.pdf; *see also* Office of the Attorney General, State of California, California's Motor Vehicle Global Warming Regulations, http://ag.ca.gov/globalwarming/motorvehicle.php.

51 For examples of efforts to reverse and investigate the denial in Congress, *see* Reducing Global Warming Pollution from Vehicles Act of 2008, S. 2555, 110th Cong. (2008); Right to Clean Vehicles Act, H.R. 5560, 110th Cong. (2008); Richard Simon, Hearing Grows Warm for EPA Chief, *L.A. Times*, Jan. 25, 2008, at A13; Staff of H. Comm. on Oversight and Government Reform, 110th Cong., Memorandum on EPA's Denial of the California Waiver (2008), http://www.cleancarscampaign.org/web-content/cleanairact/docs/Waxman-result-5-19-08.pdf.

52 For further discussion of the "multiscalar" state/federal dynamics of the case, *see* Hari M. Osofsky, Is Climate Change "International"? Litigation's Diagonal Regulatory Role, 49 *Va. J. Int'l L.* 585, 616–31 (2009).

53 *See Am. Ins. Ass'n v. Garamendi,* 539 U.S. 396 (2003) (striking down California law requiring insurance companies doing business in California to disclose any business activities in Europe during the Nazi Holocaust); *Crosby v. Nat'l Foreign Trade Council,* 530 U.S. 363 (2000) (preempting a Massachusetts law banning state agencies from contracting with companies that do business with Burma); *Zschernig v. Miller,* 389 U.S. 429 (1968) (striking down Oregon statute that had the effect of preventing a resident of East Germany from inheriting property probated in the state). For a discussion of these cases, *see* Judith Resnik, Foreign as Domestic Affairs: Rethinking Horizontal Federalism and Foreign Affairs Preemption in Light of Translocal Internationalism, 57 *Emory L. J.* 31, 74-8 (2007).

54 *Crosby v. Nat'l Foreign Trade Council*, 530 U.S. 363 (2000).

with the exclusive power of the federal government to make such foreign policy decisions. Using this same doctrine, the Court in *American Insurance Association v. Garamendi* blocked a California law merely requiring insurance companies doing business in California to disclose any business activities in Europe during the Nazi Holocaust.[55] Indeed, here the Court went even further because, unlike in *Crosby*, there was no national legislation addressing the question of whether to impose sanctions against companies that had done business in Germany during the Holocaust. Nevertheless, the Court relied on executive branch representations that California's legislation would affect settlement efforts with these companies on behalf of Holocaust survivors.[56] Using the same logic, a federal district court struck down an Illinois statute divesting from Sudan to protest atrocities in Darfur.[57]

Predictably, these efforts to impose national uniformity and clamp down on state norms have created a backlash. Most recently, in response to rulings like the one in Illinois, localities and states pressed Congress to help insulate local divestment programs from preemption attacks. The result of these efforts was the Sudan Accountability and Divestment Act.[58] As will be discussed in Chapter 6, this statute formalizes a dialectical interaction between the federal and state government by permitting localities to divest, but only if they comply with a series of federally imposed procedural and substantive mandates.[59]

[55] *Am. Ins. Ass'n v. Garamendi*, 539 U.S. 396 (2003).

[56] *See* Brief of the United States as Amicus Curiae Supporting Petitioners, *Am. Ins. Ass'n v. Garamendi*, 539 U.S. 396 (2003), 2003WL721754, at 1 (Feb. 24, 2003) (describing the federal government's encouragement of the "use of voluntary, non-adversarial mechanisms for resolving Holocaust victims' claims" and contrasting that approach with California's statutory obligations and arguing that the state laws "directly interfere with the national government's authority over foreign affairs and foreign commerce"). The brief argued that the California legislation "impermissibly intrudes" into the conduct of both "diplomatic and commercial relations with other nations – that is exclusively reserved to the President and the Congress." *Id.* at 9.

[57] *National Foreign Trade Council, Inc. v. Giannoulias*, 523 F. Supp. 2d 731 (N.D. Ill. 2007).

[58] Sudan Accountability and Divestment Act of 2007 (SADA), Pub. L. No. 110–174, 21 Stat. 2516 (2007).

[59] Such mandates include the following: First, the authority to divest is limited to companies with business operations in Sudan. SADA§ 3(d)(1). Second, the authority is

Finally, the federal government has also asserted the exclusive right to conduct foreign affairs as a rationale to block state laws regarding immigration enforcement. Here, the principal area of high profile activity in recent years has been in Arizona. The state legislature has enacted two different immigration statutes,[60] both of which have been challenged in federal court on preemption grounds.[61] As of this writing, the outcome of both cases remains in doubt, but these heated federalist clashes and the extraordinary national publicity such clashes create surely suggest that the spheres of normative authority between nation-state and substate remain fiercely contested and perhaps forever uncertain.

State Versus Nonstate Conflicts of Norms

The range of nonstate norm-generating communities is so vast as to be almost impossible even to summarize. From religious institutions to industry standard-setting bodies to not-for-profit accreditation entities to arbitral panels to university tenure committees to codes promulgated within ethnic enclaves to self-regulation regimes in semiautonomous

limited to companies with operations in four specified industries: "power production activities, mineral extraction activities, oil-related activities, or the production of military equipment." *Id.* Third, the authority does not extend to companies that have "voluntarily suspended" their activities in Sudan or that can demonstrate that their activities conform with federal policy concerning Sudan. SADA§ 3(d)(2). Fourth, companies targeted for divestment must be provided with "written notice and an opportunity to comment in writing," prior to final action. SADA§ 3(e). Fifth, targeted companies must "have direct investments in Sudan." SADA§ 3(b). Sixth, divestment authority does not extend to funds governed by federal pension law. SADA§ 3(f)(2). Finally, and perhaps most importantly, divestment is not allowed if the president certifies either that "the national interest" so requires or that Sudan has met certain conditions assuring peace and safety for civilian populations. SADA§ 12. For a discussion of SADA as an example of "dialogic federalism," *see* Perry S. Bechky, Darfur, Divestment, and Dialogue, 30 *U. Pa. J. Int'l L.* 823 (2009).

[60] 2007 Ariz. Legis. Serv. 279 (West) (giving the state the power to suspend the licenses of businesses that have twice been caught employing unauthorized aliens); 2010 Ariz. Legis. Serv. 113 (West) (authorizing police to request immigration documents from aliens).

[61] *United States v. Arizona*, 641 F. 3d 339 (9th Cir. 2011) (granting a preliminary injunction preventing Arizona from enforcing relevant portions of S.B. 1070).

communities, the sites of nonstate lawmaking are truly everywhere. And the interaction of formal state law with such nonstate lawmaking has always been a complicated dance, reminiscent of the way "high" composers from Mozart to Gershwin have incorporated and transformed more vernacular musical styles, while folk music persisted as an alternative to high art forms.[62]

In places where the state is weak or nonexistent, these nonstate lawmaking communities tend to have great power, of course.[63] One need only look at ethnic clans in Afghanistan or the warlords operating in Darfur to see how strong these forces can be. Yet, even in areas with well-developed formal governmental institutions, nonstate norms still create areas of resistance to, or semiautonomous pockets within, state law. Such quasi-legal regimes could be as mundane as placing a chair in a parking space after it has been cleared of snow to mark it as temporarily "owned" by the shoveler.[64] Or they can form the fundamental rules of an industry, as when cattle ranchers[65] or jewelry merchants[66] develop complex self-governing frameworks to try to instill cooperative behavior, or when industry standards become the de facto rule for a particular sector.[67] Such self-governance often includes significant enforcement

[62] *See* Carol Weisbrod, Fusion Folk: A Comment on Law and Music, 20 *Cardozo L. Rev.* 1439 (1999).

[63] *See* Rosa Brooks, The New Imperialism: Violence, Norms, and "The Rule of Law," 101 *Mich. L. Rev.* 2275 (2003); Elena Baylis, Beyond Rights: Legal Process and Ethnic Conflicts, 25 *Mich. J. Int'l L.* 529 (2004).

[64] *See* Patricia Ewick & Susan S. Silbey, *The Common Place of Law: Stories from Everyday Life* (1998).

[65] Robert C. Ellickson, *Order Without Law: How Neighbors Settle Disputes* (1991) (drawing on an empirical study of relations among cattle ranchers to develop a theory of nonlegal norms as a source of social control).

[66] Lisa Bernstein, Opting Out of the Legal System: Extralegal Contractual Relations in the Diamond Industry, 21 *J. Leg. Stud.* 115 (1992) (discussing the system of "private lawmaking" in the New York Diamond Dealers Club).

[67] *See, e.g.*, the International Accounting Standards Board, a private corporation that both defines and promotes international financial reporting standards, among many other examples. International Accounting Standards Board (IASB), Who we are and what we do, http://www.ifrs.org/NR/rdonlyres/1D35BB5F-6E59-446F-9861-A84F9288CBB4/0/Who_we_areJuly11.pdf (July, 2011).

clout (from gossip to public humiliation to ostracism) that is separate from governmental authority.

Sometimes, nonstate norms create forceful obligations in and of themselves and even "harden" into formal law. For example, as Janet Koven Levit has noted in the context of transnational trade finance, rules embodied in various informal standards, procedures, and agreements that bind banks and credit agencies have the force of law even without any official governmental involvement.[68] In addition, she points out that more formal lawmaking institutions such as the World Trade Organization have, over time, appropriated these norms into their official legal instruments.[69]

Other times, the nonstate regime seeks out space for autonomy within the larger state framework. Thus, as discussed in Chapter 8, a Christian university might seek to ban interracial dating as an interpretation of scriptural law in conflict with federal constitutional law.[70] Likewise, a religious ritual using peyote may run afoul of state laws of general application banning the use of controlled substances.[71]

Finally, nonstate norms can simply run on a parallel track to state law, as when arbitral bodies issue binding decisions that are generally not within the purview of state-based courts. Likewise, Sharia courts have operated within limited spheres inside nonreligious, state-based legal systems.[72] And corporate codes of conduct promulgated by entities

[68] Janet Koven Levit, A Bottom-Up Approach to International Lawmaking: The Tale of Three Trade Finance Instruments, 30 *Yale J. Int'l L.* 125 (2005). *See also*, *e.g.*, Amitai Aviram, A Paradox of Spontaneous Formation: The Evolution of Private Legal Systems, 22 *Yale L. & Pol'y Rev.* 1 (2004) (using game theory to argue that the existence of preexisting networks enhances a private legal system's ability to enforce norms); Lisa Bernstein, Private Commercial Law in the Cotton Industry: Creating Cooperation Through Rules, Norms and Institutions, 99 *Mich. L. Rev.* 1724 (2001).

[69] *See* Levit, *supra* note 68, at 128.

[70] *See Bob Jones Univ. v. United States*, 461 U.S. 574 (1983).

[71] *See Emp't Div., Dep't of Human Res. of Oregon v. Smith,* 494 U.S. 872 (1990).

[72] *See* Sameer Ahmed, Pluralism in British Islamic Reasoning: The Problem with Recognizing Islamic Law in the United Kingdom, 33 *Yale J. Int'l L. 491* (2008) (describing the role of unofficial sharia councils in British family law).

such as the Forest Stewardship Council can at times "regulate" behavior more effectively than a top-down state sanction because the threat of consumer mobilization may be more effective than the possibility of state-based enforcement.[73]

In short, state and nonstate legal and quasi-legal systems are always jostling with each other, providing yet more areas of overlapping authority and jurisdictional hybridity. And while this brief summary only barely scratches the surface, it suffices to indicate just how messy and complex our hybrid legal world really is. Moreover, only by taking seriously the principles of legal pluralism can we even begin to conceptualize in any comprehensive way this multifaceted world of legal conflict or develop schemes to manage the hybrid legal spaces that result. Accordingly, we now turn to the scholarly literature on legal pluralism and the ways in which that literature may be helpful in crafting a framework that will help us develop a jurisprudence for the hybrid world we inhabit.

Legal Pluralism and Global Legal Interactions

So, if it is true that we live in a world where a single act or actor is always potentially regulated by multiple legal or quasi-legal regimes, how should law respond? In some sense, both lawyers and legal academics, faced with this obvious reality, fall victim to what is sometimes called the "streetlight effect," named after the old joke in which a police officer sees a drunk man searching in vain under a streetlight for his keys and asks whether he is sure he lost them there. The drunk replies, no, he lost them across the street. The officer, incredulous, asks then why he is searching here, and the drunk replies, "the light is so much brighter here." Likewise, I think we all know, on some level, that jurisdictional hybridity is a reality, and accordingly our assumptions that nation-states exist in autonomous,

[73] *See* Kenneth Abbott & Duncan Snidal, Strengthening International Regulation Through Transnational New Governance: Overcoming the Orchestration Deficit, 42 *Vand. J. Transnat'l L.* 501 (2009); Errol Meidinger, The Administrative Law of Global Private-Public Regulation: The Case of Forestry, 17 *Eur. J. Int'l L.* 47 (2006).

territorially distinct spheres and that activities therefore fall under the jurisdiction of only one legal regime at a time do not begin to describe the world we encounter now, let alone the one that is emerging. And yet the light is so much brighter in this fictional world of discrete sovereignties. Accordingly, we would rather search for answers there than look for new paradigms in the far more shadowy world in which we actually live.[74]

Nevertheless, those seeking to understand the multifaceted role of law in an era of globalization need to look for alternative models. In that regard, we should take seriously the insights of legal pluralism because such insights will help open the door to a much more nuanced conceptualization of how legal norms are articulated and disseminated in a hybrid world. In general, theorists of pluralism start from the premise that people belong to (or feel affiliated with) multiple groups and understand themselves to be bound by the norms of these multiple groups.[75] Such groups can, as noted previously, include familiar political affiliations, such as nation-states, counties, towns, and so on. But many community affiliations, such as those held by transnational or subnational ethnic groups, religious institutions, trade organizations, unions, online social media groups, terrorist networks, and myriad other "norm-generating communities,"[76] may at various times exert tremendous power over our actions even though they are not part of an "official" state-based system. Indeed, as scholars of legal pluralism have long noted, "not all the phenomena related to law and not all that are lawlike have their source in government."[77]

[74] *See* David H. Freedman, The Streetlight Effect, *Discover*, July/August 2010, at 54. I am grateful to David Post for suggesting the analogy to my work.

[75] *See, e.g.*, Avigail I. Eisenberg, *Reconstructing Political Pluralism* 2 (1995) (defining pluralist theories as those that "seek to organize and conceptualize political phenomena on the basis of the plurality of groups to which individuals belong and by which individuals seek to advance and, more importantly, to develop, their interests"). For a far-from-exhaustive list of some of the pluralist literature, *see* Chapter 1, note 25.

[76] Robert Cover, Foreword: Nomos and Narrative, The Supreme Court 1982 Term, 97 *Harv. L. Rev.* 4, 43 (1983).

[77] Sally Falk Moore, Legal Systems of the World: An Introductory Guide to Classifications, Typological Interpretations, and Bibliographical Resources, in *Law and the Social*

Just as importantly, legal pluralists have studied those situations in which two or more state and nonstate normative systems occupy the same social field and must negotiate the resulting hybrid legal space. Historically, anthropologically oriented legal pluralists focused on the overlapping normative systems created during the process of colonization.[78] Early twentieth-century studies of indigenous law among tribes and villages in colonized societies noted the simultaneous existence of both local law and European law.[79] Indeed, British colonial law actually incorporated Hindu, Muslim, and Christian personal law in its administrative framework.[80] This early pluralist scholarship focused on the hierarchical coexistence of what were imagined to be quite separate legal systems, layered one on top of the other. Thus, for example, when Leopold Pospisil documented the way in which Kapauku Papuans responded to the imposition of Dutch law, it was relatively easy to differentiate the two legal fields since Dutch law and Kapauku law were quite distinct.[81] As a result, Pospisil could readily identify the degree of penetration of Dutch law, both those areas in which the Kapauku had appropriated and transformed Dutch law and those areas in which negotiations between the two legal systems were part of a broader political struggle.[82] Despite the somewhat reductionist cast of the model, these pioneering studies established the key insights of legal pluralism: a recognition that

Sciences 11, 15 (Leon Lipson & Stanton Wheeler eds., 1986). *See also* Gunther Teubner, The Two Faces of Janus: Rethinking Legal Pluralism, 13 *Cardozo L. Rev.* 1443, 1443 (1992) ("[L]egal pluralism is at the same time both: social norms and legal rules, law and society, formal and informal, rule-oriented and spontaneous."). *But see* Brian Z. Tamanaha, The Folly of the "Social Scientific" Concept of Legal Pluralism, 20 *J.L. & Soc'y* 192, 193 (1993) (arguing that such a broad view of "law" causes law to lose any distinctive meaning).

78 *See* Sally Engle Merry, Legal Pluralism, 22 *Law & Soc'y Rev.* 869, 869-72 (1988) (summarizing the literature).

79 *See, e.g.*, Bronislaw Malinowski, Crime and Custom in Savage Society (1926).

80 Sally Engle Merry, *International Law and Sociolegal Scholarship: Toward a Spatial Global Legal Pluralism* 12 (Studies in Law, Politics, & Society, Vol. 41, Austin Sarat ed., 2007).

81 *See* Leopold Pospisil, *Anthropology of Law: A Comparative Theory* (1971).

82 *See id.*

multiple normative orders exist and a focus on the dialectical interaction between and among these normative orders.[83]

In the 1970s and 1980s, anthropological scholars of pluralism complicated the picture in three significant ways. First, they questioned the hierarchical model of one legal system simply dominating the other and instead argued that systems are often semiautonomous, operating within the framework of other legal fields, but not entirely governed by them.[84] As Sally Engle Merry recounts, this was an extraordinarily powerful conceptual move because it placed "at the center of investigation the relationship between the official legal system and other forms of ordering that connect with but are in some ways separate from and dependent on it."[85] Second, scholars began to conceptualize the interaction between legal systems as bidirectional, with each influencing (and helping to constitute) the other.[86] This was a distinct shift from the early studies, which had tended only to investigate ways in which state law penetrated and changed indigenous systems and not the other way around. Third, scholars defined the idea of a "legal system" sufficiently broadly to include many types of nonofficial normative ordering and therefore argued that such legal subgroups operate not just in colonial societies, but in advanced industrialized settings as well.[87]

Of course, finding nonstate forms of normative ordering is sometimes more difficult outside the colonial context because there is no obvious indigenous system, and the less formal ordering structures tend to "blend more readily into the landscape."[88] Thus, pluralists argued that, in order to see nonstate law, scholars would first need to reject what John

[83] *See* Merry, *supra* note 78, at 873.

[84] *See, e.g.*, Sally Falk Moore, Law and Social Change: The Semi-Autonomous Social Field as an Appropriate Subject of Study, 7 *Law. & Soc'y Rev.* 719 (1973); Robert L. Kidder, Toward an Integrated Theory of Imposed Law, in *The Imposition of Law* 289 (Sandra B. Burman & Barbara E. Harrell-Bond eds., 1979).

[85] Merry, *supra* note 78, at 873.

[86] *See, e.g.*, Peter Fitzpatrick, Law and Societies, 22 *Osgoode Hall L.J.* 115 (1984).

[87] *See* Merry, *supra* note 78, at 870–71 (summarizing some of the literature).

[88] *Id.* at 873.

Griffiths called "the ideology of legal centralism," the exclusive positivist focus on state law and its system of lawyers, courts, and prisons.[89] Instead, pluralists turned to documenting "forms of social regulation that draw on the symbols of the law, to a greater or lesser extent, but that operate in its shadows, its parking lots, and even down the street in mediation offices."[90]

Meanwhile, scholars drawing more from political theory than anthropology have long focused on the fact that, prior to the rise of the state system, much lawmaking took place in autonomous institutions and within smaller units such as cities and guilds, while large geographic areas were left largely unregulated.[91] And, like the anthropologists, they have observed a whole range of nonstate lawmaking even in modern nation-states: in tribal or ethnic enclaves,[92] religious organizations,[93] corporate bylaws, social customs,[94] private regulatory bodies, and a wide variety of groups, associations, and nonstate institutions.[95] For example, in England

[89] John Griffiths, What Is Legal Pluralism?, 24 *J. Legal Pluralism & Unofficial L.* 1, 3 (1986).

[90] Merry, Legal Pluralism, *supra* note 78, at 874.

[91] *See* Eugen Ehrlich, *Fundamental Principles of the Sociology of Law* 13–38 (Walter L. Moll trans., Russell & Russell 1962) (1936) (analyzing and describing the differences between legal and nonlegal norms). *See generally* Otto Gierke, *Associations and Law: The Classical and Early Christian Stages* (George Heiman ed. & trans., 1977) (setting forth a legal philosophy based on the concept of association as a fundamental human organizing principle); Otto Gierke, *Natural Law and the Theory of Society: 1500 to 1800* (Ernest Barker trans., 1934) (presenting a theory of the evolution of the state and nonstate groups according to the principle of natural law).

[92] *See, e.g.*, Walter Otto Weyrauch & Maureen Anne Bell, Autonomous Lawmaking: The Case of the "Gypsies," 103 *Yale L.J.* 323 (1993) (delineating the subtle interactions between the legal system of the Romani people and the norms of their host countries).

[93] *See* Carol Weisbrod, *The Boundaries of Utopia* (1980); *see also* Marc Galanter, Justice in Many Rooms: Courts, Private Ordering, and Indigenous Law, 19 *J. Legal Pluralism* 1 (1981); Carol Weisbrod, Family, Church and State: An Essay on Constitutionalism and Religious Authority, 26 *J. Fam. L.* 741 (1988).

[94] *See, e.g.*, Lon L. Fuller, *Anatomy of the Law* 43–49 (1968) (describing "implicit law," which includes everything from rules governing a camping trip among friends to the customs of merchants).

[95] *See, e.g.*, Ellickson, *supra* note 65; Stewart Macaulay, Images of Law in Everyday Life: The Lessons of School, Entertainment, and Spectator Sports, 21 *Law & Soc'y Rev.*

bodies such as the church, the stock exchange, the legal profession, the insurance market, and even the Jockey Club opted for forms of self-regulation that included machinery for arbitrating disputes among their own members.[96] Moreover, "private, closely knit, homogeneous micro-societies can create their own norms that at times trump state law and at other times fill lacunae in state regulation but nonetheless operate autonomously."[97] Finally, such scholars have sometimes focused on religious communities and their ongoing tensions with state authorities.[98]

More recently, a new group of legal pluralists has emerged under the rubric of social norms theory. Interestingly, these scholars rarely refer to the anthropologists and political theorists who have long explored pluralism, perhaps because social norms theory has emerged as a branch of behavioral law and economics. The study of social norms, in its most capacious formulation, focuses on the variety of "rules and standards that impose limits on acceptable behavior."[99] Such social norms "may be the product of custom and usage, organizational affiliations, consensual undertakings and individual conscience."[100] In addition, "norm entrepreneurs," defined as individuals or groups who try to influence popular opinion in order to inculcate a social norm, may consciously try to mobilize social pressure to sustain or create social norms.[101] And while some pluralists think that this

185 (1987) (discussing the concept of legality as reflected in popular culture); Stewart Macaulay, Non-Contractual Relations in Business: A Preliminary Study, 28 *Am. Soc. Rev.* 55 (1963) (presenting empirical data on nonlegal dispute settlement in the manufacturing industry); Stewart Macaulay, Popular Legal Culture: An Introduction, 98 *Yale L.J.* 1545 (1989) (surveying the sources of popular perceptions of the law).

[96] *See* F.W. Maitland, Trust and Corporation, in Maitland: *Selected Essays* 141, 189–95 (H.D. Hazeltine, G. Lapsley & P.H. Winfield eds., 1936) (1905) (describing the sophisticated nonlegal means of enforcing order among members of these institutions).

[97] Levit, *supra* note 68.

[98] *See* Weisbrod, *The Boundaries of Utopia*, *supra* note 93.

[99] William K. Jones, A Theory of Social Norms, 1994 *U. Ill. L. Rev.* 545, 546 (1994).

[100] *Id; see also, e.g.*, David Charny, Illusions of a Spontaneous Order: "Norms," *Contractual Relationships*, 144 *U. Pa. L. Rev.* 1841, 1841 (1996) (noting that norms are said to evolve from the repeated dealings of contracting parties or industry consensus and that these norms are enforced both privately and through legal mechanisms).

[101] *See* Ethan A. Nadelmann, Global Prohibition Regimes: The Evolution of Norms in International Society, 44 *Int'l Org.* 479, 482 (1990) (defining "transnational moral

broader category of social norms dilutes legal pluralism's historic focus on more stable religious, ethnic, or tribal groupings,[102] social norms theory has the benefit of theorizing larger transnational communities that may be based on long-term rhetorical persuasion rather than face-to-face interaction.[103] Indeed, social norms theory tends to emphasize processes whereby norms are internalized through guilt, self-bereavement, a sense of duty, and a desire for esteem, or simply by slowly altering categories of thought and the set of taken-for-granted ideas that constitute one's sense of "the way things are."[104]

Those who study international public and private law have not, historically, paid much attention either to legal pluralism or to social norms theory. This is because the emphasis traditionally has been on state-to-state relations. Indeed, international law has historically emphasized bilateral and multilateral treaties between and among states, the activities of the United Nations, the pronouncements of international tribunals, and

entrepreneurs" as nongovernmental transnational organizations that (1) "mobilize popular opinion and political support both within their host country and abroad"; (2) "stimulate and assist in the creation of like-minded organizations in other countries"; (3) "play a significant role in elevating their objective beyond its identification with the national interests of their government"; and (4) often direct their efforts "toward persuading foreign audiences, especially foreign elites, that a particular prohibition regime reflects a widely shared or even universal moral sense, rather than the peculiar moral code of one society"); *see also, e.g.*, Martha Finnemore & Kathryn Sikkink, International Norm Dynamics and Political Change, 52 *Int'l Org.* 887 (1998); Harold Hongju Koh, The 1998 Frankel Lecture: Bringing International Law Home, 35 *Hous. L. Rev.* 623, 647–8 (1998).

102 *See, e.g.*, Perry Dane, The Maps of Sovereignty: A Meditation, 12 *Cardozo L. Rev.* 959, 991-2 ("There must ... be some way to tell a true competing sovereign from any other assemblage.... If every social order that the state confronts is a legal order, there is no legal order. If every legal thought is law, there is no law.").

103 Rex D. Glensy, Quasi-Global Social Norms, 38 *Conn. L. Rev.* 79, 84 (2005) ("[T]he group can consist of cattle ranchers in a county who interact on a regular basis or of millions of people who live on separate continents who, when taken individually, have a virtual statistical impossibility of interacting with each other even once in their lifetimes.").

104 Such unexamined ideas about legal reality are part of what sociolegal scholars describe as "legal consciousness." In Chapter 3 I discuss further the importance of legal consciousness.

(somewhat more controversially) the norms that states had obeyed long enough that such norms could be deemed customary.[105] This was a legal universe with two guiding principles. First, law was deemed to reside only in the acts of official, state-sanctioned entities. Second, law was seen as an exclusive function of state sovereignty.[106]

[105] *See, e.g.*, Statute of the International Court of Justice, art. 38(1), June 26, 1945, 59 Stat. 1055, 1060 (stating that the primary sources of international law are international treaties and conventions, customary practices of states accepted as law, and general principles of law common to most legal systems).

[106] Of course, this is an oversimplified vision of international law. Obviously, nonstate sources – including the idea of natural law itself – have long played a key role in the development of international legal principles. *See generally* David J. Bederman, Religion and the Sources of International Law in Antiquity, in *The Influence of Religion on the Development of International Law* 3 (Mark W. Janis ed., 1991) (tracing the role of religion in the Near East during the empires of Egypt, Babylon, Assyria, Hittites, Mittani, Israelites, Greek city-states, Indian states before 150 B.C., and Mediterranean powers from 338 to 168 B.C.). Indeed, prior to Bentham, these nonstate sources, including the universal common law of *ius gentium*, were arguably far more important than the norms generated by states. *See* Harold Hongju Koh, Why Do Nations Obey International Law?, 106 *Yale L.J.* 2599, 2605 (1997) (reviewing Abram Chayes & Antonia Handler Chayes, *The New Sovereignty: Compliance with International Regulatory Agreements* (1995) and Thomas M. Franck, *Fairness in International Law and Institutions* (1995)) (noting that medieval legal scholars viewed the law of nations, understood as *ius naturae et gentium*, as a universal law binding upon all mankind). For example, during the Middle Ages, treaties – which are usually viewed today as the positive law of state interaction – were deemed subject to the overarching jurisdiction of the church because they were sealed by oaths. *See* Arthur Nussbaum, *A Concise History of the Law of Nations* 24 (1947). Even later, no less a theorist than Vattel, while rejecting natural law's religious underpinnings (*see* Mark W. Janis, *An Introduction to International Law* 61 (4th ed. 2003)), continued to ground international law in the laws of nature. *See* E. de Vattel, *The Law of Nations; or, Principles of the Law of Nature: Applied to the Conduct and Affairs of Nations and Sovereigns* lviii (G. G. London & J. Robinson, 1797) (1792). In the nineteenth century, though positivism reigned both in the United States and abroad, transnational nonstate actors nevertheless played important roles. *See* Koh, *supra*, at 2612 (noting the work of William Wilberforce and the British and Foreign Anti-Slavery Society; Henry Dunant and the International Committee of the Red Cross; and Christian peace activists, such as America's William Ladd and Elihu Burritt, "who promoted public international arbitration and permanent international criminal courts"). And, of course, natural law principles continue to undergird many international law doctrines, such as *jus cogens* norms. *See* Janis, *supra*, at 64. Thus, the focus on nonstate norm generation is not a new phenomenon, but I argue that it is reemerging

As with the strict nineteenth-century territorial rules for jurisdiction, however, both of these sovereigntist principles have eroded over time. The rise of a conception of international human rights in the post–World War II era transformed individuals into international law stakeholders, possessing their own entitlements against the state.[107] But even apart from individual empowerment, scholars have more recently come to recognize the myriad ways in which the prerogatives of nation-states are cabined by transnational and international actors. Whereas F. A. Mann could confidently state in 1984 that "laws extend so far as, but no further than the sovereignty of the State which puts them into force,"[108] many international law scholars have, at least since the end of the cold war, argued that such a narrow view of how law operates transnationally is inadequate. Thus, the past twenty years have seen increasing attention to the important – though sometimes inchoate – processes of international norm development.[109] Such processes inevitably lead scholars to consider overlapping transnational jurisdictional assertions by nation-states, as well as norms articulated by international bodies, nongovernmental organizations (NGOs), multinational corporations and industry groups, indigenous communities, transnational terrorists, networks of activists, and so on.

as a significant branch of scholarship within international law and might even call for a reclassification of international law itself.

[107] *See, e.g.*, W. Michael Reisman, Introduction, in *Jurisdiction in International Law*, xi, xii (W. Michael Reisman ed., 1999) (noting that "since the Second World War, an increasing number of international norms of both customary and conventional provenance ... now restrict or displace specific law-making and applying competences of states"); Louis Henkin, Human Rights and State "Sovereignty," 25 *Ga. J. Int'l & Comp. L.* 31, 33 (1995–6) ("At mid-century, the international system began a slow, hesitant move from state values towards human values."). *But see* Janis, *supra* note 106, at 5–6; Georg Schwarzenberger, 1 *International Law* 34–36 (3d ed. 1957) (both noting that even after Nuremberg, international law derived primarily from state practice).

[108] F.A. Mann, The Doctrine of International Jurisdiction Revisited After Twenty Years, in 186 *Recueil Des Cours: Collected Courses of the Hague Academy of International Law* 20 (1985).

[109] *See* Berman, *supra* note 1, at 488–9 (summarizing some of this literature).

Yet, while international law scholars are increasingly emphasizing the importance of these overlapping legal and quasi-legal communities, there has been surprisingly little attention paid to the pluralism literature.[110] This is a shame, because this literature could help international law find a more comprehensive framework for conceptualizing the clash of normative communities in the modern world. Consider, for example, Sally Falk Moore's idea of the "semiautonomous social field," which she describes as one that

> can generate rules and customs and symbols internally, but that ... is also vulnerable to rules and decisions and other forces emanating from the larger world by which it is surrounded. The semi-autonomous social field has rule-making capacities, and the means to induce or coerce compliance; but it is simultaneously set in a larger social matrix which can, and does, affect and invade it, sometimes at the invitation of persons inside it, sometimes at its own instance.[111]

Notice that, following Moore's idea, we can conceive of a legal system as both autonomous and permeable; outside norms affect the system but do not dominate it fully. The framework thus captures a dialectical and iterative interplay that we see among normative communities in the international system, an interplay that rigidly territorialist or positivist visions of legal authority do not address.

Even more fundamentally, legal pluralists have observed ways in which state law and other normative orders mutually constitute each other. Thus, for example, the family and its legal order are obviously shaped by the state, but the state in turn is shaped by the family and its legal order because each is part of the other.[112] And though pluralists

[110] There are some exceptions. *See, e.g.*, William W. Burke-White, International Legal Pluralism, 25 *Mich. J. Int'l L.* 963 (2004); Benedict Kingsbury, Confronting Difference: The Puzzling Durability of Gentili's Combination of Pragmatic Pluralism and Normative Judgment, 92 *Am. J. Int'l L.* 713 (1998); Nico Krisch, The Pluralism of Global Administrative Law, 17 *Eur. J. Int'l L.* 247 (2006).

[111] Moore, *supra* note 84, at 720.

[112] *See, e.g.*, Peter Fitzpatrick, Law, Plurality and Underdevelopment, in *Legality, Ideology and the State* 159 (David Sugarman ed., 1983).

were historically thinking of the state's relationship to internal nonstate law within its borders, the framework is equally cogent in studying external dialectical interactions both with other states and with various international or transnational legal communities. Indeed, recent international law scholarship emphasizes ways in which states are changed simply by the fact that they are part of an international network of states.[113] Such an insight echoes pluralism's co-constitutive approach.

In addition, pluralism offers possibilities for thinking about spaces of resistance to state law. Indeed, by recognizing at least the semiautonomy of conflicting legal orders, pluralism necessarily examines limits to the ideological power of state legal pronouncements. Pluralists do not deny the significance of state law and coercive power, of course, but they do try to identify places where state law does not penetrate or penetrates only partially, and where alternative forms of ordering persist to provide opportunities for resistance, contestation, and alternative vision. Such an approach encourages international law scholars to treat the multiple sites of normative authority in the global legal system as a set of inevitable interactions to be managed, not as a "problem" to be "solved." And again, though pluralists historically looked only at nonstate alternatives to state power, the international law context adds state-to-state relations and their overlapping jurisdictional assertions to the mix, providing yet another set of possible alternative normative communities to the web of pluralist interactions.

Finally, pluralism frees scholars from needing an essentialist definition of "law." For example, with legal pluralism as our analytical frame, we can get beyond the endless debates both about whether international law is law at all and whether it has any real effect. Indeed, the whole debate about law versus nonlaw is largely irrelevant in a pluralism context because the key questions involve the normative commitments of a community and the interactions among normative orders that give rise

[113] *See, e.g.*, Ryan Goodman & Derek Jinks, How to Influence States: Socialization and International Human Rights Law, 54 *Duke L.J.* 621 (2004).

to such commitments, not their formal status. Thus, we can resist positivist reductionism and set nation-state law within a broader context.[114] Moreover, an emphasis on social norms allows us more readily to see how it is that nonstate legal norms can have significant impact in the world. After all, if a statement of norms is ultimately internalized by a population, that statement will have important binding force, often even more so than a formal law backed by state sanction.[115] Accordingly, by taking pluralism seriously we will more easily see the way in which the contest over norms creates legitimacy over time, and we can put to rest the idea that norms not associated with nation-states necessarily lack significance.[116] Indeed, legal pluralists refuse to focus solely on who has the formal authority to articulate norms or the coercive power to enforce them. Instead, they aim to study empirically which statements of authority tend to be *treated* as binding in actual practice and by whom.

Of course, there are differences among forms of ordering, particularly given that some legal norms have coercive power behind them and some do not.[117] And, obviously, disparities in political and economic power strongly affect how much influence any particular normative community

[114] For those who are inclined to reify state law as law and to deny all other forms of social ordering the use of the word "law," Santos argues that law is like medicine. Thus, he observes that:

> side by side with the official, professionalized, pharmochemical, allopathic medicine, other forms of medicine circulate in society: traditional, herbal, community-based, magical, non-Western medicines. Why should the designation of medicine be restricted to the first type of medicine, the only one recognized as such by the national health system? Clearly, a politics of definition is at work here, and its working should be fully unveiled and dealt with in its own terms.

Boaventura de Sousa Santos, *Toward a New Common Sense: Law, Science and Politics in the Paradigmatic Transition* 91 (2d ed. 2002).

[115] For a discussion of the importance of legal consciousness scholarship to international law thinking, *see* Chapter 3.

[116] *See id.* (critiquing a positivist rational choice approach to international law on this ground).

[117] *See, e.g.*, Santos, *supra* note 114, at 91 (arguing that we must "counteract the romantic bias of much legal pluralistic thinking" and "avoid equating simplistically all legal orders coexisting in a given geopolitical unit, and particularly...avoid denying the centrality of state law in modern sociolegal fields").

is likely to have. But even those differences are not completely determinative. After all, even if formal legal institutions have a near-monopoly on legitimate use of force (at least in many places), there are many other forms of effective coercion and inducement wielded by nonstate actors.[118] In addition, official legal norms that are contrary to prevailing customary or community norms will often have little or no real world effect, at least without the willingness (or capability) of coercive bodies to exercise sustained force to impose such norms. Thus, obedience to norms frequently reflects sociopolitical reality more than the status of those norms as "law." As a result, "[d]efining the essence of law or custom is less valuable than situating these concepts in particular sets of relations between particular legal orders in particular historical contexts."[119]

In any event, the important point is that scholars studying the global legal scene need not rehash long and ultimately fruitless debates (both in philosophy[120] and in anthropology[121]) about what constitutes law and can instead take a nonessentialist position: treating as law that which people view as law.[122] This formulation turns the what-is-law question into a descriptive inquiry concerning which social norms are recognized as authoritative sources of obligation and by whom.[123] Indeed, the question

[118] *See* Moore, *supra* note 84, at 721; *see also* Leopold Pospisil, *supra* note 81, at 97–126 (1971); Max Weber, *Law in Economy and Society* 18–19 (Max Rheinstein ed., 1954) (describing means of coercion applied by "private" organizations); Weber, *supra*, at 37-8 (describing the limits of state power to regulate activities in the economic sphere).

[119] Merry, *supra* note 78, at 889.

[120] Compare, *e.g.*, H.L.A. Hart, *The Concept of Law* (1961), with Lon. L. Fuller, *The Morality of Law* (1964), and Ronald Dworkin, *Taking Rights Seriously* (1977).

[121] Compare, *e.g.*, Malinowski, *supra* note 79, with E. Adamson Hoebel, *The Law of Primitive Man: A Study in Comparative Legal Dynamics* (1954).

[122] For a statement of this approach, *see* Brian Z. Tamanaha, A Non-Essentialist Version of Legal Pluralism, 27 *J.L. Soc'y* 296, 312-21 (2000).

[123] Such an approach echoes Paul Bohannan's focus on "double institutionalization," the process whereby secondary institutional arrangements are developed to assess which primary norms are deemed authoritative. *See* Paul Bohannan, Law and Legal Institutions, in 9 *International Encyclopedia of the Social Sciences* 73 (David L. Sills ed., 1968); *see also* Philippe Nonet & Philip Selznick, *Law and Society in Transition: Toward Responsive Law* 13 (1978) (adopting a similar formulation). Similarly, Roger Cotterrell

of what constitutes law is itself revealed as a terrain of contestation among multiple actors.[124] Thus, pluralists understand that state law never fully stamps out the alternative normative universes that exist. And so in the end there can be no effective retreat from hybridity. Accordingly, instead of insisting on a single set of authoritative norms, we can direct our attention to a more comprehensive investigation of how best to mediate the hybrid spaces where normative systems and communities overlap and clash. It is to that question that we now turn.

proposes "institutionalized doctrine" as a sufficient model of "the legal," recognizing that "doctrine" can take many guises and be institutionalized to varying degrees. *See* Roger Cotterrell, *Law's Community: Legal Theory in Sociological Perspective* 23-40 (1995).

[124] This is one of the reasons anthropologists turned away from the essentialist debate. *See* Laura Nader, *The Life of the Law: Anthropological Projects* 31 (2002).

Part II RETREATING FROM HYBRIDITY

3 The Limits of Sovereigntist Territoriality

ONE RESPONSE TO THE MESSY HYBRID WORLD OUTLINED in Chapter 2 is to seek clearer boundary lines between those norms that are heard by a decision maker and those norms that are treated as "outside" and therefore ignored. These boundary lines tend to reify territorial location as the principal rubric for determining the normative actor invested with legitimacy to speak to a dispute or assert a norm. Moreover, the territorially defined nation-state is treated as the only relevant normative community, and the nation-state is conceptualized as a unitary entity pursuing predefined sets of interests, unaffected by international, transnational, or nonstate norms. Thus, for example, we see arguments asserting that international and transnational norms are simply irrelevant to the nation-state[1] or that it is illegitimate for nation-state authorities to consider such norms in reaching decisions.[2] And in the discourse of conflict of laws – jurisdiction, choice of law, and judgment recognition – rules for establishing legal authority might be (and historically have been) demarcated along territorialist and statist lines.[3]

[1] *See, e.g.,* Jack Goldsmith & Eric Posner, *The Limits of International Law* (2005).

[2] *See, e.g.*, Roger P. Alford, Misusing International Sources to Interpret the Constitution, 98 *Am. J. Int'l L.* 57 (2004).

[3] *See* Paul Schiff Berman, Towards a Cosmopolitan Vision of Conflict of Laws: Redefining Governmental Interests in a Global Era, 153 *U. Pa. L. Rev.* 1819 (2005) (criticizing this approach).

Of course, there may well be occasions when nation-states can ill afford to defer to nonstate normative assertions. For example, nonstate communities – whether separatist ethnic groups or local warlords – may so threaten the authority of the state that no viable legal order is possible without attempting to eliminate the alternative norm altogether. In addition, there can be little doubt that, even short of exercising such authority, nation-states play dominant roles within the geopolitical order because they can deploy coercive force and therefore often wield tremendous power. Thus, an embrace of a more cosmopolitan pluralist framework in no way commits one to a belief that the nation-state is dying or should be deemed unimportant.

Nevertheless, in many instances there is no intrinsic reason to privilege nation-state communities over others. If, to use Benedict Anderson's famous phrase, nation-states are "imagined communities,"[4] then nation-state bonds are neither natural nor inevitable; they are merely one particular way of imagining community among many. As such, we must turn our attention to the ways in which conceptions of "community" are constructed within social life, how membership in a community is marked and attributed, and how notions of community are given meaning.[5] In doing so, we recognize that community formation is a psychological process, not a naturally occurring phenomenon based on external realities.[6]

Accordingly, this chapter begins by setting forth a normative case for uncoupling the assumed identity of culture, people, and place. In addition, I explore a variety of ways to conceptualize a community and suggest

[4] Benedict Anderson, *Imagined Communities: Reflections on the Origins and Spread of Nationalism* 6 (rev. ed. 2006) (arguing that nation-states are imagined communities "because the members of even the smallest nation will never know most of their fellow-members, meet them, or even hear of them, yet in the minds of each lives the image of their communion").

[5] *See* Nigel Rapport & Joanna Overing, *Social and Cultural Anthropology: The Key Concepts* 62 (2000) (discussing modern anthropological views regarding community).

[6] *See, e.g.*, Akhil Gupta & James Ferguson, Culture, Power, Place: Ethnography at the End of an Era, in *Culture, Power, Place: Explorations in Critical Anthropology* 1, 13 (Akhil Gupta & James Ferguson eds., 1997) (arguing that "community" is "a categorical identity that is premised on various forms of exclusion and constructions of otherness").

that the nation-state is only one of them. Thus I argue that, as a normative matter, we should not assume or insist that territorially defined nation-states are the only legitimate source of legal norms and therefore reject all other influence. Instead, we need a more fluid rubric for conceptualizing norm development in the global legal arena than sovereigntist territorialism allows, a rubric that acknowledges the multiple community affiliations that are simultaneously present. And, notwithstanding heated rhetoric to the contrary, I suggest that we should not be so quick to suppose that such a fluid system would necessarily run afoul of principles of democratic self-government.

Even if one rejects the strong normative arguments against sovereigntist territorialism, however, this chapter also suggests that sovereigntist territorialism simply does a poor job of describing the contemporary legal terrain. This is in part because sovereigntists often take an unduly narrow view of how legal norms operate, assuming that nation-states pursuing predefined unitary interests are the only relevant players in the equation. But, as we shall see, international, transnational, and nonstate norms can affect what nation-states view to be "in their interest" and can empower actors within bureaucracies to pursue agendas that might not otherwise have been available. Thus, when we observe the impact of law beyond sovereigntist territorial borders, we need a more capacious, cosmopolitan view than the one typically afforded by rational choice frameworks.

The Unmooring of Cultures, Peoples, and Places

Discussions of legal authority are often predicated on a seemingly unproblematic division of territory, particularly on the idea that societies, nations, and cultures occupy "naturally" discontinuous spaces. This assumption ignores the possibility that territorial jurisdiction often *produces* political and social identities rather than reflecting them.[7] Indeed, the very

[7] *See* Richard T. Ford, Law's Territory (A History of Jurisdiction), 97 *Mich. L. Rev.* 843, 844 (1999) ("Jurisdictions define the identity of the people that occupy them."). As

idea of territoriality – which we can think of as a "geographic strategy to control people and things by controlling area"[8] – is itself socially rooted.[9] Thus, conceptions of territoriality depend on "how people use ... land, how they organize themselves in space, and how they give meaning to place."[10] Absent a rigorous attempt to develop a social understanding of how space is actually constructed, the power of topography tends to obscure the topography of power.[11]

In recent years, anthropologists, among others, have increasingly challenged the assumed correlation of people, culture, and physical place. Historically, anthropology had been premised on the idea that a world of human differences could be conceptualized as a diversity of separate

Henri Lefebvre has observed, "Space is not a scientific object removed from ideology or politics; it has always been political and strategic." Henri Lefebvre, Reflections on the Politics of Space, 8 *Antipode* 30, 31 (1979).

[8] Robert D. Sack, *Human Territoriality: Its Theory and History* 5 (1986).

[9] It is the socially constructed nature of territoriality that permits theorists to discuss "deterritorialization" with respect to globalizing processes. For examples of the literature on deterritorialization, *see* Néstor García Canclini, *Hybrid Cultures: Strategies for Entering and Leaving Modernity* (Christopher L. Chiappari & Silvia L. López trans., 1995); Mike Featherstone, *Undoing Culture: Globalization, Postmodernism and Identity* (1995); *Globalization and Territorial Identities* (Zdravko Mlinar ed., 1992); Serge Latouche, *The Westernization of the World* (Rosemary Morris trans., 1996); James Lull, *Media, Communication, Culture: A Global Approach* (1995); Armand Mattelart, *Mapping World Communication: War, Progress, Culture* (Susan Emanuel & James A. Cohen trans., 1994); David Morley & Kevin Robins, *Spaces of Identity: Global Media, Electronic Landscapes and Cultural Boundaries* (1995); Arjun Appadurai, Disjuncture and Difference in the Global Cultural Economy, in *Modernity at Large: Cultural Dimensions of Globalization* 27 (1996).

[10] Sack, *supra* note 8, at 2.

[11] *See* Akhil Gupta & James Ferguson, Beyond "Culture": Space, Identity, and the Politics of Difference, in *Culture, Power, Place: Explorations in Critical Anthropology*, *supra* note 6, at 33, 35 ("The presumption that spaces are autonomous has enabled the power of topography successfully to conceal the topography of power."); *see also* Liisa H. Malkki, *Purity and Exile: Violence, Memory, and National Cosmology Among Hutu Refugees in Tanzania* 5 (1995) (referring to "ways in which the contemporary system of nation-states composes a hegemonic topography"); *cf.* Ford, *supra* note 7, at 859 ("The ideological foundation of nation-states is primarily ... organicism; nations are thought to represent 'a people' who are both distinctive and relatively homogenous. The French are united not only by language but by something called 'culture': a set of practices, significant artifacts, beliefs, styles, a certain je ne sais quoi.").

societies, each with its own culture. This central assumption made it possible, beginning in the early years of the twentieth century, to speak not only of "culture," but of "*a* culture." The implicit starting point was the presumed existence of separate, individuated worldviews that could be associated with particular "peoples," "tribes," or "nations."[12]

This individuated conception of community, still so powerful in legal discussions, no longer fits the understanding of anthropologists or the practice of ethnography. "In place of such a world of separate, integrated cultural systems ... political economy turned the anthropological gaze in the direction of social and economic processes that connected even the most isolated of local settings with a wider world."[13] As many commentators have observed, cultural difference no longer can be based on territory because of the mass migrations and transnational culture flows of late capitalism.[14] Thus, the task recently has been to understand "the way that questions of identity and cultural difference are spatialized in new ways."[15]

[12] *See* Akhil Gupta & James Ferguson, Culture, Power, Place: Ethnography at the End of an Era, in *Culture, Power, Place: Explorations in Critical Anthropology*, *supra* note 6, at 1, 1 (describing conceptions of "culture"); *see also* Ulf Hannerz, *Transnational Connections: Culture, People, Places* 20 (1996) ("The idea of an organic relationship between a population, a territory, a form as well as a unit of political organization, and ... cultures has ... been an enormously successful one, spreading throughout the world ... at least as a guiding principle."); George W. Stocking, Jr., *Race, Culture, and Evolution* 202–03 (1968) (discussing Franz Boas's influence in defining "culture").

[13] Gupta & Ferguson, *supra* note 12, at 2.

[14] *See, e.g.,* Hannerz, *supra* note 12, at 8 ("As people move with their meanings, and as meanings find ways of traveling even when people stay put, territories cannot really contain cultures."); Appadurai, *supra* note 9, at 33 (proposing a set of nonterritorial "scapes" to replace "landscapes" as fields of inquiry); Roger Friedland & Deirdre Boden, NowHere: An Introduction to Space, Time and Modernity, in *NowHere: Space, Time, and Modernity* 1, 42 (Roger Friedland & Deirdre Boden eds., 1994), ("The circulation of populations and symbols is progressively undercutting the essential relation between territory and culture, the link between place and identity."); *see also* John Tomlinson, *Globalization and Culture* 106–49 (1999) (discussing the mundane ways in which deterritorialization is experienced in everyday life).

[15] Gupta & Ferguson, *supra* note 12, at 3; *see also* Austin Sarat & Thomas R. Kearns, The Unsettled Status of Human Rights: An Introduction, in *Human Rights: Concepts, Contests, Contingencies* 1, 13 (Austin Sarat & Thomas R. Kearns eds., 2001) (noting

Accordingly, anthropologists have argued that we live increasingly in the "global cultural ecumene"[16] of a "world in creolization."[17] Similarly, sociologists have attempted to replace their traditional emphasis on bounded "societies" with "a starting point that concentrates upon analysing how social life is ordered across time and space…."[18] In both disciplines, therefore, one can see increasing efforts to explore the "intertwined processes of place making and people making in the complex cultural politics of the nation-state."[19]

Nevertheless, the assumption that a culturally unitary group (a "tribe" or a "people" or even a "citizenry") is naturally tied to "its" territory is difficult to shake because such assumptions are so deeply ingrained in the modern consciousness.[20] For example, simply the fact that contemporary maps refer to a collection of "countries" constructs a picture of space as inherently fragmented along territorial lines, where different colors correspond to different national societies, all of which are made to seem fixed in place.[21] Looking at such maps, "schoolchildren are taught such deceptively simple-sounding beliefs as that France is where the French

"a new understanding of culture in which an awareness of internal plurality, fragmentation, and contestation replaces former tendencies to speak of cultures as … unified wholes").

[16] Ulf Hannerz, Notes on the Global Ecumene, *Pub. Culture* (Spring 1989), at 66; Robert J. Foster, Making National Cultures in the Global Ecumene, 20 *Ann. Rev. Anthropology* 235 (1991); *see also* Appadurai, *supra* note 9, at 28 (arguing that "an overlapping set of ecumenes [has begun] to emerge, in which congeries of money, commerce, conquest, and migration … create durable cross-societal bonds"); Arjun Appadurai & Carol A. Breckenridge, Editors' Comments, *Pub. Culture* (Fall 1988), at 1, 1 ("[T]he emergent public cultures of many nation-states … constitute the centers of new forms of cosmopolitanism in many linguistic and cultural ecumenes.").

[17] Ulf Hannerz, The World in Creolisation, 5 *Afr.* 546 (1987).

[18] Anthony Giddens, *The Consequences of Modernity* 64 (1990).

[19] Gupta & Ferguson, *supra* note 12, at 4; *see also id.* ("[A]ll associations of place, people, and culture are social and historical creations to be explained [or justified], not given natural facts.").

[20] *See* Gupta & Ferguson, *supra* note 11, at 40 (challenging "the national habit of taking the association of citizens of states and their territories as natural").

[21] *Id.* at 34; *see also* Ford, *supra* note 7, at 866–67 (linking the emergence of jurisdiction to the development of cartography).

live, America is where the Americans live, and so on."[22] Yet we all know that not only Americans live in America, and, of course, the very question of what constitutes a "real American" is contested and variable. Nonetheless, "we assume a natural association of a culture ('American culture'), a people ('Americans'), and a place ('the United States of America')," and we therefore "present associations of people and place as solid, commonsensical, and agreed on, when they are in fact contested, uncertain, and in flux."[23] This naturalization of jurisdiction means that "space itself becomes a kind of neutral grid on which cultural difference, historical memory, and societal organization [are] inscribed."[24] As a result, although the social and political *construction* of space is a fundamental aspect of legal ordering, the constructed nature of the enterprise disappears from analytical purview.[25]

Geographers, though they too historically tended to assume a "natural" tie of a people to "their" land and a set of legal institutions,[26] are increasingly recognizing the power and politics of the construction of space in society[27] as well as the symbolic significance of

[22] Gupta & Ferguson, *supra* note 11, at 40.

[23] *Id.*

[24] *Id.* at 34.

[25] *See* Ford, *supra* note 7, at 854 (observing that "jurisdictional space may serve to obscure social relations and the distribution of resources").

[26] *See, e.g.*, Ellen Churchill Semple, *Influences of Geographic Environment* 51 (1911) ("[H]uman activities are fully intelligible only in relation to the various geographic conditions which have stimulated them in different parts of the world.... Therefore anthropology, sociology, and history should be permeated by geography."), reprinted in *Formative Influences of Legal Development* 215, 216–17 (Albert Kocourek & John H. Wigmore eds., 1918).

[27] *See* Nicholas K. Blomley, *Law, Space, and the Geographies of Power* 42 (1994) ("Recent geographic scholarship ... has adopted what might be regarded as a relational view of space. Drawing on those such as Lefebvre, some theorists regard space as both socially produced and as socially constitutive, and as deeply implicated in power relations...." (citation omitted)). For examples of such critical geography, *see* John A. Agnew, *Place and Politics: The Geographical Mediation of State and Society* (1987); *Cultural Encounters with the Environment: Enduring and Evolving Geographic Themes* (Alexander B. Murphy & Douglas L. Johnson eds., 2000); Allan Pred, *Making Histories and Constructing Human Geographies* (1990); Allan Pred & Michael John Watts,

maps.[28] Maps often function as "almost the perfect representation[s] of the state."[29] Most maps both evenly cover the territory of a country and hierarchically organize it with the most significant places "symbolically at the center, and ... states on the periphery marked down, through the use of symbols, as inferior orders of government."[30] In addition, many social and cultural groupings – such as ethnic or religious ties – might not be reflected in state-sponsored maps at all.[31] These cartographic "silences"[32]

Reworking Modernity: Capitalisms and Symbolic Discontent (1992); Edward W. Soja, *Postmodern Geographies: The Reassertion of Space in Critical Social Theory* (1989); Winichakul Thongchai, *Siam Mapped: A History of the Geo-Body of a Nation* (1994); Doreen Massey, Politics and Space/Time, *New Left Rev.*(Nov.-Dec. 1992), at 65; Allan Pred, Place as Historically Contingent Process: Structuration and the Time-Geography of Becoming Places, 74 *Annals Ass'n Am. Geographers* 279 (1984); N.J. Thrift, On the Determination of Social Action in Space and Time, 1 *Env't & Plan. D: Soc'y & Space* 23 (1983).

28 *See, e.g.*, Thongchai, *supra* note 27, at 129–30 ("[Mapping] became a lethal instrument to concretize the projected desire on the earth's surface.... A map anticipated a spatial reality, not vice versa. In other words, a map was a model for, rather than a model of, what it purported to represent."); Alan K. Henrikson, The Power and Politics of Maps, in *Reordering the World: Geopolitical Perspectives on the Twenty-First Century*, at 49, 49 (George J. Demko and William B. Wood eds., 1994) ("To formulate a political plan, diplomats must have a geographical conception, which requires the cartographic image of a map."). Indeed, maps are often persuasive precisely because, though they always constitute an attempt to portray the world in a specific way, the interests underlying that attempt tend to remain unacknowledged. *See* Diane M. Bolz, 'Follow Me ... I Am the Earth in the Palm of Your Hand,' *Smithsonian* (Feb. 1993), at 112, 113 ("[Maps] are convincing because the interest they serve is masked."). *See generally* Denis Wood, *The Power of Maps* 1 (1992) (discussing the ability of maps to represent the past and the interests served in their creation). In the thrall of such "cartohypnosis," people "accept subconsciously and uncritically the ideas that are suggested to them by maps." S.W. Boggs, Cartohypnosis, 15 *Dep't St. Bull.* 1119, 1119 (1946); *see also* Ford, *supra* note 7, at 856 ("[J]urisdiction is a function of its graphical and verbal descriptions; it is a set of practices that are performed by individuals and groups who learn to 'dance the jurisdiction' by reading descriptions of jurisdictions and by looking at maps.").

29 Henrikson, *supra* note 28, at 59.

30 *Id.*

31 *Id.*; *see also* Ford, *supra* note 7, at 853 (observing that jurisdictional lines tend to define an abstract area that is "conceived ... independently of any specific attribute of that space").

32 *See* J.B. Harley, Silences and Secrecy: The Hidden Agenda of Cartography in Early Modern Europe, 40 *Imago Mundi* 57, 57 (1988) (describing "the dialogue that arises from intentional or unintentional suppression of knowledge in maps").

may be the result of "deliberate exclusion, willful ignorance, or even actual repression."[33] As contemporary debates about the distortions caused by various "projections" of the world make clear,[34] our cartographic representations are socially constructed and politically fraught.[35]

Indeed, "[a]lthough the color map of the political world displays a neat and ordered pattern of interlocking units (with only a few lines of discord), it is not surprising that the real world of national identities is one of blotches, blends, and blurs."[36] First, many people inhabit border areas, where "[t]he fiction of cultures as discrete, objectlike phenomena occupying discrete spaces becomes implausible."[37] Such people may feel

[33] Henrikson, *supra* note 28, at 59. For example, the removal or alteration of the place-names of conquered peoples or minority groups establishes a silence of subordination. *See* Harley, *supra* note 32, at 66 ("Conquering states impose a silence on minority or subject populations through their manipulation of place names."). As one commentator has observed, cartography has always been "a teleological discourse, reifying power, reinforcing the status quo, and freezing social interaction within charted lines." J.B. Harley, Maps, Knowledge, and Power, in *The Iconography of Landscape* 277, 302–3 (Denis Cosgrove & Stephen Daniels eds., 1988).

[34] *See, e.g.*, Arno Peters, *The Europe-Centered Character of Our Geographical View of the World and Its Correction* (1979)(analyzing the size and position of countries on world maps and the Eurocentrism inherent in such maps); Arthur H. Robinson, Arno Peters and His New Cartography, 12 *Am. Cartographer* 103 (1985) (criticizing the "Peters projection"); *see also* Henrikson, *supra* note 28, at 63–4 (describing the "battle of the maps" pitting the Peters projection against the Mercator projection).

[35] *See* J.M. Roberts, *The Triumph of the West* 127 (1985) ("Maps ... are always more than mere factual statements. They are translations of reality into forms we can master; they are fictions and acts of imagination communicating more than scientific data. So they reflect changes in our pictures of reality.").

[36] David H. Kaplan, Territorial Identities and Geographic Scale, in *Nested Identities: Nationalism, Territory, and Scale* 31, 35 (Guntram H. Herb & David H. Kaplan eds., 1999).

[37] Gupta & Ferguson, *supra* note 11, at 34. Chicana writer and poet Gloria Anzaldúa has captured one experience of a "borderland" existence: "I am a border woman.... I have been straddling that *tejas*-Mexican border, and others, all my life. It's not a comfortable territory to live in, this place of contradictions. Hatred, anger, and exploitation are the prominent features of this landscape.

However, there have been compensations for this *mestiza*, and certain joys. Living on borders and in margins, keeping intact one's shifting and multiple identity and integrity, is like trying to swim in a new element.... There is an exhilaration in being a participant in the further evolution of humankind...." Gloria Anzaldúa, Preface to *Borderlands/La Frontera: The New Mestiza* (1987).

an affiliation with the state controlling the area, the nation with which most inhabitants identify, or the borderland itself.[38] Second, many others live a life of border *crossings*: migrant workers, nomads, and members of the transnational business and professional elite. For these people, it may be impossible to find a unified cultural identity. For example, "[w]hat is 'the culture' of farm workers who spend half a year in Mexico and half in the United States?"[39] Finally, many people cross borders on a relatively permanent basis, including immigrants, refugees, exiles, and expatriates.[40] For them, the disjuncture of place and culture is especially clear. Immigrants invariably transport their own culture with them to the new location and, almost as invariably, shed certain aspects of that culture when they come in contact with their new communities. Diasporas

[38] *See* Anssi Paasi, *Territories, Boundaries and Consciousness: The Changing Geographies of the Finnish-Russian Border* (1996) (studying the territorial and social consequences of imposed frontiers); Jena Gaines, The Politics of National Identity in Alsace, 21 *Can. Rev. Stud. Nationalism* 99 (1994) (discussing cultural issues emerging in Alsace resulting from the French-German struggles in the region); Oren Yiftachel, Regionalism Among Palestinian-Arabs in Israel, in *Nested Identities: Nationalism, Territory, and Scale, supra* note 36, at 237, 237 (addressing "the role of territory, geographical scale, and location as complementing other factors in the political mobilization and identity formation among the Arabs"). Residents of borderland regions, because they are often so physically removed from the state center, are often psychologically, as well as physically, isolated. *See* Stein Rokkan & Derek Urwin, *Economy, Territory, Identity: Politics of West European Peripheries* 3 (1983) ("When we say that one area is peripheral to another, this is not just an abstract matter of geographical location: the peripherality will be expressed concretely in the daily life of the inhabitants of the area, and in the nature of their links with groups in the centre."). These regions, therefore, provide fertile ground for the introduction of disparate cultural influences. Not surprisingly, states often put extra effort into securing border communities both culturally and ideologically. For example, the Dominican Republic forcibly expelled Haitians from border communities and then attempted to reeducate the remaining population to make the region more "Dominican." *See* John P. Augelli, Nationalization of Dominican Borderlands, 70 *Geographical Rev.* 19, 24 (1980) ("[T]he basic aims of the nationalization program were to stamp the Dominican national identity on both people and land of the frontier provinces...."); *see also* George W. White, Transylvania: Hungarian, Romanian, or Neither?, in *Nested Identities: Nationalism, Territory, and Scale, supra* note 36, at 267, 280–84 (discussing efforts by the Romanian and Hungarian states to eradicate the national influences of the other in the borderland of Transylvania).

[39] Gupta & Ferguson, *supra* note 11, at 34.

[40] *Id.*

therefore are both "transnational" because members of a single diaspora may live in many different countries and "extremely national" in their continued cultural and political loyalty to a homeland.[41] Indeed, such clashes of former culture and present community have led to questions about the so-called "cultural defense" to certain crimes.[42] And the divided loyalty of diaspora communities can cause host countries to view members of these communities as potential threats.[43] By creating communities

[41] Kaplan, *supra* note 36, at 38. *See generally Modern Diasporas in International Politics* (Gabriel Sheffer ed., 1986) (examining the influence of ethnic diasporas on international and trans-state politics).

[42] So-called cultural defenses use evidence about a defendant's cultural background to negate or to mitigate criminal liability (with a concomitant sentence reduction). For example, in one early use of a cultural defense in the United States, a court in Fresno, California, took into account a husband's tribal custom of marriage by capture (which involves the kidnap and rape of an intended wife) in permitting a guilty plea to misdemeanor false imprisonment rather than rape and kidnapping. *See* Rorie Sherman, "Cultural" Defenses Draw Fire, *Nat'l L.J.*, Apr. 17, 1989, at 3 (reporting recent usage of the "cultural defense," including the Fresno case, *People v. Moua*, No. 315972 (Cal. Super. Ct. 1985)). To its supporters, the "cultural defense is an argument for tolerance of foreign cultures due to a lack of moral basis for punishment." Andrew M. Kanter, Note, The *Yenaldlooshi* in Court and the Killing of a Witch: The Case for an Indian Cultural Defense, 4 *S. Cal. Interdisc. L.J.* 411, 413 (1995). *But see, e.g.*, Taryn F. Goldstein, Comment, Cultural Conflicts in Court: Should the American Criminal Justice System Formally Recognize a "Cultural Defense"?, 99 *Dick. L. Rev.* 141, 144 (1994) ("Permitting the defense promotes an unfair policy towards the majority to whom the defense is unavailable, and the defense violates principles of legality.... [O]pponents assert that a recognition of the cultural defense would, in essence, condone and even encourage [] the violence toward women that is practiced throughout the world."); Neal A. Gordon, Note, The Implications of Memetics for the Cultural Defense, 50 *Duke L.J.* 1809, 1831 (2001) ("The cultural defense is ... condescending toward other cultures – it excuses action based on foreign cultures by likening it to insanity.... [T]he defense isolates cultural groups with a patronizing wink. This isolation may lead in turn to a balkanized law and reinforce the idea that minorities should be treated differently."). Of course, there are many further questions about what gets presented as "culture" and why, as well as the relationship between supposed rationality on the one hand and assumed cultural imperatives on the other. *See, e.g.*, Leti Volpp, (Mis)Identifying Culture: Asian Women and the "Cultural Defense," 17 *Harv. Women's L.J.* 57, 58 (1994) ("The 'cultural defense' presents several complex problems inherent in essentializing a culture and its effect on a particular person's behavior.").

[43] *See* Kaplan, *supra* note 36, at 38 (noting that host communities "remain circumspect about any external loyalties and identities").

of interest rather than place, diasporas (the number of which is increasing largely as a result of labor immigration)[44] pose an implicit threat to territorially based nation-states.[45] In sum, we see that "[p]rocesses of migration, displacement and deterritorialization are increasingly sundering the fixed association between identity, culture, and place."[46]

In addition, the presumed tie between a territory and a culture fails to account for the obvious cultural differences that exist *within* a locality. "'Multiculturalism' is both a feeble recognition of the fact that cultures have lost their moorings in definite places and an attempt to subsume this plurality of cultures within the framework of a national identity."[47] Thus, even people who remain in seemingly familiar and ancestral places are likely to find that their relation to place continues to change over time. The illusion of a natural and essential connection between the place and the culture will therefore be consistently challenged.[48]

[44] *Id.*

[45] *See* Robin Cohen, Diasporas and the Nation-State: From Victims to Challengers, 72 *Int'l Aff.* 507, 517 (1996) (suggesting that people primarily identify with others on the basis of shared opinions, tastes, ethnicities, religions, and other interests and are indifferent toward their nation-state); *see also* James Clifford, Diasporas, 9 *Cultural Anthropology* 302, 307 (1994) ("Diasporas are caught up with and defined against ... the norms of nation-states...."). For a provocative attempt to frame a "diasporan model" of citizenship and the nation-state, *see* Anupam Chander, Diaspora Bonds, 76 *N.Y.U. L. Rev.* 1005 (2001).

[46] Akhil Gupta, The Song of the Nonaligned World: Transnational Identities and the Reinscription of Space in Late Capitalism, in *Culture, Power, Place: Explorations in Critical Anthropology, supra* note 6, at 179, 196.

[47] Gupta & Ferguson, *supra* note 11, at 35. Even the idea that there are "subcultures" within a society tends to preserve the idea of distinct "cultures" ... within the same geographical and territorial space. Conventional accounts of ethnicity, even when used to describe cultural differences in settings where people from different regions live side by side, rely on an unproblematic link between identity and place. While such concepts are suggestive because they endeavor to stretch the naturalized association of culture and place, they leave the tie between culture and place largely intact.

[48] For example, Gupta and Ferguson argue that for the contemporary English, "'Englishness[]' ... is just as complicated and nearly as deterritorialized a notion as Palestinian-ness or Armenian-ness, for 'England' ('the real England') refers less to a bounded place than to an imagined state of being or a moral location." *Id.* at 38; *see also*

We can see the everyday effects of deterritorialization in all areas of the world and all sectors of the economy. For example, the "local" shopping mall is not experienced as truly local at all; nearly "everyone who shops there is aware that most of the shops are chain stores," identical to stores elsewhere, and that the mall itself closely resembles innumerable other malls around the globe.[49] Thus, while experiencing a "local" place, we recognize the absent forces that structure our experience. Such forces include the steady decline in local ownership of public spaces, which can itself be linked to the globalization of capital.[50]

Similarly, we may feel the growing significance of "remote" forces on our lives, whether those forces are multinational corporations, world capital markets, or distant bureaucracies such as the European Union. As John Tomlinson has observed: "People probably come to include distant events and processes more routinely in their perceptions of what is significant for their own personal lives. This is one aspect of what deterritorialization may involve: the ever-broadening horizon of relevance in people's routine experience...."[51] The increased access to media also affects deterritorialization because one is no longer limited to the perspectives offered from within one's "home culture."[52] Thus, the "typical" life of a suburban family in the United States may become as familiar to world citizens inundated by American film and television as their own "home" life.[53] And, of course, those with less power to influence the processes of globalization – those forced to cross borders for work, those

Raymond Williams, *Towards 2000*, at 177 (1983) (illustrating the cosmopolitan existence of a typical English person experiencing everyday life); Tomlinson, *supra* note 14, at 113–16 (updating Williams's story from the early 1980s to the late 1990s).

49 Giddens, *supra* note 18, at 140–1.

50 Tomlinson, *supra* note 14, at 107–8.

51 *Id.* at 115.

52 *See id.* at 116 (describing the choice of perspectives available through new media and the resultant overlaps between national and local perspectives).

53 *See id.* at 119 ("For where *are* these places except in our cultural imagination, our repertoire of 'textual locations' built up out of all the millions of images in films ... we have encountered? And do we really *require* any of them to correspond all that closely with our 'real' locality?").

bankrupted through global competition, those affected by environmental degradation, and many others – experience this deterritorialization in even more insidious ways.

Ironically, although actual places and localities are increasingly blurred and indeterminate, *ideas* of culturally and ethnically distinct places may become even more important.[54] Imagined communities attach themselves to imagined places; displaced peoples cluster around remembered or idealized homelands in a world that seems increasingly to deny such firm territorialized anchors in their actuality. Indeed, one of the primary illusions of nationalism is the presumption that one's nation has existed from time immemorial. In case after case, however, it turns out that most national traditions are inventions of the past two hundred years, and the principle of nationality itself, "despite its trappings of misty antiquity, is a defining feature of modernity."[55] Thus, although it is admittedly difficult to imagine an international geopolitical order that is not based on a network of nation-states operating in bounded spaces, history suggests that the nation-state system is neither immutable nor inevitable. Moreover, to the extent that nations and states do not coincide, alternative conceptions of identity and community that are *not* based on state boundaries will continue to challenge the hegemony of this system.

The Nation-State as an Imagined Community

As we think about the demarcation of community boundaries, we consider more carefully what it means to say that a coherent community exists and how such a community might be defined. This consideration reveals the act of imagination necessary to equate community with state

[54] Gupta & Ferguson, *supra* note 11, at 39.

[55] Jonathan Rée, Cosmopolitanism and the Experience of Nationality, in *Cosmopolitics: Thinking and Feeling Beyond the Nation* 77, 81 (Pheng Cheah & Bruce Robbins eds., 1998). Indeed, as Rée points out, the two "national groups in Europe that have the greatest claims to many centuries of continuous existence are, significantly, those with no securely held collective territory … [: the] Romanies and [the] Jews." *Id.* at 89 n.10.

as well as the ongoing tug-of-war between nostalgic and transformative visions of community in mediating the relationship between self and world.

The concept of "community" is one of the most widely used in the social sciences. However, a precise definition has been predictably elusive. Even as far back as 1955, one study compiled ninety-four social-scientific attempts at definition and found that the only substantive overlap among them was that all the definitions dealt with human beings![56]

To many, the word "community" conjures up Norman Rockwell–like images of a small, face-to-face congregation of people sharing common values, backgrounds, and worldviews. Although such a vision seems at odds with much broader appropriations of the word, such as "the American community" or "the world community," community and state have often been juxtaposed in the anthropological and sociological literature. For example, Ferdinand Tönnies, writing in the 1880s, described ways in which gemeinschaft – the community of intimacy, close personal knowledge, and stability – was being superseded by gesellschaft – the political society dominated by social relations that were artificial, contractual, ego-focused, short-term, and impersonal.[57] Tönnies viewed the small rural community of the past as a site of solidarity and unity, while portraying contemporary society as incapable of creating such bonds.[58] His conception of gemeinschaft was firmly grounded in physical proximity, where community derives from shared territory, blood ties, and constant interaction among community members, rather than shared values or interests.[59] In contrast, according to Tönnies, the modern period of gesellschaft offered no face-to-face community, but only a set of associations

[56] George A. Hillery, Jr., Definitions of Community: Areas of Agreement, 20 *Rural Soc.* 111, 118 (1955).

[57] *See* Ferdinand Tönnies, *Gemeinschaft und Gesellschaft* [Community & Society] 202–5 (Charles Loomis trans., 1988 ed.) (describing the "order of *Gesellschaft*").

[58] *See id.* at 65 (contrasting the essential unity of individuals in the *gemeinschaft* with the essential separation of individuals in the *gesellschaft*).

[59] *Id.* at 42–4.

invented for the rational achievement of mutual goals (e.g., corporations, political parties, and trade unions).[60]

Other social scientists of the late nineteenth and early twentieth centuries echoed this juxtaposition. Henry Maine's work, though not specifically focused on the nature of community, also contrasted a society founded on personal relationships and blood-based hierarchies with a more "modern" social form based on individual freedom to enter into legal agreements.[61] Maine saw this transformation from "status" to "contract" as a shift from defining social relations through kinship networks to defining them on the basis of individual will.[62] Similarly, Emile Durkheim argued that "earlier" communities were characterized by "mechanical solidarity," in which society was founded upon likeness and unable to tolerate dissimilarity.[63] In contrast, Durkheim viewed "modern" society as based on "organic solidarity," in which differences are integrated into a collaborative, harmonious whole.[64]

For many twentieth-century scholars, community remained a term reserved only for preindustrial forms of affiliation. For example, Raymond Williams, considering the rise of modernity and its challenge to earlier conceptions of community, wrote:

> The growth of towns and especially of cities and a metropolis; the increasing division and complexity of labour; the altered and critical

[60] *Id.* at 64–5.

[61] *See* Henry Sumner Maine, *Ancient Law* 165 (1986) (1864) ("[T]he movement of the progressive societies has hitherto been a movement from Status to Contract." (emphasis omitted)).

[62] *See id.*

[63] Emile Durkheim, *The Division of Labor in Society* 88–92 (W.D. Halls trans., 1984) (1893).

[64] *Id.* at 101–5. Nevertheless, Durkheim observed that this harmony did not yet exist. *See id.* at lv (expressing the need for a "corporative institution"). In his later work, Durkheim retreated from even this qualified stance, calling instead for new communal relationships to counteract a modern tendency toward debilitating anomie. *See* Emile Durkheim, *Suicide* 361–92 (John A. Spaulding & George Simpson trans., 1951) (1897) (finding the roots of anomie in "the lack of collective forces at certain points in society" and the "state of disaggregation").

> relations between and within social classes: in changes like these any assumption of a knowable community – a whole community wholly knowable – became harder and harder to sustain.[65]

Similarly, Robert Redfield attempted to define community as necessarily small in scale, homogenous in both activities and states of mind, self-sufficient, and conscious of its distinctiveness.[66] Redfield almost seemed to find a kind of nobility and purity in these small (generally agrarian) communities. In contrast, he viewed urban societies far more negatively. To Redfield, cities were based in "impersonal institutions [and] what has been called atomization of the external world."[67]

Other anthropologists, while perhaps not quite as nostalgic as Redfield, have likewise viewed communities as inherently local. Ronald Frankenberg suggested that members of a community must have common work, economic, and religious interests.[68] Such communities, in his view, require people to live face-to-face, in a small group of people, sharing multistranded relations with one another and maintaining a sentimental attachment to a physical locality and the group itself.[69] David Minar and Scott Greer also emphasized geographical proximity.[70] They argued that the realities of living in a locale give rise to common problems, which lead to the development of organizations for joint action and activities, which in turn produces common attachments, feelings of interdependence, common commitment, and increasing homogeneity.[71] Even recent work by

[65] Raymond Williams, *The Country and the City* 165 (1973).

[66] Robert Redfield, *The Little Community and Peasant Society and Culture* 4 (1960).

[67] *Id.* at 5.

[68] *See* Ronald Frankenberg, *Communities in Britain* 238 (1966) ("Community implies having something in common.").

[69] *See id.* at 237–54 (examining the concept of community and the changes in face-to-face relationships); *see also* Nigel Rapport & Joanna Overing, *Social and Cultural Anthropology* 61 (2000) (discussing Frankenberg's and other theorists' approaches to community).

[70] *See* David Minar & Scott Greer, *The Concept of Community* 47 (1969) ("[P]lace is important to community for certainly most of the social systems to which we would apply the concept [of community] are geographic entities of one sort or another.").

[71] *See id.* (discussing the effects of living in the same locale).

communitarian theorists such as Amitai Etzioni demonstrates a similar view of community. Attempting to stem what he sees as the multicultural drift away from the common values of a liberal democracy, Etzioni clings to the notion that communities of the past shared common beliefs and values and asks contemporary members of society to recommit to those commonalities.[72]

These ideas of community do not fit comfortably with the sprawling nature of the modern industrialized state. Yet the transformation of *states* into *nation*-states requires that members of a sovereign entity come to think of themselves not simply as subjects of governmental power but as somehow bound to the other subjects within one community. Benedict Anderson therefore refers to nation-states as "imagined communities" – "*imagined* because the members of even the smallest nation will never know most of their fellow-members, meet them, or even hear of them, yet in the minds of each lives the image of their communion."[73]

This formulation does not imply that such imagined communities are somehow "false" or "fabricated" in a negative sense.[74] Anderson argues that *all* communities larger than "primordial villages" (and perhaps even those) are imagined.[75] Thus, nation-states are not illegitimate just because their inhabitants imagine and construct psychological bonds of affiliation. Nevertheless, the fact that those bonds are constructed means that they

[72] *See* Amitai Etzioni, *The Spirit of Community* 253–67 (1994) (articulating the rights and social responsibilities of individuals under a communitarian vision of society).

[73] Anderson, *supra* note 4, at 6; *see also* Ernest Gellner, *Thought and Change* 168 (1964) ("Nationalism is not the awakening of nations to self-consciousness: it *invents* nations where they do not exist…." (emphasis added)).

[74] Some commentators have a more negative view of the way in which nationalist movements fabricate many of the "traditions" they purport to restore. *See, e.g.*, Francis Fukuyama, *The End of History and the Last Man* 269 (1992) (noting the "deliberate fabrications of nationalists, who had a degree of freedom in defining who or what constituted a … nation"); Anthony D. Smith, Introduction: Ethnicity and Nationalism, in *Ethnicity and Nationalism* 1, 3 (Anthony D. Smith ed., 1992) (discussing "modernist" theories of nationalism that rely on notions of "imagined community" and "invented traditions").

[75] *See* Anderson, *supra* note 4, at 6 (suggesting that even communities characterized by "face-to-face contact" are imagined).

are neither natural nor inevitable; they are merely one particular way of imagining community among many.

This is a very different vision of community. Rather than a reified, natural structure in the relations among people, Anderson (as well as other theorists)[76] focuses on the ways conceptions of "community" are constructed within social life, on how membership in a community is marked and attributed, and on how notions of community are given meaning.[77]

[76] Social psychological research on group identities, which indicates that groups do not exist because of external factors but only because of members' identification with the group, echoes this symbolic understanding of community. *See* Henri Tajfel, *Human Groups and Social Categories* 229 (1981) (relying on a definition of intergroup community based on whether people feel they are a group). According to this research, the process of group identification proceeds in three stages: First, individuals categorize themselves as part of an ingroup, assigning themselves a social identity and distinguishing themselves from the relevant outgroup. Second, they learn the norms associated with such an identity. Third, they assign these norms to themselves, and "thus their behaviour becomes more normative as their category membership becomes salient." Michael A. Hogg & Dominic Abrams, *Social Identifications: A Social Psychology of Intergroup Relations and Group Processes* 172 (1988).

[77] *See* Rapport & Overing, *supra* note 69, at 62 (discussing modern anthropological views regarding community). In a similar vein, Gregory Bateson and Jurgen Ruesch argued that the relationships among "individual," "family," "community," "nation," and world can best be understood through a study of the social and psychological processes of human communication. *See* Gregory Bateson & Jurgen Ruesch, *Communication: The Social Matrix of Psychiatry* 5 (1951) ("[C]ommunication is the only scientific model which enables us to explain physical, intrapersonal, interpersonal, and cultural aspects of events within one system."). Likewise, Fredrik Barth observed that social groups are not naturally joined as communities; they achieve an identity by defining themselves as different from other groups and by erecting boundaries between them. *See* Fredrik Barth, Introduction to *Ethnic Groups and Boundaries* 9, 15 (Fredrik Barth ed., 1969) ("The boundaries to which we must give our attention are of course social boundaries...."). Anthony Cohen extended Barth's critique, arguing that community must be seen as a symbolic construct, not a natural one. *See* Anthony P. Cohen, *The Symbolic Construction of Community* 14 (1985) (discussing the "essentially symbolic nature of the idea of community itself"). In Cohen's vision, community derives not from the type of external characteristics Redfield and others had posited, but from internal perceptions of a boundary that separates one social group from another. Thus, communities and their boundaries exist not as geography but as "repositories of meaning" in the minds of their members, and these socially constructed repositories of meaning come to be expressed as a community's distinctive social discourse. *Id.* at 98.

Thus, community formation is viewed as a psychological process, not as a naturally occurring phenomenon based on external realities.[78]

Significantly, without this kind of expanded vision of community there is no way to conceptualize a nation-state as a community. Yet at the same time, if communities are based not on fixed attributes such as geographical proximity, shared history, or face-to-face interaction, but instead on symbolic identification and social psychology, *then there is no intrinsic reason to privilege nation-state communities over other possible community identifications that people might share*. These other identifications will be explored in the next section, but for now it is important to recognize that the very same conception of community upon which the nation-state relies also provides the basis for critiquing the hegemony of the nation-state as the only relevant community under discussion.

According to Anderson, the nation-state historically has had three distinct imagined features. First, the nation is imagined as limited, with finite boundaries.[79] He argues that "[n]o nation imagines itself coterminous

[78] *See, e.g.*, Gupta & Ferguson, *supra* note 12, at 13 (arguing that "community" is "a categorical identity that is premised on various forms of exclusion and constructions of otherness").

[79] For example, a comparison of medieval and modern maps indicates very different conceptions of boundaries and placeness. The older maps tend to depict Jerusalem at the center, Roberts, *supra* note 35, at 128; they typically indicate an incompleteness to the world, with distant lands only sketched in and then fading off without clear endpoints; and they not only are imprecise as to boundaries but seem to treat boundaries as relatively insignificant; *see* Michael Billig, *Banal Nationalism* 20 (1995) ("Mediaeval maps represent a world unobsessed with boundaries."). Kingdoms and empires are depicted in general areas, and little effort is made to define the precise point where one begins and the other ends. *See* Roberts, *supra* note 35, at 127–30 (reviewing the features of medieval maps). In contrast, the modern map, like the modern conception of sovereignty, is firmly territorial, with precisely drawn boundaries. *See* Billig, *supra*, at 20 (recognizing that modern maps depict the world as territorially divided).

Moreover, the evidence seems to indicate that the lack of clear territorial boundaries was not only part of medieval mapmaking but of medieval consciousness as well. As one commentator points out, medieval Europe consisted of a series of small overlapping power structures with no single authority controlling a "clear-cut territory or the people within it." Michael Mann, European Development: Approaching a Historical Explanation, in *Europe and the Rise of Capitalism* 6, 11 (Jean Baechler et al. eds., 1988). In addition, medieval monarchs tended to divide their estates among their

with mankind. The most messianic nationalists do not dream of a day when all the members of the human race will join their nation...."[80] Second, the nation is imagined as sovereign in order to replace the divinely ordained dynasties[81] that began to give way to modern states in the period of the Enlightenment and afterward.[82] Third, the nation is imagined as a community:

> [R]egardless of the actual inequality and exploitation that may prevail in each, the nation is always conceived as a deep, horizontal

heirs, meaning that territories would often change shape with each new generation. *See* Billig, *supra*, at 20 (discussing the transitory nature of territorial boundaries in medieval Europe). The feudal structure rested on loyalties to local lords, not to distant monarchs, and if kings raised armies, they did so through the local lords. *See id.* (discussing the methods by which kings raised armies). Not surprisingly, the mass of inhabitants of what is now France or England did not think of themselves as English or French and had little conception of a territorial nation-state to which they owed allegiance. *See, e.g.*, 1 Fernand Braudel, *The Identity of France (History and Environment)* 18 (Siân Reynolds trans., 1988) (1986) (arguing that "the *modern* notion of *la patrie*, the fatherland, had scarcely appeared in the sixteenth century"); Hugh Seton-Watson, *Nations and States: An Enquiry into the Origins of Nations and the Politics of Nationalism* 25–30 (1977) ("One can hardly speak of an English or a French nation before the thirteenth century....").

80 Anderson, *supra* note 4, at 7.

81 According to Anderson, it is no coincidence that the eighteenth century, with its rationalist secularism and its challenge to divine rule, was also the century when nationalism arose. While stopping just short of drawing a causal link between the decline of religious belief and the rise of nationalism – *see id.* at 12 ("I am not claiming that the appearance of nationalism towards the end of the eighteenth century was 'produced' by the erosion of religious certainties, or that this erosion does not itself require a complex explanation.")– Anderson does argue that the "[d]isintegration of paradise" required "a secular transformation of fatality into continuity, contingency into meaning.... [F]ew things were (are) better suited to this end than an idea of nation," *id.* at 11.

82 *See id.* (stating that the Enlightenment marked "the dawn of the age of nationalism"). Anderson links this transformation to changing conceptions of borders. Monarchy, he argues, "organizes everything around a high centre. Its legitimacy derives from divinity, not from populations, who, after all, are subjects, not citizens." *Id.* at 19. Thus, since states were defined by their centers, "borders were porous and indistinct, and sovereignties faded imperceptibly into one another." *Id.* According to Anderson, this loose sense of territoriality helps to explain how "pre-modern empires and kingdoms were able to sustain their rule over immensely heterogeneous, and often not even contiguous, populations for long periods of time." *Id.* In contrast, modern state sovereignty

> comradeship. Ultimately it is this fraternity that makes it possible, over the past two centuries, for so many millions of people, not so much to kill, as willingly to die for such limited imaginings.[83]

Thus, Anderson highlights the social, historical, and psychological forces that construct conceptions of nationhood.

Moreover, even in seemingly less multiethnic states, the composition of a nation appears to be a political, rather than a natural, process. Although many commentators have assumed that countries such as China, Korea, and Japan are ethnically homogeneous,[84] recent scholarship has challenged this claim. For example, one study argues that Japanese identity and much of Japanese officialdom have evolved through interaction with both internal others (minorities) and external others (foreigners), who were just as important for Japanese self-identification as were internal "cultural" constructions.[85] Similarly, movements to define distinctive features of Japanese culture and identity were launched in the 1970s and 1980s in opposition to Western influence because the business and administrative elite were concerned about too *little* Japanese homogeneity.[86]

is "fully, flatly, and evenly operative over each square centimetre of a legally demarcated territory." *Id.* Similarly, Giddens argues that, whereas the boundaries of empires and absolutist states were diffuse, the nation-state "is a set of institutional forms of governance maintaining an administrative monopoly over a territory with demarcated boundaries." Giddens, *supra* note 18, at 171–2. Indeed, according to Giddens, although all states seem to have been associated with territoriality, "[w]hat is specifically late European is the fixing of very precise boundaries that actually *do* effectively mark the realm of the administration of the state." *Id.* at 172.

[83] Anderson, *supra* note 4, at 7.

[84] *See, e.g.*, E.J. Hobsbawm, *Nations and Nationalism Since 1780*, at 66 (1990) ("China, Korea and Japan ... are indeed among the extremely rare examples of historic states composed of a population that is ethnically almost or entirely homogeneous.").

[85] *See* Emiko Ohnuki-Tierney, A Conceptual Model for the Historical Relationship Between the Self and the Internal and External Others: The Agrarian Japanese, the Ainu, and the Special-Status People, in *Making Majorities: Constituting the Nation in Japan, Korea, China, Malaysia, Fiji, Turkey, and the United States* 31 (Dru C. Gladney ed., 1998) [hereinafter *Making Majorities*] (examining the relationships between Japanese majority groups and foreigners).

[86] *See* Kosaku Yoshino, Culturalism, Racialism, and Internationalism in the Discourse on Japanese Identity, in *Making Majorities*, *supra* note 85, at 13, 13 (linking the "resurgence

So, how is national community formed? Anderson traces the ascendancy of the nation-state to the development of what he calls "print-capitalism."[87] He argues that the old orders of religiously unified communities, divinely determined monarchs, and static cosmologies were slowly challenged by "the impact of economic change, 'discoveries' (social and scientific), and the development of increasingly rapid communications."[88] According to Anderson, the new order of print-capitalism "made it possible for rapidly growing numbers of people to think about themselves, and to relate themselves to others, in profoundly new ways."[89]

Anderson argues that the development of the printing press and the relative ease with which literary works came to be disseminated laid the basis for national consciousness in three distinct ways. First, the spread of printed languages meant that there were "unified fields of exchange" operating "below" Latin, but "above" the locally distinct spoken vernaculars.[90] Thus, "[s]peakers of the huge variety of Frenches, Englishes, or Spanishes, who might find it difficult or even impossible to understand one another in conversation, became capable of comprehending one another via print and paper."[91] In the process, according to Anderson, these readers became aware of a broader community of readers to which they belonged that was beyond the local, but not as large as the world. Newspapers enabled the nation to be represented by the juxtaposition of stories from different "parts," which were then assimilated within one polity. The newspaper also allowed the nation to differentiate itself from others by the presentation of "international" and "foreign" news as something separate from

of cultural nationalism" to "the vast number of publications that the Japanese cultural elites produced to define and redefine the distinctiveness of Japanese society, culture, and national character").

87 *See* Anderson, *supra* note 4, at 36 (suggesting that print-capitalism offered a "new way of linking fraternity, power and time meaningfully together").

88 *Id.*

89 *Id.*

90 *Id.* at 44.

91 *Id.*

"domestic" or "national" news.[92] Second, according to Anderson, the rise of print-capitalism allowed languages to become more fixed, therefore further cementing identity based on shared linguistic tradition.[93] Third, Anderson argues that those vernaculars that were closest to the print languages rose in status and began to form something approaching an "official" language that would be understood by a broader group.[94]

Other theorists have explored the myriad ways in which national identification, once introduced, is continually reinforced in the modern era. For example, Michael Billig has studied what he calls "banal nationalism": the everyday habits of life that serve subconsciously to remind citizens of their affiliation with a particular nation-state in a world of nation-states.[95] Billig writes:

> In so many little ways, the citizenry are daily reminded of their national place in a world of nations. However, this reminding is so familiar, so continual, that it is not consciously registered as reminding. The metonymic image of banal nationalism is not a flag which is being consciously waved with fervent passion; it is the flag hanging unnoticed on the public building.[96]

Thus, Anderson's conception of nation-state as imagined community allows us to see that, although we often reserve the term "nationalist"

[92] *See* Billig, *supra* note 79, at 118–19 (describing the way in which newspapers segregate the news "so that nationhood operates ... as a context for awareness").

[93] *See* Anderson, *supra* note 4, at 44–5 (arguing that because "the printed book kept a permanent form," nations could create "that image of antiquity so central to the subjective idea of the nation").

[94] *See id.* at 45 (observing that "[c]ertain dialects inevitably were 'closer' to each print-language and dominated their final forms").

[95] *See generally* Billig, *supra* note 79 (examining the powerful presence of nationalism in everyday life).

[96] *Id.* at 8. Similarly, Gupta has observed: "In addition to practices oriented externally – that is, toward other states – some of the most important features that enable the nation to be realized are flags, anthems, constitutions and courts, a system of political representation, a state bureaucracy, schools, public works, a military and police force, newspapers, and television and other mass media." Gupta, *supra* note 46, at 185.

for extremist groups seeking recognition from a modern state,[97] the state itself often operates as a nationalist enterprise, encouraging identification in a community that matches the state's geographical borders. This nation-state nationalism is often overlooked because we assume that such nationalism is "natural." Accordingly, we believe that "[t]he separatists, the fascists and the guerrillas are the problem of nationalism. The ideological habits, by which 'our' nations are reproduced as nations, are unnamed and, thereby, unnoticed."[98]

In response to the inherently imagined nature of their existence, nations make claims upon something called national "identity." Such national identity is formed through self-categorization: articulating attributes that make "us" of one group different from "them" in another group.[99] One such attribute is the telling of a unified national "history."

[97] *See* Billig, *supra* note 79, at 5 (observing that both popular and academic writings associate nationalism "with those who struggle to create new states or with extreme right-wing politics," so that "[a]ccording to customary usage, [the American president] is not a nationalist; but separatists in Quebec or Brittany are; so are the leaders of extreme right-wing parties such as the Front National in France").

[98] *Id.* at 6. Anthony D. Smith has argued that some scholarship on nationalism relies too much on a "top down" method whereby elites manipulate "the people" into feelings of nationalist identification. Anthony D. Smith, *Nationalism and Modernism* 95–6 (1998). Instead, Smith argues that "[t]he passion that the nation could evoke, especially in time of danger, the sacrifices it could command from 'the poor and unlettered' as well as the middle classes, cannot be convincingly explained by the propaganda of politicians and intellectuals, or the ritual and pageantry of mass ceremonies." *Id.* at 130. While I believe Smith's objection to be valid, my argument here (and Billig's as well, I think) is not that the masses are manipulated by some devious elites to believe in nationalism, but rather that nationalism is a socially constructed, constitutive, and self-perpetuating phenomenon, and all members of society are simultaneously agents and recipients of nationalist sentiment. Thus, Smith's objections to a neo-Marxist view of nationalism seem to have less weight with regard to Billig's more Foucauldian approach.

[99] *See* Billig, *supra* note 79, at 60–1 (observing that feeling patriotic about one's nation requires preexisting assumptions about what a nation is and what patriotism means). Ernest Gellner and Anthony Giddens likewise emphasize that nation-states are not founded on "objective" criteria. Rather, identification with a national community is a phenomenon of social psychology. Indeed, on the first page of *Nations and Nationalism*, Gellner asserts that "[n]ationalism is primarily a political principle, which holds that

Indeed, it is no coincidence that the ascendency of nation-states was accompanied by the creation of national historical tales[100] and the rise of the professional historian.[101] These state-funded historians were a

the political and the national unit should be congruent," Ernest Gellner, *Nations and Nationalism* 1 (1983). According to Gellner, nationalism cannot exist as a concept unless it is taken for granted that the state is the legitimate political entity. *See id.* at 4 (opining that "nationalism emerges only in milieux in which the existence of the state is already very much taken for granted"). Accordingly, the national state becomes linked with a national culture that comes to be seen as the "natural repositor[y] of political legitimacy." *Id.* at 55. Gellner not only links national consciousness to the existence of the state, but also highlights the political reasons it becomes necessary to make the bridge between nation and state appear natural.

Giddens focused on the new forms of governance that arose concurrent to the rise of the nation-state. *See* Anthony Giddens, *The Nation-State and Violence* 118 (1985) ("A 'nation' ... only exists when a state has a unified administrative reach over the territory over which its sovereignty is claimed."). He defines the nation-state as "a set of institutional forms of governance maintaining an administrative monopoly over a territory with demarcated boundaries (borders), its rule being sanctioned by law and direct control of the means of internal and external violence." *Id.* at 121. In Giddens's view, the nation-state is a "bounded power-container": fixed boundaries and ability to wreak official violence are its key attributes. *Id.* at 120. He argues, moreover, that nation-states cannot exist in isolation, but only as part of a worldview that sees "a complex of other nation-states" knitted together in a world system. Giddens, *supra*, at 171.

Accordingly, we have a system of nations who go to war against each other. "In this new world of nations-at-war, there was little room for a Duke of Burgundy or an Earl of Warwick to march into the fray at the head of a private retinue." Billig, *supra* note 79, at 21. Rather, local warlords appear in places where state authority has disappeared. *See id.* (pointing to Beirut and Somalia as examples of states where warlords have emerged). Finally, the geographical boundedness of nations and the nation-state's monopolization of violence are both constantly reflected in rhetoric, symbolic imagery, and habits of thinking until they appear to be not only the primary means of organizing political community, but the most natural ways of doing so.

[100] *See, e.g.*, Linda Colley, *Britons: Forging the Nation 1707–1837*, at 5–6 (1992) (describing the "invention" of a British national identity in the eighteenth and early nineteenth centuries); Eric Hobsbawm, Introduction: Inventing Traditions, in *The Invention of Tradition* 1, 1 (Eric Hobsbawm & Terence Ranger eds., 1983) ("'Traditions' which appear or claim to be old are often quite recent in origin and sometimes invented.").

[101] *See* Friedland & Boden, *supra* note 14, at 10 ("[T]he professional historian emerged in the nineteenth century at the same time that states were struggling to create a unified nation in the territories over which they claimed sovereignty.").

mechanism by which states bolstered their power and integrated linguistically and ethnically diverse populations.[102] Thus, as Edward Said has made clear, nation-states are interpretive communities as well as imagined ones.[103]

For example, when Scots get together to celebrate their national identity, they appear to be steeped in tradition, with men wearing kilts, each clan having its own tartan, and bagpipes wailing.[104] By means of these symbols, they show their loyalty to seemingly ancient rituals – rituals whose origins go far back into antiquity. Yet, as Hugh Trevor-Roper has argued, these symbols of Scottishness were actually a creation of the Industrial Revolution.[105] Indeed, the short kilt was invented by an English industrialist to allow Highlanders to work in factories.[106] Moreover, Anthony Giddens observes that even the notion of a "tradition" is itself the product of modernity. In medieval times, by contrast, there was no separate conception of tradition "precisely because

[102] *See id.* (observing that "historians were funded by the state, which saw the creation of a 'national' history as a way to bolster its power and integrate linguistically and culturally diverse populations under its control").

[103] *See* Edward W. Said, *The World, the Text, and the Critic* 11 (1983) (tying the state to "the entire matrix of meanings we associate with 'home,' belonging and community"); *see also* Friedland & Boden, *supra* note 14, at 10 ("[T]erritorial historicity is the core of the nation-state's legitimacy and an element in the narrative of modernity."); Gupta, *supra* note 46, at 191 ("[Nationalism is] a distinctively modern cultural form [that] attempts to create a new kind of spatial and mythopoetic metanarrative...."). Such national histories "tell of a people passing through time – 'our' people, with 'our' ways of life, and 'our' culture." Billig, *supra* note 79, at 71. *See generally* Margaret Wetherell & Jonathan Potter, *Mapping the Language of Racism: Discourse and the Legitimation of Exploitation* (1992) (discussing the use of discourse in studying racism). Pop cultural forms may also tell nationalist histories. *See, e.g.*, Purnima Mankekar, *Screening Culture, Viewing Politics: An Ethnography of Television, Womanhood, and Nation in Postcolonial India* 165 (1999) (discussing the relationship between a nationally broadcast television dramatization of an important Hindu epic tale and the consolidation of Hindu nationalism in subsequent years).

[104] Hugh Trevor-Roper, The Invention of Tradition: The Highland Tradition of Scotland, in *The Invention of Tradition, supra* note 100, at 15, 15.

[105] *See id.* (characterizing the concept of a distinct Highland tradition as a retrospective invention).

[106] *Id.* at 21–2.

tradition and custom were everywhere."[107] Thus, the idea of a traditional national culture is an imagined narrative, passed on like an inheritance from one generation to the next.[108] Through such an invention of tradition, the nation becomes conceptualized in kinship terms: the nation is a "family" passing down identity over time, living in the "motherland" or "fatherland."[109]

This reference to land brings forth a final crucial attribute in the imagining of a national community: the idea of a homeland. Indeed, this tie between group identity and land is essential to the modern idea of the nation-state. After all, many peoples "have nurtured a sense of their own communal distinctiveness 'in the specific history of the group, and, above all, in the myths of group origins and group liberation.'"[110] Nationhood, however, requires the added element of place. Thus, what makes a nation-state distinctive is the imagining of an overall "country" in which lived-in localities are united within a wider homeland. The inhabitants of that homeland will generally be personally familiar with only a small part of the land, but the nation is conceived as a totality. Thus, of necessity it must be *imagined* as a totality, rather than directly apprehended. Yet, again and again, these "images of virgin territories, self-evident boundaries, and datable original occupation turn out to be mere

[107] Anthony Giddens, *Runaway World: How Globalization Is Reshaping Our Lives* 57 (2000).

[108] *See* Étienne Balibar, Is There a 'Neo-Racism'? in Étienne Balibar & Immanuel Wallerstein, *Race, Nation, Class: Ambiguous Identities* 17, 24–5 (1991) (discussing the way in which conceptions of national culture inscribe racist assumptions). For a further discussion of the "racialization" of the idea of national culture, *see* Martin Barker, *The New Racism: Conservatives and the Ideology of the Tribe* (1981); Teun A. van Dijk, *Elite Discourse and Racism* (1993).

[109] *See* Nira Yuval-Davis, *Gender & Nation* 15 (1997) (arguing that in a "naturalized image of the nation, ... nations not only are eternal and universal but also constitute a natural extension of family and kinship relations"); Gary R. Johnson, In the Name of the Fatherland: An Analysis of Kin Term Usage in Patriotic Speech and Literature, 8 *Int'l Pol. Sci. Rev.* 165, 168–71 (1987) (discussing the use of terms such as "motherland" and "fatherland" "to inspire in the listener or reader a feeling of unity with his or her fellow citizens").

[110] Billig, *supra* note 79, at 74 (citation omitted) (quoting Anthony D. Smith, *The Ethnic Revival* 65 (1981)).

mirages: territorial claims become more obscure, not clearer, the further you dig into their past."[111]

Indeed, as the social psychological literature suggests, there can be no "us" without a "them." Accordingly, the national community can only be imagined by also imagining foreigners.

> The structures of feeling that enable meaningful relationships with particular locales, constituted and experienced in a particular manner, necessarily include the marking of "self" and "other" through identification with larger collectivities. To be part of a community is to be positioned as a particular kind of subject, similar to others within the community in some crucial respects and different from those who are excluded from it.[112]

For some nations, the claim to ancient roots will often involve the nostalgic invocation of a continuous chain of racial inheritance deriving from an imagined, biologically pure past.[113] For others, it will be founded in stories about exceptionalism: that which makes our nation superior to all others on the planet. In either case, the imagined community of the nation-state is very different from the localism of the small agrarian community discussed earlier.

Thus, we see again that the nation-state is a particular type of imagined community, one that could not have existed prior to modernity and the increasing awareness of an international system. The nation-state, socially constructed and historically contingent, is only one way of parsing the modern world, however. Moreover, as Peter Spiro has argued, nation-states may have a "declining capacity to define their memberships in a way that conforms with actual community on the ground."[114] In the next section, therefore, I will consider several alternative visions of community definition.

[111] Rée, *supra* note 55 at 81; *see also* Sheldon Pollock et al., Cosmopolitanisms, 12 *Pub. Culture* 577, 579 (2000) ("Pakistan[,] ... while definitely imagined from as early as the 1920s as a homeland for the Muslims of the Indian subcontinent, had only the vaguest geographical referent for a long time in its career as a concept.").

[112] Gupta & Ferguson, *supra* note 12, at 17.

[113] Rée, *supra* note 55, at 81.

[114] Peter J. Spiro, The Boundaries of Cosmopolitan Pluralism, 51 *Wayne L. Rev.* 1261, 1264 (2005).

Conceptions of Subnational, Transnational, Supranational, and Cosmopolitan Identities

Although nation-states have become the dominant form of organizing space in the contemporary world, there are other ways of imagining community and constructing identity. As we have seen, not only are processes of placemaking always contested and unstable, but relations between places are continuously shifting as a result of the political and economic reorganization of space in the world system. Moreover, "[j]ust as the formation of nation-states was one of the defining characteristics of an earlier era, their rapid and often radical transformation is one of the defining characteristics of ours."[115] Thus, we need to look at nation-state sovereignty against the backdrop of alternative transnational, international, or subnational identities, as well as possible ways of imagining community that are not based on physical territory at all.[116] As Akhil Gupta has pointed out, "[t]he structures of feeling that constitute nationalism need to be set in the context of other forms of imagining community, other means of endowing significance to space in the production of location and 'home.'"[117]

Acknowledging community affiliations that exist apart from the nation-state therefore becomes crucial. And by analyzing the social meaning of our affiliations across space, we can think about various alternative conceptions of community that are subnational, transnational, supranational, or epistemic.[118] This is not to deny the symbolically significant, constantly reinforced, and sometimes historically rooted power of

[115] Austin Sarat & Stuart A. Scheingold, State Transformation, Globalization, and the Possibilities of Cause Lawyering: An Introduction, in *Cause Lawyering and the State in a Global Era* 3, 3 (Austin Sarat & Stuart Scheingold eds., 2001) [hereinafter *Cause Lawyering*].

[116] Gupta & Ferguson, *supra* note 12, at 17; *see also* Gupta, *supra* note 46, at 181 ("[W]e need to pay attention to the structures of feeling that bind people to geographical units larger or smaller than nations or that crosscut national boundaries.").

[117] Gupta, *supra* note 46, at 193.

[118] For further discussion of these multiple forms of community, *see* Paul Schiff Berman, The Globalization of Jurisdiction, 151 *U. Pa. L. Rev.* 311, 472–90 (2002).

the nation-state in the collective imagination of its citizens. Nor is it to deemphasize the importance of nation-state communities. It is only to say that these are not the only potentially relevant community associations people might feel. Moreover, although "the scale of the nation-state may once have enabled it to respond to many human problems, ... national boundaries no longer correspond (if they ever did) to capital formation, personal opportunities, or risk."[119] Thus, we should recognize the possibility that other affiliations may sometimes be more deeply felt than bonds of loyalty to nation-states. As Roger Cotterrell has argued, "'Community' has to be drained of any residual romanticism and its different types identified insofar as they have a bearing on regulatory issues. Relations of community need to be seen as much more varied, flexible, fluid and changeable than is envisaged in most appeals to 'community.'"[120]

Meanwhile, if territorial location is of less significance now than it once was, we increasingly face normative questions about whether legal rules based on territory are desirable. Again, this is not to say that territory is unimportant, but it is difficult to deny that we are increasingly affected by activities and decisions that take place far from us in a spatial sense. Such deterritorialized effects have always been present to some extent, of course. One need only look at the history of empire to realize that the strings of governance were often pulled by far-off rulers. But at least in the premodern world such political arrangements, perhaps because of the slow pace of transportation and communications, rarely meant strong centralized control of distant realms. Rather, the social construction of space was organized around many centers, with a patchwork of overlapping and incomplete rights of government.[121] And, although

[119] Judith Resnik, Foreign as Domestic Affairs: Rethinking Horizontal Federalism and Foreign Affairs Preemption in Light of Translocal Internationalism, 57 *Emory L.J.* 31 (2007).

[120] Roger Cotterrell, What Is Transnational Law?, 37 *Law & Soc. Inq.* (2012), manuscript at 19; *see generally* Roger Cotterrell, *Law, Culture, and Society* (2006).

[121] *See, e.g.*, John Gerard Ruggie, Territoriality and Beyond: Problematizing Modernity in International Relations, 47 *Int'l Org.* 139, 149 (1993) (noting that premodern states were not based principally on territorial sovereignty and that, instead, medieval Europe

cross-border interaction obviously is not a new phenomenon, in an electronically connected world the effects of any given action may immediately be felt elsewhere with no relationship to physical geography at all.

Indeed, the globalization of capital, the movement of people and goods across borders, the reach of global corporate activity, the impact of worldwide NGOs, and the development, of so many international or transnational tribunals all make it far more likely that local communities will be affected by activities and entities with no local presence. As a thought experiment, one can imagine an "effects map," in which one identifies a territorial locality and plots on a map every action that has an effect on that locality.[122] Five hundred years ago, such effects would almost surely have been clustered around the territory, with perhaps some additional effects located in a particular distant imperial location. One hundred years ago, those effects might have begun spreading out. But today, while locality is surely not irrelevant, the effects would likely be diffused over many corporate, governmental, technological, and migratory centers. In a world of such extraterritorial effects, it is unrealistic to expect legal rules based on territory to be satisfactory, and it would not be surprising to see such rules evolve in the course of the increasingly deterritorialized twenty-first century.[123]

Concerns About Democratic Legitimacy

Of course, some maintain that only territorially defined nation-state communities can legitimately claim to exercise democratically grounded power. Such arguments have been much rehearsed in the scholarly literature,[124] and a full explication of these debates is far

was in some ways an archetype for nonexclusive territorial rule; its "patchwork of overlapping and incomplete rights of government ... [was] inextricably superimposed and tangled") (internal quotations and citation omitted).

[122] This thought experiment is derived from David G. Post, Against "Against Cyberanarchy," 17 *Berkeley Tech. L.J.* 1365, 1371–3 (2002).

[123] For an extended argument along these lines, *see* Chapter 7.

[124] *See, e.g.*, Eric A. Posner & Cass R. Sunstein, The Law of Other States, 59 *Stan. L. Rev.* 131, 133 n.4 (2006) (citing articles).

beyond the scope of this book. Here I make only a few observations, which I think are sufficient at least to complicate the claim that the imperatives of democratic sovereignty necessarily render consideration of transnational, international, or nonstate jurisdictional assertions illegitimate.

First, it is no threat to sovereignty for a nation-state to decide that its sovereign interests are advanced overall by making agreements with other nations that limit what it can otherwise do. Thus, for example, international jurisdictional assertions that derive from such agreements do not implicate concerns about democratic sovereignty.

Second, both international human rights norms and international, transnational, or nonstate institutions may actually strengthen domestic democracy, properly understood. This is because constitutional democracy already includes within it the idea that "all people (and not merely the majority) can associate themselves with the project of self-government."[125] Thus, obedience to human rights norms that minimally protect minority interests or multilateral institutions that help guard against capture of government by majority factions actually enhance democracy rather than subvert it.[126] And while such regimes beyond the nation-state will not always have these salutary effects, that is an argument to amend or reject those particular regimes, not to reject the possible efficacy of such norms or institutions altogether.

[125] Christopher L. Eisgruber, *Constitutional Self-Government* 19 (2001); *see also* Ronald Dworkin, *Freedom's Law: The Moral Reading of the American Constitution* (1996) (criticizing what he terms "the majoritarian premise" – the idea that when a group must make a collective decision, fairness requires the decision favored by a majority of its members – and arguing instead for a "constitutional" conception of democracy that requires rights to autonomy and equality as a precondition to democratic legitimacy); Lawrence G. Sager, The Incorrigible Constitution, 65 *N.Y.U. L. Rev.* 893, 897–909 (1990) (criticizing majoritarian theories of popular sovereignty on the ground that they are irreconcilable with the Constitution itself, which explicitly places limits on majoritarianism).

[126] *See, e.g.*, Robert O. Keohane, Stephen Macedo, & Andrew Moravcsik, Democracy-Enhancing Multilateralism, 63 *Int'l Org.* 1 (2009) (discussing international institutions); Jamie Mayerfeld, The Democratic Legitimacy of International Human Rights Law 19 *Ind. Int'l & Comp. L. Rev.* 49 (2009) (discussing international human rights).

Third, at least when foreign, international, or nonstate norms are formally incorporated in domestic law, such incorporation usually occurs through domestic political actors on either the national or local level. Indeed, as Judith Resnik has documented, at least in the United States local actors are, and have been, major sources through which "foreign" law has become part of U.S. traditions.[127] Moreover, when city councils or state legislatures debate and enact provisions incorporating foreign or international norms, there can be no objection from a majoritarian or federalist perspective.[128] And while the actions of judges tend to be more controversial, once one accepts the basic democratic legitimacy of countermajoritarian judges' exercising judicial review, then it is difficult to see why there is an additional democratic legitimacy argument against those same judges' issuing opinions that may sometimes be influenced by nonstate norms, such as international or foreign law (there may be normative objections to the content of particular rulings, but that is not an argument about democratic legitimacy). As Mark Tushnet has argued, "The rules made by supranational institutions become domestic U.S. law only through the operation of U.S. domestic institutions subject to the checks-and-balances system."[129] Thus, there seems to be little reason to think that the sky is falling.

For similar reasons, because the judges involved are domestic political actors, it is unclear why there are sovereignty or democracy objections to judges' considering the law of a foreign jurisdiction when resolving a choice-of-law question with multistate elements.[130] Indeed, there should be even fewer objections in the choice-of-law context because

[127] *See* Resnik, *supra* note 119 at 43–62.

[128] *See id.* at 63 ("[A]s a political theory, sovereigntism has no special relationship to majoritarianism. Sometimes, sovereigntist positions win popular initiatives to try to erect formal boundaries, and other times, such attempts fail.").

[129] Mark Tushnet, Transnational/Domestic Constitutional Law, 37 *Loy. L.A. L. Rev.* 239, 263 (2003).

[130] *See* Graeme B. Dinwoodie, A New Copyright Order: Why National Courts Should Create Global Norms, 149 *U. Pa. L. Rev.* 469, 577 (2000) ("The national courts that develop international norms are connected to a national legislative or political unit that can revisit apparent judicial over-reaching.").

statutory rules promulgated by legislatures are rarely enacted with an eye to international disputes or conduct.[131] And, even when legislators do consider activities abroad, they do so to pursue domestic policy priorities, with little consideration of multistate implications. Yet, the mere fact that a dispute is multinational necessarily means that it implicates interests that are different from a purely domestic dispute, including the state's interest in being part of a well-functioning, interlocking global system. Accordingly, judges may actually be effectuating broader sovereign interests by incorporating nonstate norms in their decisions in multistate cases.[132]

Finally, and most fundamentally, legal norms have always migrated across territorial boundaries, and precepts that come to be thought of as constitutive of a community can often be traced historically to ideas borrowed from foreign sources.[133] Accordingly, even as some seek legislatively to enjoin judges from relying on foreign or international law, others deploy foreign and international law in legal and political arguments, or they formally announce solidarity with international treaties as a way of cementing transnational community affiliations. "Ideas, norms, and practices do not stop at the lines that people draw across land,"[134] and international norms are always translated into local vernacular. This process of "vernacularization,"[135] and the debate about ideas, norms, and practices

[131] *Id.* at 548–9.

[132] *See* Berman, *supra* note 3, at 1864 ("[A]s courts consider multiple community affiliations and develop hybrid rules for resolving multistate disputes, they do so not because they are ignoring the policy choices of their home state, but because they are effectuating their state's broader interest in taking part in a global community.").

[133] *See* Judith Resnik, The Internationalism of American Federalism: Missouri and Holland, 73 *Missouri L. Rev.* 1105, 1125 (2008) ("Certain legal precepts are now seen to be foundational to the United States. But one should label them 'made in the USA' knowing that – like many other 'American' products – some of their parts are designed abroad.").

[134] Judith Resnik, et al., Ratifying Kyoto at the Local Level: Sovereigntism, Federalism, and Translocal Organizations of Government Actors (TOGAS), 50 *Arizona L. Rev.* 709, 725 (2008).

[135] *See* Sally Engle Merry, *Human Rights & Gender Violence: Translating International Law into Local Justice* 1 (2006) ("In order for human rights ideas to be effective ... they

that goes along with it, are and always have been part of democratic discourse, not in opposition to it.[136] As Seyla Benhabib has argued,

> The spread of cosmopolitan norms ... has yielded a ... political condition [in which] the local, the national and the global are all imbricated in one another. Future democratic iterations will make their interconnections and interdependence deeper and wider. Rather than seeing this situation as undermining democratic sovereignty, we can view it as promising the emergence of new political configurations and new forms of agency....[137]

Accordingly, there is no particular reason to see the recognition of norms beyond the nation-state as somehow in opposition to democratic legitimacy. Rather, such normative assertions and their effects become part of the rich discourse of a robust democratic debate.

Why Sovereigntist Territorialism Fails to Describe the Global Legal System

These arguments about nation-state communities, territoriality, and democratic legitimacy are sure to be convincing to some and unconvincing to others. But regardless of where one comes down concerning these various normative arguments, the most important point to remember is that a total rejection of foreign, international, or nonstate influence and authority is unlikely to be fully successful in a world of global interaction and cross-border activity. Indeed, seen from the point of view of U.S. historical practice, "sovereigntists have a dismal track record, in that American law is constantly being made and remade through exchanges, some frank and some implicit, with normative views from abroad. Laws – like

need to be translated into local terms and situated within local contexts of power and meaning. They need, in other words, to be remade in the vernacular.").

[136] *See* Resnik, Foreign as Domestic Affairs, *supra* note 119, at 63 ("[O]ne must learn not to equate 'the foreign' with democratic deficits because democratic iterations are a regular route by which 'the foreign' becomes domestic.").

[137] Seyla Benhabib, *Another Cosmopolitanism* 74 (Robert Post, ed., 2006).

people – migrate. Legal borders, like physical ones, are permeable, and seepage is everywhere."[138]

Nevertheless, sovereigntist territorialism still seems to many to be an accurate way of understanding the legal world. This is because these commentators and observers fundamentally misconceive how non-territorial norms are most likely to operate. They use only a positivist conception of formal law enforced coercively by a sovereign wielding physical power, pursuing a unitary set of predetermined interests. But that is not the only way (and often not even the most important way) that legal norms are developed and have impact. For example, because international law generally is not backed by coercive force, it of course often does not literally bind state actors. But international law may nevertheless have a large impact by slowly changing attitudes in large populations, effecting shifts in ideas of appropriate state behavior. Further, international legal norms may well empower constituencies within a domestic polity and provide them with a language for influencing state policy, thereby affording them leverage that they would not otherwise have had at their disposal.

Such subtle processes may not, at least on the surface, seem to play a role in constraining state behavior. And they cannot necessarily be measured in immediately quantifiable ways. But, over time, we may see changes that are more profound than those brought about by an ephemeral coercive statute enacted by a legislature. Thus, if we want to study whether international (or transnational or nonstate) law has real effects, we need to analyze these processes rather than limit our gaze to the question of whether it binds states coercively. In order to explore this point, I conclude this chapter by briefly discussing *The Limits of International Law* by Jack Goldsmith and Eric Posner, a relatively recent book that seeks to make the case against the efficacy of international law in particular, and I describe why the sovereigntist vision Goldsmith and Posner espouse is inadequate to conceptualize a world of law beyond borders.

[138] Resnik, Foreign as Domestic Affairs, *supra* note 119, at 64.

Goldsmith and Posner, like many other sovereigntists, deploy a set of simplifying assumptions in an attempt to demonstrate that legal norms beyond the nation-state, and in particular international law, have no independent valence whatsoever.[139] Rather, in this so-called realist vision each state single-mindedly pursues its rational state interest and therefore obeys alternative legal norms only to the extent that such norms serve those preexisting interests. Thus, they argue, international law is sometimes important, but only as a mechanism by which nation-states negotiate power, not as an independent limitation on the prerogatives of state governments. Yet, like the economist in the old joke who, in order to open a can in the forest, must first assume a can opener, this vision depends almost entirely on a set of simplifying assumptions.

First, we must assume that state interests exist independently of the social context within which the interests are formed. But a policymaker's idea of what is in the state's interest is always and necessarily affected by ideas of appropriate action, and these ideas are likely to be shaped – even if unconsciously – by legal norms, including the norms of international, transnational, substate, and nonstate law.[140] Moreover, as noted previously, such government officials, especially in a democracy, are at least somewhat responsive to popular opinion, and such opinion is also likely to be shaped by a variety of forces, again including the moral pull of alternative legal norms. As sociolegal scholars have long described, legal

[139] This position is most often associated with so-called international relations realists. *See* Anne-Marie Slaughter Burley, International Law and International Relations Theory: A Dual Agenda, 87 *Am. J. Int'l L.* 205, 206 (1993) (describing the "Realist challenge" embodied in "the defiant skepticism ... that international law could ever play more than an epiphenomenal role in the ordering of international life"). From the realist perspective, states in the international realm always act only in their own national interest. Thus, law is irrelevant. The only relevant laws are the "laws" of politics, and politics is a "struggle for power." *See* Hans J. Morgenthau, *Politics Among Nations: The Struggle for Power and Peace* 4, 26–7 (1949) ("International politics cannot be reduced to legal rules and institutions.").

[140] As Andrew Moravcsik puts it: "Societal ideas, interests, and institutions influence state behavior by shaping state preferences, that is, the fundamental social purposes underlying the strategic calculations of governments." Andrew Moravcsik, Taking Preferences Seriously: A Liberal Theory of International Politics, 51 *Int'l Org.* 513, 513 (1997).

norms can contribute to changes in legal consciousness that in turn alter the categories of our thought, such that they help determine what we are likely to see as a viable policy option in the first place. Indeed, even law and economics long ago adopted a framework that includes behavioral psychology within its analysis.[141]

Second, this perspective assumes that, in any given setting, a state actually has a single, definable set of interests. Thus, even as many have attacked rational choice theory for its reliance on the idea that *individuals* have unitary definable interests,[142] the sovereigntist vision espoused by Goldsmith, Posner, and others tends to multiply the problem by asserting that *entire states* have such interests. Yet, given that states are made up of multiple bureaucrats with various spheres of authority, political ideologies, institutional loyalties, and interests that range from the goal of reelection, to the need to curry favor with particular interest groups, to the aim of career advancement, the idea that a state could have a single interest is simply unfathomable. And that is not even counting the myriad forces outside government – NGOs, editorial writers, campaign contributors, political movements, and so on – that all exert influence on government actors and all may themselves be influenced by and may consciously deploy the norms of international, transnational, substate, and nonstate law in order to press varying agendas.

As a result of their radically simplifying assumptions, Goldsmith and Posner end up arguing against a straw man. Only the most diehard internationalists would suggest that a state already completely united behind both a set of interests and a strategy for attaining those interests will practice self-denial solely because that strategy contravenes international law. So, of course, if one starts from the premise that there are preexisting unitary interests, it will be difficult to find examples where international legal norms appear to have any effect.

[141] *See generally Behavioral Law and Economics* (Cass R. Sunstein ed., 2000) (containing contributions by law and economics scholars whose arguments are grounded in behavioral psychology principles).

[142] *See generally id.* (providing numerous examples demonstrating that individual interests are variable, rather than static, and depend on context).

But it is ludicrous to assume that coercively preventing states from doing that which they have already decided to do is the only way of evaluating the efficacy of international, transnational, and nonstate law. Indeed, even in the domestic context, legal norms are effective largely because people imbibe those norms and adopt them as their own, not because a police officer stands behind the next corner waiting to pounce. And law's impact is not found only in literal obedience to rules, but in the everyday categories of our discourse. When we casually refer to "private" property, "married" couples, the "rights" of people, and so on, we are adopting and deploying law's power even if we are not aware of the fact. Thus, over time, what a state considers to be in its interest is likely to change, and those changes will often be at least partly the product of changes in legal consciousness, which is in turn shaped by international law. Moreover, various actors within the state bureaucracy (or those seeking to affect bureaucratic decision making) will use international, transnational, and nonstate norms to craft political arguments within their own polities. Again, such arguments will, at least sometimes, effectively shift popular or political consensus.

Let us consider each of these ways in which the sovereigntist vision is skewed.

International Legal Consciousness

Goldsmith and Posner deny that international and transnational law has any independent power that would tend to pull a state toward compliance in opposition to that state's interests. But once we unpack the idea of a state interest, we recognize that conceptions of proper policy do not simply arise in a vacuum. Rather, they are developed by human beings operating with various sets of assumptions, ideas about justice, conceptions of global strategy, and beliefs about morality. These assumptions, ideas, and cognitive categories are themselves shaped in part by what sociolegal scholars have long termed legal consciousness.[143] Accordingly,

[143] *See, e.g.*, Patricia Ewick & Susan S. Silbey, *The Common Place of Law: Stories from Everyday Life* 45 (1998); *see also* Jean Comaroff, *Body of Power, Spirit of Resistance:*

the legal norms that are "in the air" at any given moment of history – including international, transnational, and nonstate norms – may well affect how both policy makers and ordinary citizens think about the state's interests.

Thus, coercive power is not the only way that law can have an effect, either domestically or internationally. Indeed, as Martha Finnemore has noted, "[s]ocially constructed rules, principles, norms of behavior, and shared beliefs may provide states, individuals, and other actors with understandings of what is important or valuable and what are effective and/or legitimate means of obtaining those valued goods."[144] As a result, law has an impact not merely (or perhaps even primarily) because it prevents us from doing what we want. Rather, law changes what we want in the first place.

Yet, while self-proclaimed "constructivist" international relations scholars have long made such arguments, they have not drawn on the extensive domestic sociolegal scholarship on legal consciousness. That is a shame because legal consciousness scholars have sought to study empirically just how it is that legal categories become reflected in ordinary discourse and thought. Indeed, such scholars have examined the ways in which law operates as much by influencing modes of thought as by determining conduct in any specific case.[145] From this perspective, law is

Culture and History of a South African People 4–5 (1985) (presenting the argument that consciousness is "embedded in the practical constitution of everyday life, part and parcel of the process whereby the subject is constructed by external sociocultural forms"); Robert W. Gordon, Critical Legal Histories, 36 *Stan. L. Rev.* 57, 109 (1984) ("[T]he power exerted by a legal regime consists less in the force that it can bring to bear against violators of its rules than in its capacity to persuade people that the world described in its images and categories is the only attainable world in which a sane person would want to live."); David M. Trubek, Where the Action Is: Critical Legal Studies and Empiricism, 36 *Stan. L. Rev.* 575, 604 (1984) ("Law, like other aspects of belief systems, helps to define the role of an individual in society and the relations with others that make sense.").

144 Martha Finnemore, *National Interests in International Society* 15 (1996).

145 *See, e.g.*, Kristin Bumiller, *The Civil Rights Society* 30–2 (1988) (examining "the role of legal ideology in structuring mass consciousness"); Ewick & Silbey, *supra* note 143, at 45 (1998) (defining "legal consciousness" and arguing that "every time a person

a constitutive part of culture, shaping and determining social relations[146] and providing "a distinctive manner of imagining the real."[147]

For example, "[l]ong before we ever think about going to a courtroom, we encounter landlords and tenants, husbands and wives, barkeeps and hotel guests – roles that already embed a variety of juridical notions."[148] Indeed, we cannot escape the categories and discourses that law supplies.[149] These categories may include ideas of what is public and what is private, who is an employer and who is an employee, what precautions are "reasonable," who has "rights," and so on.[150] In short, "it is just about impossible to describe any set of 'basic' social practices

interprets some event in terms of legal concepts or terminology – whether to applaud or to criticize, whether to appropriate or to resist – legality is produced" and "repeated invocation of the law sustains its capacity to comprise social relations"); Michael W. McCann, *Rights at Work: Pay Equity Reform and the Politics of Legal Mobilization* 7 (1994) ("Legal (or rights) consciousness... refers to the ongoing, dynamic process of constructing one's understanding of, and relationship to, the social world through use of legal conventions and discourses."); Sally Engle Merry, *Getting Justice and Getting Even: Legal Consciousness Among Working-Class Americans* 5 (1990) (arguing that "[l]egal consciousness is expressed by the act of going to court as well as by talk about rights and entitlements" and that such "[c]onsciousness develops through individual experiences"); Susan S. Silbey, Making a Place for Cultural Analyses of Law, 17 *Law & Soc. Inquiry* 39, 42 (1992) (noting that "law contributes to the articulation of meanings and values of daily life").

146 *See, e.g., id.* at 41 (arguing that "law is a part of the cultural processes that actively contribute in the composition of social relations").

147 Clifford Geertz, *Local Knowledge: Further Essays in Interpretive Anthropology* 173 (1983).

148 Austin Sarat & Jonathan Simon, Beyond Legal Realism? Cultural Analysis, Cultural Studies, and the Situation of Legal Scholarship, 13 *Yale J.L. & Human.* 3, 20 (2001).

149 Gordon, *supra* note 143, at 105 ("[I]n actual historical societies, the law governing social relations – even when never invoked, alluded to, or even consciously much thought about – has been such a key element in the constitution of productive relations that it is difficult to see the value... of trying to describe those relations apart from law.").

150 Indeed, according to Sarat and Kearns: "Perhaps the most stunning example of law's constitutive powers is the willingness of persons to conceive of themselves as legal subjects, as the kind of beings the law implies they are – and needs them to be. Legal subjects think of themselves as competent, self-directing persons who, for example, enter bargained-for exchanges as free and equal agents." Austin Sarat & Thomas R. Kearns, Beyond the Great Divide: Forms of Legal Scholarship and Everyday Life, in *Law in Everyday Life* 21, 28 (Austin Sarat & Thomas R. Kearns eds., 1993).

without describing the legal relations among the people involved – legal relations that don't simply condition how the people relate to each other but to an important extent define the constitutive terms of the relationship...."[151]

Because legal categories and ideas suffuse social life,[152] scholars have studied both how people think about the law and the ways in which largely inchoate ideas about the law can affect decisions they make.[153] For example, legal consciousness can be observed in "the way people conceive of the 'natural' and normal way of doing things, their habitual patterns of talk and action, and their commonsense understanding of the world."[154] These understandings are often taken for granted. This is because legal consciousness may be so much a part of an individual's worldview that it is present even when law is seemingly absent from an understanding or construction of life events. Thus, "[w]e are not merely

[151] Gordon, *supra* note 143, at 103.

[152] *See* Mark C. Suchman & Lauren B. Edelman, Legal Rational Myths: The New Institutionalism and the Law and Society Tradition, 21 *Law & Soc. Inquiry* 903, 907 (1996) ("Law and Society scholarship depicts the law as a culturally and structurally embedded social institution.").

[153] Indeed, various authors have explored the legal consciousness of average citizens. *See, e.g.*, Bumiller, *supra* note 145; Ewick & Silbey, *supra* note 143; Malcolm M. Feeley, *The Process Is the Punishment: Handling Cases in a Lower Criminal Court* (1979); McCann, *supra* note 145; Merry, *supra* note 145; Barbara Yngvesson, *Virtuous Citizens, Disruptive Subjects: Order and Complaint in a New England Court* (1993); Patricia Ewick & Susan S. Silbey, Conformity, Contestation, and Resistance: An Account of Legal Consciousness, 26 *New Eng. L. Rev.* 731 (1992); Laura Beth Nielsen, Situating Legal Consciousness: Experiences and Attitudes of Ordinary Citizens About Law and Street Harassment, 34 *Law & Soc'y Rev.* 1055 (2000); Austin Sarat, "...The Law Is All Over": Power, Resistance, and the Legal Consciousness of the Welfare Poor, 2 *Yale J. L. & Human.* 343 (1990); Austin Sarat & William L. F. Felstiner, Lawyers and Legal Consciousness: Law Talk in the Divorce Lawyer's Office, 98 *Yale L.J.* 1663 (1989).

[154] Merry, *supra* note 145, at 5; *see also* Gordon, *supra* note 143, at 101 (arguing that we should "treat legal forms as ideologies and rituals whose 'effects' – effects that include people's ways of sorting out social experience, giving it meaning, grading it as natural, just, and necessary or as contrived, unjust and subject to alteration – are in the realm of consciousness"); Sarat & Simon, *supra* note 148, at 19 ("Law is part of the everyday world, contributing powerfully to the apparently 'stable, taken-for-granted quality of that world and to the generally shared sense that as things are, so must they be.'") (quoting Sarat & Kearns, *supra* note 150, at 30).

the inert recipients of law's external pressures. Rather, we have imbibed law's images and meanings so that they seem our own."[155] Law is an often unnoticed, but nevertheless crucial, presence in our ideas of what is fair, appropriate, or natural.[156]

This focus on law in everyday life[157] recognizes that people interpret their experiences by drawing on a collaboration of law and other social structures.[158] These interpretations may be widely varied and will, of course, depend partly on social class, prior contacts with the law, and political standing.[159] Nevertheless, legal consciousness constitutes an ongoing interaction between official norms as embodied in the commonsense categories of daily life and each individual's ongoing participation

155 Sarat & Kearns, *supra* note 150, at 29.

156 *See* Gordon, *supra* note 143, at 111 ("In short, the legal forms we use set limits on what we can imagine as practical options: Our desires and plans tend to be shaped out of the limited stock of forms available to us: The forms thus condition not just our power to get what we want but what we want (or think we can get) itself."). Indeed, scholars have noted that people's judgments about praise and blame will often match the corresponding legal categories, even when those people are not familiar in detail with legal rules and doctrines. *See generally The Allocation of Responsibility* 109, 155–8 (Max Gluckman ed., 1972) (collecting essays by multiple authors analyzing similarities between industrialized societies and primitive African tribes in terms of their legal systems and behavioral patterns).

157 *See, e.g., Law in Everyday Life* (Austin Sarat & Thomas R. Kearns eds., 1993).

158 David M. Engel & Frank W. Munger, Rights, Remembrance, and the Reconciliation of Difference, 30 *Law & Soc'y Rev.* 7, 14 (1996) (asserting that their "study points to the mutuality and inseparability of law, culture, identity and experience" and that "[l]aw is one of the elements that constitute the categories and routines of everyday life"); Sarat, *supra* note 153, at 346 (arguing that welfare recipients, for example, "use legal ideas to interpret and make sense of their relationship to the welfare bureaucracy even as they refine those ideas by making claims the meaning and moral content of which are often at variance with dominant understandings").

159 *See, e.g.*, Davina Cooper, Local Government Legal Consciousness in the Shadow of Juridification, 22 *J. L. & Soc'y* 506, 510 (1995) ("[L]aw is understood experientially, in ways shaped by class, education, geography, and occupational positioning."); Carroll Seron & Frank Munger, Law and Inequality: Race, Gender… and, of Course, Class, 22 *Ann. Rev. Soc.* 187, 202 (1996) (asserting that "the relationship between lawyers and the evolution of … the class system [] should be a prime area for continuing development of theory and research").

in the process of constructing legality.[160] Accordingly, legal consciousness includes the ways in which individuals themselves deploy, transform, or subvert official legal understandings and thereby "construct" law on the ground.[161] We all take part in the construction of legal consciousness, even as we are also inevitably affected by the legal categories of the social structures around us.

Thus, when Goldsmith and Posner complain that the international law constructivist literature lacks "a mechanism for how moral and legal talk influences national behavior,"[162] legal consciousness scholarship provides part of an answer. And while it is difficult to definitively prove a direct causal link between a legal conception and an individual's categories of thought, that does not mean that such processes are not very powerful determinants of how we think. Moreover, the mere fact that changes in legal consciousness are difficult to quantify and predict does not render them any less important in analyzing state behavior concerning international law. Indeed, there are simply too many instances when we do see state actors internalize the norms of international law to dismiss them as flukes or explain them away as mere strategic behavior.

[160] "Legality" is defined as those meanings, sources of authority, and cultural practices that are in some sense legal although not necessarily approved or acknowledged by official law. The concept of legality offers the opportunity to consider "how, where and with what effect law is produced in and through commonplace social interactions.... How do our social roles and statuses, our relationships, our obligations, prerogatives, and responsibilities, our identities, and our behaviors bear the imprint of law?" Ewick & Silbey, *supra* note 143, at 20; *see also* Sarat & Kearns, *supra* note 150, at 55. ("Law is continuously shaped and reshaped by the ways it is used, even as law's constitutive power constrains patterns of usage.").

[161] *See, e.g.*, Austin D. Sarat, Redirecting Legal Scholarship in Law Schools, 12 *Yale J.L. & Human.* 129, 140 (2000) (reviewing Paul Kahn, *The Cultural Study of Law* (1999)) ("Contests over meaning in courts or communities... become occasions for [socio-legal scholars to observe] the play of power. Meanings that seem natural, or taken-for-granted, are described as hegemonic, but because the construction of meaning through law is, in fact, typically contested, scholars show the many ways in which resistance occurs.") (citation omitted).

[162] Goldsmith & Posner, *supra* note 1, at 171.

Perhaps the best-known example of a change in international legal consciousness concerns the very idea of crimes against humanity. At the time of the Nuremberg prosecutions, it was not at all clear that the pre-war atrocities committed by the German government against German citizens constituted an international crime punishable outside Germany itself.[163] Yet, the statute of the Nuremberg tribunal and the decisions of the tribunal itself effectively established such a crime.[164] Then, subsequent to Nuremberg, almost every state for the first time voluntarily subjected itself to the Genocide Convention,[165] further enshrining the idea that individuals might have international rights against their own nation-states. Today, this idea is sufficiently well accepted that we commonly see international prosecutions for crimes against humanity committed within state borders,[166] and the International Criminal Court

[163] *See* Diane F. Orentlicher, Settling Accounts: The Duty to Punish Human Rights Violations of a Prior Regime, 100 *Yale L.J.* 2537, 2555 (1991) ("To the extent that they reached Nazi offenses against German nationals, the Nuremberg prosecutions represented a radical innovation in international law. With few and limited exceptions, international law had not previously addressed a state's treatment of its own citizens, much less imposed criminal sanctions for such conduct.").

[164] *See* Charter of the International Military Tribunal, Aug. 8, 1945, 59 Stat. 1544, 82 U.N.T.S. 279, Art. 6(c) (establishing individual responsibility for crimes against humanity committed "*before* or during the war") (emphasis added); International Military Tribunal, Opinion & Judgment, The Law Relating to War Crimes and Crimes Against Humanity, *available at* http://www.yale.edu/lawweb/avalon/imt/proc/judlawre.htm. At the time, this issue raised serious retroactivity concerns precisely because the statute was effectively establishing a new international crime. Accordingly, the Tribunal finessed this issue, interpreting the statute to give the Tribunal jurisdiction over only those crimes against humanity that were deemed sufficiently related to the other two crimes in the statute: crimes against peace and war crimes. *See id.* ("To constitute crimes against humanity, the acts relied on before the outbreak of war must have been in execution of, or in connection with, any crime within the jurisdiction of the Tribunal.").

[165] *See* Convention on the Prevention and Punishment of the Crime of Genocide, Dec. 9, 1948, art. 2, S. Exec. Doc. O, 81–1, at 7 (1949), 78 U.N.T.S. 277, 280. For a list of ratifying countries, *available at* http:// www.ohchr.org/english/countries/ratification/1.htm.

[166] *See, e.g.*, Ruti Teitel, The Law and Politics of Contemporary Transitional Justice, 38 *Cornell Int'l L.J.* 837, 841–2 (2005) (considering the work of the International Criminal Tribunal for the Former Yugoslavia and noting that war crimes, crimes against humanity, and genocide "have been made subject to international jurisdiction, although some

has jurisdiction over such crimes.[167] Significantly, though the United States has not ratified the International Criminal Court statute,[168] the basic idea of a crime against humanity under international law is no longer seriously in doubt,[169] signifying an important shift from World War II to the present day.[170]

In addition, there is evidence that even military officers, who might be supposed to resist any limits on their strategic behavior, may come to imbibe and espouse international norms. For example, in the U.S. military, every proposed bombing target is vetted by lawyers who work to ensure that the minimum possible collateral damage is created, in accordance with international law.[171] Likewise, military lawyers and current and former military officers were among the loudest opponents of the George W. Bush administration's lack of concern for abiding by the

were committed domestically, reflecting radical developments in the construction of international criminal jurisdiction").

167 Rome Statute of the International Criminal Court, Jul. 17, 1998, U.N. Doc. A/CONF.183/9, 37 *I.L.M.* 999.

168 *See* http://treaties.un.org/Pages/ViewDetails.aspx?src=TREATY&mtdsg_no=XVIII-10&chapter=18&lang=en (listing ratification history of the statute).

169 For example, the United States supported the creation of the International Criminal Tribunal for the Former Yugoslavia (ICTY), *see* Wayne Sandholtz, The Iraqi National Museum and International Law: A Duty to Protect, 44 *Colum. J. Int'l L.* 185, 204 (2005) ("The United States supported the creation of the ICTY and has contributed to its work, not least by providing experienced investigators and prosecutors to the ICTY Office of The Prosecutor."), whose enabling statute included crimes against humanity in its jurisdictional reach. Statute of the International Criminal Tribunal for the Former Yugoslavia art. 5, May 25, 1993, 32 *I.L.M.* 1192, 1193–4. In addition, U.S. courts have regularly recognized crimes against humanity as a violation of the Law of Nations that is cognizable under the Alien Tort Statute (ATS), 28 U.S.C. §1350. *See, e.g.*, Beth Stephens, *Sosa v. Alvarez-Machain:* "The Door Is Still Ajar" for Human Rights Litigation in U.S. Courts, 70 *Brook. L. Rev.* 533, 537& n.18 (2004) (noting U.S. cases interpreting the ATS that have "recognized a small core of actionable human rights violations in addition to torture, including summary execution, disappearance, war crimes, *crimes against humanity*, slavery, and arbitrary detention") (emphasis added).

170 *See, e.g.*, David Luban, A Theory of Crimes Against Humanity, 29 *Yale J. Int'l L.* 85, 86 (2004) ("The phrase 'crimes against humanity' has acquired enormous resonance in the legal and moral imaginations of the post–World War II world.").

171 Secretary of the Air Force, Air Force Instruction 13–1AOC, Vol. 3 § 8.4 (2005), *available at* http://www.e-publishing.af.mil/pubfiles/af/13/afi13–1aocv3/afi13–1aocv3.pdf.

Geneva Conventions in detaining and interrogating terrorism suspects.[172] These acts are not explainable simply by suggesting that this is a "cooperation game" where military officers wish to obey international law solely to ensure that U.S. targets or captured soldiers in the future are treated similarly. Instead, it seems clear that these officials have internalized the values of international law and see them as part of what is required, both morally and strategically. Similarly, in the environmental context, we have seen multinational corporations supporting the Kyoto Protocol on global climate change,[173] either because they want to take part in the growing

[172] For example, in six memoranda dated from February 5 to March 13, 2003, the Air Force, Army, Navy, and Marine Offices of the Judge Advocate General protested "extreme" interrogation techniques being permitted in the so-called war against terrorism. Memorandum from Jack L. Rives, Major Gen., U.S. Air Force, Deputy Judge Advocate Gen., to Air Force Gen. Counsel (Feb. 5, 2003), *available at* http://balkin.blogspot.com/jag.memos.pdf; Memorandum from Jack L. Rives, Major Gen., U.S. Air Force, Deputy Judge Advocate Gen., to Air Force Gen. Counsel (Feb. 6, 2003), *available at* http://balkin.blogspot.com/jag.memos.pdf; Memorandum from Michael F. Lohr, Rear Admiral, U.S. Navy, Judge Advocate Gen., to Air Force Gen. Counsel (Feb. 6, 2003), *available at* http://balkin.blogspot.com/jag.memos.pdf; Memorandum from Kevin M. Sandkuhler, Brigadier Gen., U.S. Marine Corps, Staff Judge Advocate to Commandant of the Marine Corps, to Air Force Gen. Counsel (Feb. 27, 2003), *available at* http://balkin.blogspot.com/jag.memos.pdf; Memorandum from Thomas J. Romig, Major Gen., U.S. Army, Judge Advocate Gen., to Air Force Gen. Counsel (Mar. 3, 2003), *available at* http://balkin.blogspot.com/jag.memos.pdf; Memorandum from Michael F. Lohr, Rear Admiral, U.S. Navy, Judge Advocate Gen., to Air Force Gen. Counsel (Mar. 13, 2003), *available at* http://balkin.blogspot.com/jag.memos.pdf. As Air Force Major General Jack Rives wrote in one of the memoranda: "[T]he use of the more extreme interrogation techniques simply is not how the U.S. armed forces have operated in recent history. We have taken the legal and moral 'high-road' in the conduct of our military operations regardless of how others may operate. Our forces are trained in this legal and moral mindset beginning the day they enter active duty. It should be noted that law of armed conflict and code of conduct training have been mandated by Congress and emphasized since the Viet Nam conflict when our POWs were subjected to torture by their captors. We need to consider the overall impact of approving extreme interrogation techniques as giving official approval and legal sanction to the application of interrogation techniques that U.S. forces have consistently been trained are unlawful." Memorandum from Jack L. Rives, Major Gen., U.S. Air Force, Deputy Judge Advocate Gen., to Air Force Gen. Counsel (Feb. 5, 2003), *available at* http:// balkin.blogspot.com/jag.memos.pdf.

[173] Kyoto Protocol to the U.N. Framework Convention on Climate Change, Dec. 10, 1997, 37 *I.L.M.* 22.

international trade in pollution credits,[174] or because they seek future profits from investments in renewable energy.[175] Such activities suggest that corporations, through the mechanism of capitalist self-interest, have come to internalize (and seek profit from) an international environmental norm. Further, such norm internalization by nongovernmental entities can in turn influence governmental actors.

Finally, obedience to international legal norms, even if sometimes detrimental to state interests in the short term – because one is restrained from taking certain actions – may further state interests in the longer term by allowing the state to have legitimacy and a certain morally persuasive position in the eyes of other states. Indeed, it is significant that Goldsmith and Posner almost entirely exclude so-called soft law[176] or soft power[177]

[174] *See* Ricardo Bayon, Trading Futures in Dirty Air: Here's a Market-Based Way to Fight Global Warming, *Wash. Post*, Aug. 5, 2001, at B02 (arguing that President Bush should sign on to the Kyoto Protocol in part because the emerging market in pollution credits is poised to be extremely profitable); Jay Newton-Small & Jonathan D. Salant, GM, DuPont Adapt to Kyoto Environmental Standards, Bloomberg News Serv., Nov. 15, 2004, *available at* http:// www.bloomberg.com/apps/news?pid=71000001&refer=us&sid=aSedVkbj0CwQ ("Enron Corp., DuPont, American Express Power Co. and other U.S. companies urged Bush to salvage parts of the treaty, saying they viewed regulation as inevitable and they wanted credit for cutting their emissions."); *see also* Marianne Lavelle, A Shift in the Wind on Global Warming, *U.S. News & World Rep.*, Mar. 19, 2001, at 39, 39 ("Many businesses active on global warming envision ... a market-based trading system that would allow farmers and others who cut carbon emissions to get credits they could sell to carbon-emitting businesses. Perhaps that's why traditional manufacturers...have joined forces with pro-regulatory groups like the Pew Center for Global Climate Change.").

[175] *See* William Drozdiak, U.S. Firms Become "Green" Advocates: Global Warming Talks Near End, *Wash. Post*, Nov. 24, 2000, at E1 ("Aidan Murphy, vice president at Shell International, says the Kyoto treaty has prompted the British-Dutch oil company to shift some of its focus away from petroleum toward alternative fuel sources.").

[176] For discussions of "soft law," *see*, for example, Kenneth W. Abbott & Duncan Snidal, Hard and Soft Law in International Governance, 53 *Int'l Org.* 421 (2000); Christine Chinkin, Normative Development in the International Legal System, in *Commitment and Compliance: The Role of Non-Binding Norms in the International System* 21 (Dinah Shelton ed., 2000); Dinah Shelton, Compliance with International Human Rights Soft Law, in *International Compliance with Nonbinding Accords* 9 (Edith Brown Weiss ed., 1997).

[177] *See, e.g.*, Joseph S. Nye, *The Paradox of American Power: Why the World's Only Superpower Can't Go It Alone* 9 (2002) (defining soft power as "getting others to want what you want").

from their analysis. Yet it is difficult to see how a state could hope to further its long-term interests without being able to convince others to follow certain policies simply through the power of persuasion and moral authority. The problem is that Goldsmith and Posner, because they simply assume a set of interests, provide no way of choosing between these short-term and longer-term interests. As Martha Finnemore has pointed out:

> [I]t is all fine and well to assume that states want power, security, and wealth, but what kind of power? Power for what ends? What kind of security? What does security mean? How do you ensure or obtain it? Similarly, what kind of wealth? Wealth for whom? How do you obtain it?[178]

Goldsmith and Posner, like the neorealists and neoliberals before them, have no answer to these questions. And, even worse, their framework does not allow such questions to be raised.

To be sure, one can certainly find instances when international law does appear to envision itself as a coercive set of rules meant to constrain states. For example, the UN Charter lays out a use-of-force regime that is clearly intended to prevent states from engaging in certain belligerent acts.[179] And we can readily concede that states might sometimes refuse to follow such constraints – as with the George W. Bush doctrine of preemptive war – though such refusal may carry severe consequences to the nonconforming state.[180] Thus, when sovereigntists argue that such international law regimes do not, in the end, stop states from pursuing their own interests, such a statement may be true in a certain limited category of cases.

But just as importantly, many aspects of the international normative order do not lend themselves to this type of framework. Indeed, by

[178] Finnemore, *supra* note 144, at 1–2.

[179] *See* U.N. Charter art. 2, para. 4("All Members shall refrain in their international relations from the threat or use of force against the territorial integrity or political independence of any state, or in any other manner inconsistent with the Purposes of the United Nations.").

[180] For example, other countries may withhold funds or manpower, and forging compromise on a host of other issues may become more difficult.

excluding soft law, Goldsmith and Posner limit their field of vision to the formal, state-centered international law regimes that are arguably playing a less and less important role in the transnational order.[181] Moreover, in many cases, it is not that the international regime is constraining states but that the international regime creates the impetus for action in the first place. For example:

> Prior to the actions of UNESCO [the United Nations Educational, Scientific, and Cultural Organization], most states, especially less developed countries, had no notion that they needed or wanted a state science bureaucracy. Similarly, European heads of state were not particularly concerned about treatment of the war wounded until Henri Dunant and the International Committee of the Red Cross made it an issue. Global poverty alleviation, while long considered desirable in the abstract, was not considered a pressing responsibility of states, particularly of developed states, until the World Bank under Robert McNamara made it a necessary part of development.[182]

Thus, the persuasive power of international norms caused states to develop interests they might not otherwise have had.

In each of these instances, international law is shaping the consciousness of state actors, not operating to constrain them from taking actions they would otherwise pursue. Similarly, as Thomas Berger argues, in Germany and Japan today, antimilitarism is as crucial to national identity as militarism was in the World War II era.[183] These are changes in the states' conceptions of their own interests, influenced by the international legal regime that Germany in particular has long championed. Again, the important impact of such international regimes has no place in the Goldsmith-Posner framework.

[181] *See* Paul Schiff Berman, From International Law to Law and Globalization, 43 *Colum. J. Transnat'l L.* 485 (2005) (discussing this expansion of international law to include less formal transnational and international mechanisms).

[182] Finnemore, *supra* note 144, at 12.

[183] Thomas U. Berger, *Cultures of Antimilitarism: National Security in Germany and Japan* 8–9 (1998).

Indeed, Goldsmith and Posner go so far as to deny that the existence of a legal norm or agreement necessarily changes the constitutive terms of the relationships among nation-states. According to Goldsmith and Posner, even a treaty exerts no "normative pull."[184] Rather, "[s]tates refrain from violating treaties (when they do) for the same basic reason they refrain from violating nonlegal agreements: because they fear retaliation from the other state or some kind of reputational loss, or because they fear a failure of coordination."[185] But once Goldsmith and Posner acknowledge that reputational loss could factor into nation-state decision making, they have essentially conceded that the treaty regime does indeed have a normative pull. This is because the potential reputational loss is made greater by the existence of the treaty regime itself. The treaty effectively alters the terms of the relationship among the parties and necessarily changes their bargaining positions. The same is true of customary international law. Once a norm is named a customary international law norm, then violation of that norm will have far more serious reputational costs. This is not to say that states will never violate such a customary norm, but rather that the naming of the norm itself makes violating the norm that much more difficult without suffering consequences. Again, the international legal framework changes the constitutive relationship among nation-states.

Goldsmith and Posner respond by saying that such reputational costs do not amount to a true normative pull, and they liken a treaty to a nonbinding letter of intent, which they argue does not itself cause parties to follow its terms.[186] But, of course, that is precisely how seemingly nonbinding letters of intent *do* work. By stating an intent to do something, a party vastly increases the likelihood of doing it because the statement of the intent to be bound changes expectations of the parties and increases reputational costs for noncompliance.[187]

[184] Goldsmith & Posner, *supra* note 1, at 90.

[185] *Id.*

[186] *See id.* at 90–1.

[187] *See, e.g.*, Oscar Schachter, *International Law in Theory and Practice* 100 (1991) (arguing that states tend to view the nonbinding agreements that they enter into in good faith

Thus, we need a richer account of how law actually operates, both domestically and internationally, than the positivist vision of sovereigntism often assumes. We imbibe legal norms and cognitive categories even when we are not consciously aware of the norm in question. We are persuaded by legal norms even when those norms are not literally enforceable. We act in accordance with law because doing so has become habitual, not because we seek to avoid sanction. We conceive of our interrelations with others in terms of law because our long-term interests require that we do so, even when our short-term interest might seem to counsel otherwise. And the existence of a legal norm alters the constitutive terms of our relationships with others as well as the costs of noncompliance. All of these may be overcome in some circumstances. Indeed, people sometimes violate domestic law just as states sometimes violate international law. But in neither case does that mean that the law in question has no significant constraining force. And only by thinking more broadly about changes in legal consciousness and the complicated social, political, and psychological factors that enter into the conceptualization of state interests can we begin to understand how international, transnational, and nonstate law operates.

Multiple Constituencies and the Deployment of International Law

Sovereigntists tend to treat the state as a unitary "personality" with a single set of interests. But, of course, the real world is far more messy, with a vast number of constituencies both within the governmental bureaucracy and outside it. This cacophony of voices is important both because it challenges the seductive simplicity of the vision offered by sovereigntists and

as political or moral obligations upon which other states will rely and expect compliance); Peter M. Haas, Why Comply, or Some Hypotheses in Search of an Analyst, in *International Compliance with Nonbinding Accords*, *supra* note 184, at 31, 33 (arguing that activities such as monitoring a state's compliance with a nonbinding agreement and direct verification of compliance may induce that state to comply in order to avoid detection and potential criticism).

because many of these voices, when advocating policy positions, can use the moral authority or persuasive power of international, transnational, or nonstate norms for leverage. These norms therefore become a tool of empowerment for particular actors. And given that any state policy decision is inevitably the result of a contest among various bureaucratic power centers, all of which are themselves influenced by outside pressure groups, lobbyists, NGOs, and the like, a more complex understanding of international law would need to explore ways in which international legal norms empower specific interests both within and without the state policy-making apparatus and provide arguments and leverage that they might not otherwise have had.

For example, although the well-known efforts of Spanish judge Baltasar Garzón (described in Chapter 2) to try former Chilean leader Augusto Pinochet[188] were not literally "successful" because Pinochet was never extradited to Spain,[189] they strengthened the hands of human rights

[188] Judge Garzón issued an arrest order based on allegations of kidnappings, torture, and planned disappearances of Chilean citizens and citizens of other countries. Spanish Request to Arrest General Pinochet, Oct. 16, 1998, reprinted in *The Pinochet Papers: The Case of Augusto Pinochet in Spain and Britain* 57–9 (Reed Brody & Michael Ratner eds., 2000) [hereinafter *The Pinochet Papers*]; *see also* Anne Swardson, Pinochet Case Tries Spanish Legal Establishment, *Wash. Post*, Oct. 22, 1998, at A27 ("As Chilean president from 1973 to 1990, Garzón's arrest order said, Pinochet was 'the leader of an international organization created… to conceive, develop and execute the systematic planning of illegal detentions [kidnappings], torture, forced relocations, assassinations and/or disappearances of numerous persons, including Argentines, Spaniards, Britons, Americans, Chileans and other nationalities.'"). On October 30, 1998, the Spanish National Court ruled unanimously that Spanish courts had jurisdiction over the matter both on the principle of universal jurisdiction (that crimes against humanity can be tried anywhere at any time) and on the passive personality principle of jurisdiction (that courts may try cases if their nationals are victims of crime, regardless of where the crime was committed). S Audiencia Nacional, Nov. 5, 1998 (No. 173/98), reprinted in *The Pinochet Papers*, *supra*, at 95, 95–107. For an English translation of the opinion, *see The Pinochet Papers*, *supra*, at 95, 95–107. The Office of the Special Prosecutor alleged that Spaniards living in Chile were among those killed under Pinochet's rule. *Id.* at 106.

[189] Pinochet was physically in Great Britain. The British House of Lords ultimately ruled that Pinochet was not entitled to head-of-state immunity for acts of torture and could be extradited to Spain. *Regina v. Bow St. Metro.* Stipendiary Magistrate, *Ex parte*

advocates within Chile itself and provided the impetus for a movement that led to a Chilean Supreme Court decision stripping Pinochet of his lifetime immunity.[190] Likewise, Spanish efforts to prosecute members of the Argentine military bolstered reformers within the Argentine government, most notably then-President Néstor Kirschner. Judge Garzón sought extradition from Argentina of dozens of Argentines for human rights abuses committed under the Argentine military government in the 1970s[191] and successfully extradited from Mexico one former Argentine navy lieutenant who was accused of murdering hundreds of people.[192] In the wake of Garzón's actions, sovereigntist observers complained that such transnational prosecutions were illegitimate because Argentina had previously conferred amnesty on those who had been involved in the period of military rule and therefore any prosecution would infringe on Argentina's sovereign "choice" to grant amnesty.[193]

Pinochet (No. 3), [2000]1 *A.C.* 147, 204–5 (*H.L.* 1999) (appeal taken from Q.B. Div'l Ct.) (holding that the International Convention Against Torture, incorporated into United Kingdom law in 1988, prevented Pinochet from claiming head-of-state immunity after 1988, because the universal jurisdiction contemplated by the Convention is inconsistent with immunity for former heads of state). Nevertheless, the British government refused to extradite, citing Pinochet's failing health. *See* Jack Straw, Sec'y of State Statement in the House of Commons (Mar. 2, 2000), in *The Pinochet Papers*, *supra* note 188, at 481, 482 ("[I]n the light of th[e] medical evidence... I... conclude[d] that no purpose would be served by continuing the Spanish extradition request."). Pinochet was eventually returned to Chile.

[190] *See* Chile's Top Court Strips Pinochet of Immunity, *N.Y. Times*, Aug. 27, 2004, at A3 ("Chile's Supreme Court stripped the former dictator Augusto Pinochet of immunity from prosecution in a notorious human rights case on Thursday, raising hopes of victims that he may finally face trial for abuses during his 17-year rule.").

[191] *See* Larry Rohter, Argentine Congress Likely to Void "Dirty War" Amnesties, *N.Y. Times*, Aug. 21, 2003, at A3 (recounting Garzón's extradition request).

[192] Emma Daly, Spanish Judge Sends Argentine to Prison on Genocide Charge, *N.Y. Times*, June 30, 2003, at A3 ("In an unusual act of international judicial cooperation, and a victory for the Spanish judge Baltasar Garzón, Mexico's Supreme Court ruled this month that the former officer, Ricardo Miguel Cavallo, could be extradited to Spain for crimes reportedly committed in a third country, Argentina.").

[193] *See* David B. Rivkin Jr. & Lee A. Casey, Crimes Outside the World's Jurisdiction, *N.Y. Times*, July 22, 2003, at A19 (noting that Argentina had granted amnesty to Cavallo and arguing that "Judge Garzón is essentially ignoring Argentina's own history and desires").

But the amnesty decision was not simply a unitary choice made by some unified "state" of Argentina; it was a politically contested act that remained controversial within the country.[194] And the Spanish extradition request itself gave President Kirschner more leverage in his tug-of-war with the legal establishment over the amnesty laws. Just a month after Garzón's request, both houses of the Argentine Congress voted by large majorities to annul the laws.[195] Meanwhile the Spanish government decided that it would not make the formal extradition request to Argentina that Garzón sought, but it did so primarily because Argentina had begun to scrap its amnesty laws and the accused would therefore be subject to domestic human rights prosecution.[196] President Kirschner therefore could use Spain's announcement to increase pressure on the Argentine Supreme Court to officially overturn the amnesty laws.[197]

Finally, on June 14, 2005, the Argentine Supreme Court did in fact strike down the amnesty laws, thus clearing the way for domestic human rights prosecutions.[198] Not only was the pressure exerted by Spain instrumental

[194] The Argentine army, for example, made known its desire for amnesty for human rights abuses through several revolts in the late 1980s. The Argentine Congress granted amnesty after one such uprising in 1987. *See* Joseph B. Treaster, Argentine President Orders Troops to End Revolt, *N.Y. Times*, Dec. 4, 1988, § 1, at 13 (describing an army revolt in Buenos Aires).

[195] Argentina's Day of Reckoning, *Chi. Trib.*, Apr. 24, 2004, at C26.

[196] Elizabeth Nash, Garzón Blocked over "Dirty War" Extraditions, *The Independent*, Aug. 30, 2003, at 14; *see also* Al Goodman, Spain Blocks Trials of Argentines, CNN.com, Aug. 29, 2003, *available at* http://www.cnn.com/2003/WORLD/europe/08/29/spanish.argentina/index.html (quoting the Spanish attorney for the victims saying that the Spanish government's decision sends a "powerful message" to Argentina's Supreme Court to overturn the amnesty laws).

[197] *See* Héctor Tobar, Judge Orders Officers Freed: The Argentine Military Men Accused of Rights Abuses in the '70s and '80s May Still Face Trials, *L.A. Times*, Sept. 2, 2003, at A3 ("President Nestor Kirchner used Spain's announcement to increase pressure on the Argentine Supreme Court to overturn the amnesty laws that prohibit trying the men here.").

[198] Corte Suprema de Justicia [CSJN], 14/6/2005, "Simón, Julio Héctor y otros s/ privación ilegítima de la libertad," causa No. 17.768, S.1767.XXXVIII (Arg.); *see also* Press Release, Human Rights Watch, Argentina: Amnesty Laws Struck Down (June 14, 2005), *available at* http:// hrw.org/english/docs/2005/06/14/argent11119.htm.

in these efforts, but it is significant that the Argentine Court cited as legal precedent a 2001 decision of the Inter-American Court of Human Rights striking down a similar amnesty provision in Peru as incompatible with the American Convention on Human Rights and hence without legal effect.[199] So, in the end, the "sovereign" state of Argentina made political and legal choices to repeal the amnesty laws just as it had previously made choices to create them. But in this change of heart we can see the degree to which international legal pronouncements, even if they are without any literal constraining effect, may significantly alter the domestic political terrain.

Likewise, official international institutions, such as the UN, can also pressure local bureaucracies, for example, by creating international commissions of inquiry concerning alleged atrocities or by threatening prosecutions in international courts. Such declarations can empower reformers within local bureaucracies, who can then argue for institutional changes as a way of staving off international interference. For example, in the aftermath of the violence in East Timor that followed its vote for independence, there were grave concerns that the Indonesian government would not pursue human rights investigations of the military personnel allegedly responsible for the violence.[200] Thus, an International Commission of Inquiry was established, and UN officials warned that an international court might be necessary.[201] As with Chile and Argentina, such actions strengthened the hand of reformers within Indonesia, such

[199] Corte Suprema de Justicia [CSJN], 14/6/2005, "Simón, Julio Héctor y otros s/ privación ilegítima de la libertad," causa No. 17.768, S.1767.XXXVIII (Arg.); *see also* Press Release, *supra* note 198.

[200] *See, e.g.,* Laura A. Dickinson, The Dance of Complementarity: Relationships Among Domestic, International, and Transnational Accountability Mechanisms in East Timor and Indonesia, in *Accountability for Atrocities: National and International Responses* 319, 358–61 (Jane E. Stromseth ed., 2003) (discussing ways in which international pressure on Indonesia in the period just after East Timor gained its independence strengthened the hand of reformers within the Indonesian government to push for robust domestic accountability mechanisms for atrocities committed during the period leading up to the independence vote).

[201] *Id.* at 358–9.

as then-attorney general Marzuki Darusman. With the specter of international action hanging over Indonesia, Darusman made several statements arguing that, for nationalist reasons, a hard-hitting Indonesian investigation was necessary in order to forestall an international takeover of the process.[202] Not surprisingly, when this international pressure dissipated after the terrorist attacks of September 11, 2001, so did the momentum to provide real accountability in Indonesia for the atrocities committed.[203] Thus, we can again see that international legal activity (or the lack of it) alters the domestic terrain. Indeed, as examples throughout this book suggest, even a country as militarily and economically powerful as the United States will often be affected by the global environment.

Finally, there can be little doubt that local actors, outside official government bureaucracies or judicial institutions, can at times leverage international legal norms to press causes within their countries.[204] For example, as late as 1994, women in Hong Kong were unable to inherit land.[205] That year a group of rural indigenous women joined forces with urban women's groups to demand legal change. As detailed by Sally Engle Merry and Rachel E. Stern, "[t]he indigenous women slowly shifted from seeing their stories as individual kinship violations to broader examples of discrimination."[206] Ultimately, the women learned to protest these unjust customary laws in the language of international human rights and

[202] *See id.* at 360 (documenting the response of the Indonesian government, which appointed an investigative team, identified priority cases, named suspects, and collected evidence).

[203] *See id.* at 364–6 (discussing the shifting priorities of the Bush administration following the 9/11 attacks and tracing the impact of outside pressure in efforts to hold individuals accountable for the violence in East Timor).

[204] Of course, such local actors not only "use" international law as "given" to them, but also, through their social movements, shape the international legal norms themselves. For an argument that human rights discourse has been fundamentally shaped by Third World resistance to development, *see* generally Balakrishnan Rajagopal, *International Law from Below: Development, Social Movements, and Third World Resistance* (2003).

[205] Sally Engle Merry & Rachel E. Stern, The Female Inheritance Movement in Hong Kong: Theorizing the Local/Global Interface, 46 *Current Anthropology* 387, 387 (2005).

[206] *Id.* at 399.

gender equality.[207] Having done so, they were successful at getting the inheritance rules overturned.[208] While we might regret the fact that these women were forced to "translate" their grievances into an internationally recognized language in order to be heard, the success of the movement in accessing political power surely attests to the strength and importance of the international law discourse.

This same story has been replicated numerous times around the world. Assisted by a global network of NGOs and activists, indigenous movements use international norms to influence local political or judicial actors. In June 2005 communities from across the Niger Delta filed a case in the Federal High Court of Nigeria against several oil companies to stop the practice of "gas flaring," which poses severe health risks and contributes to greenhouse gas emissions.[209] Though nominally brought under the Nigerian Constitution, the complaint explicitly references the African Charter on Human and People's Rights and argues for a right to a "clean, poison-free, pollution free and healthy environment."[210] Other environmental groups seek to have sites placed on UNESCO's World Heritage Committee list of protected sites so that they can then pressure their local governments to take steps to limit environmental damage to the sites.[211]

[207] *See id.* at 390 (explaining the evolution of the Anti-Discrimination Female Indigenous Residents Committee from a group that perceived the prohibition of female inheritance as a personal wrong perpetrated by relatives to a group arguing that the male-only inheritance laws failed to comply with international agreements, such as the Convention on the Elimination of Discrimination Against Women and the International Covenant on Civil and Political Rights).

[208] *Id.* at 394.

[209] *Gbemre v. Shell Petroleum Dev. Co. Nig.*, Suit No. FHC/B/CS/153/2005. On November 14, 2005, the Federal High Court of Nigeria in Benin City ruled that Royal Dutch Shell, Chevron, Exxon Mobil, and other oil companies must end natural gas flaring in Nigeria, claiming that the practice was wasteful and violated the local communities' constitutional rights to life and dignity. A copy of the judicial order is *available at* http://www.climatelaw.org/media/media/gas.flaring.suit.nov2005/ni.shell.nov05.decision.pdf.

[210] Complaint at 4, *Gbemre v. Shell Petroleum Dev. Co. Nig.*, Suit No. FHC/B/CS/153/2005, *available at* http://www.climatelaw.org/media/gas.flaring.suit/case.pleadings.20June2005.pdf.

[211] For example, the countries of Belize, Nepal, and Peru have petitioned the World Heritage Committee to place the Belize Barrier Reef, Mount Everest, and Huarascan

Consumer groups organize worldwide boycotts on the rhetorical strength of rights discourse.[212] Meanwhile, many African countries, responding in part to pressure from international human rights activists, have enacted laws forbidding the practice known as female genital cutting.[213] And of course, it is not only social movements that use the language and institutions of international law to access domestic power. Thus, transnational corporations have deployed the rhetoric of international free trade law and have used bodies such as the NAFTA tribunals or the World Trade Organization to avoid being subject to domestic regulation.[214] And even lower domestic courts within the European Union have more readily embraced the jurisprudence of the European Court of Justice, perhaps

National Park on its list of World Heritage in Danger Sites, because of threats to the sites due to global climate change. *See* Press Release, Climate Justice, UNESCO Danger-Listing Petitions Presented (Nov. 17, 2004), *available at* http://www.climatelaw.org/media/UNESCO.petitions.release. "Danger-listing" is a legal mechanism under the Convention Concerning the Protection of the World Cultural and Natural Heritage, Nov. 16, 1972, 27U.S.T. 37, 1037 U.N.T.S. 151, which requires State Parties to the Convention to take action to transmit World Heritage Sites to future generations.

212 *See* Paul Schiff Berman, The Globalization of Jurisdiction, 151 *U. Pa. L. Rev.* 311, 480–82 (2002) (discussing such efforts). As the *Economist* has observed, "a multinational's failure to look like a good global citizen is increasingly expensive in a world where consumers and pressure groups can be quickly mobilised behind a cause." Multinationals and Their Morals, *Economist*, Dec. 2–8, 1995, at 18–19. For discussion of how noncompliance with entrenched international law norms may result in lost economic opportunities for subnational units, crucial to economic prosperity in a globalized economy, *see* Peter J. Spiro, Globalization and the (Foreign Affairs) Constitution, 63 *Ohio St. L.J.* 649, 672–3 (2002), in which he outlines ways that consumers, nongovernmental organizations, and states can pressure corporations to boycott investment and development in regions that fail to follow standards of international law.

213 Leigh A. Trueblood, Female Genital Mutilation: A Discussion of International Human Rights Instruments, Cultural Sovereignty and Dominance Theory, 28 *Denv. J. Int'l L. & Pol'y* 437, 464–5 (2000) (describing how the efforts of international organizations, NGOs, and other groups have led many countries, including Cameroon, Egypt, Kenya, Sudan, Burkina Faso, and Ivory Coast, to pass legislation designed to limit or prevent female genital cutting).

214 *See, e.g.*, Benjamin W. Putnam, Note, The Cross-Border Trucking Dispute: Finding a Way Out of the Conflict Between NAFTA and U.S. Environmental Law, 82 *Texas L. Rev.* 1287, 1307–8 (2004) (describing cases in which regulated entities cite NAFTA to avoid the requirements of domestic environmental laws).

in part as a way to leverage power that had previously been retained by national high courts.[215]

REGARDLESS OF WHETHER OR NOT ONE THINKS THE PROLIFERATION AND deployment of international norms in domestic political and legal debates are a good thing, it is difficult to deny the reality. Thus, the interaction between the international and the local cannot simply be viewed as sovereigntists like Goldsmith and Posner tend to view it: a state pursuing a single set of interests either completely constrained or completely unconstrained by international norms. Rather, as part of the multivalent, messy process by which various state constituencies vie to have their preferred policies adopted, international, transnational, and nonstate norms can be a powerful tool. And though one might think that I should not include nonstate norms in this list because they are not law at all, consider the idea of international human rights itself, which is to a large degree a creature of religiously based conceptions of natural law standing above the state. Thus, these norms provide a set of moral, rhetorical, and strategic arguments that may empower constituencies that might not otherwise have a voice, or they may be used by already powerful forces to protect their own interests. In any event, only by going beyond the simplistic model of the unitary state pursuing a single set of interests can we see the power of nonstate law (international, transnational, subnational) coursing below the surface.

Indeed, even a country as economically and militarily powerful as the United States cannot do it alone.[216] Consider some of the examples discussed in Chapter 2. After the French court issued judgment against Yahoo!,[217] the service provider filed suit in federal district court in

[215] *See* Karen J. Alter, *Establishing the Supremacy of European Law: The Making of an International Rule of Law in Europe* (2001).

[216] *See, e.g.*, Nye, *supra* note 177, at 17.

[217] Tribunal de Grande Instance de Paris [T.G.I.][ordinary court of original jurisdiction] Paris, May 22, 2000, Ordonnance de refere, UEJF et Licra c/ Yahoo! Inc. et Yahoo France, *available at* http://www.juriscom.net/txt/jurisfr/cti/tgiparis20000522.htm.

California seeking a declaration that the judgment would be unenforceable pursuant to the First Amendment.[218] Leaving aside the merits of this suit (which was ultimately dismissed on procedural grounds),[219] what would it mean, in practical terms, for the United States to declare its unwillingness to enforce the French order? As it turns out, very little. Certainly if Yahoo! wants to continue to operate in France or the European Union or anywhere else that recognizes the French judgment, it will need to comply with the French ruling, regardless of U.S. judicial or governmental declarations. Indeed, given Yahoo!'s professed desire to build a company with a "global footprint,"[220] it is not surprising that the company "voluntarily" complied with the French order,[221] while still continuing to challenge its legitimacy. Even from a governmental perspective, the United States would need to step gingerly lest other countries begin to refuse to enforce U.S. judgments, thus impeding U.S. regulatory interests. The reality of global commercial activity means that simply refusing to pay attention to the regulatory decisions of other countries is not feasible.

Moreover, there will be many occasions when a pure territorialist scheme will thwart U.S. regulatory interests. For example, the federal government has doggedly pursued efforts to shut down and/or prosecute Internet sites operating from foreign locations that send unsolicited commercial e-mail, offer online gambling, distribute child pornography,

[218] *Yahoo!, Inc. v. La Ligue Contre Le Racisme et L'Antisémitisme,* 169 F. Supp. 2d 1181 (N.D. Cal.2001), rev'd en banc on other grounds, 433 F.3d 1199 (9th Cir. 2006).

[219] *See Yahoo!, Inc. v. La Ligue Contre Le Racisme et L'Antisémitisme*, 433 F.3d 1199 (9th Cir. 2006).

[220] *See* Press Release, Yahoo! Inc., Yahoo! Reports Fourth Quarter, Year End 2000 Financial Results (Jan. 10, 2001), at http://docs.yahoo.com/docs/pr/4q00pr.html (stating that Yahoo! "remained committed to broadening its global footprint and maintaining a leadership position worldwide").

[221] *See* Press Release, Yahoo! Inc., Yahoo! Enhances Commerce Sites for Higher Quality Online Experience (Jan. 2, 2001), at http://docs.yahoo.com/docs/pr/release675.html (announcing new product guidelines for its auction sites that prohibit "items that are associated with groups deemed to promote or glorify hatred and violence").

and disseminate online viruses, among others.[222] Adhering to a regulatory environment that reifies territory will tend to hinder such efforts. Antitrust regulation poses another prominent example.[223] And with regard to governing the international financial system, U.S. regulators have joined global networks, such as the International Organization of Securities Commissioners or the Basel Committee on Banking Supervision, which now work to develop de facto international regulatory and enforcement regimes.[224]

What about the decisions of international bodies? Recall the NAFTA ruling that Mississippi courts had violated international standards of due process in adjudicating a dispute between a U.S. and a Canadian company.[225] While such a ruling has no binding authority on Mississippi, will Mississippi simply ignore it in future cases raising similar issues? Probably not. First, although the NAFTA panel cannot literally overrule Mississippi civil procedure, it can assess fines against the federal government,[226] which in turn can put pressure on the states to change their policies. And though the United States could, theoretically, simply refuse to pay, such an action would effectively scuttle NAFTA itself, to

[222] *See, e.g.*, The FBI's Cyber Division: Hearing Before the Subcomm. on Courts, the Internet and Intellectual Property of the H. Comm. on the Judiciary, 108th Cong. (2003) (testimony of Jana D. Monroe, Asst. Dir., Cyber Division, FBI), *available at* http:// www.fbi.gov/congress/congress03/Monroe071703.htm (detailing such efforts).

[223] *See, e.g.*, *F. Hoffmann-LaRoche Ltd. v. Empagran S.A.*, 542 U.S. 155 (2004) (limiting the extraterritorial scope of the Sherman Act).

[224] For example, a Memorandum of Understanding signed by the members of the International Organization of Securities Commissioners creates "the first global multilateral information-sharing arrangement among securities regulators," which "sets a new international benchmark for cooperation critical to combating violations of securities and derivatives laws." IOSCO (2008). For more discussion of these sorts of transnational regulatory networks in the financial sector, *see, e.g.*, David Zaring, Rulemaking and Adjudication in International Law, 46 *Colum. J. Trans. L.* 563 (2008); David Zaring, Informal Procedure, Hard and Soft, in International Administration, 5 *Chi. Int'l L.J.* 547 (2005).

[225] *See Loewen Group, Inc. v. United States,* ICSID (W. Bank) Case No. ARB(AF)/98/3.

[226] *See* North American Free Trade Agreement, U.S.-Can.-Mex., art. 1135, Jan. 1, 1994, 107 Stat. 2057 (outlining remedies available).

the detriment of U.S. business interests. Second, Mississippi may face economic hardship if Canadian and Mexican businesses refuse to locate there for fear of being sued on a tilted playing field. Thus, there may also be internal pressure to modify local practices. Third, perhaps more speculatively, it is difficult to believe as a matter of legal consciousness that Mississippi judges could be completely unaffected by a judicial ruling that they violated international due process standards, even if that judicial ruling were issued in a distant location. Such effects are likely to increase as international and domestic judges interact more, both in formal and in informal settings.[227] After all, if one actually knows the judges leveling the criticism or will need to face them in social settings in the near-future, it becomes that much harder to ignore their disapprobation.

Finally, one might think it easier to ignore the rules or decisions of nonstate actors who probably have the least leverage over official governmental policy. But even here, a refusal to recognize or accept other normative communities may be impossible. After all, what would it mean for even a powerful state to refuse to recognize the quasi-legal norms articulated and enforced through yearly meetings of a small group of international trade finance bankers?[228] The bankers will meet regardless of U.S. pronouncements, they will still set rules for trade finance, and U.S. bankers will continue to comply with those rules, at least if they want to be part of the global marketplace. The objection of a nation-state is therefore largely irrelevant.

Of course, there are many times when a nation-state can ignore the wishes of foreign regulatory entities, particularly if there is a great disparity of wealth or power in the relationship among the entities. For example, the George W. Bush administration defied international law and opinion in its continued worldwide detention and rendition

[227] *See, e.g.*, Anne-Marie Slaughter, Judicial Globalization, 40 *Va. J. Int'l L.* 1103 (2000) (describing potential impact of such interactions).

[228] For a discussion of the creation of these banking norms, *see* Janet Koven Levit, A Bottom-Up Approach to International Lawmaking: The Tale of Three Trade Finance Instruments, 30 *Yale J. Int'l L.* 125 (2005).

practices.[229] But even such defiance was not necessarily without substantial consequences. The U.S. policy of exceptionalism likely made it more difficult to achieve security in Iraq,[230] get cooperation from potential allies in tracking down and extraditing terrorism suspects,[231] or use moral suasion to convince repressive governments to obey human rights norms,[232] among many other consequences. And that is not even counting the possibility that other countries may attempt to initiate prosecutions against U.S. government operatives who engaged in such controversial practices.[233]

Indeed, as Peter Spiro has pointed out, the Bush administration provides an unlikely confirmation of the power of law beyond the

[229] *See, e.g.*, Leila Nadya Sadat, Ghost Prisoners and Black Sites: Extraordinary Rendition Under International Law, 37 *Case W. Res. J. Int'l L.* 309, 309–11 (2006) (summarizing the detention and rendition policies and international reaction).

[230] *See, e.g.*, Scott Wilson & Sewell Chan, As Insurgency Grew, So Did Prison Abuse, *Wash. Post*, May 10, 2004, at A1 (stating that Brigadier General Mark Kimmitt, spokesman for the U.S. military in Iraq, acknowledged that "the evidence of abuse inside Abu Ghraib has shaken public opinion in Iraq to the point where it may be more difficult than ever to secure cooperation against the insurgency.... [and] that winning over Iraqis before the planned handover of some sovereign powers next month had been made considerably harder by the photos").

[231] *See, e.g.*, Laura A. Dickinson, Using Legal Process to Fight Terrorism: Detentions, Military Commissions, International Tribunals, and the Rule of Law, 75 *S. Cal. L. Rev.* 1407, 1450 (2002) (discussing the reluctance of some nations to cooperate with the United States due to their perceptions of the illegitimacy of the use of military tribunals); Craig Whitlock, Testimony Helps Detail CIA's post-9/11 Reach: Europeans Told of Plans for Abductions, *Wash. Post*, Dec. 16, 2006, at A1 (quoting State Department legal adviser John B. Bellinger III's statement that ongoing disputes with U.S. allies about detention practices have "undermined cooperation and intelligence activities").

[232] For a discussion of how U.S. practices have undermined American effectiveness in promoting human rights abroad, *see Hamdan v. Rumsfeld,* 344 F. Supp. 2d 152, 163 (D.D.C. 2004), rev'd, 415 F.3d 33, 43 (D.C. Cir. 2005) (citing Lawyers Comm. for Human Rights, *Assessing the New Normal: Liberty and Security for the post-September 11 United States* (2003)), and Deborah Pearlstein & Priti Patel, *Human Rights First, Behind the Wire: An Update to Ending Secret Detentions* (2005); *see also* Brief of Diego C. Asencio et al. as Amici Curiae in Support of the Petitioners, *Rasul v. Bush,* 542 U.S. 466 (2004) (Nos. 03–334, 03–343) (filed by former U.S. diplomats, making this argument).

[233] *See, e.g.*, Tracy Wilkinson & Maria De Cristofaro, Italy Indicts 33 in Abduction Case; 26 Americans Charged in Alleged CIA Rendition, *Chi. Trib.*, Feb. 17, 2007, at 11, *available at* 2007 WLNR 3186956 (Westlaw News Room).

nation-state.[234] Whereas in its early years, the administration seemed positively gleeful in its refusal to submit to international legal norms,[235] by its second term, many retreats were noticeable. Thus, although the administration had firmly refused to endorse the International Criminal Court,[236] by 2005 the United States supported a UN Security Council referral to the court on Darfur.[237] Indeed, the State Department legal adviser went so far as to "acknowledge that [the court] has a role to play in the overall system of international justice."[238] In July 2008 Bush joined a G-8 pledge to reduce greenhouse gases.[239] And, as will be discussed in Chapter 9, the administration ultimately attempted to impose an International Court of Justice judgment on the states. Finally, Bush launched a major push late in his second term to win Senate ratification of the UN Convention on the Law of the Sea, a treaty that by its terms delegates self-executing decision making authority to an international tribunal.[240]

[234] *See* Peter J. Spiro, Wishing International Law Away, 119 *Yale L. J. Online* 23, 25–7 (2009).

[235] *Id.* at 25 ("The Bush Administration withdrew from the Kyoto process on climate change; vigorously opposed emerging international regimes in such areas as biological weapons and small arms trafficking; and denounced the U.S. signature to the Rome Statute establishing the International Criminal Court. In the wake of 9/11, the Administration evinced a determination not to be bound by international law norms with respect to anti-terror policies. It invaded Iraq notwithstanding a clear majority view in the international community that the action violated norms relating to the use of force.").

[236] *See, e.g.,* Jennifer K. Elsea, U.S. Policy Regarding the International Criminal Court, Cong. Res. Svc., Aug. 29, 2006, at 2 ("While most U.S. allies support the ICC, the Bush Administration firmly opposes it and has renounced any U.S. obligations under the treaty.").

[237] Although the United States formally abstained from the Security Council referral, following the vote, U.S. Representative Anne Woods Patterson made clear that the United States "strongly supported bringing to justice those responsible for the crimes and atrocities that had occurred in Darfur and ending the climate of impunity there," adding that "Violators of international humanitarian law and human rights law must be held accountable." *See* U.N. Security Council Press Release, Security Council Refers Situation in Darfur, Sudan, to Prosecutor, Mar. 31, 2005, at 3.

[238] Jess Bravin, U.S. Warms to Hague Tribunal, *Wall St. J.*, June 14, 2006, at A4.

[239] *See* G8 Hokkaido Toyako Summit Leaders Declaration, Jul. 8, 2008, *available at* http://www.mofa.go.jp/policy/economy/summit/2008/doc/doc080714__en.html.

[240] *See* United Nations Convention on the Law of the Sea annex VI, Dec. 10, 1982, 1833 U.N.T.S. 397.

Spiro observes similar shifts on the national security front: "In the wake of the Iraq debacle, the use of ground forces was never a serious option against rogue regimes in Iran and North Korea. On the anti-terror front, the Bush White House backed down from its earlier bluster. On such issues as torture, rendition, black sites, and above all Guantánamo, the Administration retreated from positions that had previously been presented as non-negotiable."[241] And although the administration never attributed its change of heart on these and other issues to a softening in its stance toward international law, it seems clear that "defiance was costing too much in terms of the war on terror and the national interest generally."[242]

In short, if one wants to be a player on the world geopolitical scene and wishes to secure a favorable climate for one's own business interests in the world, it will be difficult to insist on pure sovereignty-based territorialist prerogatives for long. And, of course, countries with less military or economic power will tend to be even more buffeted by the activities of international, foreign, and nonstate entities physically dispersed around the globe.

Thus, sovereigntist territorialism is a limited vision on almost every level. It does not begin to capture the realities of our world or how people actually experience place and community; it does not recognize the ways in which legal and quasi-legal norms actually shape behavior over time; and it does not reflect how even powerful actors must navigate an interconnected globe. Accordingly, we must look elsewhere for a more capacious, fluid conception of law beyond borders.

[241] *See* Spiro, *supra* note 234, at 26.
[242] *Id.*

4 Universalism and Its Discontents

IN CONTRAST TO A REASSERTION OF SOVEREIGNTIST territorial prerogative, a universalist vision tends to respond to normative conflict by seeking to erase normative difference altogether.[1] Indeed, international legal theory has long yearned for an overarching set of commitments that would establish a more peaceful and harmonious global community.[2] More recently, some have suggested that the nation-state legal regimes of the world are increasingly converging and developing a "world law."[3] This supposed new world order variously focuses on the religiously based natural law principles of international human rights or the neoliberal ideology of free trade and its need to harmonize rules that regulate commerce.

[1] It is, perhaps, possible to have a universalist vision that focuses exclusively on developing overarching procedural mechanisms, institutions, and practices for managing hybridity. Indeed, one might see the effort to construct global administrative law principles as an initiative along these lines. *See, e.g.*, Nico Krisch, The Pluralism of Global Administrative Law, 17 *Eur. J. Int'l L.* 247 (2006). That sort of universalism would, of course, be more compatible with the pluralist perspective offered in this book.

[2] *See, e.g.*, Immanuel Kant, *Perpetual Peace* (Helen O'Brien trans., 1927) (1795).

[3] *See, e.g.*, Harold J. Berman, World Law, 18 *Fordham Int'l L.J.* 1617 (1995); *see also* Harold J. Berman, Is Conflict of Laws Becoming Passé? An Historical Response 43, 44 (Emory Univ. Sch. of Law Pub. Law & Legal Theory Research Paper Series, Paper No. 05–42, 2005), *available at* http://ssrn.com/abstract=870455 ("[W]ill increasing harmonization of the civil and criminal law of the nation-states of the world substantially reduce the scope of that branch of law that we call conflict-of-laws?").

As with territorialism, one cannot discount the importance of universalism. Certainly since World War II we have seen the creation of a dizzying array of international institutions, multilateral and bilateral treaties, conventions, cross-border regulatory coordination efforts, and the like. In one way or another, all of this activity represents the desire to harmonize conflicting norms. And on many fronts, in both public and private law, norms are in fact converging to a degree, whether through hegemonic imposition or global embrace. Moreover, such harmonization has important benefits because it tends to lower transaction costs and uncertainty as to what norms will be applied to any given activity. Yet, again as with territorialism, there are reasons to question both the desirability and – more importantly – the feasibility of universalism, at least in some contexts. Because universalism has fewer adherents than sovereigntist territorialism, I will spend far less time discussing the limitations of the universalist vision. Accordingly, I will just briefly touch upon the normative and descriptive problems that a universalist perspective encounters, before comparing it with what I deem to be a preferable, more cosmopolitan, approach.

Self, Other, and the Negotiation of Difference

Universalism is based on the premise that people are fundamentally the same despite differences in culture and circumstance. Likewise, sociological studies of communication often start from the idea that interpersonal interaction requires both parties in an encounter to believe (or at least assume) that the other is not truly other at all.[4] According to this view, most associated with Alfred Schutz,[5] differences in individual perspectives

[4] My discussion here relies heavily on Z.D. Gurevitch, The Other Side of Dialogue: On Making the Other Strange and the Experience of Otherness, 93 *Am. J. Sociology* 1179 (1988).

[5] *See* Alfred Schutz, *On Phenomenology and Social Relations* (H.R. Wagner ed., 1970) [hereinafter Schutz, *On Phenomenology*]; Alfred Schutz, *Collected Papers*. I: *The Problems of Social Reality* (Maurice Natanson ed., 1962) [hereinafter Schutz, *Problems*]; Alfred Schutz, *The Stranger: An Essay in Social Psychology*, 49 *Am. J. Sociology* 499 (1944).

are overcome only if each party tacitly believes that he/she could effectively trade places with the other. As Schutz describes it, "I am able to understand other people's acts only if I can imagine that I myself would perform analogous acts if I were in the same situation."[6] Thus, differences in perspective are reduced to differences in situation. Any possibly more fundamental differences are suppressed in order to facilitate dialogue.

As a result, the deliberate "assuming away" of the unfamiliar is seen as a constant part of everyday life. The unfamiliar is relegated to the category of "strange," and "strangeness" necessarily is placed elsewhere, somewhere other than the interaction at hand.[7] Moreover, Harold Garfinkel and other ethnomethodologists have argued that individuals do not simply passively maintain these assumptions but are constantly engaged in a joint enterprise aimed at sustaining this familiarity.[8] In all of these studies, the emphasis is on "the human production of common worlds of meaning as the only axis on which dialogue rotates."[9]

But is that all there is to the experience of the other? Is it really imperative constantly to assume that our fellow human beings are fundamentally identical to us? After all, as Z. D. Gurevitch has argued, "[u]nder this principle, if a dialogue is to take place, strangeness as a phenomenon of everyday interaction must be considered negatively, namely, as that part of an encounter that must be constantly 'assumed away' by the participants."[10] Thus, we are left with a world in which people are classified either as familiar or as strangers. And, even more problematic, these studies suggest that it will be simply impossible to bridge the communication gap with those deemed strangers. Yet, as Georg Simmel noted long ago, the stranger is never truly distant,[11] so there will need to be some way of bridging gaps short of assuming away strangeness altogether.

[6] Schutz, *On Phenomenology*, *supra* note 5, at 181.

[7] *See* Gurevitch, *supra* note 4, at 1180 (summarizing arguments in Schutz, *Problems*).

[8] *See* Harold Garfinkel, Studies of the Routine Grounds of Everyday Activities, 11 *Social Problems* 225 (1964).

[9] Gurevitch, *supra* note 4, at 1180.

[10] *Id.* at 1181–2.

[11] *See generally* Georg Simmel, The Stranger, in *The Sociology of Georg Simmel* 402–8 (K.H. Wolff ed., 1950).

Uniformity Versus Fragmentation

Turning to legal regimes, which model of communication across difference should we embrace: one that erases difference and assumes commonality or one that seeks communication across difference? This is a crucial question because a universalist or harmonization vision asks us to see ourselves principally as citizens of a broader (or a global) community and therefore dissolves the multirootedness of community affiliation into one overarching identity. But universalism is inherently problematic. Even if such a perspective were feasible, it does not seem desirable because it fails to capture the extreme emotional ties people still feel to distinct national or local communities. As Thomas Franck put it, "The powerful pull of loyalty exerted by the imagined nation demonstrates that, even in the age of science, a loyalty system based on romantic myths of shared history and kinship has a capacity to endure."[12] Therefore, universalism tends to ignore the very attachments people hold most deeply.

In addition, universalism inevitably erases diversity. Indeed, the whole point of a universalist or harmonization solution is to combat diversity or fragmentation. Yet, although one can appreciate the goal, erasing diversity may involve the silencing of less powerful voices in the global conversation. Thus, the presumed universal may also be the hegemonic. This argument is most often heard by those who resist international human rights norms because they may run roughshod over important local practices, customs, or perspectives. For example, in response to the presumed universality of the Universal Declaration of Human Rights, some scholars wonder what such a declaration can mean "in a universe of competing values and moralities? Is there an objective technique for evaluating systems of morals and cultures? Given the specificity of cultural standards and values, and given the predisposition of human beings to generalize from their situated perspectives and realities, how can we ensure that

[12] Thomas M. Franck, Clan and Superclan: Loyalty, Identity and Community in Law and Practice, 90 *Am. J. Int'l L.* 359, 374 (1996).

our presumptions and assertions of universality are not veiled projections onto others of our moral categories?"[13] Such arguments have arisen most famously in debates about eradicating the practice of female genital cutting. On the one hand, many condemn and combat the practice as a violation of women's human rights. At the same time, others suggest that such a position fails to understand the local meaning of the practice. As one scholar argues, "In the eyes of the Neo-Agrarian cultures of today's Africa, the customary ritual practices of both male and female circumcision are seeable by their practitioners as the supernaturally prescribed, and therefore, indispensable condition of being human. So it is only within the terms of our contemporary culture that the eradication of these specific cultural practices ... can be seeable as the indispensable condition of being human.... "[14] Thus, critics contend that the presumed universal tends to become a Western or northern imperialist imposition on less powerful communities.

Of course, in this debate we can see replayed the insistence on universal imposition, on the one hand, and the pristine integrity of the local community, on the other. Both positions are therefore retreats from hybridity. In contrast, a cosmopolitan pluralist vision would focus on the interactions between these two positions: the ways in which local actors deploy the universalist language of human rights to advance positions strategically, the ways in which so-called local voices interact with seemingly international ones to create change to internationalist regimes and assumptions, and so on. Only through this sort of interactive vision can we avoid reifying either the universal or the local.

Even outside the realm of human rights, we may see concerns about harmonization schemes that impose standardized economic, business, or

[13] L. Amede Obiora, Bridges and Barricades: Rethinking Polemics and Intransigence in the Campaign Against Female Circumcision, 47 *Case W. Res. L. Rev.* 275, 277–8 (1997) (footnotes omitted).

[14] Sylvia Wynter, "Genital Mutilation" or "Symbolic Birth"? Female Circumcision, Lost Origins, and the Aculturism of Feminist/Western Thought, 47 *Case W. Res. L. Rev.* 501, 504–5 (1997).

technology practices on communities. Indeed, we need not look far to find passionate resistance to fiscal austerity measures uniformly imposed by the International Monetary Fund.[15] Similarly, critics contend that efforts to harmonize the intellectual property system give short shrift to the needs of developing countries,[16] and that the global free trade system harms local actors[17] while paying insufficient attention to environmental[18] or labor concerns[19] or the needs of indigenous communities.[20]

Communities may also seek to maintain their own legal regimes in areas that are particularly important to their own distinctive cultural histories. For example, returning to the *Yahoo!* case, can we really expect to solve the problem of whether to prohibit Nazi memorabilia or Holocaust denial material through universal harmonization? After all, France may have very good reasons, rooted in France's ambiguous experience with Nazism, to ban such material, while the United States, without that history, may have equally good reasons to insist on a more absolutist speech protection regime. Clearly any universal rule in this area would run roughshod over one or the other community's core values.

Meanwhile, annual meetings of the world's industrialized countries have become sites for the expression of uncertainty and resentment about the effect of international trade and monetary policy on local labor forces, the environment, and nation-state sovereignty.[21] Likewise,

[15] *See, e.g.*, Padraic Halpin, Voters Hammer Irish Government, *Reuters*, Nov. 26, 2010 (citing IMF-imposed austerity measures for ruling party's electoral loss).

[16] *See, e.g.*, Amy Kapczynski, Harmonization and Its Discontents: A Case Study of TRIPS Implementation in India's Pharmaceutical Sector, 97 *Cal. L. Rev.* 1572 (2009).

[17] *See, e.g.*, Frank J. Garcis, Trade and Inequality: Economic Justice and the Developing World, 21 *Mich. J. Int'l L.* 975 (2000).

[18] *See, e.g.*, Carmen G. Gonzalez, Beyond Eco-Imperialism: An Environmental Justice Critique of Free Trade, 78 *Denv. U. L. Rev.* 979 (2001).

[19] *See, e.g.*, Aaron B. Sukert, Marrionettes of Globalization: A Comparative Analysis of Legal Protections for Contingent Workers in the International Community, 27 *Syracuse J. Int'l L. & Com.* 431 (2000).

[20] *See, e.g.*, Dinah Shelton, Protecting Human Rights in a Globalized World, 25 *B.C. Int'l & Comp. L. Rev.* 273 (2002).

[21] *See, e.g.*, After Genoa, *Nation*, Aug. 6, 2001, at 3–4 (quoting French president Chirac as saying, "[t]here is no demonstration drawing 100,000, 150,000 people without

when a United Nations Working Group released a preliminary report advocating an international regulatory regime for the Internet,[22] alarm bells were sounded, with commentators resisting what was termed "UN Control of the Internet."[23] Similarly we see persistent grumbling in Europe about "Belgian bureaucrats" imposing pan-European rules on local communities.[24]

Beyond simply erasing less powerful voices, we might also think that preserving legal diversity is a good in and of itself because it means that multiple forms of regulatory authority can be assayed in multiple local settings. Just as states in a federal system function as "laboratories" of innovation,[25] so too the preservation of diverse legal spaces makes innovation possible. As will be discussed in more detail in Chapter 7, for example, maintaining multiple jurisdictions with multiple normative agendas creates a more robust field for alternative approaches to common problems. And, to the extent that a first approach turns out to be less than ideal, there is room for better approaches to emerge. In contrast, if there is one overarching normative system, innovation is likely to be slower and more difficult. Even more fundamentally, a decision-making body

having a valid reason"); Michael Hardt & Antonio Negri, What the Protesters in Genoa Want, *N.Y. Times*, July 20, 2001, at A21 (arguing that "[t]he protests themselves have become global movements, and one of the clearest objectives is the democratization of globalizing processes"); Jerry Useem, There's Something Happening Here, *Fortune*, May 15, 2000, at 234 (describing a "new breed of economic activism [that] has appeared not only in Seattle but also in Davos, Switzerland; the City, London; and now Washington, D.C.").

[22] *See* Victoria Shannon, A Compromise of Sorts on Internet Control, *N.Y. Times*, Nov. 16, 2005, at C2.

[23] *See, e.g.*, Harold Furchtgott-Roth, Keep the United Nations Away from the Internet, *N.Y. Sun*, Oct. 11, 2005, *available at* http://www.nysun.com/business/keep-the-united-nations-away-from-the-internet/21329/.

[24] *See, e.g.*, Stephen Castle, European Farmers' Anger Spills Into the Streets of Brussels, *N.Y. Times*, Oct. 5, 2009, at B9.

[25] *See, e.g.*, *United States v. Lopez,* 514 U.S. 549, 580–81 (1995) (Kennedy, J., concurring) ("[T]he theory and utility of our federalism are revealed" when "considerable disagreement exists about how best to accomplish [a] goal" because "the States may perform their role as laboratories for experimentation to devise various solutions where the best solution is far from clear.").

that does not have competition is likely to grow less restrained and less amenable to democratic input. In contrast, when decision makers are forced to consider the existence of other possible decision makers, they may tend to adopt, over time, a more restrained view of their own "jurispathic" power.[26]

Relatedly, we may think that a legal system that provides mechanisms for mediating diversity without dissolving difference necessarily also provides an important model for mediating diversity in day-to-day social life. For example, one argument for a strongly speech-protective interpretation of the First Amendment is that the effort required to tolerate the provocative speech of others is the same effort required to tolerate others more generally.[27] Thus, a legal system that demands tolerance of diversity rather than its erasure is more likely to create the context for a tolerant society than one that, in contrast, seeks uniformity as its goal.

Finally, some critics have suggested that the very goal of harmonization may be misguided, at least in the commercial context. For example, Paul Stephan has pointed out two common outcomes of the harmonization process,[28] neither of which is normatively desirable. First, Stephan contends that international-harmonization efforts are often the product of rent seeking by various industry groups. He suggests that many harmonization efforts in commercial law are initiated by particular industries seeking particular legal rules. The resulting international norms are usually drafted by industry experts and, not surprisingly, benefit the industry seeking the change. Second, he observes a tendency among the various

[26] Robert Cover, The Uses of Jurisdictional Redundancy: Interest, Ideology, and Innovation, 22 *Wm. & Mary L. Rev.* 639 (1981).

[27] *See, e.g.*, Thomas I. Emerson, *Toward a General Theory of the First Amendment* 14 (1966) (arguing that free speech "contemplates a mode of life that, through encouraging toleration, skepticism, reason and initiative, will allow man to realize his full potentialities. It spurns the alternative of a society that is tyrannical, conformist, irrational and stagnant. It is this concept of society that was embodied in the first amendment").

[28] Paul B. Stephan, The Futility of Unification and Harmonization in International Commercial Law, 39 *Va. J. Int'l L.* 743, 744 (1999).

parties to an international harmonization effort to adopt relatively vague standards in order to smooth over major policy disagreements. These standards, because they are couched in such general language, become a license for domestic decision makers to exercise broad discretion in interpreting international norms. As a result, the law may well become even less certain than it was before, thus foiling the harmonization effort altogether. Accordingly, Stephan argues that "[t]he political economy of [the harmonization] process results too often either in rules written for the benefit of particular industries and other interest groups, or in the suppression of conflict that in turn increases legal risk."[29] Instead, he envisions a system that would allow parties virtually unlimited power to choose among national rules through private contractual agreements.[30] Stephan's alternative may or may not be attractive, but his criticism of international harmonization should at least raise doubts regarding the efficacy of the enterprise.

Nevertheless, even if one rejects these normative arguments and embraces universalism as a goal, it is difficult to believe that, as a practical matter, harmonization processes will ever fully bridge the significant differences that exist among states, let alone the variety of nonstate orders at play in the world. This is because, as discussed previously, many differences both in substantive values and in attitudes about law arise from fundamentally different histories, philosophies, and worldviews. People are therefore likely to be either unable or unwilling to trade in their perspectives for the sake of universal harmony. Moreover, even if they were so inclined, it would be difficult to develop a process for determining which norms should be elevated to universal status and which should give way. Thus, when harmonization is possible, it is usually a slow, laborious undertaking, limited to codifying normative convergences that have already occurred over time. As a result, harmonization is generally backward-looking, and in a rapidly changing

[29] *Id.*

[30] *Id.* at 789.

world, harmonization processes will tend to lag behind social, technological, and economic realities.[31] Accordingly, even the most optimistic universalist would have to acknowledge that normative conflict is at the very least a constant transitional reality that will require more pluralist processes to address.

[31] *See* Graeme B. Dinwoodie, A New Copyright Order: Why National Courts Should Create Global Norms, 149 *U. Pa. L. Rev.* 469, 569 (bemoaning the lack of dynamism in classical public international lawmaking and advocating an alternative approach to mediating legal diversity).

Part III EMBRACING HYBRIDITY

5 Toward a Cosmopolitan Pluralist Jurisprudence

ALTHOUGH SOVEREIGNTIST TERRITORIALISM AND universalism are obviously different strategies, they both represent a retreat from hybridity. Yet, hybridity is difficult to escape in a world of overlapping jurisdictions and normative diversity, where – as the pluralists would say – multiple conflicting legal systems occupy the same social field. The question therefore often becomes, Are there other approaches to managing pluralism? And though the next chapter surveys a range of specific procedural mechanisms, institutions, and practices for doing so, here I briefly outline some principles that underlie a more cosmopolitan pluralist approach.

First, as should be obvious by now, a cosmopolitan pluralist approach to managing multiplicity should not attempt to erase the reality of that multiplicity. Indeed, arguably the desire to "solve" hybridity problems is precisely what has made conflict of laws such a conceptually unsatisfying field for so long. Each generation seeks a new way (or often the revival of an old way) to divine an answer to what is at its root an unanswerable question: which territorially based state community's norms should govern a dispute that, by definition, is not easily situated territorially and necessarily involves affiliations with multiple communities?

Yet, unlike the universalist approach discussed in the previous chapter, a cosmopolitan pluralist vision does not require people to be conceptualized as fundamentally identical in order to be brought within the same normative system. Nor does it relegate outsiders to irrelevance, as sovereigntist territorialism does. Instead, it attempts to navigate a different path altogether.

This effort to chart a course between universalizing and particularizing poles echoes long-standing debates in comparative law,[1] where some, labeled functionalists, have sought to identify (or forge) commonalities across legal systems in order to solve problems,[2] while others, the contextualists, vociferously argued for the "redemptive, empowering" idea of fundamental difference.[3] Faced with a required choice between these poles, it is clear that an effort like mine to construct or identify procedural mechanisms, institutional designs, and discursive practices for managing without eliminating pluralism is still functionalist in the sense that it seeks solutions to problems of difference. And it celebrates universalizing procedural mechanisms for doing so, much as Jürgen Habermas has attempted, leaving itself open to the critique that this is simply a universalization of Western proceduralist liberalism in disguise.

To some extent, this is no doubt true, and some may resist the vision I am pursuing on such grounds. But I wonder whether, even if it is within a universalizing proceduralist regime, we might mitigate some of the problems of universalism by seeking solutions without assuming commonality or seeking harmonization while preserving the insistence on difference that contextualists rightly emphasize? In short, are we doomed either to requiring commonality or to essentializing difference? Are those truly the only possible approaches? Think of how we encounter a stranger. Do we necessarily see that stranger as fundamentally the same as we are or fundamentally different? Might not we see (and celebrate) important

[1] I am grateful to Russell Miller for pointing out the similarities in comparative laws scholarship.

[2] *See, e.g.*, Konrad Zweigert & Hein Kötz, *Introduction to Comparative Law* (1977, 3d ed. 1998).

[3] Pierre Legrand, The Same and the Different, in *Comparative Legal Studies: Traditions and Transitions* 240, 241–42 (Pierre Legrand and Roderick Munday eds., 2003). For a nice discussion of the neo-functionalist impulses in much contemporary comparative constitutionalism, *see* Ruti Teitel, Comparative Constitutional Law in a Global Age, 117 *Harv. L. Rev.* 2570 (2004).

differences while seeking ways to bridge those gaps so that we might communicate with each other and live peaceably side by side?

Perhaps we might draw from Hannah Arendt, who offers a different way of conceptualizing the encounter with the stranger. Instead of assuming commonality, she seeks, in "Understanding and Politics," the quality that "makes it bearable to live with other people, strangers forever, in the same world, and makes it possible for them to live with us."[4] Note that for Arendt the task is how to "bear with" strangers, even while recognizing that they will forever be strange.[5] Arendt's strategy for bearing with strangers is more than just mutual indifference and more than just toleration as well. It "involves a mental capacity appropriate for an active relation to that which is distant,"[6] which Arendt locates in King Solomon's gift of the "understanding heart."[7] Understanding, according to Arendt, "is the specifically human way of being alive, for every single person needs to be reconciled to a world in which he was born a stranger and in which, to the extent of his distinct uniqueness, he always remains a stranger."[8] And what does "understanding" entail for Arendt? This is a bit difficult to pin down, but she makes clear that it is not gained through direct experience of the other, and it is not just knowledge of the other.[9] Instead, understanding starts from the individual situated apart from others. Thus, instead of "feeling your pain," understanding involves determining what aspects of the pain people feel has to do with politics, and what politics can do to resolve our common dilemmas. Moreover, "understanding can be challenged and is compelled to respond to an alternative argument or interpretation."[10] In short, understanding

[4] Hannah Arendt, Understanding and Politics (the Difficulties of Understanding), in *Hannah Arendt, Essays in Understanding* 322 (Jerome Kohn ed., 1994).

[5] In focusing on Arendt's idea of "bearing with strangers," I draw from the analysis in Phillip Hansen, Hannah Arendt and Bearing with Strangers, 3 *Contemp. Pol. Theory* 3 (2004).

[6] *Id.* at 3.

[7] Arendt, *supra* note 4, at 322.

[8] *Id.* at 308.

[9] *See id.* at 313.

[10] Jean Bethke Elshtain, Judging Rightly, 47 *First Things* 49 (1994) (reviewing Arendt, *supra* note 4).

in Arendt's formulation looks a lot less like empathy and a lot more like judging.[11]

While assuming sameness leads to a universalist harmonization approach, Arendt's more distanced conception of the encounter with the stranger is akin to the cosmopolitan vision I am pursuing as an alternative. Likewise, consider Iris Marion Young's idea of "unassimilated otherness," which she posits as the relation among people in the ideal "unoppressive city."[12] Young envisions ideal city life as the "'being-together' of strangers."[13] These strangers may remain strangers and continue to "experience each other as other."[14] Indeed, they do not necessarily seek an overall group identification and loyalty. Yet, they are open to "unassimilated otherness."[15] They belong to various distinct groups or cultures and are constantly interacting with other groups. But they do so without seeking either to assimilate or to reject those others. Such interactions instantiate an alternative kind of community,[16] one that is never a hegemonic imposition of sameness but that nevertheless prevents different groups from ever being completely outside one another.[17] In a city's public spaces, Young argues, we see glimpses of this ideal: "The city consists in a great diversity of people and groups, with a multitude of subcultures and differentiated activities and functions,

[11] Arendt, *supra* note 4, at 313.

[12] *See* Iris Marion Young, The Ideal of Community and the Politics of Difference, in *Feminism/Postmodernism* 300, 317 (Linda J. Nicholson ed., 1990) ("Our political ideal is the unoppressive city.").

[13] *Id.* at 318.

[14] *Id.*

[15] *Id.* at 319.

[16] Young resists using the word "community" because of the "urge to unity" the term conveys, but acknowledges that "[i]n the end it may be a matter of stipulation" whether one chooses to call her vision "community." *Id.* at 320; *see also* Jerry Frug, The Geography of Community, 48 *Stan. L. Rev.* 1047, 1049 (1996) ("Unlike Young, I do not cede the term community to those who evoke the romance of togetherness.").

[17] *See* Young, *supra* note 12, at 319 (positing that a group of strangers living side by side "instantiates social relations as difference in the sense of an understanding of groups and cultures that are different, with exchanging and overlapping interactions that do not issue in community, yet which prevent them from being outside of one another").

whose lives and movements mingle and overlap in public spaces."[18] In this vision, there can be community without sameness, shifting affiliations without ostracism. And although Young does not describe her ideal as cosmopolitan, this idea of "unassimilated otherness" and multiple community affiliations fits comfortably with what I describe as a cosmopolitan pluralist vision.

Second, and relatedly, a cosmopolitan pluralist framework recognizes that normative conflict is unavoidable and so, instead of trying to erase conflict, it seeks to manage it through procedural mechanisms, institutions, and practices that might at least draw the participants to the conflict into a shared social space. This approach draws on Ludwig Wittgenstein's idea that agreements are reached principally through participation in common forms of life, rather than agreement on substance.[19] Or, as the political theorist Chantal Mouffe has put it, we need to transform "enemies" – who have no common symbolic space – into "adversaries."[20] Adversaries, according to Mouffe, are "friendly enemies": friends because they "share a common symbolic space but also enemies because they want to organize this common symbolic space in a different way."[21] Ideally, law – and particularly legal mechanisms for managing multiplicity – can function as the sort of common symbolic space that Mouffe envisions and can therefore play a constructive role in transforming enemies into adversaries. This is akin to Young's ideal city.

Of course, Mouffe might well disagree with my application of her idea to law. Indeed, in *The Democratic Paradox*, she writes that "one cannot oppose, as so many liberals do, procedural and substantial justice without recognizing that procedural justice already presupposes acceptance of certain values."[22] Her point is well taken; certainly my

[18] *Id.*

[19] Ludwig Wittgenstein, *Philosophical Investigations* § 241 (G.E.M. Anscombe trans., 3d ed. 1958).

[20] Chantal Mouffe, *The Democratic Paradox* 13 (2000).

[21] *Id.*

[22] *Id.* at 68.

focus on procedural mechanisms, institutions, and practices necessarily limits the range of pluralism somewhat because it requires participants to accept the principles underlying the values of procedural pluralism itself. This is, to a large extent, a vision consonant with liberal principles, and many may reject it on that basis. Alas, there is no way to extricate oneself from this concern if one wants to have any type of functioning legal system for negotiating normative difference. Thus, I argue only that a cosmopolitan pluralist framework is *more likely* able to draw participants together into a common social space than a territorialist or universalist framework would. As philosopher Stuart Hampshire has argued, because normative agreement is impossible, "fairness and justice in procedures" are the only virtues that offer even the possibility for broader sharing.[23] Accordingly, the key is to create spaces for such broader sharing, spaces for turning enemies into adversaries, without insisting on normative agreement.[24]

Third, in order to help create this sort of shared social space, procedural mechanisms, institutions, and practices for managing pluralism should encourage decision makers to wrestle explicitly with questions of multiple community affiliation and the effects of activities across territorial borders, rather than shunting aside normative difference. As a result, a cosmopolitan pluralist framework invites questions that otherwise might not be asked: How are communities appropriately defined in today's world? To what degree do people act on the basis of affiliations with nonstate or supranational communities? How should the various norm-generating communities in the global system interact so as to provide opportunities for contestation and expression of difference? Such questions must be considered carefully in order to develop

[23] Stuart Hampshire, *Justice Is Conflict* 53 (2000).

[24] *Cf.* Jeremy Waldron, Tribalism and the Myth of the Framework, in *Karl Popper: Critical Appraisals* 203, 221 (Philip Catton & Graham Macdonald eds., 2004)("Humans are enormously curious about each other's ideas and reasons, and, when they want to be, they are resourceful in listening to and trying to learn from one another across what appear to be insurmountable barriers of cultural comprehensibility, often far beyond what philosophers and theorists of culture give them credit for.").

mechanisms that will take seriously the multifaceted interactions of such communities.

Thus, a cosmopolitan conception makes no attempt to deny the multirooted nature of individuals within a variety of communities, both territorial and nonterritorial. Accordingly, although a cosmopolitan conception might acknowledge the potential importance of asserting universal norms in specific circumstances, it does not require a universalist belief in a single world community. As a result, cosmopolitanism offers a promising rubric for analyzing law in a world of diverse normative voices. And these multiple identifications can include identities based on citizenship within nation-states themselves.

Martha Nussbaum has stressed that cosmopolitanism does not require one to give up local identifications, which, she acknowledges, "can be a source of great richness in life."[25] Rather, following the Stoics, she suggests that we think of ourselves as surrounded by a series of concentric circles:

> The first one encircles the self, the next takes in the immediate family, then follows the extended family, then, in order, neighbors or local groups, fellow city-dwellers, and fellow countrymen – and we can easily add to this list groupings based on ethnic, linguistic, historical, professional, gender, or sexual identities. Outside all these circles is the largest one, humanity as a whole.[26]

Therefore, we need not relinquish special affiliations and identifications with the various groups of which we may feel a part.[27]

In this vision, people could be "cosmopolitan patriots," accepting their responsibility to nurture the culture and politics of their home community, while recognizing that such cultural practices are always shifting, as people move from place to place or are increasingly affected by spatially

[25] Martha C. Nussbaum, Patriotism and Cosmopolitanism, in *For Love of Country: Debating the Limits of Patriotism* 2, 9 (Joshua Cohen ed., 1996).

[26] *Id.*

[27] *See id.* ("We need not think of [local affiliations] as superficial, and we may think of our identity as constituted partly by them.").

distant actors.[28] "The result would be a world in which each local form of human life is the result of long-term and persistent processes of cultural hybridization – a world, in that respect, much like the world we live in now."[29]

Thus, cosmopolitanism is emphatically not a model of international citizenship in the sense of international harmonization and standardization, but is instead a recognition of multiple refracted differences where (as in Young's ideal city) people acknowledge links with the "other" without demanding assimilation or ostracism. Cosmopolitanism seeks "flexible citizenship," in which people are permitted to shift identities amid a plurality of possible affiliations and allegiances, including nonterritorial communities.[30] The cosmopolitan worldview shifts back and forth from the rooted particularity of personal identity to the global possibility of multiple overlapping communities. "[I]nstead of an ideal of detachment, actually existing cosmopolitanism is a reality of (re)attachment, multiple attachment, or attachment at a distance."[31]

Fourth, thinking in cosmopolitan pluralist terms forces consideration of so-called conflicts values, particularly the independent benefit that may accrue when domestic judicial and regulatory decisions take into account a broader interest in a smoothly functioning overlapping international legal order, reflecting what Justice Blackmun called "the systemic value of reciprocal tolerance and goodwill."[32] For example, as discussed in more detail in Chapter 9, U.S. courts give full faith and credit to judgments

[28] Kwame Anthony Appiah, Cosmopolitan Patriots, in *Cosmopolitics: Thinking and Feeling Beyond the Nation* 91, 91–2 (Pheng Cheah & Bruce Robbins eds., 1998) [hereinafter *Cosmopolitics*].

[29] *Id.* at 92.

[30] *See* Aihwa Ong, *Flexible Citizenship: The Cultural Logics of Transnationality* 6 (1999) (describing how "the cultural logics of capitalist accumulation, travel, and displacement that induce subjects to respond fluidly and opportunistically to changing political-economic conditions" foster a form of transnationality she calls "flexible citizenship").

[31] Bruce Robbins, Introduction, Part I: Actually Existing Cosmopolitanism, in *Cosmopolitics*, *supra* note 28, at 1, 3.

[32] *Société Nationale Industrielle Aérospatiale v. U.S. Dist. Court for the S. Dist. of Iowa*, 482 U.S. 522, 555 (1987) (Blackmun, J., concurring in part and dissenting in part).

rendered in other states even if those judgments would be illegal if issued by the crediting state.[33] Thus, the conflicts value of respecting an interlocking national system outweighs individual parochial interests. And though the domestic example is made easier by the existence of a constitutional command,[34] such considerations should always be part of any mechanism for addressing the overlap of plural legal systems. Moreover, taking account of these sorts of systemic values should be seen as a necessary part of how communities pursue their interests in the world, not as a restraint on pursuing such interests. After all, if it is true that communities cannot exist in isolation from each other, then there is a long-term parochial benefit from not insisting on narrow parochial interest and instead establishing mechanisms for trying to defer to others' norms where possible.

Fifth, even a system that respects conflicts values will, of course, sometimes find a foreign law so anathema that the law will not be enforced. Or a local religious practice may be so contrary to state values that it will be deemed illegal. Or creating a zone of autonomy for a particular minority group might so threaten the stability of the larger community that it cannot be countenanced. Thus, embracing cosmopolitan pluralism in no way requires a full embrace of illiberal communities and practices or the recognition of autonomy rights for every minority group across the board. But when such "public policy" exceptions are invoked within a cosmopolitan

[33] *See, e.g., Estin v. Estin,* 334 U.S. 541, 546 (1948) (stating that the full faith and credit clause "ordered submission ... even to hostile policies reflected in the judgment of another State, because the practical operation of the federal system, which the Constitution designed, demanded it"); *see also Milwaukee County v. M.E. White Co.,* 296 U.S. 268, 277 (1935) ("In numerous cases this Court has held that credit must be given to the judgment of another state, although the forum would not be required to entertain the suit on which the judgment was founded.... "); *Fauntleroy v. Lum,* 210 U.S. 230, 237 (1908) (stating that the judgment of a Missouri court was entitled to full faith and credit in Mississippi even if the Missouri judgment rested on a misapprehension of Mississippi law).

[34] U.S. Const., art. IV, § 1 ("Full Faith and Credit shall be given in each State to the public Acts, Records, and judicial Proceedings of every other State. And the Congress may by general Laws prescribe the Manner in which such Acts, Records and Proceedings shall be proved, and the Effect thereof.").

pluralist framework, they should be treated as unusual occasions requiring strong normative statements regarding the contours of the public policy.[35] This means that, as Robert Cover envisioned, a jurispathic act that "kills off" another community's normative commitment[36] is always at least accompanied by an equally strong normative commitment. The key point is to make decision makers self-conscious about their necessary jurispathic actions.[37] Such an approach has the best chance of preventing adversaries from turning into enemies.

Finally, a cosmopolitan pluralist framework must always be understood as a middle ground between sovereigntist territorialism, on the one hand, and universalism, on the other. The key, therefore, is to try to articulate and maintain a balance between these two poles. As such, successful mechanisms, institutions, or practices will be those that simultaneously celebrate both local variation and international order and recognize the importance of preserving both multiple sites for contestation and an interlocking system of reciprocity and exchange. Of course, actually doing that in difficult cases is a Herculean and perhaps impossible task. Certainly, mutual agreement about contested normative issues is unlikely and, as discussed previously, possibly even undesirable. Thus, the challenge is to develop ways to seek mutual accommodation while keeping at least some "play" in the joints so that diversity is respected as much as possible. Such play in the joints also allows for the jurisgenerative possibilities inherent in having multiple lawmaking communities and multiple

[35] *See, e.g.*, Convention on the Recognition and Enforcement of Foreign Arbitral Awards, June 10, 1958, 21 U.S.T. 2517, 330 U.N.T.S. 38 (requiring courts to enforce the judgment or arbitral award unless there is fraud or if doing so would be repugnant to the public policy of the enforcing forum).

[36] *See* Robert Cover, Foreword: Nomos and Narrative, The Supreme Court 1982 Term, 97 *Harv. L. Rev.* 4, 53 (1983)(describing judges as inevitably "people of violence" because their interpretations "kill" off competing normative assertions).

[37] Judith Resnik, Living Their Legal Commitments: Paideic Communities, Courts, and Robert Cover, 17 *Yale J.L. & Human.* 17, 25 (2005) ("[Cover] wanted the state's actors ... to be uncomfortable in their knowledge of their own power, respectful of the legitimacy of competing legal systems, and aware of the possibility that multiple meanings and divergent practices ought sometimes to be tolerated, even if painfully so.").

norms.[38] Always the focus is on trying to forge the sort of shared social space that Mouffe describes for transforming enemies into adversaries and Young describes as the ideal city.

Taken together, these principles provide a set of criteria for evaluating the ways in which legal systems interact. In addition, the principles could inform a community (whether state-based or not) that wishes to design mechanisms, institutions, or practices for addressing multiple assertions of norms. Of course, such criteria are not exclusive. For example, a procedure or practice that manages pluralism well but denies certain norms of fundamental justice might be deemed problematic, regardless of its embrace of pluralism. Thus, my goal is not to say that embracing pluralism always overrides other concerns. After all, as mentioned previously, many legal and quasi-legal orders are repressive and profoundly illiberal, and their norms may be resisted on these grounds. The important point is simply that pluralist questions should always at least be part of the debate. In order to see what this would entail, the next chapter surveys a broad range of jurisdictional, regulatory, institutional, and doctrinal arrangements that are not usually grouped together and that are not usually evaluated on the basis of the criteria set forth in this chapter. Nevertheless, despite the very different doctrinal contexts in which these mechanisms, institutions, and practices arise, they can usefully be understood and evaluated as approaches to the management of pluralism.

[38] *See* Seyla Benhabib, *Another Cosmopolitanism* 49 (2006).

6 Procedural Mechanisms, Institutional Designs, and Discursive Practices for Managing Pluralism

GIVEN THE REALITY OF PLURALISM, WE SHOULD NOT BE AT all surprised to find, across a wide variety of doctrinal areas, the development of procedural mechanisms, institutions, and practices that serve to manage the overlapping of legal or quasi-legal communities. In this chapter, I survey eight such mechanisms, institutions, and practices: dialectical legal interactions, margins of appreciation, limited autonomy regimes, subsidiarity schemes, hybrid participation arrangements, mutual recognition regimes, safe harbor agreements, and regime interaction. Each has been the subject of scholarship (sometimes voluminous) in its own right, but they have not, to date, been viewed collectively; nor have they, for the most part, been considered through a cosmopolitan pluralist lens. Indeed, just thinking of them as mechanisms for managing pluralism may offer a different perspective on their efficacy or functionality. For example, these mechanisms, institutions, and practices are often the product of necessary political compromise between sovereigntist territorialism and universalism, and they are therefore deemed "half a loaf" solutions by advocates on both sides: less attractive than what they were hoping for, but better than nothing. Viewing such mechanisms, institutions, and practices through a cosmopolitan pluralist lens, however, might cause us to consider whether they are not, instead, "loaf-and-a-half" solutions, which, through their compromises, actually result in a *better* set of procedures for managing pluralism than if either sovereigntist territorialism or universalism had prevailed in toto. In any event, though I provide no more than brief summaries here, I believe that, taken together, these examples demonstrate the importance of cosmopolitan pluralism as an intellectual framework for studying law and globalization in the twenty-first century.

One point is necessary before proceeding, however. Describing *mechanisms* for managing pluralism does not tell us how best actually to *manage* pluralism in particular cases. Thus, each of the mechanisms described in this chapter encounters excruciatingly difficult and probably impossible to resolve problems as to how best to determine when norms of one community should give way to norms of another and when, in contrast, pluralism can be maintained. This sort of line-drawing question can never be resolved definitively or satisfactorily because there is at root level no way to "solve" problems of pluralism; the debates are ongoing. But in any event it is beyond the scope of this book to suggest solutions to specific cases of plural conflict. Instead, I argue that creating (or preserving) mechanisms, institutions, and practices that self-consciously acknowledge the reality of pluralism and seek provisional compromises may sometimes be the best we can do. In addition, simply recognizing the importance of these mechanisms as sites for continuing debates about pluralism, legal conflicts, and mutual accommodation is a crucial first step.

Dialectical Legal Interactions

To begin, we may view the built-in dialectical interactions among different decision makers, whether international, state, substate, or nonstate, as a core mechanism for responding to normative pluralism. For instance, as discussed in Chapter 3, some who study international law fail to find real "law" in the international realm because they are looking for hierarchically based commands backed by coercive power.[1] In contrast, a cosmopolitan pluralist approach understands that interactions among various tribunals and regulatory authorities are more likely to take on a dialectical quality

[1] *See, e.g.*, Jack L. Goldsmith & Eric A. Posner, *The Limits of International Law* (2005).

that is neither the direct hierarchical review traditionally undertaken by appellate courts, nor simply the dialogue that often occurs under the doctrine of comity.[2] In the international context, for example, we may see treaty-based courts exert an important influence even as national courts retain formal independence, much as U.S. federal courts exercising habeas corpus jurisdiction may well influence state court interpretations of U.S. constitutional norms in criminal cases.[3] In turn, the decisions of national courts may also come to influence international tribunals. This dialectical and iterative process,[4] if it emerges, will exist without an official hierarchical relationship based on coercive power.

Three examples illustrate the point. First, of course, is the relationship between NAFTA panels and U.S. state courts discussed previously. In *Loewen Group v. United States*, a NAFTA tribunal reviewed the procedures of the Mississippi courts concerning contract and antitrust claims brought by a local entity against a Canadian corporation.[5] The tribunal criticized the trial as "so flawed that it constituted a miscarriage of justice amounting to manifest injustice as that expression is understood in international law."[6] In addition, the tribunal criticized the $400 million punitive damages award issued by the trial court as "grossly disproportionate" to the damage actually suffered.[7] And while in the end the NAFTA panel refrained (on standing grounds) from assessing damages against the United States,[8] there is little reason to think that liability in similar situations will not be imposed in the future.

[2] For a detailed analysis of such dialectical regulation, *see* Robert B. Ahdieh, Between Dialogue and Decree: International Review of National Courts, 79 *N.Y.U. L. Rev.* 2029 (2004).

[3] *See id.* at 2034.

[4] *See* Seyla Benhabib, *Another Cosmopolitanism* 48 (2006) ("Every iteration involves making sense of an authoritative original in a new and different context. The antecedent thereby is reposited and resignified via subsequent usages and references.").

[5] *Loewen Group, Inc. v. United States*, ICSID Case No. ARB(AF)/98/3, 4 J. World Investment 675, 702, 42 (NAFTA Ch. 11 Arb. Trib. 2003), *available at* http://naftaclaims.com/Disputes/USA/Loewen/LoewenFinalAward.pdf.

[6] *Id.* at 687, 54.

[7] *Id.* at 700, 113.

[8] *See id.* at 730, 238–240.

Thus, the question becomes, How will a domestic court, faced with a multinational dispute in the future, respond both to the NAFTA precedents already in place and the threat of possible NAFTA panel review? Although these NAFTA panels lack formal authority over the domestic courts they review, they do have the power to assess damages against federal authorities for violations of the trade agreement, even if those violations occurred in the context of a domestic court judgment. Thus, we see plural sources of normative authority: the domestic court that issued an initial judgment, the NAFTA tribunal that reviews this judgment for fidelity with the principles of the treaty, and the federal authorities who, in response to pressure from the NAFTA tribunal, may in turn put pressure on the domestic court. Robert Ahdieh has argued that, given these realities, we are likely to see, over time, a dialectical relationship form between the domestic and international tribunals, in which those courts pay attention to each other's interpretations and, while not literally bound by each other's decisions, develop a joint jurisprudence partly in tandem and partly in tension with each other.[9]

In order to see how such a dialectical relationship might evolve, consider interactions between the European Court of Human Rights (ECHR) and the constitutional courts of European member states. Here, the relationship may seem more hierarchical because, over the past several decades, the ECHR has increasingly come to seem like a supranational constitutional court, and its authority as ultimate arbiter of European human rights disputes has largely been accepted.[10] Yet, even in this context there appears to be room for hybridity. As Nico Krisch has documented, domestic courts occasionally fail to follow ECHR judgments, asserting fundamental principles embedded in their own constitutional order and in general claiming the power to determine the ultimate limits to be placed on the authority of the ECHR.[11] Typical of this dialectical

[9] *See* Ahdieh, *supra* note 2, at 2080–2.

[10] *See* Nico Krisch, The Open Architecture of European Human Rights Law 71 *Mod. L. Rev.* 183 (2008).

[11] *See generally id.*

relationship is the statement by the German constitutional court that ECHR judgments have to be "taken into account" by German courts but may have to be "integrated" or adapted to fit the domestic legal system.[12] Moreover, the German court has gone so far as to say that ECHR decisions must be disregarded altogether if they are "contrary to German constitutional provisions."[13]

Yet, although such statements make it sound as if conflict between the ECHR and domestic courts is the norm, the reality has actually been quite harmonious. As Krisch points out, "despite national courts' insistence on their final authority, the normal, day-to-day operation of the relationship with the [ECHR] has lately been highly cooperative, and friction has been rare."[14] The picture that emerges is one in which domestic courts and the ECHR engage in a series of both informal and interpretive mutual accommodation strategies to maintain a balance between uniformity and dissention. Likewise, as Lisa Conant has observed, nation-state courts have sought to "contain" the impacts of European Court of Justice decisions in national legal orders, even while formally accepting both the supremacy of EU law and the ECJ's role in authoritatively interpreting that law.[15] These sorts of dialectical relationship, forged and developed over many years, may well reflect the path yet to be taken by the NAFTA tribunals and domestic courts, as well as the many other intersystemic interactions at play in the world today.

Finally, consider the Canadian Constitution, which explicitly contemplates a dialectical interaction between national courts and provincial legislatures concerning constitutional interpretation. Section 33's so-called "notwithstanding" clause permits Parliament or a provincial legislature to authorize the operation of a law for a five-year period, even after it has been declared invalid by a court.[16] As with the ECHR example, this

[12] As quoted in *id.* at 19.

[13] *Id.*

[14] *Id.*

[15] *See* Lisa Conant, *Justice Contained: Law and Politics in the European Union* (2002).

[16] *See* Canadian Charter of Rights and Freedoms, Part I of the Constitution Act, 1982, being Schedule B to the Canada Act 1982, ch. 11, § 33 (U.K.).

provision potentially has a disciplining effect on the court and encourages a more nuanced iterative process in working out constitutional norms. It is true of course that the notwithstanding clause, though often invoked rhetorically, has only rarely actually been used by provincial governments to continue a judicially invalidated law.[17] Yet, this relative infrequency of use may not be evidence of a failed constitutional innovation. Instead, it may indicate just the opposite: that the various institutional actors have sufficiently internalized this mechanism for managing pluralism such that, as in the ECHR example, the precipice is rarely reached.[18]

In contrast to the dialectical interplay contemplated by the "notwithstanding clause," the U.S. Supreme Court has, on multiple occasions, interpreted the U.S. Constitution to contain an implicit foreign affairs preemption doctrine that *cuts off* such interplay.[19] Thus, as

[17] For example, the Quebec Parliament overrode the Canadian Supreme Court's invalidation of provisions of a language law. *See Ford v. Quebec*, [1988] 2 S.C.R. 712. However, outside Quebec the notwithstanding clause has never been used to overturn a judicial decision. *See* James Allan & Grant Huscroft, Constitutional Rights Coming Home to Roost? Rights Internationalism in American Courts, 43 *San Diego L. Rev.* 1, 21 (2006). In addition, according to one account, the clause has been disavowed by successive prime ministers because "its use has come to be seen as undermining the Charter, in part because judicial decisions interpreting the Charter have come to be seen as synonymous with the Charter itself." *Id.* at 20.

[18] On the other hand, it is possible that "the notwithstanding clause ... frees Canadian courts to be *less* deferential to elected legislatures than they otherwise would have been in the absence of such a clause, because it allows judges to act on the basis that their decisions are not final." *Id.* at 21–2. In any event, the important point for this chapter is that the clause is structured as a mechanism for managing the hybridity of multiple communities within a federal system. For an account supporting the approach of the notwithstanding clause from the perspective of political theory, *see* Jennifer Nedelsky, Reconceiving Rights and Constitutionalism 7 *J. of Human Rights* 139, 147 (2008).

[19] *See American Insurance Ass'n v. Garamendi*, 539 U.S. 396 (2003) (striking down California law requiring insurance companies doing business in California to disclose any business activities in Europe during the Nazi Holocaust); *Crosby v. National Foreign Trade Council*, 530 U.S. 363 (2000) (prohibiting Massachusetts from banning state expenditures on imports made with forced labor); *Zschernig v. Miller*, 389 U.S. 429 (1968) (striking down Oregon statute that had the effect of preventing a resident of East Germany from inheriting property probated in the state). For a discussion of these cases, *see* Judith Resnik, Foreign as Domestic Affairs: Rethinking Horizontal Federalism and Foreign Affairs Preemption in Light of Translocal Internationalism, 57 *Emory L.J.* 31 (2007).

discussed in Chapter 2, the Court has refused to allow localities to take actions that were deemed to encroach upon the exclusive national prerogative to conduct foreign affairs. Yet, one might think that, "[i]n our democratic federation, local efforts to effectuate protection of rights have a presumptive validity authorized by the commitments to multiple voices protected in a federal system."[20] At the very least, courts should carefully interrogate the claimed justification for preemption to ensure that the local action at issue poses a real, rather than conjectural, threat to the federal government's conduct.[21] After all, pluralism is built into the structure of federalism, and so actions of localities to import international or foreign norms or signal solidarity with them should not easily be displaced.

Indeed, at times we can see the explicit creation of dialectical legal regimes to manage federalist interactions. For example, take California's efforts to impose more stringent automobile fuel efficiency standards than the federal government's. At first glance, this might seem to be simply a direct state challenge to federal authority. However, the entire regime under which California can apply for a waiver to impose stricter standards is itself a creature of federal law, because it is the Clean Air Act that grants California this special status in regulating automobile emissions[22] and arguably has contributed to California's regulatory leadership in this area.[23] Similarly, amendments to the Clean Air Act established in 1990 a formal mechanism whereby northeastern states were granted the ability to cooperate in the control of ozone, but the Environmental

[20] *Id.* at 86.

[21] *See id.* at 87 ("Judges ought to adopt a posture of non-encroachment by insisting on exacting evidence of particular and specific imminent harms before invalidating actions by localities or states as they determine their own expenditures of funds and rules.").

[22] *See* Clean Air Act, 42 U.S.C. §7543(e)(2)(A) (2006).

[23] *See* Ann E. Carlson, Iterative Federalism and Climate Change, 103 *Nw. U. L. Rev.* 1109 (2009) ("California's leadership on climate change issues is not merely the product of state leadership. California's climate change regulations are a direct result of federal law, which has played a central role both in allowing the state to regulate and in demanding stricter regulation of air pollution.").

Protection Agency (EPA) was given the power to approve or disapprove any recommendations the consortium might have.[24]

Significantly, these provisions, both of which explicitly create formalized dialectical (or multiscalar) relations between state and federal authority, may be preferable to a regime that granted either the states or the federal government sole authority.[25] As Ann Carlson argues,[26] the federal statutes have, as an initial matter, tended to encourage the states to ratchet up their environmental protection beyond what they otherwise might have done. However, the dialectical scheme has gone further and actually encouraged the deputized states to become leaders on environmental compliance. Moreover, by granting such authority to only one or a small group of states, the dialectical scheme reaps the benefits of permitting a greater field for experimentation than a top down solution would ordinarily provide, at the same time achieving greater national uniformity than would occur if each state were free to go its own way. Thus, the pluralist approach of these provisions walks a middle ground between fully decentralized and fully centralized power and arguably achieves a better outcome than either.

Likewise, as discussed in Chapter 2, the Sudan Accountability and Divestment Act of 2007 is a federal statute that authorizes states to divest from companies doing business in Sudan, but only under certain conditions and in limited ways, and only until the president certifies that the human rights abuses committed by Sudan have eased.[27] Again, the federal restrictions address concerns about national uniformity in foreign affairs, but the act does not embrace the jurispathic doctrine of foreign affairs preemption, under which the U.S. Supreme Court altogether

[24] *See* 42 U.S.C. §7511c(a).

[25] *See* Hari Osofsky, The Future of Environmental Law and Complexities of Scale: Federalism Experiments with Climate Change Under the Clean Air Act, 32 *Wash. U. J. L. & Pol'y* 79 (2010).

[26] *See* Carlson, *supra* note 23.

[27] *See* Sudan Accountability and Divestment Act of 2007, *Pub. L. No.* 110–174, 21 *Stat.* 2516 (2007).

foreclosed Massachusetts's efforts to divest from companies doing business in Burma.[28] Instead, the pluralist approach of the statute provides a port of entry for states to contribute to the formulation of national foreign policy while guarding against complete devolution of foreign affairs power. As Perry Bechky has observed, "state divestment may call attention to an under-attended concern, influence societal attitudes about that concern, and build domestic political support for a more vigorous national response thereto. Congress may reasonably conclude that it wishes to hear state speech about Darfur as it continually reassesses the degree of priority to afford Darfur amongst the many concerns competing for Congressional attention."[29] Accordingly, the statutory scheme provides greater opportunity for intersystemic dialogue, public debate, and creative norm generation by multiple actors than if either a localist or nationalist solution had fully triumphed.

These examples all involve dialectical interactions between formal state or international legal institutions. However, the same dialectical interactions are possible with regard to nonstate normative standards. For example, the decisions of arbitral panels may, over time, exert influence on the decisions of more formal state or international bodies, and vice versa. In a different context, states may incorporate or adapt standards of conduct that are part of accreditation schemes promulgated by NGOs or industry groups.[30] And more broadly, we might see the creation of monitoring schemes in general as a kind of pluralist approach because instead of dictating rules, such monitoring generates oversight and publicity that can instigate change without a formal hierarchical relationship or coercive enforcement.

[28] *Crosby v. National Foreign Trade Council*, 530 U.S. 363 (2000).

[29] Perry S. Bechky, Darfur, Divestment, and Dialogue, 30 *U. Pa. J. Int'l L.* 823, 826 (2009).

[30] *See, e.g.*, Jody Freeman, The Private Role in Public Governance, 75 *N.Y.U. L. Rev.* 543, 618–19 (2000) (describing government incorporation of accreditation standards on health maintenance organizations (HMOs) first promulgated by a not-for-profit entity); *see also* Laura A. Dickinson, *Outsourcing War and Peace* (2011) (proposing such an accreditation scheme for disciplining private military contractors).

Margins of Appreciation

One of the interpretive mechanisms employed by the ECHR to maintain space for local variation is the oft-discussed "margin of appreciation" doctrine.[31] Unlike the dialectical legal encounter between the ECHR and the German Constitutional Court discussed previously, the margin of appreciation doctrine is an explicit interpretive device employed by the ECHR to give play to local variation. The idea here is to strike a balance between deference to national courts and legislators, on the one hand, and maintaining "European supervision" that "empower[s the ECHR] to give the final ruling" on whether a challenged practice is compatible with the convention, on the other.[32] Thus, the margin of appreciation allows domestic polities some room to maneuver in implementing ECHR decisions in order to accommodate local variation. How big that margin is depends on a number of factors including, for example, the degree of consensus among the member states. For example, in a case involving parental rights of transsexuals, the ECHR noted that because there was as yet no common European standard and "generally speaking, the law appears to be in a transitional stage, the respondent State must be afforded a wide margin of appreciation."[33]

Affording this sort of variable margin of appreciation usefully accommodates a limited range of pluralism. It does not permit domestic courts to ignore fully the supranational pronouncement (though, as discussed previously, domestic courts have sometimes asserted greater independence). Nevertheless, it does allow space for local variation, particularly when the law is in transition or when no consensus exists among member

[31] A particularly useful, succinct summary can be found in Lawrence R. Helfer & Anne-Marie Slaughter, Toward a Theory of Effective Supranational Adjudication, 107 *Yale L.J.* 273, 316–17 (1997). My discussion here largely tracks theirs.

[32] *Sunday Times v. United Kingdom*, 30 Eur. Ct. H.R. (ser. A) at 36 (1979).

[33] *X v. United Kingdom*, No. 75/1995/581/667, slip op. at 13 (Eur. Ct. H.R. Apr. 22, 1997); *see also Otto-Preminger Inst. v. Austria*, 295-A Eur. Ct. H.R. (ser. A) at 19 (1994) (finding that the lack of a uniform European conception of rights to freedom of expression "directed against religious feelings of others" dictates a wider margin of appreciation).

states on a given issue. Moreover, by framing the inquiry as one of local consensus, the margin of appreciation doctrine disciplines the ECHR and forces it to move incrementally, pushing toward consensus without running too far ahead of it.

Finally, the margin of appreciation functions as a signaling mechanism, through which "the ECHR is able to identify potentially problematic practices for the contracting states before they actually become violations, thereby permitting the states to anticipate that their laws may one day be called into question."[34] And, of course, there is reverse signaling as well, because domestic states, by their societal evolution away from consensus, effectively maintain space for local variation. As Laurence Helfer and Anne-Marie Slaughter have observed, "The conjunction of the margin of appreciation doctrine and the consensus inquiry thus permits the ECHR to link its decisions to the pace of change of domestic law, acknowledging the political sovereignty of respondent states while legitimizing its own decisions against them."[35] A similar sort of interaction could be established by a constitutional court adopting some form of the classic concept/conception distinction[36] with regard to the adoption of norms by other actors. Thus, an entity such as the ECHR could, for example, articulate a particular concept of rights, while recognizing that the way this right is implemented is subject to various alternative conceptions.

[34] Helfer & Slaughter, *supra* note 31, at 317; *see also* Laurence R. Helfer, Consensus, Coherence and the European Convention on Human Rights, 26 *Cornell Int'l L.J.* 133, 141 (1993). For an example of this type of signaling, *see* J.G. Merrills, *The Development of International Law by the European Court of Human Rights* 81 (2d ed. 1993) (interpreting the ECHR's statement in *Rees v. United Kingdom*, 106 Eur. Ct. H.R. (ser. A) at 19 (1986), that "'[t]he need for appropriate legal measures [to protect transsexuals] should therefore be kept under review having regard particularly to scientific and societal developments'" as a "strong hint that while British practice currently satisfied [the Convention], the court's duty to interpret the Convention as a living instrument may lead it to a different conclusion in the future").

[35] Helfer & Slaughter, *supra* note 31, at 317.

[36] *See, e.g.*, Ronald Dworkin, *Law's Empire* 71 (1986) (discussing the difference between "concept" and "conception" as "a contrast between levels of abstraction at which the interpretation of the practice can be studied").

Other legal regimes could also usefully adopt margins of appreciation. For example, the controversial agreement on Trade-Related Aspects of Intellectual Property Rights (TRIPs) could be interpreted to incorporate a margin of appreciation. Such a flexible approach might allow developing countries more leeway in trying to make sure that access to knowledge in their countries is not unduly thwarted by stringent intellectual property protection.

Limited Autonomy Regimes

A different kind of margin of appreciation problem involves the interactions between state and nonstate law. Here, as with the supranational/national dialectic, we have two different normative orders that can neither ignore nor eliminate the other. Thus, the question becomes, What mechanisms of pluralism can be created to mediate the conflicts? As noted previously, this problem classically arises in the context of religion or ethnicity, though it is in no way limited to such communities. Nevertheless, an overview of mechanisms for managing religious and ethnic (or linguistic-group) pluralism may shed light on the possibility of building institutions to address nonstate normative communities in a variety of settings.

In a useful summary, Henry Steiner has delineated three distinct types of autonomy regime.[37] The first allows a territorially concentrated ethnic, religious, or linguistic minority group limited autonomy within the nation-state.[38] The precise contours of this autonomy can vary considerably from situation to situation. However, such schemes can include the creation of regional elective governments, command of local police, control over natural resources, management of regional schools,

[37] *See* Henry J. Steiner, Ideals and Counter-Ideals in the Struggle Over Autonomy Regimes for Minorities, 66, *Notre Dame. L. Rev.* 1539, 1541–3 (1991).

[38] *See, e.g.*, Will Kymlicka, *Politics in the Vernacular: Nationalism, Multiculturalism, and Citizenship* 156 (2001) (arguing that the creation of linguistically homogeneous, separate institutions for minority subgroups within a larger federal structure will foster the participation of minority groups in democracy by giving them the autonomy to control cultural policy).

and so on.[39] With regard to language, communities may be empowered to create language rights within their regions.[40] Or, as with indigenous tribal communities in the United States and elsewhere, the minority community can be explicitly granted sovereign status, though the full extent of that sovereignty is often contested.

Of course, nonstate normative communities may be dispersed throughout a state, making it difficult to create specific local zones of autonomy. In such cases, other potential autonomy regimes may be more effective.[41] A second possibility, therefore, involves direct power-sharing arrangements.[42] "Such regimes carve up a state's population in ethnic terms to assure one or several ethnic groups of a particular form of participation in governance or economic opportunities."[43] Thus, we may see provisions that set aside a fixed number of legislative seats, executive branch positions, or judicial appointments to a particular religious or ethnic minority group.[44] In addition, legislators who are members of a particular minority group may be granted the ability to veto proposed measures adversely affecting that group.[45] Alternatively, states may enact

[39] *See* Steiner, *supra* note 37, at 1541 (listing examples).

[40] *See, e.g.*, Wouter Pas, A Dynamic Federalism Built on Static Principles: The Case of Belgium, in *Federalism, Subnational Constitutions, and Minority Rights* 157, 158–9 (G. Alan Tarr, Robert F. Williams, & Josef Marko eds., 2004) ("[I]n 1970, the Belgian State was divided into four territorial linguistic regions: The Dutch-speaking region, the French-speaking region, the bilingual region of Brussels-Capital, and the German-speaking region.... The authorities in each region may, in principle, only use the official language of that region in their dealings with citizens. In some municipalities, where a significant number of the inhabitants speak another language, special provisions were enacted to give individuals the right to continue to use their own language in their relations with the local authorities.").

[41] *See, e.g.*, Cristina M. Rodriguez, Language and Participation, 94 *Cal. L. Rev.* 687, 744 (2006) ("Devolution to minority-run institutions will not help secure rights for disparate ethnic groups spread out over a nation's territory....").

[42] *See, e.g.*, Arend Lijphart, The Power-Sharing Approach, in *Conflict and Peacemaking in Multiethnic Societies* 491 (Joseph V. Montville ed., 1990); Ivo D. Duchacek, Federalist Responses to Ethnic Demands: An Overview, in *Federalism and Political Integration* (Daniel Judah Elazar ed., 1979).

[43] Steiner, *supra* note 37, at 1541.

[44] *Id.* at 1541–2.

[45] *Id.*

rules requiring formal consultation before decisions are taken on issues that particularly impact on minority communities.[46]

Finally, a third autonomy regime contemplates the reality that members of an ethnic community may invoke the idea of a personal law that is carried with the individual, regardless of territorial location. This personal law is often religious in character, and it reflects a primary identification with one's religious or ethnic group, rather than the territorially delimited community of the nation-state.[47] Accordingly, state law may seek to create what are essentially margins of appreciation to recognize forms of autonomy for these identities.[48] "Like power sharing, a personal law can provide an important degree of autonomy and cohesion even for minorities that are territorially dispersed."[49]

The question of accommodation to personal law is not a new one; nor is it limited to religious groups. In ancient Egypt, foreign merchants in commercial disputes were sometimes permitted to choose judges of their own nationality so that foreigners could settle their dispute "in accordance with their own foreign laws and customs."[50] Greek city-states adopted similar rules.[51] Later, legal systems in England and continental Europe applied personal law to foreign litigants, judging many criminal and civil matters not on the basis of the territorial location of the actors, but on their citizenship.[52] In the ninth century, for example, King Edgar allowed Danes to be judged by the laws of their homeland.[53] Likewise, William the Conqueror granted eleventh-century French immigrants the right to be judged by rules based on their national identity.[54] Foreign

[46] *Id.* at 1542.

[47] *See, e.g.*, Chibli Mallat, On the Specificity of Middle Eastern Constitutionalism, 38 *Case W. Res. J. Int'l L.* 13, 47–55 (2006) (contrasting the "personal model" with the "territorial model").

[48] Chibli Mallat calls this scheme "'communitarian' (or personal) federalism." *Id.* at 51.

[49] Steiner, *supra* note 37, at 1543.

[50] Coleman Phillipson, The International Law and Custom of Ancient Greece and Rome 193 (1911).

[51] *See* Douglas M. MacDowell, *The Law in Classical Athens* 220, 222–4 (1978).

[52] *See* Marianne Constable, *The Law of the Other* 7 (1994).

[53] *Id.* at 8.

[54] *Id.* at 10.

merchants trading under King John, in the twelfth and thirteenth centuries, were similarly governed by the law of their home communities.[55]

As noted previously, the relationship between state and personal law frequently arose in colonial settings where Western legal systems were layered on top of the personal laws and customs of indigenous communities. Indeed, in the colonial context, margins of appreciation and other forms of accommodation were often invoked as governing legal principles. For example, English courts of law and chancery were empowered to exercise jurisdiction only "as far as circumstances [would] admit."[56] Likewise, with respect to personal laws, the Straits Settlements Charter of 1855 allowed the courts of judicature to exercise jurisdiction as an ecclesiastical court "so far as the several religions, manners and customs of the inhabitants will admit."[57] By the end of the colonial era, indigenous law was recognized as law proper by all of the colonial powers.[58]

Today, particularly in countries with a large minority Muslim population, many states maintain space for personal law within a nominally Westphalian legal structure. These nation-states – ranging from Canada to Egypt to India to Singapore – recognize parallel civil and religious legal

[55] *Id.* at 13.

[56] *Saik v. Drashid*, [1946] 1 *Malayan L.J.* 147, 152 (App. Ct. Sept. 13, 1941).

[57] Roland Braddell, *Braddell's Law of the Straits Settlements* 17 (3rd ed. 1982). Interestingly, in the era prior to the age of empire, English courts would only defer to indigenous laws of Christian communities. For example, in Calvin's Case, 7 Co. Rep. 1 a, [18a] (1608), reprinted in 77 *Eng. Rep.* 377, 398 (1932), Lord Coke stated: "If a King conquers a Christian kingdom... he may at his pleasure alter the laws of the kingdom, but until he [does] so, the ancient laws... remain. But if a Christian king should conquer the kingdom of an infidel, and bring them under his subjugation, [then] ipso facto, the laws of the infidels are abrogated, for that they are not only against Christianity but against the law of God and of nature, contained in the Decalogue...." However, by at least 1774, that distinction appears to have fallen into disrepute. *See, e.g.*, *Campbell v. Hall, Lofft.* 655, 716 (1774), reprinted in 98 *Eng. Rep.* 848 (1932): ("Don't quote the distinction [between Christians and non-Christians] for the honour of my Lord Coke.").

[58] David Pearl, *Interpersonal Conflict of Laws* 26 (1981). Pearl excludes Germany, but notes that even Germany established an internal conflicts of law regime, which seems implicitly to recognize some sort of autonomous legitimacy for indigenous practices. *Id.*

systems, often with their own separate courts.[59] And civil legal authorities are frequently called on to determine the margin of appreciation to be given to such personal law. For example, the Indian Supreme Court has famously attempted to bridge secular and Islamic law in two decisions involving Muslim women's right to maintenance after divorce.[60] At the same time, issues arise concerning the extent to which members of a particular religious or ethnic community can opt *out* of their personal law and adopt the law of the nation-state. For example, in 1988 a Sri Lankan court decided that a Muslim couple could adopt a child according to state regulation but could not confer inheritance rights on their adopted child because Islamic law did not recognize adoption.[61] Even outside the context of Islamic law, the U.S. Supreme Court has at times deferred to the independent parallel courts maintained by American Indian populations located within U.S. territorial borders.[62] And beyond judicial bodies, we will increasingly see other governmental entities, such as banking regulators, forced to oversee forms of financing that conform to religious principles.[63] Of course, sometimes deference to religious or ethnic affiliations can be insufficiently protective of other values, such as the rights of women.[64] Nevertheless, these sorts of negotiations, like all the limited

[59] *See* Bharathis Anandhi Venkatraman, Islamic States and the United Nations Convention on the Elimination of All Forms of Discrimination Against Women: Are the Shari'a and the Convention Compatible? 44 *Am. U. L. Rev.* 1949, 1984 (1995); DeNeen L. Brown, Canadians Allow Islamic Courts to Decide Disputes, *Wash. Post*, Apr. 28, 2004, at A14 (discussing an Islamic Court of Civil Justice in Ontario, staffed by arbitrators trained in both Sharia and Canadian civil law).

[60] *See Mohammed Ahmed Khan v Shah Bano Begum*, 1985 AIR SC 945; *Danial Latifi & Anr v Union of India*, 2001 AIR SC 3958.

[61] *See, e.g., Ghouse v. Ghouse*, 1988 1 Sri LR 25.

[62] *See Santa Clara Pueblo v. Martinez*, 436 U.S. 49 (1978).

[63] *See, e.g.*, Tavia Grant, Sharia-Compliant Finance Is Increasingly Popular, *Toronto Globe & Mail*, May 7, 2007, *available at* http://www.theglobeandmail.com/servlet/story/RTGAM.20070507.wrislam07/EmailBNStory/robNews/home.

[64] *See, e.g.*, Resnik, *supra* note 19, at 48–9 (criticizing *Santa Clara Pueblo* on this ground); Mary Anne Case, Feminist Fundamentalism as an Individual and Constitutional Commitment, 19 *American University Journal of Gender, Social Policy and the Law* 549 (2011) (arguing that feminist commitments should be deemed as fundamental, and as deserving of deference, as religious ones).

autonomy regimes surveyed in this section, reflect official recognition of essential hybridity that the state cannot wish away.

Subsidiarity Schemes

Subsidiarity is another mechanism for managing the interactions among different legal or quasi-legal authorities. The Catholic Church first developed subsidiarity as an ordering principle designed to prevent so-called higher levels of authority from interfering unduly with the "internal life of the community."[65] Thus, it was deemed "an injustice and at the same time a grave evil and a disturbance of right order to transfer to the larger and higher collectivity functions which can be performed and provided for by lesser and subordinate bodies."[66] This principle seeks to push authority for decision making "down" to the most local or smallest unit of governance that is feasible.[67]

Subsidiarity has also, of course, become an integral concept for managing relations between national and supranational governing bodies in Europe.[68] For example, Article 5 of the European Community (EC)

[65] *See Catechism of the Catholic Church* ¶ 1883 (1994) ("A community of a higher order should not interfere in the internal life of a community of a lower order, depriving the latter of its functions, but rather should support it in case of need and help to coordinate its activity with the activities of the rest of society, always with the view to the common good") (quoting Centesimus Annus).

[66] Pope Pius XI, Quadragesimo Anno ¶ 79.

[67] For discussions of the Catholic Church understanding of subsidiarity, *see generally* Robert A. Sirico, Subsidiarity, Society, and Entitlements: Understanding and Applications, 11 *Notre Dame J.L. Ethics & Pub. Pol'y*, 549, 550 (1997) (quoting Catechism of the Catholic Church); Thomas C. Kohler, Quadragesimo Anno, in *A Century of Catholic Social Thought: Essays on "Rerum Novarum" and Nine Other Key Documents* 27, 31 (George Weigel & Robert Royal eds., 1991); Joseph P. Rompala, "Once More unto the Breach, Dear Friends": Recurring Themes in Welfare Reform in the United States and Great Britain and What the Principle of Subsidiarity Can Do to Break the Pattern, 29 *J. Legis.* 307, 331 (2003).

[68] The literature on subsidiarity within the European context is voluminous. Indeed, as early as 1993 Joseph Weiler was already calling academic subsidiarity commentary a "growth industry," J.H.H. Weiler, Journey to an Unknown Destination: A Retrospective and Prospective of the European Court of Justice in the Arena of Political Integration,

Treaty provides that any action falling within the concurrent competence of the community and the member states should only be taken by the EC "if and in so far as the objectives of the proposed action cannot be sufficiently achieved by the Member States and can therefore, by reason of the scale or effects of the proposed action, be better achieved by the Community."[69] Interestingly, *sovereignty* – a concept steeped in absolutist rhetoric – has, by some accounts, been replaced by *subsidiarity* – which is a more flexible mechanism for managing pluralism – as "the core idea that serves to demarcate the respective spheres of the national and the international."[70]

Unlike sovereignty, a subsidiarity regime does not pose an outright bar to governance at the "higher" level of authority. But it does not offer

31 *J. Common Mkt. Stud.* 417, 437 (1993), and there is no indication that interest in subsidiarity has weakened since. Among many useful treatments, *see*, for example, George A. Bermann, Taking Subsidiarity Seriously: Federalism in the European Community and the United States, 94 *Colum. L. Rev.* 331 (1994); Peter L. Lindseth, Democratic Legitimacy and the Administrative Character of Supranationalism: The Example of the European Community, 99 *Colum. L. Rev.* 628, 668–70 (1999); Mattias Kumm, The Legitimacy of International Law: A Constitutional Framework of Analysis, 15 *Eur. J. Int'l L.* 907, 920–4 (2004); N.W. Barber, The Limited Modesty of Subsidiarity, 11 *Eur. L.J.* 308 (2005); Phil Syrpis, In Defence of Subsidiarity, 24 *Oxford J. Legal Stud.* 323 (2004) (reviewing Antonio Estella, *The EU Principle of Subsidiarity and Its Critique* (2002)); Kees van Kersbergen & Bertjan Verbeek, Subsidiarity as a Principle of Governance in the European Union, 2 *Comp. Eur. Pol.* 142, 151 (2004); Deborah Z. Cass, The Word That Saves Maastricht? The Principle of Subsidiarity and the Division of Powers Within the European Community, 29 *Common Mkt. L. Rev.* 1107 (1992); A.G. Toth, The Principle of Subsidiarity in the Maastricht Treaty, 29 *Common Mkt. L. Rev.* 1079 (1992).

[69] Treaty establishing the European Community, Dec. 24, 2002, 2002 O.J. (C 325) 33, at Art. 5; *see also* Treaty Establishing the European Economic Community, Mar. 25, 1957, art. 5, 298 U.N.T.S. 11 (entered into force Jan. 1, 1958) ("In areas which do not fall within its exclusive competence, the Community shall take action, in accordance with the principle of subsidiarity, only if and insofar as the objectives of the proposed action cannot be sufficiently achieved by the Member States and can therefore, by reason of the scale or effects of the proposed action, be better achieved by the Community.")

[70] Kumm, *supra* note 68, at 920–1; *see also, e.g.*, Neil MacCormick, Democracy, Subsidiarity, and Citizenship in the "European Commonwealth," 16 *L. & Phil.* 331, 338 (1997) (arguing that Europe is now "postsovereign," having evolved beyond sovereignty).

a blank check either. The idea is to foster careful and repeated *consideration* of other potential lawmaking communities. Thus, "at its core the principle of subsidiarity requires any infringements of the autonomy of the local level by means of pre-emptive norms enacted on the higher level to be justified by good reasons."[71] Accordingly, it is not enough for, say, a supranational governance rule simply to be a good idea; the supranational lawmaking community also must consider whether the rule is one that is appropriately enacted at the supranational level, given contrary local policies.

For example, consider the case of a higher-level authority that enacts an emissions cap in order to combat global climate change but runs up against a lower-level authority that performed its own cost-benefit analysis and determined that it was better for the local economy not to create such a stringent restriction.[72] Here the collective action problems inherent in the lower-level authority's parochial cost-benefit analysis would probably justify intervention at the higher level. In contrast, a higher-level rule limiting nicotine consumption might not override a more permissive local rule because the locality can plausibly decide it wants to bear the higher healthcare costs or other consequences that might result.

As with all mechanisms for managing hybridity, the line-drawing problems are potentially difficult and often politically contested, but even just the habits of mind generated by *thinking* in terms of subsidiarity can help ensure that lawmaking communities at least take into account other potentially relevant lawmaking communities.[73] Moreover, subsidiarity can

[71] Kumm, *supra* note 68, at 921.

[72] This hypothetical example derives from one offered by Kumm, *supra* note 68, at 923–4.

[73] I realize that my discussion of subsidiarity has a functionalist cast and therefore may seem to deemphasize other concerns, such as democratic legitimacy or the nation-state's claims to loyalty as against supranational institutions. *See, e.g.*, Lindseth, *supra* note 68, at 669 (arguing that a functionalist approach "is clearly inadequate to understanding the full import of the subsidiarity principle" because it tends to ignore important issues of legitimacy); Paul D. Marquardt, Subsidiarity and Sovereignty in the European Union, 18 *Fordham Int'l L.J.* 616, 618 (1994) ("[T]he underlying logic of subsidiarity reduces the claim of rightful governance to a technocratic question of

help "local populations ... better preserve their sense of social and cultural identity,"[74] while still allowing for the possibility that higher-level governmental authority might sometimes be necessary. Finally, even though a subsidiarity regime sets the default in favor of the local, requiring articulated justifications to override the presumption, subsidiarity-related concerns can sometimes actually strengthen the perceived legitimacy of the higher-level authority as well. This is because, when the higher authority *does* override local regulation, it presumably does so only after carefully considering local practices and only after articulating reasons to justify such an override.[75] Accordingly, the institutional processes of subsidiarity aim to ensure dialogue among multiple legal communities, leading ideally to increased acceptance by each. Not surprisingly, subsidiarity has been proposed as a more general model for international law as well.[76] Indeed, though I discuss it in more detail in Chapter 7, the complementarity regime of the International Criminal Court – whereby the Court only takes jurisdiction if the local state is unwilling or unable to investigate – can be seen as a form of subsidiarity scheme.

Hybrid Participation Arrangements

Sometimes hybridity can be addressed not so much through the relationships among multiple communities and their decision makers as through

functional efficiency that will eventually undercut the nation-state's claims to loyalty."). However, the sort of dialogue that mechanisms for managing hybridity encourage need not be "technocratic" and can in fact engage with precisely the questions of legitimacy and community ties that critics want. Thus, I argue only for mechanisms that enhance dialogue; I do not circumscribe the content of that dialogue. Nevertheless, to the extent that critics of a functionalist account of subsidiarity are trying to raise a sovereigntist objection to supranationalism in general, the pluralist framework I pursue in this chapter clearly rejects such a position as both normatively undesirable and impractical. *See* Chapter 3.

[74] Bermann, *supra* note 68, at 341.

[75] *See* Kumm, *supra* note 68, at 922 ("If there are good reasons for deciding an issue on the international level, because the concerns addressed are concerns best addressed by a larger community, then the international level enjoys greater jurisdictional legitimacy.").

[76] *See, e.g.*, *id.* at 921.

hybridizing the decision-making body or process itself. For example, from 1190 until 1870, English law used the so-called mixed jury, or *jury de medietate linguae,* with members of two different communities sitting side by side to settle disputes when people from the two communities came into conflict.[77] Sir Edward Coke attributed this practice "to the Saxons, for whom 'twelve men versed in the law, six English and an equal number of Welsh, dispense justice to the English and Welsh.'"[78] Regional differences, however, were not the only type of community variation recognized in the mixed-jury custom. Mixed juries were also used in disputes between Jews and Christians,[79] city and country dwellers,[80] and merchants and nonmerchants.[81] In the United States, the custom of mixed juries was imported from England and used in disputes between settlers and indigenous people[82] and in other interjurisdictional disputes at least through the beginning of the twentieth century.[83] Karl Llewellyn's

[77] Deborah A. Ramirez, The Mixed Jury and the Ancient Custom of Trial by Jury De Medietate Linguae: A History and Proposal for Change, 74 *B.U. L. Rev.* 777, 781 (1994); *see also* Constable, *supra* note 52, at 8 (describing the practice of mixed juries in early England).

[78] Constable, *supra* note 52, at 17 (quoting *Sir* Edward Coke, *The First Part of the Institutes of the Laws of England* § 234 (1628)).

[79] *See id.* at 18–21 (noting that half-Jewish, half-Christian juries heard suits between Jews and non-Jews in England during the twelfth and thirteenth centuries); Ramirez, *supra* note 77, at 783–4 (arguing that mixed juries originated in part from the king's desire to protect Jewish capital, which was subject to high assessments and escheatment to the crown, rather than lose it to Christians in an unfair trial).

[80] *See* Constable, *supra* note 52, at 17 (recounting an action involving a country dweller in twelfth-century London that required that at least one of the jurors be of "the county in which the foreigner dwells" (citation omitted)).

[81] *See id.* at 23–5 (exploring the evolution of "mixed merchant juries" in early England); Ramirez, *supra* note 77, at 784–6 (recognizing the king's regard for foreign merchants, which prompted the use of mixed juries in order to promote a "perception of fairness" to outsiders and attract their capital and goods).

[82] *See* Katherine A. Hermes, Jurisdiction in the Colonial Northeast: Algonquian, English, and French Governance, 43 *Am. J. Legal Hist.* 52, 64–5 (1999) (discussing the implementation of a mixed-jury system in colonial Pennsylvania, Rhode Island, and Massachusetts).

[83] *See* Ramirez, *supra* note 77, at 790 (noting that "[a]t various times between 1674 and 1911, Kentucky, Maryland, Massachusetts, Pennsylvania, New York, Virginia, and South Carolina each provided for mixed juries").

proposal that merchant experts sit as a tribunal to hear commercial disputes relies on a similar idea that specialized communities may possess relevant knowledge or background that should be called upon in rendering just verdicts.[84]

The principles underlying mixed juries can still be found today. Indeed, the line of U.S. Supreme Court decisions involving peremptory challenges of jurors could be seen as responding in part to a felt imperative that jury panels reflect both racial and gender diversity.[85] Nor is this a misplaced imperative, given that racially mixed juries tend to deliberate longer, consider more facts, raise more questions, and discuss more racial issues than all-white juries.[86] In addition, racially mixed juries make fewer factual errors than single-race juries, and when factual inaccuracies do arise, they are more likely to be corrected in the racially mixed juries than in single-race juries.[87]

In the human rights arena, hybrid domestic/international courts maintain the tradition of the mixed jury.[88] Such hybrid courts have been employed in transitional justice settings in Kosovo, East Timor, Sierra Leone, and Cambodia. In these courts, domestic judges – ideally drawn from the multiple political, racial, or ethnic groups involved in the larger

[84] *See* Zipporah Batshaw Wiseman, The Limits of Vision: Karl Llewellyn and the Merchant Rules, 100 *Harv. L. Rev.* 465, 512–15 (1987). (describing Llewellyn's merchant-tribunal proposal).

[85] *See Batson v. Kentucky*, 476 U.S. 79, 89 (1986) (ruling that prosecutors may not challenge jurors solely on the basis of race); *J.E.B. v. Alabama*, 511 U.S. 127, 130–1 (1994) (extending *Batson* to peremptory challenges based on gender).

[86] *See* Samuel R. Sommers & Phoebe C. Ellsworth, How Much Do We Really Know About Race and Juries? A Review of Social Science Theory and Research, 78 *Chi.-Kent L. Rev.* 997, 1028 (2003).

[87] *Id.*; *see also* Hiroshi Fukurai, Social De-Construction of Race and Affirmative Action in Jury Selection, 11 *Berkeley La Raza L.J.* 17, 20 (1999) ("[j]ury research shows that racially heterogeneous juries are more likely than single race juries to enhance the quality of deliberations. A number of empirical studies ... show that racially mixed juries minimize the distorting risk of bias.").

[88] *See, e.g.*, Laura A. Dickinson, The Promise of Hybrid Courts, 97 *Am. J. Int'l L.* 295 (2003).

geopolitical conflict – sit alongside international judges, and domestic and international lawyers also work together to prosecute the cases.[89]

Scholars suggest that, at least in theory, hybrid courts hold the promise of addressing some of the problems encountered in postconflict settings by wholly international courts, on the one hand, and wholly domestic courts, on the other.[90] Such problems can be grouped into three categories: legitimacy, capacity building, and norm penetration.[91] With regard to legitimacy concerns, the rationale for hybrid courts is largely the same as for mixed juries. If there is broad representation from the various communities involved in the dispute, then the outcome of the trial is more likely to be palatable to a cross-section of the population. Moreover, the presence of judges from the broader international community may contribute to a sense of fairness both for others watching the process from afar and for domestic populations who fear that local judges will rule on the basis of sectarian prejudices. On the other hand, however, the presence of local judges may protect against rejection of the court as wholly "foreign," a perception that has, for example, bedeviled the International Criminal Tribunal for the former Yugoslavia (ICTY). The hybrid court may therefore be seen as the best available compromise. Turning to capacity building, a hybrid court physically located in the region may be preferable to an international court elsewhere because resources both for physical infrastructure and for training will be more likely to flow into the country.[92] Finally, scholars argue, hybrid courts may help train a cadre of domestic lawyers in international legal standards and give them the tools necessary to develop and adapt those international norms in local settings. Meanwhile, the international actors are more likely to understand better the local nuances that may complicate the application of universal norms.[93]

[89] *See id.* at 295.

[90] *See e.g., id.* at 300.

[91] *See id.* at 301–5.

[92] Of course, sometimes trials in the postconflict locale may be too dangerous, thus necessitating a more distant situs for the court.

[93] *See* Dickinson, *supra* note 88, at 301–5.

It should be noted that, at least so far, the hybrid courts have failed to fully live up to their promise.[94] And of course the introduction of international, foreign, or hybrid components to a postconflict legal system does not necessarily promote legitimacy or credibility but instead can provoke additional suspicion. Thus, hybrid processes are at times viewed as shams or as representative of foreign idealism, of a thinly veiled preference for one side over another, or as a local political ploy meant to push through the decisions of the group in power under the guise of intergroup consensus.[95]

On the other hand, such criticisms of hybrid arrangements would seem to be even more salient with regard to wholly international tribunals, and so a hybrid arrangement may still be preferable to wholly international or wholly domestic courts for many of the reasons set forth previously. Moreover, some of the problems the courts have encountered are traceable to failures of implementation (inadequate funding, for example); they do not necessarily call into question the usefulness of the institutional model as a whole. In any event, a hybrid court will often be the only viable political compromise, reflecting – as in almost all the examples surveyed in this chapter – the impracticality of wholly universalist or wholly territorialist responses and the resulting need for some sort of hybrid mechanism. And, as Stephen Krasner has theorized, the sort of "shared sovereignty"[96] reflected in the hybrid court structure can be particularly important when domestic institutions are weak because it can "gird new political structures with more expertise, better-crafted policies, and guarantees against abuses of power."[97] Following this logic,

[94] *See, e.g.*, Justice Should Be Done, but Where? The Relationship Between National and International Courts, 101 *Am. Soc'y Int'l L. Proc.* 289, 297–300 (Mar. 28–31, 2007) (remarks of Laura A. Dickinson) (discussing shortcomings).

[95] I am grateful to Elena Baylis for emphasizing this important caveat.

[96] Such a "shared sovereignty" arrangement, according to Krasner, "involves the creation of institutions for governing specific issue areas within a state – areas over which external and internal actors voluntarily share authority." Stephen D. Krasner, Building Democracy After Conflict: The Case for Shared Sovereignty, 16 *J. Democracy*, Jan. 2005, at 69, 76.

[97] *Id.* at 70.

the Dayton Accords effectively made the Bosnian Constitutional Court a hybrid court, authorizing the president of the European Court of Human Rights to appoint three non-Bosnian judges to the nine-member court.[98] A different kind of hybrid is the Israeli Supreme Court, which has, since its inception, customarily had at least one member who is an expert in Jewish law.[99]

We can also see hybrid arrangements outside the judicial context. For example, pursuant to an oil pipeline agreement between Chad and the World Bank, the two parties share control and governance of the project.[100] As a condition for its participation, the World Bank insisted on a revenue management plan aimed at ensuring that the proceeds from the oil would be used for socioeconomic development.[101] To that end, the plan contains important limitations on how the expected oil revenue can be invested and spent.[102] In addition, oversight of the revenue plan is shared. Both the World Bank and the government of Chad must approve the annual expenditure of revenues, and there is a nine-member

[98] *See* General Framework Agreement for Peace in Bosnia and Herzegovina with Annexes, Dec. 14, 1995, 35 I.L.M. 75, annex 4, art. VI, para. 1(a), at 117, 123.

[99] *See, e.g.,* Donna E. Arzt, Growing a Constitution: Reconciling Liberty and Community in Israel and the United States, 19 *L. & Soc. Inquiry* 253, 257 (1994).

[100] For a useful description of the terms of the project, *see* Emeka Duruigbo, The World Bank, Multinational Oil Corporations, and the Resource Curse in Africa, 26 *U. Pa. J. Int'l Econ. L.* 1, 38–46 (2005).

[101] *See id.* at 40.

[102] For example, "In the course of the first ten years of production, that is, between 2004 and 2013, income taxes will constitute sixteen percent of total revenues to Chad and the rest will come from royalties and dividends. The government is given discretion on how to spend the revenues from income taxes subject to the limitation that they be used for general development purposes. The government has less liberty when it comes to royalties and dividends. A Special Revenue Account is created in which they would be deposited. A distribution formula has also been specified. Ten percent of the money will be kept in international financial institutions as a fund for future generations. Eighty-five percent of the remaining ninety percent will be deposited in local commercial banks and is dedicated to the financing of programs in five important sectors namely, education, health and social services, rural development, infrastructure, and environment and water resources. The remaining fifteen percent would be devoted to the development of the oil-producing Doba region." *Id.* at 41–2.

oversight committee – seven of whom represent the government while two represent civil society.[103] The committee annually publishes a review of operations, and those operations are subject to external audit.[104] Finally, the World Bank's International Advisory Group and Inspection Panel retains oversight power.[105] Whether such measures will result in effective hybrid governance remains to be seen. But significantly, most of the criticisms of the plan thus far tend to focus on the particular terms of the shared sovereignty arrangement, not the hybrid structure itself.[106]

It is not only officially constituted courts, governments, and international institutions that may benefit from hybrid participation arrangements in the international sphere. Consider, for example, the dilemmas raised by questions of Internet standard setting and governance. Of course, global governance of the Internet is a problematic and contested area because of the wide variety of potentially relevant community norms (both state and nonstate) and the concern that any global governmental body would inevitably fail to reach consensus on many issues and might lack democratic legitimacy.

In navigating these complexities, the Internet Engineering Task Force (IETF) has, for more than two decades, played an important role in Internet-standard setting and technical architecture design.[107] Given the fact that potentially significant values and policy choices can be embedded into the technical architecture of the Internet,[108] the IETF is an important – though by no means the only – place where Internet governance battles play out.

Since at least 1992, the IETF has self-consciously sought ways to manage its inherently hybrid space effectively as a nonstate entity embedding standards into a global technology. Its approach has been

[103] *Id.* at 42.
[104] *Id.*
[105] *Id.*
[106] For a summary of criticisms, *see id.* at 43–6.
[107] *See* Overview of IETF, *available at* http://www.ietf.org/overview.html.
[108] *See* Lawrence Lessig, *Code and Other Laws of Cyberspace* 6 (1999).

completely nonterritorial, relying on the "rough consensus" of volunteer network designers, operators, vendors, and researchers who join e-mail lists to discuss potential standards and attend triennial meetings held in different locations around the world.[109] Meetings are open to all, and anyone connected to the Internet can join the e-mail mailing lists that discuss proposed protocols. Moreover, everyone who attends meetings has an equal right to participate. At least one scholar celebrates the IETF for instantiating Jürgen Habermas's ideal of deliberative democracy.[110] On the other hand, though the IETF admirably draws from a wide range of territorial communities, the participants might be said to hail largely from a single elite community of technologists who, for the most part, speak the same language and share the same goals.[111] Indeed, it may well be these shared community norms (and the fact that most Internet standards decisions are likely to be non-zero-sum games[112]) that make "rough consensus" even possible.[113] Nevertheless, the IETF's global egalitarian ethic at the very least attempts to manage hybridity through broad-based participation from members of multiple territorial communities, while eschewing both nation-state and top-down international governmental approaches. Moreover, it is interesting to consider that this open, relatively nonhierarchical approach to standard setting in a hybrid environment helped to establish the Internet as a wildly successful global phenomenon.[114]

[109] *See* A. Michael Froomkin, Habermas@Discourse.Net: Toward a Critical Theory of Cyberspace, 116 *Harv. L. Rev.* 749, 792–4 (2003).

[110] *See id.* at 797 ("The Internet Standards-making institutions and processes are international phenomena that conform relatively well to the discourse required to actualize Habermas's discourse ethics. The participants in the IETF engage in constant discourse, continually reflect on their actions, and routinely document their reflections in a self-conscious manner.").

[111] *See id.*

[112] *See id.*

[113] *See id.*

[114] *See* Philip J. Weiser, Internet Governance, Standard Setting, and Self Regulation, 28 *N. Ky. L. Rev.* 822, 828 (2001).

Mutual Recognition Regimes

Given that harmonization is often difficult with regard to the substantive norms applied to products or services that cross borders, a more pluralist strategy for achieving some level of intersystemic regulation involves so-called mutual recognition regimes.[115] Under a policy of mutual recognition, different communities retain their own standards for internally produced products but agree to recognize another jurisdiction's standards for products imported from that jurisdiction. Thus, material entering, say, France from the United States would be subject to U.S. law despite its presence in France. Such a regime still leaves space for communities to adopt their own norms but then seeks to manage the hybridity that the movement across territorial borders inevitably creates.

Of course, as the French *Yahoo!* case discussed previously makes clear, communities will not always be willing even to go this far in ceding their own regulatory control, particularly if the norms involved are deemed fundamental. Not surprisingly then, most mutual recognition regimes set conditions on the recognition of foreign laws, regulations, standards, and certification procedures in order to ensure that such recognition will be "compatible" with local regulation. Making such a determination requires consideration of when normative differences are "legitimate" or "acceptable" and when they are so different that they cannot be recognized. And, as with margins of appreciation or permissible invocation of personal law, though the line-drawing problems can be formidable, the basic inquiry seeks to draw disparate communities into dialogue with

[115] For useful discussions of mutual recognition regimes, *see, e.g.*, Kalypso Nicolaidis & Gregory Shaffer, Transnational Mutual Recognition Regimes: Governance Without Global Government, 68 *L. & Contemp. Probs.* 263 (2005); Gregory Shaffer, Reconciling Trade and Regulatory Goals: The Prospects and Limits of New Approaches to Transatlantic Regulatory Governance Through Mutual Recognition and Safe Harbor Agreements, 9 *Colum. J. Eur. L.* 29 (2002) [hereinafter Shaffer, Reconciling Trade and Regulatory Goals]; Kalypso Nicolaidis, Regulatory Cooperation and Managed Mutual Recognition: Developing a Strategic Model, in *Transatlantic Regulatory Cooperation* 596 (George Bermann et al. eds., 2000).

each other and pave the way for working cooperation without imposing uniformity. Indeed, mutual recognition regimes tend to elide distinctions between domestic and international regulation by "intermingling domestic laws to constitute the global."[116]

In order to see how the line drawing works, we can consider two cases. In one, the European Court of Justice ruled that, under a mutual recognition regime, Germany must recognize French standards for marketing the liqueur cassis (and therefore cannot ban French imports on consumer protection grounds) because Germany can vindicate its consumer protection concerns through labeling.[117] On the other hand, the WTO Appellate Body permitted the United States to ban the importation of shrimp caught without devices to protect turtles, as required by U.S. law, in part because no other approach would satisfy the U.S. government's global environmental protection concerns. Nevertheless, the Appellate Body did require the United States to provide foreign governments or exporters with an opportunity to comment on U.S. regulatory decisions that could affect them.[118] Thus, the mutual recognition regime, even when it does not force full recognition of the foreign norm, can at least open up space for debate about conflicting norms.

As these two cases indicate, mutual recognition regimes often provide for international oversight or adjudication. Alternatively, national courts may be forced to consider the degree to which a foreign standard should apply to a cross-border transaction, leading to choice-of-law questions of the sort considered in Chapter 8. In addition, transnational networks of regulatory officials may work together to negotiate and monitor the day-to-day operation of such regimes. Finally, private third-party NGOs or monitoring firms can also be employed to help police the agreements.

[116] *See* Nicolaidis & Shaffer, *supra* note 115, at 3.

[117] *See* Case 120/78, *Rewe-Zentrale AG v. Bundesmonopolverwaltung für Branntwein*, [1979] E.C.R. 649, para. 14, (1979) 3 *C.M.L.R.* 494, 510 (1979).

[118] Report of the Appellate Body, United States – Import Prohibition of Certain Shrimp and Shrimp Products; Report of the Appellate Body, WT/DS58/AB/R (Oct. 12, 1998), *available at* http:// docsonline.wto.org/.

Safe Harbor Agreements

Like mutual recognition regimes, safe harbor agreements can manage pluralism by creating an intermediate plane between the conflicting normative requirements of two different communities. Instead of fully harmonizing norms, safe harbor principles require that firms doing business abroad abide by some (though not all) of the standards of that foreign community.[119] In return, the foreign community agrees not to impose further regulatory burdens.

The U.S.-EC data privacy initiative is the best-known example of a state-to-state safe harbor agreement. The Safe Harbor Principles on data privacy subject U.S. businesses to a higher standard of privacy protection than they would need to follow domestically. However, if firms do comply, then under the agreement, the firms will not be subject to challenge under potentially even more stringent EU privacy directives. Significantly, these principles create no legal obligations within the United States. "The United States and EC may thereby claim that they formally retain autonomy to enact whatever privacy legislation that they deem appropriate. However, any firm that engages in cross-border exchange is subject to pressure to abide by the Principles."[120] As such, the Safe Harbor Principles seek to retain space for local law while recognizing and facilitating the inevitability of cross-community interaction.

Safe harbors can also function as a way in which formal law incorporates less formal or less institutionalized lawmaking processes. For example, the Arrangement on Officially Supported Export Credits, adopted widely among industrialized countries, is not officially a binding legal document, having been adopted by design as a "gentleman's agreement" of participants.[121] However, adherence to the arrangement

[119] *See* Shaffer, Reconciling Trade and Regulatory Goals, *supra* note 115, at 57–8.

[120] *Id.* at 58.

[121] For a discussion of this Arrangement, *see* Janet Koven Levit, A Bottom-Up Approach to International Lawmaking: The Tale of Three Trade Finance Instruments, 30 *Yale J. Int'l L.* 125, 157–67 (2005).

now functions as a safe harbor for the WTO's Agreement on Subsidies and Countervailing Measures.[122] Accordingly, through the mechanism of the safe harbor, a formal international lawmaking body can enshrine a system of deference to a less formal, practice-based industry arrangement.

Regime Interaction Within the International System

Thus far, most of the examples in this chapter have involved what are sometimes called "vertical" interactions between international and transnational decision makers, on the one hand, and decision makers that are more "local," on the other. And while mutual recognition and safe harbor agreements tend to be "horizontal," they are generally formed among states (though there is no intrinsic reason why any two communities could not form similar agreements). Thus, missing so far in the analysis is the "horizontal" interactions within what might broadly be described as the international system. Significantly, a focus on such regime interactions helpfully takes us away from an emphasis on judicial decision making to a broader view of how different groups of actors may interrelate on the international stage.

For the better part of a decade, public international law scholars and practitioners have been preoccupied with conflicts between and among different functional international legal regimes.[123] As Jeffrey L. Dunoff has neatly summarized,[124] these conflicts tend to take the form of the following fact patterns:

(i) when norms from two or more international legal regimes are potentially applicable to a situation, such as when human rights

[122] *See id.* at 165.

[123] I am grateful to Jeff Dunoff for his contributions to this section. The paragraphs that follow draw heavily upon Jeffrey L. Dunoff, A New Approach to Regime Interaction, in *Regime Interaction in International Law: Facing Fragmentation* 136 (Margaret A. Young, ed., 2012).

[124] *See id.* at 139–41.

and/or international humanitarian law is applicable in specific cases;[125]

(ii) when a court or other body embedded in one legal regime is asked to interpret or apply a norm originating in a different regime, such as when a WTO panel is asked to apply an environmental norm from international law;[126]

(iii) when the same or a related fact pattern goes before multiple courts or institutions, such as the MOx plant litigation that went before four different international tribunals;[127] the Swordfish case that was filed at both the WTO and the International Tribunal for the Law of the Sea (ITLOS);[128] disputes arising from the Georgia-Russia conflict over Southern Ossetia and Abkhazia, which are currently pending before the ICJ and European Court of Human Rights; cases arising out of armed conflict in the Democratic Republic of the Congo that were filed before the International Court of Justice and the African Commission on Human People's Rights; certain alleged human rights violations;[129] and certain investment disputes;[130] or

(iv) when different international tribunals or courts adopt different approaches to the meaning or application of a legal concept, such as when the ICJ and the ICTY disagree over the correct legal test for

[125] For a sampling of the academic debate, *see* Alexander Orakhelashvilli,The Interaction Between Human Rights and Humanitarian Law: Fragmentation, Conflict, Parallelism, or Convergence?, 19 *Eur. J. Int'l L.* 125 (2008).

[126] Petros C. Mavroidis, No Outsourcing of Law? WTO Law as Practiced by WTO Courts, 102 *Am. J. Int'l L.* 421 (2008); Joost Pauwelyn, *Conflict of Norms in Public International Law* (2003); Jeffrey L. Dunoff, The WTO in Transition: Of Constituents, Competence and Coherence, 33 *Geo. Wash. Int'l L. Rev.* 979 (2001); Joel P. Trachtman, The Domain of WTO Dispute Resolution, 40 *Harv. Int'l L. J.* 333 (1999).

[127] *See, e.g.*, Robin Churchill & Joanne Scott, The MOx Plant Litigation: The First Half Life, 53 *Int'l & Comp. L. Q.* 643 (2004).

[128] *See, e.g.*, Marcos Orellana, The Swordfish Dispute Between the EU and Chile at the ITLOS and the WTO, 71 *Nordic J. Int'l L.* 55 (2002).

[129] Laurence R. Helfer, Forum Shopping for Human Rights, 148 *U. Pa. L. Rev.* 285 (1999).

[130] Steven R. Ratner, Regulatory Takings in Institutional Context: Beyond the Fear of Fragmented International Law, 102 *Am. J. Int'l L.* 475 (2008); Susan Franck, The Legitimacy Crisis in Investment Treaty Arbitration: Privatizing Public International Law Through Inconsistent Decisions, 73 *Fordham L. Rev.* 1521 (2005).

> the attribution of conduct by nonstate actors to states[131] and when the ICTY, the International Criminal Tribunal for Rwanda (ICTR), and the ICC disagree over the permissibility of "witness-proofing" before trial.[132]

Yet, while all these interactions are important, they all focus on litigation before juridical bodies. Not only is this an incomplete picture, but it may be that a juridical focus is distorting because it tends to produce a conceptualization of regime interaction in terms of discrete transactions or disputes. The analogy is to standard models of private domestic litigation involving parties who interact in a discontinuous event, such as a car accident. However, most regime interactions do not arise out of discrete transactions. Instead, as Dunoff notes, most international regime interaction occurs in ongoing relationships among actors and institutions from different regimes, and these interactions take place outside international courthouses.[133]

Consider, for example, the Joint United Nations Programme on HIV and AIDS (UNAIDS), the focal point for international responses to the human immunodeficiency virus/acquired immunodeficiency syndrome (HIV/AIDs) pandemic. UNAIDS is a joint venture of ten different "cosponsors" from a broad spectrum of international legal regimes, including the United Nations Office of the High Commissioner for Refugees; United Nations Children's Fund; World Food Programme;

[131] *See, e.g.*, Richard Goldstone & Rebecca Hamilton, *Bosnia v. Serbia*: Lessons from the Encounter of the International Court of Justice with the International Criminal Tribunal for the Former Yugoslavia, 21 *Leiden J. Int'l L.* 95 (2008); Antonio Cassesse, The Nicaragua and Tadic Tests Revisited in Light of the ICJ Judgement on Genocide in Bosnia, 18 *Eur. J. Int'l L.* 649 (2007).

[132] *Prosecutor v. Dyilo*, Case No. ICC-01/04–01/06, Decision on Practices of Witness Familiarization and Witness Proofing (Nov. 8, 2006); *Prosecutor v. Milutinovic*, Case No. IT-05–87-T, Decision on Ojdanic Motion to Prohibit Witness Proofing (ICTY Dec. 12, 2006); *Prosecutor v. Karemara*, Case No. ICTR-98–44-T, Decision Defence Motions to Prevent Witness Proofing (Dec. 15, 2006).

[133] For a more complete taxonomy and discussion of international regime interactions, *see* Dunoff, *supra* note 123.

United Nations Development Programme; United Nations Population Fund; United Nations Office on Drugs and Crime; International Labour Organization; United Nations Educational, Scientific and Cultural Organization; World Health Organization (WHO); and World Bank. Each body sponsors extensive AIDS programs and activities. In an effort to minimize duplication and maximize the efficient and effective use of international resources, the organizations have jointly developed an agreed-upon "division of labor." Following extensive consultation and negotiation, different entities have been identified as the lead body in specific areas of operational activity, such as strategic planning, prevention, treatment, and monitoring. This division of labor is designed to exploit the comparative advantage of each of the UNAIDS organizations and to facilitate the delivery of unified and consolidated programming.

In other contexts, we see similar sorts of cooperative iterative interactions among different legal regimes. For example, the Stockholm Convention on Persistent Organic Pollutants (POPs Convention), which entered into force in 2004, bans the use of certain pesticides, but DDT was not banned altogether, because of its effectiveness in combating malaria.

In order to resolve the normative clash between two epistemic communities – environmentalists who wanted the ban and health officials who did not – the treaty expressly contemplates a continuing series of interactions between the two groups. First, the treaty provides that parties may produce and use DDT only in accordance with WHO recommendations and guidelines. Thus, any changes in guidelines produced within the public health regime automatically produce regulatory changes within the chemicals regime. In addition, states using DDT are required to provide to the secretariat and the WHO information about the amount of DDT used, the conditions under which it is used, and the way such use relates to the country's disease management strategy. Most importantly, the POPs Convention expressly provides that every three years the treaty parties will consult the WHO to determine whether there is still a need to permit the use of DDT for vector control. The clear expectation is that if and when the WHO determines that there is no longer a need to use DDT for malarial control the chemicals regime will be changed to ban DDT.[134] Thus, as Dunoff points out, "the treaty explicitly structures an ongoing series of interactions between actors in the chemicals regime ... and actors in the public health regime ... over global efforts to create global regulations for dangerous pesticides."[135]

Accordingly, the international legal space is increasingly marked by ongoing collaborations among international actors from diverse international regimes, ranging from human rights to international finance to the environment. These iterative, sustained, and dynamic operational interactions can be understood as an adaptive strategy that arises in response to the fragmented nature of the international legal order and that permits the international community to address particular problems in a comprehensive and holistic fashion. Although operational interactions are not as dramatic as, say, the conflicts involved in high-profile international judicial opinions, operational interactions are more common than the interactions that give rise to international litigations. Moreover, robust and dynamic operational interactions can generate impressive substantive initiatives.

Even more interesting are what Dunoff calls "conceptual" interactions. The basic insight here is that when international actors create rules or engage in operational activities, they at the same time create social knowledge. Many regime interactions are designed to create (or change) such social knowledge. Consider, by way of illustration, the emerging relationship between the climate change and human rights regimes. For nearly two decades, the climate debate has focused on the nature, causes, and consequences of climate change. However, in recent years a potentially significant effort has been launched by human rights bodies to

[134] As of June 2009, the WHO position on the use of malaria remained unchanged; it "still supports the use of DDT for malaria control ... provided that WHO guidelines are followed strictly," and the treaty provisions on DDT had not been changed. WHO Re-affirms Its Position on DDT for Malaria Control (June 2009).

[135] Dunoff, *supra* note 123, at 161.

change the terms of climate discourse.[136] An important element of this strategy is the instigation of multiple interactions between the climate regime and the human rights regime by human rights bodies.[137]

From a pluralist perspective, we should understand these initiatives as an effort to spark a normative dialogue between the human rights and climate regimes. The goal is to prompt a reconceptualization of the climate issue, to shift the debate from one that is largely scientific and economic to one that is rooted in rights-based approaches that would supply "a set of internationally agreed values around which policy responses can be negotiated and motivated" and "contribute ... to the construction of better policy responses at both the national and international level."[138] In short, actors in the human rights community are provoking an ongoing set of *conceptual* regime interactions intended to change the way we come to understand climate change, the problems it poses, and the range of appropriate responses.

[136] For discussions, *see* Daniel Bodansky, Climate Change and Human Rights: Unpacking the Issues, 38 *Ga. J. Int'l & Comp. L.* 511 (2010); John H. Knox, Climate Change and Human Rights Law, 50 *Va. J. Int'l L.* 163 (2009).

[137] For example, in 2007 the UN deputy high commissioner for human rights addressed the Bali Conference and urged the need to use a human rights perspective when discussing environmental issues. At roughly the same time, a diverse range of international actors, ranging from the United Nations Development Programme and the OAS to Oxfam International and Kofi Annan's Global Humanitarian Forum, began to explore the interface between climate change and human rights. In 2008, the Human Rights Council asked the Office of the High Commissioner for Human Rights (OHCHR) to prepare a "detailed analytical study of the relationship between climate change and human rights." In undertaking the study, the OHCHR opened up a dialogue with a variety of other UN bodies, international organizations, national human rights institutes, nongovernmental organizations, and academic experts. In January 2009, the OHCHR released a study concluding that climate change interferes with a wide range of human rights and that States have an obligation under international human rights law to protect those rights from the adverse effects of climate change, including in particular through international cooperation. Moreover, the climate/human rights dialogue has started to migrate into other fora. For example, the Special Rapporteur on adequate housing has addressed how climate change challenges the right to housing and visited the Maldives to witness firsthand the effects of climate change.

[138] Marc Limon, Human Rights and Climate Change: Constructing a Case for Political Action, 33 *Harv. Envt'l L. Rev.* 439, 451–2 (2009).

Thus, we can spot hybrid procedural mechanisms or institutions far beyond the traditional juridical arena. Moreover, focusing on such non-judicial activities shifts attention from one-shot "transactional" interactions to ongoing "relational" regime interactions, and to the features that sharply distinguish relational interactions from the transactional interactions at issue in most litigations. Unlike litigations, which are necessarily retrospective and center upon a single dispute, relational interactions have a highly dynamic and forward-looking character. And, unlike litigations, which are typically bilateral, are designed to narrow the issues in dispute, and ultimately seek authoritative resolution, relational interactions often expand the range of issues under consideration, the fora where the issues are considered, and the number of relevant actors. This expansion, in turn, dramatically increases the possibility of trade-offs and mutual accommodation that permits all parties to benefit – precisely the results that litigation may sometimes be less able to generate. Accordingly, hybrid mechanisms for discursive interactions often go far beyond traditional legal forms.

EVEN THIS NECESSARILY BRIEF SURVEY OF DIFFERENT MECHANISMS, institutions, and practices for managing pluralism leads to several important insights. First, the range of interactions discussed makes it clear that hybrid legal spaces are the norm rather than the exception, and as a practical matter we may not be able to wish them away. Second, we should view the various procedural mechanisms, institutions, and practices surveyed as important sites for managing pluralism, not just as necessary but regrettable compromises. Indeed, such cosmopolitan pluralist approaches may, at least on some occasions, actually be preferable. Third, when evaluating the efficacy of any particular procedural mechanism, we should, in addition to any other criteria that might be considered, take into account how well the mechanism provides space for hybridity and jurisgenerative iterations and mediates among multiple communities. In other words, the management of pluralism should be seen as an independent value. Fourth, this survey provides a useful menu of options for communities attempting to negotiate pluralism. Indeed, many of the mechanisms and institutions considered here could usefully be adopted by state or nonstate communities. Alternatively, new mechanisms could be created along similar lines. Finally, identifying these mechanisms as sites for contestation establishes a research agenda whereby the microinteractions inherent in each mechanism can be detailed and studied to see how precisely these mechanisms operate in practice. Only this sort of detailed case study will allow us to understand the ways in which such mechanisms operate to channel contestation and provoke creative innovation. In short, the cosmopolitan pluralist framework I propose here illuminates an entire field of inquiry and asks scholars to consider the processes whereby normative gaps among communities can be bridged, shared social spaces can be created, and enemies can be transformed into adversaries, all without displacing contestation or dissolving difference. This is a difficult task, to be sure, but there can be no hope of meeting the challenge without first conceptualizing the independent value of pluralism.

Part IV CONFLICT OF LAWS IN A HYBRID WORLD

THE THREE CLASSIC LEGAL DOCTRINES OFTEN GROUPED together under the rubric of conflict of laws – jurisdiction, choice of law, and judgment recognition – are specifically meant to manage hybrid legal spaces. Jurisdiction involves the decision of a community to assert legal dominion over an act or actor. Choice-of-law analysis considers which community's legal norms should apply to a dispute involving members of multiple communities. And recognition of judgments asks communities to decide whether to enforce prior judgments of other communities, even when those judgments would not (or could not) have been issued by the enforcing community as an original matter. Each of these doctrines, therefore, is crucial to analyzing how law confronts the potential norms of foreign communities and conceptualizes ideas of space, place, distance, territory, sovereignty, and pluralism. Yet, neither sociolegal scholars studying the interaction of legally defined communities nor scholars interested in the multiplicity of legal and quasi-legal norms under conditions of globalization have focused sufficiently on these conflicts doctrines. This is unfortunate, and so one aim of these next three chapters is merely to stake a claim to conflict of laws as a crucial area of interdisciplinary inquiry. Indeed, it is largely on the terrain of conflict of laws that communities delineate self and other and consider the alternative normative communities that are all around. In addition, by attending to changes in legal doctrine in these areas over time, we will glimpse the tectonic societal shifts that these legal rules both reflect and create.

But beyond simply identifying conflict of laws as a fruitful subject of further study, I also want to argue that conflict of laws provides a potentially useful framework for viewing disputes among multiple normative orders. If taken seriously, a conflicts analysis could offer a forum for creative engagement with questions of community affiliation, extraterritorial effects, and the development of hybrid norms.

Throughout this book, we have observed the myriad ways in which a pure sovereigntist vision consisting of lines of demarcated legal authority fails to describe accurately the much more complex reality on the ground. Nevertheless, some look simply to reassertions of hierarchical legal authority to clean up this messiness. Thus, even when jurisdictional overlap or regulatory interdependence is undeniable, we see what Robert Ahdieh has termed "the standard dualist response."[1] Law seeks to delimit each entity's jurisdiction and authority more effectively and thereby eliminate such overlaps. This paradigm of jurisdictional line drawing has been prevalent both in the international/transnational realm[2] and in discussions of federalism,[3] as courts and scholars try to separate distinct spheres for

[1] Robert B. Ahdieh, Dialectical Regulation, 38 *Conn. L. Rev.* 863 (2006) at 867.

[2] For example, debates in the United States about judicial citation of foreign authority have often centered around delineating when it is permissible and when impermissible to reference foreign or international law. *See, e.g.*, Melissa A. Waters, Creeping Monism: The Judicial Trend Toward Interpretive Incorporation of Human Rights Treaties, 107 *Colum. L. Rev.* 628 (2007). Similarly, theories of jurisdiction and choice of law have long sought to provide a single answer to the question of which law should apply to a cross-border dispute. Compare *Pennoyer v. Neff*, 95 U.S. 714 (1877) (holding that states have complete authority within their territorial boundaries but no authority outside those boundaries), with *Int'l Shoe Co. v. Washington*, 326 U.S. 310, 316 (1945) (establishing a test for determining whether an assertion of personal jurisdiction comports with the due process clause of the U.S. Constitution on the basis of whether the defendant had sufficient contacts with the relevant state "such that maintenance of the suit does not offend 'traditional notions of fair play and substantial justice'" (quoting *Milliken v. Meyer*, 311 U.S. 457, 463 (1940))); compare *Restatement (First) of Conflict of Laws* §378 (1934) ("The law of the place of wrong determines whether a person has sustained a legal injury.") with *Restatement (Second) of Conflict of Laws* § 6 cmt. c (1971) (providing a more flexible inquiry aimed at determining the place with the "most significant relationship" to the dispute in question).

[3] Robert A. Schapiro, Toward a Theory of Interactive Federalism, 91 *Iowa L. Rev.* 243 (2005).

state and federal authority. As Ahdieh notes, "Such reactions are hardly surprising. At heart, they reflect some visceral sense of law's project as one of categorization, clear definition, and line-drawing."[4]

Yet, this single-minded focus on certainty and clarity not only fails to describe a globalized world of inevitable cross-border jurisdictional overlap; it also ignores the crucial question of whether leaving open space for such overlapping regulatory authority might actually be beneficial. In the next three chapters, therefore, I wish to engage in a thought experiment. What if, instead of approaching problems of jurisdictional overlap by insisting on separate sovereign spheres among state, federal, international, transnational, and nonstate authority, we sought to maximize interaction among various communities, both state and nonstate? What impact might such a change of lens have on the way we approach the core questions of conflict of laws: jurisdiction, choice of law, and judgment recognition?

Indeed, it seems to me that conflict of laws is a potential site for the sort of interaction across difference that was discussed in Chapter 5 with regard to Hannah Arendt, Iris Young, and Chantal Mouffe. This is because a conflict-of-laws decision, if taken seriously, neither assumes away difference nor annihilates difference through the jurispathic act of rejecting one normative commitment in favor of another one. Instead, we could use conflicts doctrines to acknowledge that we are all members of multiple overlapping normative communities, that some of these communities are state based and some are not, and that all of these communities may assert norms that have real impact on the world stage of law. And even when the alternative norms are so far beyond the pale that they cannot in the end be followed, using a conflicts framework means that such a decision will always be the exception, not the rule, and will need to be accompanied by an overriding normative commitment. Thus, even when acting jurispathically, communities will at least be engaging with the alternative norm and offering a strong normative justification

[4] Ahdieh, Dialectical Regulation, *supra* note 1, at 867.

for rejecting it. This vision of conflict of laws may help to better negotiate the inevitable divide between self and other by requiring communities both to acknowledge competing community norms and to wrestle explicitly with the question of how much to assimilate or give deference to those competing norms. Such an approach does not destroy difference in the vain search for uniform rules; instead it fosters engagement among strangers and negotiation of unassimilated otherness.

To explore how such a conflicts framework might work, I provide some examples, beginning with more conventional cases involving the interaction of state communities with each other and then considering a variety of conflicts issues raised by the norms of nonstate communities: religious communities, international communities, and ethnic communities. In each of these instances, the point is not to employ doctrine to "solve" conflicts disputes for all time. Rather, I hope to show simply that it might, at least at times, be fruitful to consider these debates through a conflicts lens, particularly when that lens takes seriously questions of community affiliation and the possibility of nonstate lawmaking.

7 The Changing Terrain of Jurisdiction

LAW HAS GENERALLY TAKEN A VERY NARROW VIEW OF jurisdiction by linking it to coercive power. If a community can literally seize a party (or its assets), then that party is usually deemed to be within the community's jurisdiction. As such, jurisdiction has historically been tied to physical territory. Anyone within the territorial borders was subject to jurisdiction; anyone outside them was not. In this scenario, the territorially distant stranger is conceptualized as forever strange and therefore not even a part of the legal dialogue.

In line with this vision, debates about jurisdiction generally revolve around either political theory questions concerning when a judicial or administrative exercise of authority is legitimate or legal policy questions about the most efficient or effective system for solving specific legal dilemmas. Even approaches that advocate decentralized authority or the creation of transnational norms do so largely on the basis of literature from political philosophy and law.

There is more to the assertion of jurisdiction or the extraterritorial imposition of norms, however, than simply questions of political legitimacy or efficient dispute resolution. The assertion of jurisdiction, like all legal acts, can also be viewed as a meaning-producing cultural product. What does it mean, after all, to say that some person, corporation, or activity is subject to a community's jurisdiction? And how does the idea of jurisdiction relate to conceptions of geographic space, community membership, citizenship, boundaries, and self-definition? Although largely ignored in jurisdictional debates, these foundational issues must be considered seriously if we are to develop a richer descriptive or normative account of the role of legal jurisdiction in a global era.

This chapter begins to develop such an account by isolating four specific aspects of jurisdiction that are often overlooked: the way in which jurisdictional rules reflect and construct social conceptions of space, the role of jurisdictional rules in establishing community dominion over a transgressor, the process by which the assertion of jurisdiction symbolically extends community membership to those brought within its ambit, and the way in which assertions of jurisdiction can open space for the articulation of norms that challenge sovereign power. Only by expanding our conception of jurisdiction will we be in a position to construct a more nuanced model for understanding and addressing a world of law beyond borders. I then apply a more cosmopolitan pluralist conception of jurisdiction to state-based and non-state-based assertions of jurisdiction, and I explore the potential uses of jurisdictional redundancy and overlap in managing the inevitable hybrid legal spaces we see all around us.

Jurisdiction and the Social Construction of Space

It has become commonplace for cultural critics and others to identify the ways in which social structures shape and constrain conduct, yet the link between social structures and physical spaces has received less attention.[5] Nevertheless, "[t]he production of space and place is both the medium and the outcome of human agency and social relations."[6] This cultural construction of space includes the boundaries drawn between "public"

[5] For two notable exceptions within legal scholarship, *see* Terry S. Kogan, Geography and Due Process: The Social Meaning of Adjudicative Jurisdiction, 22 *Rutgers L.J.* 627 (1991); Richard T. Ford, Law's Territory (A History of Jurisdiction), 97 *Mich. L. Rev.* 843 (1999). Kogan's work specifically addressed the social significance of adjudicative jurisdiction and so is particularly relevant here. My discussion in this section is heavily indebted to Kogan's argument.

[6] Allan Pred, *Making Histories and Constructing Human Geographies* 10 (1990).

and "private" spaces; the decisions a community makes about land use and zoning; the appropriation and transformation of "nature" as both a concept and a physical description; the local autonomy of governmental units; the use of specialized locations for the conduct of economic, cultural, and social practices; the creation of patterns of movement within a community; and "the formation of symbolically laden, meaning-filled, ideology-projecting sites and areas."[7]

In addition, *topological* space, which consists of the formal boundary lines we have chosen, is distinctively different from *social* space, which includes the meanings given to space (both local and nonlocal), to the distances between delineated spaces, and to the time necessary to traverse those distances.[8] For example, a one-hundred-mile automobile trip may seem like a greater journey to residents of the northeastern United States, who are accustomed to relatively short distances between destinations, than to residents of the West, where cities and towns are more dispersed. Similarly, a one-thousand-mile trip carries a very different social meaning today, in the age of relatively inexpensive air travel, than it did one hundred years ago, even if the topological space remains the same.[9] And of course America's well-documented postwar demographic shift from city to suburb is not merely a change of topology, but a politically and symbolically significant cultural transformation.[10]

[7] *Id.*

[8] Kogan, *supra* note 5, at 634.

[9] John Tomlinson describes this shift as follows: "In a globalized world, people in Spain really do continue to be 5,500 miles away from people in Mexico, separated, just as the Spanish conquistadors were in the sixteenth century, by a huge, inhospitable and perilous tract of ocean. What connectivity means is that we now experience this distance in different ways. We think of such distant places as routinely accessible, either representationally through communications technology or the mass media, or physically, through the expenditure of a relatively small amount of time (and, of course, of money) on a transatlantic flight. So Mexico City is no longer meaningfully 5,500 miles from Madrid: it is eleven hours' flying time away." John Tomlinson, *Globalization and Culture* 4 (1999).

[10] For the sociopolitical history of American suburbanization, *see* Joel Garreau, *Edge City: Life on the New Frontier* (1992); Kenneth T. Jackson, *Crabgrass Frontier: The Suburbanization of the United States* (1985).

Moreover, the construction of legal spaces and the delineation of boundaries are always embedded in broader social and political processes.[11] "Legal categories are used to construct and differentiate material spaces which, in turn, acquire a legal potency that has a direct bearing on those using and traversing such spaces."[12] For example, in the history of European conquest of Australia, the naming of particular spaces – rivers, mountains, capes, bays, and so on – became a central point of political contest.[13] The Europeans believed that the aboriginals did not classify or name the landscape and transformed that purported "spatial deficiency" into a "legal deficiency": if the aboriginals did not name their places, so the thinking went, their "grasp of it [was] so tenuous ... [that] it was hardly a crime to take possession of it."[14]

The social meaning of geographical space also includes the way in which an individual or community perceives those who are *outside* the community's topological or social boundaries. As people develop attitudes of familiarity toward the spaces in which they reside and conduct their daily activities, they may also come to view unfamiliar people and locations as frighteningly alien. Alternatively, the outside "other" can be seen as inviting, friendly, and hospitable, or as mysterious, exotic, and romantic.[15] There are a seemingly infinite variety of attitudes one may

[11] *See* Nicholas K. Blomley, *Law, Space, and the Geographies of Power*, at xi (1994) ("The legal representation of space must be seen as constituted by – and in turn constitutive of – complex, normatively charged and often competing visions of social and political life under law.").

[12] *Id.* at 54.

[13] *See* Paul Carter, *The Road to Botany Bay: An Exploration of Landscape and History* (1988) (describing European exploration and subsequent naming of various Australian geographical features).

[14] *Id.* at 64; *see also* Robert D. Sack, *Human Territoriality: Its Theory and History* 6–8 (1986) (describing similarly loose conceptions of territoriality among members of the Chippewa people at the time Europeans settled in the United States).

[15] As Stuart Hall has described: "To be English is to know yourself in relation to the French, and the hot-blooded Mediterraneans, and the passionate, traumatized Russian soul. You go round the entire globe: when you know what everybody else is, then you are what they are not. Identity is always, in that sense, a structured representation which only achieves its positive through the narrow eye of the negative." Stuart Hall,

hold toward unfamiliar social spaces. Such attitudes are embedded in context and shaped and influenced by manifold factors including politics, socioeconomic relationships, and the extent of contact that one has with the "other." [16]

Thus, jurisdictional rules have never simply emerged from a utilitarian calculus about the most efficient allocation of governing authority. Rather, the exercise of jurisdiction has always been part of the way in which societies demarcate space, delineate communities, and draw both physical and symbolic boundaries. Such boundaries do not exist as an intrinsic part of the physical world; they are a social construction. As a result, the choice of jurisdictional rules reflects the attitudes and perceptions members of a community hold toward their geography, the physical spaces in which they live, and the way in which they define the idea of community itself.

In order to convey this basic idea, it might be useful to give an admittedly oversimplified, functionalist account of the change in American jurisdictional rules over time. In this account, the territorially based jurisdictional principle articulated in the nineteenth century by the U.S. Supreme Court in *Pennoyer v. Neff*[17] – which held that states have complete authority within their territorial boundaries but no authority outside those boundaries[18] – derives in part from a particular understanding of social space in the United States at that time. As historian Robert Wiebe has famously observed, "America during the nineteenth century was a society of island communities."[19] With weak communication and limited interaction, these "islands" felt widely dispersed, and it is not surprising

The Local and the Global: Globalization and Ethnicity, in *Culture, Globalization and the World-System: Contemporary Conditions for the Representation of Identity* 19, 21 (Anthony D. King ed., 1997).

[16] Kogan, *supra* note 5, at 637.

[17] 95 U.S. 714 (1877).

[18] *See id.* at 722 (ruling that a State has power to decide the "civil *status* and capacities of its inhabitants" and to regulate how property may be handled, but that "no State can exercise direct jurisdiction and authority over persons or property without its territory").

[19] Robert H. Wiebe, *The Search for Order: 1877–1920*, at xiii (1967).

that local autonomy became "[t]he heart of American democracy."[20] Even though France had long since developed a centralized public administration, Wiebe argues that Americans still could not even conceive of a distant managerial government. In such a climate, geographical loyalties tended to inhibit connections with a whole society. "Partisanship ... grew out of lives narrowly circumscribed by a community or neighborhood. For those who considered the next town or the next city block alien territory, such refined, deeply felt loyalties served both as a defense against outsiders and as a means of identification within."[21]

As the nineteenth century progressed, so this story goes, massive socioeconomic changes introduced an onslaught of seemingly "alien" presences into these island communities. Immigrants were the most obvious group of outsiders, but perhaps just as frightening was the emergence of powerful distant forces such as insurance companies, major manufacturers, railroads, and the national government itself. Significantly, these threats appear to have been conceived largely in spatial terms. According to Wiebe, Americans responded by reaffirming community self-determination and preserving old ways and values from "outside" invasion.[22]

Given such a social context, it is not surprising that the jurisdictional rules of the period emphasized state territorial boundaries. Indeed, it is likely that the burdens of litigating in another state far exceeded simply the time and expense of travel, substantial as those burdens were. Just as important was the *psychic* burden of being forced to defend oneself in a foreign state, which may have felt little different from the idea of defending oneself in a foreign country. An 1874 Pennsylvania state court decision issued shortly before *Pennoyer* illustrates the extent of this psychic burden.[23] In the case, a resident of New York had contested jurisdiction in Pennsylvania. The court acknowledged that the Pennsylvania courthouse

[20] *Id.*

[21] *Id.* at 27.

[22] *Id.* at 52–8. For a fictional account of this period that gives texture to this description, *see* Willa Cather, *My Antonia* (1926) (1918).

[23] *Coleman's Appeal*, 75 Pa. 441 (1874).

was only "a few hours' travel by railroad" from New York but nevertheless ruled that the defendant could not be sued personally, in part because "nothing can be more unjust than to drag a man thousands of miles, perhaps from a distant state, and in effect compel him to appear."[24] The court disregarded the relatively slight literal burden in the case at hand and instead focused on the specter of being "dragged" to a "distant state" located "thousands of miles" away. Indeed, the decision seemed to equate other states with foreign countries, referring to a "defendant living in a remote state or foreign country ... [who] becomes subject to the jurisdiction of this, to him, foreign tribunal."[25] These passages indicate that the psychic significance of defending oneself in another state was at least as important as the literal difficulties of travel.

Both the literal and psychic burdens associated with out-of-state litigation changed as a result of the urban Industrial Revolution at the turn of the twentieth century, a revolution that profoundly altered American social space. Increasingly, economic and governmental activities were administered from afar by impersonal managers at centralized locations. In such a world, another state was likely to be viewed less as a foreign country and more as yet another distant power center, just one of many "anonymous, bureaucratic, regulatory bodies in an increasingly complex society."[26]

In addition, advances in transportation and communications helped to weaken territoriality as the central category in which Americans understood their space. "As long as daily lives were focused to a large extent on the local, a state boundary symbolized the edge of the world and everything outside that boundary was alien and foreign."[27] With increased mobility, however, Americans regularly crossed state boundaries by train, by car, and by airplane, a trend that inevitably diminished the sense that

[24] *Id.* at 457 (1874).

[25] *Id.* Indeed, for juridical purposes, other states had, since the founding, been treated much as foreign countries were, even for some time after the Civil War.

[26] Kogan, *supra* note 5, at 651 (citations omitted).

[27] *Id.* at 652.

other places were alien. The rise of radio and television meant that events in other states could become a regular part of one's daily consciousness. "Physical distance as a social barrier began to be bypassed through the shortening of communication 'distance.'"[28] These communication and transportation advances reinforced the functional interdependence that characterized the United States throughout the twentieth century. As a result, almost all of us are now regularly affected by people, institutions, and events located far away.

In this altered social space, the call to defend a lawsuit in the courts of another state remained an imposition, but the burdens were no longer perceived in stark territorial terms. In other words, though many economic and practical burdens remained, the psychic burden was no longer as strong. Thus, it is not surprising that, in 1945, the U.S. Supreme Court substituted a flexible "fairness" test for the more rigidly territorial scheme of *Pennoyer*.[29]

As previously stated, this is an oversimplified account of the shift in American jurisdictional rules. For the purposes of this discussion, however, it makes the essential point clearly enough: changes in political and social conceptions of space form at least part of the context for changes in jurisdictional understandings. Thus, although some might ask why we need to rethink our ideas about legal jurisdiction, the reality is that jurisdictional rules are always evolving, and this evolution has always responded to changing social constructions of space, distance, and community.

With the rise of global capitalism, the Internet, international trade and human rights norms, and so on, the question becomes whether the sense of social space has shifted once again. Arguably, people around the world now share economic space to a greater degree than ever before, in large part because of the increase in online interaction. Modern electronic communications, recordkeeping, and trading capacities have allowed the world financial markets to become so powerful that the

[28] Joshua Meyrowitz, *No Sense of Place: The Impact of Electronic Media on Social Behavior* 116 (1985).

[29] *Int'l Shoe Co. v. Washington*, 326 U.S. 310 (1945).

actions of individual territorial governments often appear to be ineffectual by comparison. Essential services, such as computer programming, can easily be "shipped" across nation-state boundaries and can even be produced multinationally. The international production and distribution of merchandise mean that communities around the country – and even around the world – increasingly purchase the same name-brand goods and shop at the same stores. Online communities (to the extent that we are willing to call them communities) ignore territoriality altogether and instead are organized around shared interests. People fly more than ever, carry telephones and laptops with them as they travel, and keep in touch by e-mail.

All of these changes radically reshape the relationship of people to their geography.[30] As Joshua Meyrowitz observed more than twenty

[30] Some have conceptualized this shift as a change in the way we experience and represent space and time. *See, e.g.*, Anthony Giddens, *The Consequences of Modernity* 64 (1990) (describing the problem of today's higher-level "time-space distanciation," which has stretched local and distant social forms); Tomlinson, *supra* note 9, at 4–5 (describing the way airline journeys transform "spatial experience into temporal experience"). In that regard, it is interesting to link this change to shifts in the arts. For example, in visual arts, Friedland and Boden have observed that the fall of the linear perspective of early Renaissance painting occurred along with the rediscovery of Euclidean geometry and the emergence of spatial representation, such as maps. Roger Friedland & Deirdre Boden, NowHere: An Introduction to Space, Time and Modernity, in *NowHere: Space, Time and Modernity* 1, 2 (Roger Friedland & Deirdre Boden eds., 1994) (citing Denis Cosgrove, Prospect, Perspective, and the Evolution of the Landscape Idea, in 10 *Transcripts of the Institute of British Geographers* 45, 46–8 (1985)). In the late nineteenth century, the impressionists "fragmented light (and thus time)." *Id.* at 1–2. Then, postimpressionists such as Cézanne built "a new language, abandoning linear and aerial perspective and making spatial dispositions arise from the modulations of color." *Id.* at 2 (citing Charles Taylor, *Sources of the Self: The Making of the Modern Identity* 468 (1989)). The cubists went still further, "providing simultaneous images of the same moment from different points in space and multiple views of a single scene at various points in time." *Id.* at 2; *see also* Stephen Kern, Cubism, Camouflage, Silence, and Democracy: A Phenomenological Approach, in *NowHere: Space, Time and Modernity*, *supra*, at 163, 167 (describing how artists such as "Picasso and Braque gave space the same colors, texture and substantiality as material objects and made objects and space interpenetrate so as to be almost indistinguishable"). Likewise the development of the modern novel – with books such as Marcel Proust, *Remembrance of Things Past* (C.K. Scott Moncrieff & Terence Kilmartin trans., 1954); James Joyce, *Finnegans Wake*

years ago, electronic media create "a nearly total dissociation of physical place and social 'place.' When we communicate through telephone, radio, television, or computer, where we are physically no longer determines where and who we are socially."[31] Meyrowitz pointed out that, historically, communication and travel were synonymous, and it was not until the invention of the telegraph that text messages could move more quickly than a messenger could carry them.[32] Thus, "informational differences between different places began to erode."[33] Moreover, many of the boundaries that define social settings by including and excluding participants – including walls, doors, barbed wire, and other physical and legal barriers – are less significant in a world where "the once consonant relationship between access to information and access to places has been greatly weakened."[34]

Given such changes, it is possible that the psychic burden of foreign jurisdiction is less significant today because of our increased contact with foreign places. On the other hand, we may feel the need to cling even more tenaciously to localism in the face of the encroaching global economic system.[35] Moreover, in either scenario the "we" is problematic. After all, different social groups, and different individuals, have very different degrees of exposure to and control over global flows of information, capital, and human migration.[36] Nevertheless, the important point is

(1939); and Virginia Woolf, *Mrs. Dalloway* (1925) – also mined changes in the equation between space and time.

[31] Meyrowitz, *supra* note 28, at 115.

[32] *See id.* at 116 (describing the impact of telegraphic technology).

[33] *Id.*

[34] *Id.* at 117.

[35] *Cf.* Giddens, *supra* note 30, at 65 ("The development of globalised social relations probably serves to diminish some aspects of nationalist feeling linked to nation-states (or some states) but may be causally involved with the intensifying of more localised nationalist sentiments.").

[36] Doreen Massey refers to this as the "power geometry of time-space compression." Doreen Massey, *Space, Place, and Gender* 149 (1994). She contrasts those who are "in charge" of time-space compression – "the jet-setters, the ones sending and receiving the faxes and the e-mail, holding the international conference calls ... distributing the films, controlling the news, organizing the investments" – with those who do a lot of physical

that if jurisdictional rules both reflect and construct social space, further investigation is needed in order to comprehend better the relationships among community affiliation, physical location, and personal identity in a world where the importance of territorial borders and of geographical distance is being challenged.

Jurisdiction and the Assertion of Community Dominion

When a transgressor behaves in some way contrary to society's moral code, the community can view the transgressor in one of two ways. First, the community can close ranks by defining itself in opposition to the transgressor and by treating the transgression purely as an *external* threat. Or, second, the community can claim dominion over the transgression by conceptualizing the transgressor as a member of the community who has committed what might be considered an *internal* offense.

The definition of a threat as internal or external is, in part, a question of jurisdiction. When a community exercises legal jurisdiction, it is symbolically asserting its dominion over an actor. This jurisdictional reach can serve to transform what otherwise might have been considered an external threat into an internal adjudication. Accordingly, the assertion of jurisdiction can be seen as one way that communities domesticate chaos.

In earlier work I have written about the surprisingly widespread and elaborate practice in medieval Europe and ancient Greece of putting on trial animals and inanimate objects that caused harm to human beings.[37]

moving but are not "in charge" of the process in the same way. *Id.* These people include those such as undocumented migrant workers who cross borders illegally, or those who lose their jobs to less expensive labor abroad, or those whose livelihood is affected by global currency fluctuations. Thus, social conceptions of space, distance, and community definition are, of course, themselves varied and contested.

[37] *See* Paul Schiff Berman, An Observation and a Strange but True "Tale": What Might the Historical Trials of Animals Tell Us About the Transformative Potential of Law in American Culture? 52 *Hastings L.J.* 123 (2000) (using a discussion of animal trials to explore overlooked social benefits of legal proceedings); Paul Schiff Berman, Note, Rats, Pigs, and Statues on Trial: The Creation of Cultural Narratives in the Prosecution of Animals and Inanimate Objects, 69 *N.Y.U. L. Rev.* 288 (1994) (surveying the history

Although such trials may seem far removed from any discussion of contemporary jurisdictional rules, I believe they illuminate the symbolic content of such rules. In deciding how to respond to acts of violence or depredation caused by animals, communities were faced with a choice of whether to view the acts as internal or external threats. Random acts of violence caused by insensate agents undoubtedly generated a deep feeling of lawlessness: not so much the fear of laws' being broken, but the far worse fear that the world might not be a lawful place at all.[38] To combat such a fear, it may have been essential to view the animals not as uncontrollable natural forces belonging to the outside world, but as members of the community who could actually break the community's laws. By asserting dominion over the animals, members of communities could assure themselves that, even if the social order had been violated, at least there was *some* order, and not simply undifferentiated chaos.

Just as the animal trials implicitly communicated a symbolic message that nonhuman transgressors were nevertheless subject to human control, so too our contemporary notions of jurisdiction continue to be linked to the way we define both the limits of the community and who should be within its dominion. This exercise of jurisdiction, in and of itself, can be part of the process of healing after the breach of a social norm. For example, a person injured by a defective product may feel powerless to affect the behavior of a distant, seemingly uncontrollable corporation. Indeed, while animals may have been viewed as an uncontrollable "other" in medieval Europe, the products of global capitalism today likewise may seem to be external forces of destruction that obey only their own law. By bringing the corporation within local jurisdiction, the individual and the community may feel they have regained some control over their world.

of animal trials and analyzing their role in helping a community heal after a breach of the social order).

[38] Nicholas Humphrey, Foreword to E.P. Evans, *The Criminal Prosecution and Capital Punishment of Animals*, at xxv (1987) (1907) (articulating the strong fear of Greeks and medieval Europeans that "God was playing dice with the universe").

Finally, the need to assert community dominion may also be a significant part of the desire to use legal and quasi-legal proceedings to respond to atrocities such as war crimes, genocide, or crimes against humanity. For example, the French trial of accused Nazi war criminal Klaus Barbie arguably was concerned less with punishing the individual (who, after all, was extremely old and in failing health at the time of the trial) than about asserting France's authority and sense of control after a horrific and chaotic human tragedy.[39] Thus, the impulse to assert jurisdiction over a territorially distant outsider who "invades" a community is tied to the need to assert dominion in order to domesticate external chaos.

Jurisdiction and the Extension of Community Membership

The previous section discussed how the exercise of jurisdiction functions in part as a symbolic assertion of community *dominion*. A corollary to this observation is that the exercise of jurisdiction also symbolically extends a form of community *membership*. As discussed previously, a true outsider is either fought as an external threat or ignored entirely. By exercising jurisdiction, a community constructs a narrative whereby the outsider is not truly an outsider but is in some way a member of that community and subject to its norms.

A rather extreme example of this phenomenon is the death sentence issued by an Islamic leader against author Salman Rushdie. Chances are that if I had written the same novel as Rushdie, I would not have been treated in the same way. Instead, it is likely that I would have been dismissed as a total outsider or targeted in an ad hoc fashion as a purely external threat. The death sentence therefore reflects the fact that Rushdie was considered a *member* of the Islamic community. Even this violent exercise of jurisdiction acted to extend community membership.

[39] *See* Guyora Binder, Representing Nazism: Advocacy and Identity at the Trial of Klaus Barbie, 98 *Yale L.J.* 1321, 1322 (1989) (describing the intent of the trial as "pedagogical").

Similarly, by prosecuting war criminals or human rights abusers we are insisting that the defendants are members of the world community. Accordingly, the assertion of jurisdiction can be seen as an educative tool and not simply an exercise of coercive power. The community, in effect, tells the defendants that they share a membership bond with others and therefore cannot simply impose their will with impunity. Meanwhile, the assertion of jurisdiction also implicitly delivers a message to the public that the defendants are neither subhuman nor the agents of chaotic fate but are instead members of the world community to be considered in their full humanity and punished according to human law.

This idea of jurisdiction as the assertion of community membership may also have relevance in evaluating the usefulness of alternative legal procedures aimed at restorative justice, such as the use of truth commissions as a mechanism for societal reconciliation.[40] For example, the Truth and Reconciliation Commission (TRC) proceedings in South Africa attempted to restore psychic membership in the South African community to both victims and perpetrators. The TRC required that those perpetrators seeking amnesty both acknowledge the community's jurisdiction by appearing before the commission and address that community by recounting their misdeeds in an open forum.[41] Likewise, victims who for

[40] For example, truth commissions have been established in countries including Argentina, Bolivia, Chile, El Salvador, Guatemala, Haiti, the Phillipines, Rwanda, Somalia, South Africa, Uganda, and Uruguay. *See* Priscilla B. Hayner, *Unspeakable Truths: Confronting State Terror and Atrocity* 291–7 (2001) (listing twenty truth commissions established since 1982); Martha Minow, *Between Vengeance and Forgiveness: Facing History After Genocide and Mass Violence* 53–4 (1998) (describing the establishment of truth commissions in African and South American countries); Michael P. Scharf, The Case for a Permanent International Truth Commission, 7 *Duke J. Comp. & Int'l L.* 375, 377–8 (1997) (providing a brief history of truth commissions and detailing their establishment in particular countries). Indeed, "truth commissions have proliferated, and now every nation emerging from dictatorship or war wants one. This year Nigeria, Ghana, Sierra Leone, Peru, Panama, East Timor, Yugoslavia, Bosnia and South Korea all began commissions or have them under way." Tina Rosenberg, Designer Truth Commissions, *N.Y. Times*, Dec. 9, 2001, § 6 (Magazine), at 66; *see also* Hayner, *supra*, at 36 (discussing the possibility of truth commissions in Indonesia, Colombia, and Bosnia).

[41] *See* Minow, *supra* note 40, at 55–7 (describing the conditions attached to the TRC's grant of amnesty).

years were not recognized as full-fledged members of the South African community were given an opportunity to speak about their pain and to enter into the community's legal system instead of remaining outside it. The TRC proceedings, therefore, implicitly expressed the hope that victims, perpetrators, and spectators could all be integrated into the new South African community.

Even in more commonplace legal proceedings, the idea of asserting community membership through jurisdiction may be important. For example, while a community may need to assert its dominion over the products of a distant corporation in order to feel some control over seemingly random misfortune, a multinational corporation may come to conceive of itself as a corporate citizen of many different localities because of the potential exercise of local jurisdiction. Accordingly, the exercise of jurisdiction may encourage corporate officials to rethink their sense of responsibility to communities far beyond the boundaries of their corporate headquarters.

In addition, the ability to assert the jurisdiction of a court may give people some sense of *their own* membership in the community. Prison inmates bringing civil rights actions against abusive guards, for example, may feel validated simply because they are able to invoke the jurisdiction of a court. Regardless of outcome, the fact that the inmates' grievances are aired and considered, however briefly, may give marginal members of society a greater sense of community affiliation.[42] As a result, the assertion of community dominion may be beneficial both for the community, which can assert its control over otherwise uncontrollable behavior, and for the individual, who achieves a form of community membership through the legal process. Even a criminal defendant is implicitly deemed to be a member of the community who has gone astray (and therefore retains certain rights), rather than a purely external pariah (who has no rights).[43]

[42] *See* Roland Acevedo, Thoughts of an Ex-Jailhouse Lawyer, *N.Y. L.J.*, Aug. 5, 1998, at 2 (describing the psychological benefit prison inmates receive from being able to bring a lawsuit in court even if the suit is ultimately unsuccessful).

[43] *But see* David Garland, *The Culture of Control: Crime and Social Order in Contemporary Society* 1–3 (2001) (charting the retreat in the United States and Britain, since the early

The assertion of community membership is relevant to discussions of Internet jurisdiction as well. As discussed previously, the growth of electronic communications is closely linked to our increasing global economic and psychological interdependence.[44] Online interaction contributes to our awareness of outsiders and our sense of connection with them. People develop friendships and business relationships regardless of physical proximity; they may even fall in love online. Many of the psychic bonds that in a previous era were shared only within the confines of one's local community now stretch far beyond any single geographical location. Given this change in economic and psychological interdependence, it would not be surprising to see the definition of community membership change as well. And if jurisdiction is one of the ways we express our intuitions about community membership, then jurisdictional rules, in turn, must evolve. Otherwise, we will risk being trapped in a legal doctrine that no longer represents the reality of modern life, just as the United States was trapped during the first half of the twentieth century when courts struggled to expand the strict territorial rule of *Pennoyer*.

Jurisdiction and the Assertion of Alternative Norms

We are accustomed to thinking of jurisdictional assertions as the unique province of a sovereign entity. The assertion of jurisdiction, however, can also open space for the articulation of norms that function as alternatives to, or even resistance to, sovereign power. Thus, we can go even further than just thinking about assertions of jurisdiction beyond geographical borders. In addition, we can get beyond the border that defines jurisdictional assertions as the unique province of sovereignty. For example, in seventeenth-century England, common law courts began to issue writs of

1970s, from a crime control model concerned with criminal rehabilitation to an "official policy of punitive sentiments and expressive gestures that appear oddly archaic and downright anti-modern").

[44] *See* Meyrowitz, *supra* note 28, at 115–17 (discussing the relationship between electronic media and the erosion of social boundaries).

prohibition in order to prevent the rival Court of High Commission from hearing certain cases.[45] In response, some critics argued that the common law courts were overreaching and that the question of which court had proper jurisdiction to hear a case could only be resolved by the king because the authority of all judges derived from him.[46] In *Prohibitions del Roy*, Lord Coke describes himself as having replied to such characterizations of the king's authority:

> [T]rue it was, that God had endowed his Majesty with excellent Science, and great Endowments of Nature; but his Majesty was not learned in the Laws of his Realm of England.... With which the King was greatly offended, and said, that then he should be under the Law, which was Treason to affirm, as he said; to which I said, that Bracton saith, *Quod Rex non debet esse sub homine, sed sub Deo et Lege* [that the King should not be under man, but under God and the Law].[47]

Thus, Coke refused to place the king beyond or above the domain of law.

By challenging the king and affirming the jurisdiction of the common law courts, Coke asserted the primacy of law even over sovereign power. In doing so, however, he also stripped the courts of the very "institutional protection ... that ordinarily stands behind" courts and enforces their orders.[48] After all, who is to enforce legal jurisdiction when the king stands in opposition? This story makes clear both that courts can exercise power separate from (and perhaps contrary to) the governing power of

[45] *See* Catherine Drinker Bowen, *The Lion and the Throne: The Life and Times of Sir Edward Coke* 295 (1956) (explaining how Sir Edward Coke attacked the Ecclesiastical High Commission through writs of prohibition); 12 Edward Coke, *Reports of Sir Edward Coke* 42 (E. Nutt et al. eds., 4th ed. 1738) (1655) (discussing the use of writs in *Nicholas Fuller's Case*).

[46] *See, e.g.*, 12 Coke, *supra* note 45, at 63 (describing the debate as to who had authority to decide jurisdiction in *Prohibitions del Roy*, 77 Eng. Rep. 1342 (K.B. 1607)); *see also* Bowen, *supra* note 45, at 303–4 (discussing the debate over the king's "absolute power and authority" to decide legal disputes).

[47] 12 Coke, *supra* note 45, at 65.

[48] Robert Cover, The Folktales of Justice: Tales of Jurisdiction, in *Narrative, Violence, and the Law: The Essays of Robert Cover* 173, 186 (Martha Minow et al. eds., 1992) [hereinafter Cover, Folktales of Justice].

the state and that the exercise of such power is risky and always contingent on broader acceptance by communities (and coercive authorities) over time. Nevertheless, despite the risk, the rhetorical assertion of jurisdiction itself can have an important effect.[49] For example, Coke's memorialization of this jurisdictional assertion in his treatise was undoubtedly part of the Enlightenment movement to limit the power of kings and assert a higher rule of law. Thus, one can see a direct line from Coke to Thomas Paine, who declared that, in the new United States of America, "law is King."[50]

It is, of course, commonplace to say that courts lack their own enforcement power, making them dependent on the willingness of states and individuals to follow judicial orders. This observation is often used as an argument for the irrelevance of international law itself. As we saw in Chapter 3, because such "law" is subject to the realpolitik demands of pure power, so the argument goes, it is not really law at all. Domestic law is substantially similar, however, because courts can only exercise authority to the extent that someone with coercive power chooses to carry out the legal judgments issued.[51]

[49] There is some evidence that Coke's version of his actions is not accurate and that he actually capitulated to the king's authority. *See* Bowen, *supra* note 45, at 305–6 (observing that some historians have rejected Coke's account, relying on other seventeenth-century evidence, which indicates that Coke actually threw himself on the mercy of the king). Even if this is so, however, the rhetorical assertion of jurisdiction in his treatise might still have persuasive value over time.

[50] Thomas Paine, *Common Sense*, in *The Complete Writings of Thomas Paine* 1, 29 (Philip S. Foner ed., 1945) (1776).

[51] Of course, the question of whether there is a fundamental difference between international and domestic law has been a subject of debate within political theory. *See generally* Kimberly Hutchings, Political Theory and Cosmopolitan Citizenship, in *Cosmopolitan Citizenship* 3 (Kimberly Hutchings & Roland Dannreuther eds., 1999) (providing an overview of the various positions in this debate). That debate is beyond the scope of this chapter. I note only that many of the international relations realist objections to international law have been made by American legal realists and critical legal studies scholars with regard to domestic law as well. *See, e.g.*, Laura A. Dickinson, Using Legal Process to Fight Terrorism: Detentions, Military Commissions, International Tribunals, and the Rule of Law, 75 *S. Cal. L. Rev.* 1407, 1477–8 (2002) (linking international relations realist claims to arguments made by critical legal theorists about domestic law).

Thus, the essence of law is that it makes aspirational judgments about the future, the power of which depends on whether the judgments accurately reflect evolving norms of the communities that must choose to obey them. If this is so, then we might view extraterritorial lawmaking as substantially similar to lawmaking within territorial bounds. To take the French prosecution of Yahoo! as an example, it is true that the court's command is only enforceable if an American authority will agree to enforce it, but the same court's decision against Yahoo!'s French subsidiary is similarly dependent on the enforcement power of a sovereign. After all, if the executive branch of the French government were to refuse to enforce the order against the subsidiary, that order would have no more force than the order against the American parent.

In addition, if the assertion of jurisdiction is always an assertion of community dominion, then judicial decisions rely not only on that particular community's acquiescence, but also the willingness of other communities to recognize and enforce the jurisdictional assertion. This is a sort of "natural law of jurisdiction"[52] in which jurisdictional assertions depend solely on the rhetorical force of their articulation of norms to entice allegiance. Thus, a court asked to enforce a prior court's judgment would always need to consider whether the prior judgment properly spoke for a relevant community and whether the substantive norms articulated in the judgment are attractive in order to determine whether the jurisdictional assertion and the substantive norms should be recognized.

This more capacious understanding of jurisdiction provides a more appropriate framework for understanding law in a global era than sovereignty does. Indeed, as discussed previously, sovereigntist territoriality may be a concept ill-suited to an understanding of law beyond borders because sovereignty tends to focus our attention on who possesses coercive enforcement power. In contrast, jurisdiction implicates the more expansive idea of norm articulation and persuasion. After all,

[52] Robert M. Cover, The Supreme Court, 1982 Term – Foreword: Nomos and Narrative, 97 *Harv. L. Rev.* 4, 58 (1983) [hereinafter Cover, Nomos and Narrative].

the word "jurisdiction" derives from Latin roots literally meaning "to speak the law," and we must therefore look not so much at the power to *enforce* legal norms as at the ability to *articulate* them. This is a crucial distinction because in a world of law beyond borders the mere speaking of legal norms may, over time, persuade others to enforce them.

As a result, we can transform the idea of jurisdiction as solely a tool of territorially based enforcement power into the more capacious understanding of jurisdiction as a discursive space. Of course enforcement power (and who controls it) is important. But ultimately enforcement depends on whether those who assert jurisdiction can rhetorically persuade those who possess coercive power (the police force, the military) to enforce the judgment issued. Thus, it is not only the state that might assert jurisdiction, but any community that purports to use the language of law to articulate a norm as a group. Acknowledging community affiliations that exist apart from the nation-state therefore becomes crucial. And by analyzing the social meaning of our affiliations across space, we can think about various alternative conceptions of community.[53]

From this perspective, law is not merely the coercive command of a sovereign power, but a language for imagining alternative future worlds. Moreover, various norm-generating communities – not just the sovereign – are always contesting the shape of such worlds.[54] Jurisdiction becomes the way a community – any community – seizes the language of law, attempts to construct itself as a coherent community, and offers a norm, thereby asserting its "soft" power.[55] The assertion of jurisdiction is therefore a mechanism that opens up an opportunity for negotiation across distance.

This idea of legal jurisdiction as rhetorical persuasion is played out repeatedly in a world of law and globalization, because entities without

[53] For further discussion of these multiple forms of community, *see* Paul Schiff Berman, The Globalization of Jurisdiction, 151 *U. Pa. L. Rev.* 311, 480–82 (2002), at 472–95.

[54] *See* Cover, Nomos and Narrative, *supra* note 52, at 43.

[55] *See* Joseph S. Nye Jr., *The Paradox of American Power: Why the World's Only Superpower Can't Go It Alone* 9 (2002).

literal enforcement power often exert normative force through the assertion of jurisdiction. Such assertions of jurisdiction often have real impact despite the lack of enforcement power. Accordingly, we lose much of the story if we focus solely on the coercive commands of a sovereign state.

Constructing a Cosmopolitan Pluralist Framework for Jurisdiction

Having identified four ways in which the assertion of jurisdiction both constructs and reflects social meaning, what remains to be investigated more fully is the extent to which accepted notions of legal jurisdiction actually accord with the social meanings at play in the contemporary world. Territorially fixed boundaries remain the primary way of differentiating jurisdictional space, and nation-states remain the primary jurisdictional communities. How well does this legal conception actually map onto social space? The answer to such a question cannot be left in the legal arena, where the discussion is often limited to debates about historical precedent, political philosophy, or economic efficiency. Instead, the relationship between jurisdiction and social understandings of space, borders, and community is a topic that should engage theorists from a variety of disciplines. Such theorists might help forge a more complex account of the world onto which jurisdictional rules are imposed. They also might point the way to alternative conceptions of jurisdiction grounded in, and reflective of, this more complex view of the world. New conceptions of jurisdiction could allow for a more cosmopolitan and pluralist understanding of the variety of community affiliations people experience in their lives.

State-Sanctioned Courts

As to more traditional, state-based, legal authority, courts could use an analysis of community affiliation and effects as the touchstone for jurisdictional determinations, rather than focusing solely on the counting of contacts with a territorially bounded locale. Such a change in focus would alter jurisdictional jurisprudence in a number of respects. For example, under most current jurisdictional analyses, a court assumes that the plaintiff is appropriately within the court's jurisdiction because the plaintiff, by bringing the lawsuit, has voluntarily submitted to its jurisdiction and is physically present within its territorial bounds. A court employing a community-based jurisdictional analysis, however, would need to determine whether either (1) the plaintiff can appropriately be defined as a member of the community asserting jurisdiction or (2) even if the plaintiff is not a community member, the issue the plaintiff raises is of such significance to the community that jurisdiction can be justified.[56]

As to the first inquiry – the plaintiff's community membership – a number of factors may be relevant. Some are familiar from current jurisdictional analyses: What is the plaintiff's citizenship? Where is the plaintiff usually found? But others are significantly different. For example, while jurisdictional inquiries often look only to the citizenship or primary residence of the party,[57] a community-based model might find relevant community ties anywhere the party resides for a significant period, regardless of whether or not it is a primary residence. In addition, the presence of a relevant subcommunity within the jurisdiction might be a factor (for example, if the plaintiff has ties to others within the community based on common kinship, ethnicity, or interests).

[56] This inquiry is sometimes captured by a court's consideration of the plaintiff's standing to bring suit. The doctrine of standing, however, often incorporates other inquiries – such as whether the plaintiff suffered sufficient harm – that are distinct from an investigation of the nexus between the dispute and the community where the court sits. *See, e.g.*, *Whitmore v. Arkansas*, 495 U.S. 149, 155–6 (1990) (listing the various requirements to establish proper standing).

[57] *See, e.g.*, *Milliken v. Meyer*, 311 U.S. 457, 463 (1940) ("The state which accords [a defendant] privileges and affords protection to him and his property by virtue of his domicile may also exact reciprocal duties."); *cf. Restatement (Second) of Conflict of Laws* § 11 (1971) ("Every person has a domicil at all times and ... no person has more than one domicil at a time.").

Even if the plaintiff does not possess such ties, jurisdiction would still be appropriate if the issue raised in the suit is of great importance to the community. For example, as we have seen, grave human rights violations might trigger various forms of universal or transnational jurisdiction.[58] Jurisdiction might also be appropriate over a defendant who is a member of the community even if the plaintiff is not, because the community still has an obligation to police one of its own.

Turning to the defendant, under a community-based analysis jurisdiction is proper if (1) the defendant can be deemed a member of the same community as the plaintiff or (2) the defendant can be deemed a member of the forum community. Thus, for example, if plaintiff and defendant are bound by ethnic ties or are linked through transnational networks, jurisdiction might be appropriate even if the defendant lacked specific ties with the territorial location of the court. Conversely, even if plaintiff and defendant were not particularly linked, if the defendant can be deemed a member of the community where the court sits, jurisdiction would also be proper.

In order to determine the community affiliation of the defendant, courts again could consider a variety of factors. These include the citizenship and residence of the defendant, the amount of activity the defendant conducts in the forum community, and the extent of the defendant's impact on the community. The jurisdictional analysis in criminal cases would be similar, focusing on the defendant's own community identification as well as the extent of the defendant's community activities or the impact of the defendant's activities on the community. Such traditional factors as "purposeful availment" or "volitional contacts" could be substantially retained but recast as an analysis of whether the defendant has become aligned with or bound to the community at issue.

[58] Although, as discussed in Chapters 4 and 5, a cosmopolitan conception of jurisdiction rejects a universalist approach that seeks to make world community citizenship the only relevant jurisdictional affiliation, it in no way denies the importance of local communities' asserting universal jurisdiction in specific cases.

In all of these inquiries, the determination of community affiliation contains both a subjective and an objective element. The felt and expressed bonds of individuals are relevant to the calculus, but such bonds might have objective indicia, such as citizenship, travel patterns, telephone records, social activities, financial transactions, and so forth. In addition, a community severely affected by transnational activity might see fit to assert community dominion even over a distant actor, based solely on the impact of the defendant's activities.

Under current U.S. law, there is a great deal of uncertainty regarding jurisdiction over territorially distant corporations whose products enter the "stream of commerce," become incorporated in a larger product, and end up causing harm someplace far away.[59] This question is only difficult, however, if one is focused on contacts with a territory. A community-based analysis, in contrast, would likely result in the assertion of jurisdiction over such a territorially distant defendant if its products regularly end up in a given community and cause harm there. In such circumstances, courts following this approach would recognize that the reality of global capitalism means that companies form transnational bonds with consumers territorially removed from them.

Indeed, territorial location is often largely irrelevant to the actual dispute, and yet territory takes on inflated significance in jurisdictional

[59] *See Asahi Metal Indus. Co. v. Superior Court, 480 U.S. 102 (1987)*. In *Asahi*, four Justices indicated that simply placing a product into the stream of commerce would not be sufficient to establish jurisdiction wherever that product happened to end up. *Id.* at 112 (O'Connor, J., joined by Rehnquist, C.J., Powell, Scalia, JJ.). Instead, these Justices would require some sort of "additional conduct" by the defendant that would demonstrate that the defendant had the specific "intent or purpose to serve the market" in the state exercising jurisdiction. *Id.* Four other Justices (including Justice Brennan) disagreed, arguing that simply placing a product into the stream of commerce was sufficient. *Id.* at 117 (Brennan, J., concurring in part and concurring in the judgment). The ninth Justice, Justice Stevens, found that, based on the facts of the case, jurisdiction was improper under either test and therefore declined to choose between them. *Id.* at 121–22 (Stevens, J., concurring in part and concurring in the judgment). As a result, neither rationale achieved a majority, and as of this writing the Supreme Court has not directly addressed the stream of commerce question again.

inquiries. For example, in France's efforts to prosecute Yahoo!, location was largely a red herring. To begin with, no one doubted that the French court could assert jurisdiction over Yahoo.fr, Yahoo!'s French subsidiary; the dispute only concerned yahoo.com. But, of course, that distinction, which was based on territory, was immaterial to Internet users because those wishing to access the proscribed materials could just as easily type "yahoo.com" as "yahoo.fr" into their browsers, thereby circumventing any restrictions placed on yahoo.fr. Thus, the different "locations" of yahoo.fr and yahoo.com were, from a practical perspective, completely unimportant. Similarly, focusing on minutiae such as the physical location either of Yahoo!'s Web servers (an arbitrary and easily changeable detail) or of the safety deposit box housing the share certificate indicating Yahoo.com's ownership of Yahoo.fr completely sidesteps the core question of whether Yahoo! should be deemed within the dominion of France. Thus, a territorial analysis tends to preclude any engagement with the fundamental issues surrounding how best to negotiate normative differences among multiple communities. And, as discussed previously, focusing on territorial location tends to result in jurisdictional stalemate because either U.S. law reaches "into" France extraterritorially or France's prosecution reaches "into" the United States extraterritorially, with no territorially based means of resolving the conundrum.

In contrast, a cosmopolitan conception, because it deemphasizes territorial location and recognizes the importance of multiple communities, would focus on relevant community affiliation, regardless of territory. Such an analysis would suggest piercing the corporate form and analyzing Yahoo!'s substantive connections to French customers and the global Internet market, which were numerous.[60] Thus, the French court's assertion of jurisdiction can be justified on those grounds (though significantly they were not the stated basis of the judgment). But whatever the

[60] *See* Paul Schiff Berman, Towards a Cosmopolitan Vision of Conflict of Laws: Redefining Governmental Interests in a Global Era, 153 *U. Pa. L. Rev.* 1819, 1878 (2005); Joel R. Reidenberg, Yahoo and Democracy on the Internet, 42 *Jurimetrics* 261, 267 (2002).

ultimate result, it seems clear that the territorial formalisms with which the debate was fought simply cannot provide a rational framework for making jurisdictional judgments.

Other aspects of traditional inquiries would also be less important under a more cosmopolitan, community-based approach. For example, the purported inconvenience to the defendant of having to defend a suit far from home can be part of the analysis of whether a defendant should be deemed a member of the community, but it no longer takes on such significance as an independent factor. This is appropriate because in a world of rapid transportation, instant wireless communication, and even virtual courtrooms, defending a lawsuit in a distant physical location is far less burdensome (both literally and psychically) than it once was. Likewise the "foreseeability" of being brought into a particular court, though often invoked in U.S. Supreme Court doctrine,[61] is of little help given that, in an increasingly interconnected world, it is always foreseeable that activity in one place will have effects in many faraway locations. Moreover, as many scholars have pointed out, "foreseeability" is a circular test because whether one foresees being subject to jurisdiction in a particular court depends in large part on what courts have previously determined is reasonably foreseeable.[62] Thus, little is lost by jettisoning this analytical metric.

[61] *See, e.g.*, *World-Wide Volkswagen Corp. v. Woodson*, 444 U.S. 286, 297 (1980) ("[T]he foreseeability that is critical to due process analysis is ... that the defendant's conduct and connection with the forum State are such that he should reasonably anticipate being haled into court there.").

[62] *See, e.g.*, David Wille, Personal Jurisdiction and the Internet – Proposed Limits on State Jurisdiction over Data Communications in Tort Cases, 87 *Ky. L.J.* 95, 136 (1998) ("The purposeful availment requirement stems from the notion that defendants should be able to plan their conduct knowing where that conduct will subject them to jurisdiction. But ... [d]efendants only have reasonable expectations about where they will be haled into court because courts have created such expectations." (citation omitted)); Burk, Federalism in Cyberspace, 25 *Conn. L. Rev.* 1095, 1118 (1996) (opining that a forseeability inquiry amounts to nothing more than the idea that "defendants should reasonably anticipate being haled into any court into which they should reasonably anticipate being haled"); *cf.* Luther L. McDougal III, Judicial Jurisdiction: From a Contacts to an Interest Analysis, 35 *Vand. L. Rev.* 1, 10 (1982) (noting the impossibility of predicting how a court will rule on the "fairness" element of minimum contacts). For

Nevertheless, it is important to emphasize that a community-based analysis would not necessarily result in broader assertions of jurisdiction than under current jurisdictional schemes. For example, the requirement that the plaintiff have community ties with the forum might well make so-called forum shopping more difficult because plaintiffs could not simply choose the community with the most convivial law regardless of social ties. Likewise, a community-based approach might not permit transient-presence jurisdiction, where the defendant is present within the physical boundaries of a territory only briefly, or for an unrelated reason.[63] Such transient-presence jurisdiction is generally permissible under territorial schemes, leading to such ludicrous activities as service of process in an airplane as it flies over a territorial jurisdiction.[64] By inquiring about substantive ties to a community rather than formal contacts with a location, a community-based approach would render such jurisdictional assertions more amenable to challenge. Finally, there might be occasions when a contacts-based inquiry would find, say, that a couple of Web "hits" in a jurisdiction would be sufficient to render a defendant subject to suit there. A community-based approach, however, would go beyond counting contacts to inquire about the substantive bonds formed between the member of the forum community and the territorially distant actor.

To see how such an approach might play out, we can point to two examples, one that broadens the jurisdictional reach and one that narrows it. First, a more cosmopolitan jurisdictional inquiry would require governmental actors to obey their community's norms regardless of where, territorially, those actions take place. This means that in the famous "Does

a discussion of this problem within a more general analysis of circularity in constitutional adjudication, *see* Michael Abramowicz, Constitutional Circularity, 49 *UCLA L. Rev.* 1, 64–5 (2001).

[63] *See, e.g.*, *Burnham v. Superior Court,* 495 U.S. 604, 610–19 (1990) (Scalia, J., joined by Rehnquist, C.J., White, Kennedy, J.J.) (finding jurisdiction based on mere transient presence consonant with traditional practice at the time of the adoption of the Fourteenth Amendment).

[64] *See, e.g.*, *Grace v. MacArthur,* 170 F. Supp. 442, 447 (E.D. Ark. 1959) (permitting assertion of jurisdiction in such circumstances).

the Constitution follow the flag?" debate, the answer would emphatically be yes. Accordingly, a facility completely controlled and operated by the United States, whether in Guantánamo Bay, Cuba, or at Abu Ghraib prison in Iraq, would be subject to U.S. constitutional norms.

An important statement of this principle can be found in *United States v. Tiede*. In that case, a foreign national accused of hijacking a Polish aircraft abroad was tried under German substantive law in Berlin in a court created by the United States. The U.S. court held that, despite the use of German substantive law, the foreign national was entitled to jury trial as a matter of U.S. constitutional right because the U.S. court must act in accordance with the Constitution even when situated beyond U.S. territorial borders.[65] According to the court, "[i]t is a first principle of American life – not only life at home but life abroad – that everything American public officials do is governed by, measured against, and must be authorized by the United States Constitution."[66]

While this sort of analysis would broaden jurisdictional reach, in other cases we see the opposite. Thus, some U.S. courts, in analyzing their jurisdiction over defendants on the basis of content posted online, have eschewed a focus on the number of "contacts" with a locality and have instead analyzed the community affiliation of the defendant. Accordingly, a defendant who operates a Website that does not create substantive community ties in a distant jurisdiction might not be subject to suit there even if there are Internet contacts with that jurisdiction. For example, in *Young v. New Haven Advocate*, Virginia courts were denied

[65] *United States v. Tiede,* 86 F.R.D. 227 (U.S. Ct. Berlin 1979) at 247–51.

[66] *Id.* at 244; *see also DKT Mem'l Fund Ltd. v. Agency for Int'l Dev.,* 887 F.2d 275, 307–8 (D.C. Cir. 1989) (Ginsburg, R.B., J., dissenting in part) ("[J]ust as our flag carries its message… both at home and abroad, so does our Constitution and the values it expresses." (alteration in original) (citation and internal quotation marks omitted)); *cf. United States v. Balsys,* 524 U.S. 666, 701–2 (1998) (Ginsburg, J., dissenting) (expressing the view that "the Fifth Amendment privilege against self-incrimination prescribes a rule of conduct generally to be followed by our Nation's officialdom" and "should command the respect of United States interrogators, whether the prosecution reasonably feared by the examinee is domestic or foreign").

jurisdiction over Connecticut newspapers, regardless of Internet contacts, because content of the newspapers' Websites was "decidedly local."[67]

Most important, the cosmopolitan pluralist approach to jurisdiction requires that courts make explicit an inquiry that current jurisdictional rules obscure. If jurisdiction is in part about the assertion of community dominion over a distant actor, then courts should consider the nature of the community that has allegedly been harmed, the relationship of the dispute to that community, and the social meaning of asserting dominion over the actor in question. Accordingly, the jurisdictional inquiry becomes a site for discussion about both the nature of community affiliation and the changing role of territorial borders. The precise contours of the jurisdictional norms that would develop from this process are impossible to predict and would undoubtedly evolve over time. The crucial point, however, is that these discussions would not be truncated by a formulaic test that bears scant relationship to the core questions underlying the social meaning of jurisdiction.

Nonstate Communities

A truly pluralist conception of jurisdiction also allows us to make sense of *nonstate* assertions of jurisdiction. Consider Robert Cover's invocation of the bold (or utopian) impulse of a nonstate actor to assert jurisdiction:

> Imagine yourself a tribunal. Pretend you have an audience – a community of some sort that will recognize you as a tribunal. Now, go all the way. What grandeur of transformation of the normative universe

[67] *Young v. New Haven Advocate,* 315 F.3d 256 (4th Cir. 2003); *see also Bensusan Restaurant Corp. v. King,* 126 F.2d 25 (2d Cir. 1997) (concluding that Missouri cabaret could not be sued in New York for domain name trademark violation because cabaret was of "local character"); *Cybersell, Inc. v. Cybersell, Inc.,* 130 F.3d 414 (9th Cir.1997) (analyzing whether Florida corporation, through its Website, had created any substantive ties to Arizona, rather than focusing on the number of contacts). *See also* Berman, The Globalization of Jurisdiction, *supra* note 53, at 512–33 (discussing the implications of a community affiliation analysis).

> would you perform? Will you simply issue a general writ of peace? A warrant for justice notwithstanding facts and law? Will you order everyone to be good? Perhaps, perhaps you will judge the dead? Or even bring God as a defendant? The possibilities are endless and the question arises whether or why one should or should not try something outlandish, impossible, or just plain daring.[68]

The idea of imagining oneself a tribunal sounds fanciful. After all, we might think, people cannot simply construct their own legal jurisdiction. But that is true only if we accept a reified conception of jurisdiction based on state sovereigns acting within an unchanging set of legal boundaries. Such a conception, however, has been challenged throughout this book both because it is normatively unjustifiable as a way of capturing actual community identifications and social understandings of space, and because it fails to describe adequately the increasingly extraterritorial and nonstate nature of actual legal practice. Moreover, by imagining the creation of jurisdiction we can see the transformative way in which alternative assertions of legal jurisdiction can be linked to the articulation and development of alternative norms and community definitions.

Looking more closely at the process of jurisdiction creation, we can imagine a nonstate community coming together and purporting to adjudicate a dispute.[69] Obviously, its judgment is not self-executing; some entity with police power must enforce it. Thus, the question becomes not whether a community can assert jurisdiction, but whether other communities are willing to give deference to the judgment rendered and enforce it as if it were their own. This is the process of judgment recognition

[68] Cover, Folktales of Justice, *supra* note 48, at 187.

[69] Robert Cover offers the example of a group of Jews in a small city in Galilee in 1538. This group attempted to constitute a Jewish court even though its authority to do so was dubious. Significantly, the leaders of the group apparently determined that they could not assert jurisdiction on their own. Thus, they proclaimed their act in a message sent to Jerusalem seeking recognition. *Id.* at 190–2. Cover suggests that such approval was necessary not only as a matter of religious doctrine, but also because, without assent from Jerusalem, it was hardly likely that the rest of Judaism would take the experiment seriously. *Id.* at 193.

familiar to those who study conflict of laws (and which will be discussed in chapter 9). A tribunal asserts jurisdiction over a dispute, and then other jurisdictions must decide whether to confer legitimacy on that tribunal by recognizing and enforcing its judgment. Thus, even at the moment that a community daringly invents its own legal jurisdiction, it is immediately forced to acknowledge that its invention is limited by the willingness of others to accept the judgment as normatively legitimate.[70]

In order to make this interplay between lawmaking entities more concrete, consider a run-of-the-mill slip-and-fall case involving two citizens of a state.[71] It makes some sense to think that such a case should be heard by the courts of that state. But what if the slip-and-fall case is between two members of an insular immigrant community that happens to be located within that state? Assume that the community's norms call for a remedy that does not exist under the state law: something alien, but not extreme, perhaps a ritual delivery of food and a public apology. Further assume that the injured party would prefer this remedy to the damages that might be available in state court. In this case, it is not clear why the state court should assert jurisdiction (or if it does, why it should not defer to the community-based remedy).

This scenario is not hypothetical. Indeed, sharia courts, established by Muslim communities in Western states, often pose precisely this challenge. And if the parties and the dispute are internal to this community, it may be that imposition of state law based solely on territory may simply be an inappropriate imperialism. On the other hand, if the jurisprudential practices of the insular community are so illiberal or beyond the pale (for example, if the punishment for a relatively minor offense were stoning), then even the deference that might be owed to a nonstate jurisdiction could be overcome.

[70] As Cover points out, though law is a bridge to an alternative set of norms, the bridge begins not in "alternity" but in reality. Therefore, there are real constraints on the engineering of that bridge. *See id.* at 187 ("If law ... is a bridge from *reality* to a new world there must be some constraints on its engineering. Judges must dare, but what happens when they lose that reality?").

[71] I am grateful to Peter Spiro for suggesting this hypothetical.

Of course, if one of the parties to our slip-and-fall case is *not* a member of the insular community, then it is far more likely (and acceptable) for the court to impose territorially based law. Yet, even here a cosmopolitan pluralist approach would seek ways to mediate between the conflicting norms, both in formal mediation processes and in any subsequent judicial intervention.

We have already seen how formal international tribunals, though established by agreements of nation-states, can contribute to the generation of international standards that ultimately limit state prerogatives. Here the process of jurisdictional assertion and rhetorical persuasion has helped to develop norms over time. For example, one of the great accomplishments of the war crimes tribunals established after World War II was "the capacity of the event to project a new legal meaning into the future."[72] As Charles Wyzanski, who originally opposed the creation of the Nuremberg tribunals, later acknowledged, "the outstanding accomplishment of the trial, *which could never have been achieved by any more summary executive action*, is that it crystalized the concept that there already is inherent in the international community a machinery both of the expression of international criminal law and for its enforcement."[73] Significantly, Wyzanski's statement reveals that he came to believe not only that the tribunals were legitimate, but also that they served a norm-creating function that went beyond the realm of political

[72] Cover, Folktales of Justice, *supra* note 48, at 196. Robert Jackson, chief prosecutor at the Nuremberg trials, made a similar argument at the time: "We have also incorporated [the trial's] principles into a judicial precedent. 'The power of the precedent,' Mr. Justice Cardozo said, 'is the power of the beaten path.' One of the chief obstacles to this trial was the lack of a beaten path. A judgment such as has been rendered shifts the power of the precedent to the support of these rules of law. No one can hereafter deny or fail to know that the principles on which the Nazi leaders are adjudged to forfeit their lives constitute law – and law with a sanction." Report of Robert H. Jackson, United States Representative to the International Conference on Military Trials 437 (Int'l Org. & Conference Series II, U.S. Dep't of State Publ'n No. 3080, 1945).

[73] Charles E. Wyzanski Jr., Nuremberg in Retrospect, 178 *Atlantic Monthly* 56 (1946) (emphasis added), reprinted in *The New Meaning of Justice* 137, 144 (1965).

or military power and that could not have been achieved through the use of such power. Thus, sometimes the assertion of legal jurisdiction, even more than the assertion of military or political muscle, may help inculcate norms for the future.[74]

Moreover, these norms, once created and developed into a functioning body of human rights law, are not so easily circumscribed. Therefore, although it has been said that the Nuremberg and Tokyo trials after World War II themselves represented mere victors' justice,[75] the norms established in those trials have helped spawn a large body of human rights norms and a working consensus (fragile though it sometimes is) regarding enforcement of those norms.[76] I have already discussed the case of Augusto Pinochet, in which a Spanish judge asserted jurisdiction over the former Chilean dictator and almost succeeded in convincing the world to accede to that assertion. Other transnational human rights actions, both criminal and civil, have been attempted or are pending around the world, and the International Criminal Court, though controversial, has been established. This normative universe of human rights enforcement through legal apparatus is a direct result of the jurisdiction creation at Nuremberg.

Formal international trials such as those held at Nuremberg are not the only ways in which nonstate legal jurisdiction can be created and exercised, however. As discussed previously, nonstate communities also assert lawmaking power through more informal networks and organizations and through the slow accretion of social custom itself. And even day-to-day human encounters such as interacting with strangers on a public street, waiting in lines, and communicating with subordinates or superiors are all governed by what Michael Reisman has called "microlegal

[74] For an article using Cover's work to support the idea that international trials help create and develop norms, *see* Dickinson, *supra* note 51, at 1477–90.

[75] *See, e.g.*, Montgomery Belgion, *Victors' Justice* 42–131 (1949) (arguing that the alleged crimes were acts of war in which both sides were engaged and therefore did not warrant criminal punishment).

[76] *See* Cover, Folktales of Justice, *supra* note 48, at 196–7 (noting the precedents created by the Nuremberg and Tokyo trials).

systems."[77] Thus, law is found not only in the formal decisions of judges, legislators, and administrators, but also

> any place and any time that a group gathers together to pursue an objective. The rules, open or covert, by which they govern themselves, and the methods and techniques by which these rules are enforced is the law of the group. Judged by this broad standard, most lawmaking is too ephemeral to be even noticed. But when conflict within the group ensues, and it is forced to decide between conflicting claims, law arises in an overt and relatively conspicuous fashion. The challenge forces decision, and decisions make law.[78]

In some circumstances, official legal actors may delegate lawmaking authority to nonstate entities or recognize the efficacy of nonstate norms. For example, commercial litigation, particularly in the international arena, increasingly takes place before nonstate arbitral panels.[79] Likewise, nongovernmental standard-setting bodies, from Underwriters Laboratories (which tests electrical and other equipment) to the Motion Picture Association of America (which rates the content of films) to the International Accounting Standards Board (which sets global standards for financial reporting) to the Internet Corporation for Assigned Names and Numbers (which administers the Internet domain name system), construct detailed normative systems with the effect of law. Regulation of much financial market activity is left to private authorities such as

[77] For discussions of verbal and nonverbal cues that govern social behavior, *see* Michael Reisman, Lining Up: The Microlegal System of Queues, 54 *U. Cin. L. Rev.* 417 (1985); Michael Reisman, Looking, Staring and Glaring: Microlegal Systems and Public Order, 12 *Denv. J. Int'l L. & Pol'y* 165 (1983); Michael Reisman, Rapping and Talking to the Boss: The Microlegal System of Two People Talking, in *Conflict and Integration: Comparative Law in the World Today* 61 (Chuo Univ. ed., 1988).

[78] Walter Otto Weyrauch & Maureen Anne Bell, Autonomous Lawmaking: The Case of the "Gypsies," 103 *Yale L.J.* 323, 328 (1993) (quoting Thomas A. Cowan & Donald A. Strickland, *The Legal Structure of a Confined Microsociety*, at (Univ. of Cal., Berkeley, Internal Working Paper No. 34, 1965)).

[79] *See, e.g.*, Yves Dezalay & Bryant G. Garth, *Dealing in Virtue: International Commercial Arbitration and the Construction of a Transnational Legal Order* 5–9 (1996) (noting the "tremendous growth" in international commercial arbitration over the past twenty-five to thirty years).

stock markets or trade associations such as the National Association of Securities Dealers. And, to take a rather mundane example, lawmaking authority over sports events is generally left to nonstate entities (such as referees) whose decisions are not usually reviewable except within the system established by the sports authority or league.[80]

Significantly, the jurisdiction of all of these nonstate actors may be formally limited to their particular bounded communities, but the norms they articulate often seep into the decisions of state legal institutions. The most obvious example of state law's recognition of nonstate lawmaking is in the common law's ongoing incorporation of social custom and practice. Thus, after a period in which English common-law courts struggled with admiralty courts for jurisdiction over commercial cases with overseas elements, Lord Mansfield deftly reconceptualized large parts of mercantile law as part of the common law itself.[81] As scholars have recognized, "[d]ecisionmakers work under a continuing pressure to incorporate customary rules into their decisions."[82] Sometimes such incorporation is explicit, as when a statute is interpreted (or even supplanted) by reference to industry custom,[83] or when a law of sales

[80] *See, e.g.*, *Ga. High Sch. Ass'n v. Waddell*, 285 S.E.2d 7, 9 (Ga. 1981) (holding that a dispute over a referee's decision affecting the outcome of a high school football game was nonjusticiable). *But see PGA Tour, Inc. v. Martin*, 532 U.S. 661, 690 (2001) (ruling that a golf association had violated the Americans with Disabilities Act by preventing a partially disabled golfer from using a golf cart to compete); Bart Aronson, *Pinstripes and Jailhouse Stripes: The Case of "Athlete's Immunity,"* Find Law Corporate Counsel Center (Nov. 3, 2000), *available at* http://writ.corporate.findlaw.com/aronson/20001103.html (criticizing the blanket refusal to apply criminal law sanctions to athletes' actions during sporting events).

[81] *See, e.g.*, J. Milnes Holden, *The History of Negotiable Instruments in English Law* 114 (1955, reprint edition 1996)("His practice was to incorporate customs into his judgments, and so to establish them as binding rules for the future."). I am grateful to Clyde Spillinger for suggesting the Mansfield example.

[82] Weyrauch & Bell, *supra* note 78, at 330.

[83] *See, e.g.*, Lon L. Fuller, *Anatomy of the Law* 57–9 (1968) (arguing that the act of interpretation permits courts to adjust official legal norms to match custom or usage); James Willard Hurst, *Law and Economic Growth: The Legal History of the Lumber Industry in Wisconsin 1836–1915*, at 289–94 (1964) (describing the ways in which local norms in the Wisconsin lumber industry played a significant role in the way contract law was applied).

that would accord with merchant reality was adopted in the Uniform Commercial Code,[84] or when the rules promulgated by a small community of trade finance bankers were ultimately appropriated by the World Trade Organization in their official legal instruments.[85] Even when the impact of nonstate norms is unacknowledged, however, state-sponsored law may only be deemed legitimate to the extent that its official pronouncements reflect the "common understandings of private laws and customs."[86] Indeed, the invention of legal fictions often indicates that official norms are being adjusted to reflect more closely the dictates of nonstate norms and practices.

In addition, nonstate assertions of jurisdiction may sometimes take the guise of more formal legal proceedings. For example, in 1933, as five communists accused by Hitler of setting fire to the Reichstag building in Berlin were tried in Germany, Arthur Garfield Hays – counsel for the American Civil Liberties Union – helped to organize a "countertrial" in London.[87] This "trial" used the formalities of legal process to enact a "publicly deliberative drama."[88] According to Hays, the countertrial helped "to engage 'public opinion' and to set a 'valuable precedent' by which the actions of the German tribunal could be measured."[89] Even the German court ultimately felt the need to refute the findings of the London proceedings in order to combat the international impact

[84] *See* Zipporah Batshaw Wiseman, The Limits of Vision: Karl Llewellyn and the Merchant Rules, 100 *Harv. L. Rev.* 465, 503–19 (1987) (describing Karl Llewellyn's initial drafts of what later became Article 2 of the Uniform Commercial Code).

[85] *See* Janet Koven Levit, A Bottom-Up Approach to International Lawmaking: The Tale of Three Trade Finance Instruments, 30 *Yale J. Int'l L.* 125, 165 (2005) (describing the incorporation of an informal "Gentleman's Agreement" on export credits as a safe harbor in the WTO's Agreement on Subsidies and Countervailing Measures).

[86] Weyrauch & Bell, *supra* note 78, at 329.

[87] *See* Louis Anthes, Publicly Deliberative Drama: The 1934 Mock Trial of Adolph Hitler for "Crimes Against Civilization," 42 *Am. J. Legal Hist.* 391, 398–9 (1998) (describing the trial).

[88] *Id.* at 393. Anthes defines this term as "the improvising of legal formality to foster debate." *Id.*

[89] *Id.* at 399.

of the countertrial.[90] According to Arthur Koestler, the countertrial "was a unique event in criminal history" because it caused the German court to "concentrate its efforts on refuting accusations by a third, extraneous party."[91]

The following year, Hays and others organized a trial styled the "Case of Civilization Against Hitler" as part of a rally at Madison Square Garden in New York City.[92] Twenty thousand people in attendance and thousands more listening live over the radio heard an indictment, testimony from nearly two dozen witnesses, a summation by a former New York Court of Appeals judge, and a judgment of the court pronounced by a local minister.[93] Newspaper accounts the following day reported that Hitler had been found guilty of a high "crime against civilization"[94] and that the trial "rendered solemn judgment that the Nazi government stood convicted before the world."[95] Thus, nonstate assertions of jurisdiction may mobilize popular opinion in resistance to state-sanctioned norms and may also create a context for telling a counternarrative about historical events.

The Women's International War Crimes Tribunal 2000 represents a more recent, though similar, use of legal forms to construct an alternative history. This self-styled "peoples' tribunal" – convened in Tokyo December 8–12, 2000 – heard evidence concerning the criminal liability for crimes against humanity of both Japan and its high-ranking military and political officials for rape and sexual slavery arising out of Japanese military activity in the Asia-Pacific region during the 1930s and 1940s.[96]

[90] *See id.* (noting that in doing so, the German court was apparently seeking "to minimize the loss of international goodwill").

[91] Arthur Koestler, The Invisible Writing: Being the Second Volume of Arrow in the Blue, an Autobiography 200 (1954).

[92] *See* Anthes, *supra* note 87, at 391–4 (describing the trial in terms of both culture and politics).

[93] *Id.* at 391–2.

[94] Nazis "Convicted" of World "Crime" by 20,000 in Rally, *N.Y. Times*, Mar. 8, 1934, at 1.

[95] *Id.*

[96] Christine M. Chinkin, Women's International Tribunal on Japanese Military Sexual Slavery, 95 *Am. J. Int'l L.* 335, 335 (2001).

Frustrated by the denials of Japanese government officials[97] and by failure in lawsuits before state-sanctioned courts,[98] survivors of these alleged offenses turned to international nongovernmental organizations.[99] After initial conferences were held in Tokyo and Seoul, an International Organizing Committee for the tribunal was formed.

Indictments were presented by prosecution teams from ten countries: North and South Korea, China, Japan, the Philippines, Indonesia, Taiwan, Malaysia, East Timor, and the Netherlands. Indeed, "[t]he shared experience of Japanese colonization brought North and South Korean prosecutors together with a joint indictment – an expression of common purpose that continues to be unthinkable at the governmental level."[100] The prosecution presented evidence for three days. More than seventy-five survivors were present. Many of those present gave evidence, and other survivors recorded video interviews or signed affidavits that were entered into evidence by the prosecution. The panel of judges "represented a broad geographical distribution, expertise in diverse and relevant areas of domestic and international law, a mix of practitioner, judicial, and academic expertise, and ... an equitable gender balance."[101]

After the closing of evidence and argument, the judges began deliberating, assisted by a team of legal advisers. They prepared a preliminary judgment, which was presented to an audience of more than one thousand people. The judgment found Emperor Hirohito "guilty of the charges on the basis of his command responsibility."[102] In addition,

[97] *See id.* (describing Japan's continued official denial of legal responsibility).

[98] *See, e.g.*, Japan Overturns Sex Slave Ruling, *BBC News* (Mar. 29, 2001), *available at* http://news.bbc.co.uk/1/hi/world/asia-pacific/1249236.stm (discussing the decision by Hiroshima's High Court to overturn the only successful claim for compensation in Japanese courts).

[99] *See* Chinkin, *supra* note 96, at 336 (noting that the primary NGO was a group called Violence Against Women in War Network, Japan, "which was founded in 1998 after the International Conference on Violence Against Women in War and Armed Conflict Situations was held in Tokyo in 1997").

[100] *Id.*

[101] *Id.* at 338.

[102] *Id.*

the panel ruled that Japan was "responsible under international law applicable at the time of the events for violation of its treaty obligations and principles of customary international law relating to slavery, trafficking, forced labor, and rape, amounting to crimes against humanity."[103] The judges subsequently proposed a range of reparations and made other recommendations.

Other nonstate tribunals have similarly sought to inculcate the norms embodied in international human rights law. For example, the 1967 International War Crimes Tribunal convened by Bertrand Russell and Jean-Paul Sartre purported to adjudicate whether the United States had violated international law in prosecuting the Vietnam War.[104] Likewise, "private citizens of high moral authority" from several countries established a Permanent People's Tribunal in Italy in the 1970s.[105] This tribunal existed for a number of years and examined a series of alleged violations of international law to which there had been inadequate official response, including the Soviet military intervention in Afghanistan, that of Indonesia in East Timor, and the genocide of Armenians by the Turks in the period from 1915 through 1919.[106] In 1984, another People's Tribunal was convened to gather evidence concerning the Armenian genocide.[107] A recent film, *The Trials of Henry Kissinger* (based on a 2001 book of the same name by Christopher Hitchens), assembles historians, politicians, and others to assess the former U.S. secretary of state's criminal responsibility for U.S. military activities in Vietnam and Cambodia.[108]

[103] *Id.*

[104] *See* Cover, Folktales of Justice, *supra* note 48, at 198–201 (describing this nonstate tribunal as arising from a lack of state opposition to the war). For the report of this tribunal, *see Against the Crime of Silence: Proceedings of the Russell International War Crimes Tribunal* (John Duffett ed., 1968).

[105] Richard Falk, The Rights of Peoples (in Particular Indigenous Peoples), in *The Rights of Peoples* 17, 28 (James Crawford ed., 1988).

[106] *Id.* at 28–9.

[107] *See generally* The Permanent Peoples' Tribunal, a Crime of Silence: The Armenian Genocide (1985).

[108] *See* Ronnie Scheib, Film Review: The Trials of Henry Kissinger, *Variety*, July 15–21, 2002, at 27 ("Is Henry Kissinger, America's revered elder statesman and Nobel Peace Prize

In some ways, of course, such assertions of jurisdiction are purely symbolic acts. Yet, by claiming authority to articulate norms, these tribunals insisted that "'law is an instrument of civil society' that does not belong to governments, whether acting alone or in institutional arenas."[109] Moreover, the reports issued by such tribunals provide a valuable alternative source of evidence and jurisprudence pertaining to contested applications of international law. And even these "quasi-legal" fora can constitute a form of public acknowledgment to the survivors that serious crimes were committed against them.[110]

Thus, calling the tribunals "extralegal" or "symbolic" does nothing to lessen their claims to produce norms or to affect people. After all, even state entities pursue trials that are largely symbolic, such as the French trial against Klaus Barbie[111] and the proposed Spanish trial of Augusto Pinochet. We have also noted previously the rise of truth commissions, the primary aim of which is storytelling in order to create a record of past abuses.[112] Lawsuits in the United States seeking reparations for slavery[113]

winner, a war criminal? That's the question posed by this startling BBC docu[mentary] that starts with the accusations leveled by Christopher Hitchens in his recent book.").

109 Chinkin, *supra* note 96, at 339 (quoting Falk, *supra* note 105, at 29).

110 Of course, such tribunals' impact undoubtedly depends in part on the power and resources of the entities or individuals sponsoring and publicizing them.

111 Indeed, Guyora Binder has argued that many of those most interested in the trial viewed its role as pedagogical or symbolic. *See* Binder, *supra* note 39, at 1322 (observing that the trial was viewed by some as "an occasion for self-improvement"). Binder quotes French government officials referring to the proceedings as "a pedagogic trial," Israeli governmental officials describing the trial as "justice that has educational significance," a *New York Times* editorial expressing hope that the trial would "educate a new generation," a statement from a representative of French Resistance veterans that he hoped the trial would "deepen our understanding," and a comment from Nazi hunter Simon Wiesenthal that "the trial would be 'a proper history lesson,' and that its true significance was 'symbolic.'" *Id.*

112 *See, e.g.*, Hayner, *supra* note 40, at 32 (listing twenty-one truth commissions convened between 1974 and 2001); Minow, *supra* note 40, at 52–4 (recounting the creation of several truth commissions contemporaneously with the establishment of South Africa's in 1995).

113 *See, e.g.*, Joe R. Feagin & Eileen O'Brien, The Growing Movement for Reparations, in *When Sorry Isn't Enough: The Controversy over Apologies and Reparations for Human*

serve as another example of the way in which juridical mechanisms can be used to affect collective memory. Finally, one might see the creation of the International Criminal Court[114] (a new form of international jurisdictional assertion) as evidence that the norms these nonstate tribunals sought to inculcate have taken hold.

Of course, some communities may embrace norms that many would find undesirable. For example, white supremacist militia groups might well attempt to assert jurisdiction over their perceived enemies. Other communities might seek to impose norms that conflict with evolving international human rights standards. Hierarchy and oppression abound within many communities, and merely uttering the talismanic word "community" does not transform human behavior into sweetness and light. Thus, any theory of jurisdiction that requires deference to these sorts of alternative normative visions would likely prove unacceptable.

Yet, it is important to recognize that, in order for the legal norms of a nonstate community to be enforced, such norms must be adopted by those with coercive power. Thus, the enforcement arena would provide a powerful incentive to communities not to move too far away from a developing international consensus. In a sense, this is how even state-sanctioned courts operate because they lack their own enforcement power. Courts always issue decisions at the sufferance of their "sovereign," and if they choose to defy the entity that enforces their judgments, they must appeal to a broad base of popular support or risk being treated as politically irrelevant.

Likewise, a nonstate jurisdictional assertion – such as the decision to apply the norms of merchants, or the pronouncements of the permanent people's tribunals, or the regulations of the Internet domain name system

Injustice 341 (Roy L. Brooks ed., 1999) (describing the reparations movement within the United States).

[114] Despite U.S. resistance to the International Criminal Court, an overwhelming percentage of the world's countries have signed the ICC treaty, and the court held its first assembly in September 2002, Elizabeth Becker, U.S. Presses for Total Exemption from War Crimes Court, *N.Y. Times*, Oct. 9, 2002, at A6.

issued by the Internet Corporation for Assigned Names and Numbers – must make a strong case to the governments of the world and other political actors that the assertion of community dominion is appropriate and that the substantive norms expressed are worth adopting. It is true that nonstate entities can effect compliance even though they lack the tools of legitimized violence, through social norms, the reputational interests of repeat players, the power of consuming publics, the ability to enact technological standards, and so on. However, at least some of their impact depends on the degree to which state entities are willing to delegate or recognize their authority.

In any event, a cosmopolitan pluralist conception of jurisdiction does not imply that all assertions of jurisdiction (much less all normative rules imposed) are justified; it only argues that we extend the term "jurisdiction" to these nonstate norm-producing acts. In this way, multiple communities can attempt to claim the mantle of law, making it more likely that we will at least *notice* these alternative visions, regardless of whether such visions are ultimately adopted broadly or roundly rejected.[115] In a more freewheeling jurisdictional inquiry, law functions as a site for discourse among strangers across both physical and normative space.

The Value of Jurisdictional Redundancy

As we have seen, many of the legal conundrums of a hybrid world arise because of jurisdictional redundancy. That is, as noted throughout this book, multiple legal communities frequently seek to assert jurisdiction over the same act or actor. Yet, while this jurisdictional overlap is often viewed as a problem because it potentially creates conflicting obligations and uncertainty, we might also view jurisdictional redundancy as a necessary adaptive feature of a multivariate, pluralist legal system. Indeed, jurisdictional redundancy may itself be thought of as a mechanism for

[115] *Cf.* Cover, Folktales of Justice, *supra* note 48, at 176 (referring to law as the bridge in normative space that connects reality to "alternity").

managing pluralism because the existence of overlapping jurisdictional claims often leads to a nuanced negotiation – either explicit or implicit – between or among the various communities making those claims.

In focusing on the pluralist opportunities inherent in jurisdictional redundancy, I echo the insights of Robert Cover in his article "The Uses of Jurisdictional Redundancy."[116] Although his essay was focused particularly on the variety of "official" law pronouncers in the U.S. federal system, Cover celebrated the benefits that accrue from having multiple overlapping jurisdictional assertions. Such benefits include a greater possibility for error correction, a more robust field for norm articulation, and a larger space for creative innovation.[117] Moreover, we might think that when decision makers are forced to consider the existence of other possible decision makers, they will tend to adopt, over time, a more restrained view of their own "jurispathic" power.[118] Instead, they may come to see themselves as part of a larger tapestry of decision making in which they are not the only potentially relevant voice. Finally, though Cover acknowledged that it might seem perverse "to seek out a messy and indeterminate end to conflicts which may be tied neatly together by a single authoritative verdict," he nevertheless argued that we should "embrace" a system "that permits tensions and conflicts of the social order" to be played out in the jurisdictional structure of the system.[119] Thus, Cover's pluralism, though here focused on U.S. federalism, can be said to include the creative possibilities inherent in multiple overlapping jurisdictional assertions by both state and nonstate entities in whatever context they arise. More recently, Judith Resnik has noted the "multiple ports of entry" that a federalist system creates[120] and has argued that what constitutes

[116] Robert M. Cover, The Uses of Jurisdictional Redundancy: Interest, Ideology, and Innovation, 22 *Wm. & Mary L. Rev.* 639 (1981).

[117] *See id.*

[118] *See id.* at 664–8 (describing the idea that judges are inevitably jurispathic because in making a decision they "kill" competing legal visions).

[119] *Id.* at 682.

[120] *See* Judith Resnik, Law's Migration: American Exceptionalism, Silent Dialogues, and Federalism's Multiple Ports of Entry, 115 *Yale L.J.* 1564 (2006).

the appropriate spheres for "local," "national," and "international" regulation and adjudication changes over time and should not be essentialized.[121] Not surprisingly, other commenters have at times advocated what amounts to a federalist approach to national/supranational relations.[122]

With regard to state-to-state jurisdictional redundancy, consider the way in which Spanish efforts to assert jurisdiction over members of the Argentine military strengthened the hand of human rights reformers in Argentina itself. Likewise, the earlier efforts to assert jurisdiction over Pinochet[123] provided the impetus for a movement that led to a Chilean Supreme Court decision stripping Pinochet of his lifetime

[121] *See* Judith Resnik, Afterword: Federalism's Options, 14 *Yale L. & Pol'y Rev.* 465, 473 (1996) ("My point is not only that particular subject matter may go back and forth between state and federal governance but also that the tradition of allocation itself is one constantly being reworked; periodically, events prompt the revisiting of state or federal authority, and the lines move.").

[122] *See, e.g.*, Mattias Kumm, The Legitimacy of International Law: A Constitutional Framework of Analysis, 15 *Eur. J. Int'l L.* 907, 922 (2004) (arguing that subsidiarity should be a general principle to be applied both with regard to federally structured entities and with regard to the "management of the national/international divide").

[123] Judge Garzón issued an arrest order based on allegations of kidnappings, torture, and planned disappearances of Chilean citizens and citizens of other countries. Spanish Request to Arrest General Pinochet, Oct. 16, 1998, reprinted in *The Pinochet Papers: The Case of Augusto Pinochet in Spain and Britain* 57–9 (Reed Brody & Michael Ratner eds., 2000) [hereinafter *The Pinochet Papers*]; *see also* Anne Swardson, Pinochet, Pinochet Case Tries Spanish Legal Establishment, *Wash. Post*, Oct. 22, 1998, at A27 ("As Chilean president from 1973 to 1990, Garzón's arrest order said, Pinochet was 'the leader of an international organization created ... to conceive, develop and execute the systematic planning of illegal detentions [kidnappings], torture, forced relocations, assassinations and/or disappearances of numerous persons, including Argentines, Spaniards, Britons, Americans, Chileans and other nationalities.'"). On October 30, 1998, the Spanish National Court ruled unanimously that Spanish courts had jurisdiction over the matter on the basis of both the principle of universal jurisdiction (that crimes against humanity can be tried anywhere at any time) and the passive personality principle of jurisdiction (that courts may try cases if their nationals are victims of crime, regardless of where the crime was committed). S Audiencia Nacional, Nov. 5, 1998 (No. 173/98), reprinted in *The Pinochet Papers, supra*, at 95, 95–107. For an English translation of the opinion, *see The Pinochet Papers, supra*, at 95, 95–107. The Office of the Special Prosecutor alleged that Spaniards living in Chile were among those killed under Pinochet's rule. *Id.* at 106.

immunity.[124] In 2006 the Chilean court further ruled that Chile was subject to the Geneva Conventions during the period of Pinochet's rule and that neither statutes of limitations nor amnesties could be invoked to block prosecutions for serious violations of the conventions, such as war crimes or crimes against humanity.[125] To date, 148 people, including nearly 50 military officers, have been convicted for human rights violations committed during this era, and more than 400 more suspects, mostly from the armed forces, have been indicted or are under investigation.[126] One might even see Italy's assertion of jurisdiction over U.S. Central Intelligence Agency agents for allegedly abducting a terrorist suspect as a source of alternative norms concerning the appropriate role for civil liberties in the conduct of antiterrorism operations. Such norms may have broader influence over time.

Turning to international assertions of jurisdiction, we can see again that even the potential jurisdictional assertion of an alternative norm-generating community can put pressure on local politics. For example, although international courts do not generally have the power to force states to surrender suspects, the International Criminal Tribunal for the former Yugoslavia instituted so-called Rule 11bis proceedings, whereby public hearings were held at the indictment phase.[127] Such hearings publicized the various cases and the atrocities alleged, thereby helping pressure states to turn over suspects. Likewise, the prosecution of Slobodan Milosevic may well have played at least some role in weakening his hold on power in Serbia, ultimately bringing about his ouster from government. And even without formal court proceedings, the United Nations can influence local political realities by asserting forms of jurisdiction,

[124] *See* Chile's Top Court Strips Pinochet of Immunity, *N.Y. Times*, Aug. 27, 2004, at A3 ("Chile's Supreme Court stripped the former dictator Augusto Pinochet of immunity from prosecution in a notorious human rights case on Thursday, raising hopes of victims that he may finally face trial for abuses during his 17-year rule.").

[125] Slaking a Thirst for Justice, *Economist* Apr. 14, 2007, at 39–40.

[126] *Id.*

[127] This Rule concerns, *inter alia*, the procedure by which the Trial Chamber issues arrest warrants.

as in the Indonesia/East Timor example discussed in Chapter 3, where a UN Commission of Inquiry empowered the reform-minded Indonesian attorney general to pursue human rights abusers in Indonesia. Or, conversely, international pressure could also trigger local backlash.

Complementarity regimes are a more formalized way of harnessing the potential power of jurisdictional redundancy. Here the idea is that when two legal communities claim jurisdiction over an actor, one community agrees not to assert jurisdiction, but only so long as the other community takes action. This is a hybrid mechanism because one community does not hierarchically impose a solution on the other, but it does assert influence on the other's domestic process through its mere presence as a potential jurisdictional actor in the future.

The best known complementarity regime in the world today is the one enshrined in the statute of the International Criminal Court. As noted previously, the court cannot prosecute someone unless the suspect's home country is unwilling or unable to investigate.[128] As with most mechanisms for managing pluralism, this one has been criticized by both sides in the nation-state sovereignty/international human rights debate. Thus, sovereigntist voices in the United States condemn the ICC as an encroachment on state prerogatives,[129] despite the fact that ICC jurisdiction over U.S. citizens is easily staved off so long as our domestic or military authorities simply conduct the type of investigations that a democratic citizenry would normally expect in response to allegations of serious human rights abuses. On the other hand, international human rights advocates fear the complementarity regime will permit too many potential suspects to skirt international justice.[130] This concern, however,

[128] Rome Statute of the International Criminal Court art. 17, July 17, 1998, 2187 U.N.T.S. 90, at Art. 17.

[129] *See, e.g.*, Miles A. Pomper, Helms Gives Blunt Message to U.N. Security Council: Don't Tread on U.S., 58 *CQ Weekly*, No. 4, Jan. 22, 2000, *available at* 2000 WLNR 201231 (reporting that Sen. Jesse Helms "criticized the proposed International Criminal Court as an intrusion on sovereignty and stated that the U.S. should be free to pursue unilateral military action overseas").

[130] *See, e.g.*, Hans-Peter Kaul, Preconditions to the Exercise of Jurisdiction, in *The Rome Statute of the International Criminal Court: A Commentary* (Antonio Cassese et al., eds.

discounts the catalytic impact that even the *potential* of international prosecutions can have.

The important catalytic function of complementarity has not been lost on the ICC prosecutor, Luis Moreno Ocampo. In one of his first speeches upon assuming office, Ocampo noted that "as a consequence of complementarity, the number of cases that reach the Court should not be a measure [of] its efficiency. On the contrary, the absence of trials before this Court, as a consequence of the regular functioning of national institutions, would be a major success."[131] Ocampo therefore announced that he would take a "proactive approach to complementarity" and encourage (and perhaps even aid) national governments in undertaking their own investigations and prosecutions.[132]

According to William Burke-White, this idea of proactive complementarity, if it is truly pursued, would create a hybrid system of judicial enforcement for the prosecution of the most serious international crimes, under which the ICC and national governments share the ability and the duty to act and would therefore necessarily be engaged in a broad series of interactions directed toward accountability. Indeed, the ICC could become a contributor to the effective functioning of national judiciaries and investigative bodies. The result of such a policy, Burke-White argues, "could produce a virtuous circle in which the Court stimulates the exercise of domestic jurisdiction through the threat of international intervention."[133]

2003) 583, 613 (referring to the rejection of universal jurisdiction as a "painful weakness" of the ICC regime).

[131] Statement of the Prosecutor (16 June 2003), *available at* http://www.icc-cpi.int/otp/otp_ceremony.html.

[132] Statement of the Prosecutor to the Diplomatic Corps (12 February 2004), *available at* http://www.icc-cpi.int/library/organs/otp/LOM_20040212_En.pdf.

[133] William W. Burke-White, Proactive Complementarity: The International Criminal Court and National Courts in the Rome System of International Justice, 49 *Harv. Int'l L.J.* 53, 57 (2008); *see also* Brian Concannon Jr., Beyond Complementarity: The International Criminal Court and National Prosecutions, A View from Haiti, 32 *Colum. Hum. Rts. L. Rev.* 201 (2000) (discussing ways in which the International Criminal Court's complementarity regime, supplemented with other forms of aid, can support local prosecutions).

Of course, we should not assume that international jurisdictional assertions always work as a force for increased human rights protections. Indeed, as Kim Lane Scheppele has documented, Security Council resolutions adopted after the terrorist attacks of September 11, 2001, and backed by threat of sanctions, required countries to enact antiterrorism legislation and adjust antiterrorism policies regardless of domestic, constitutionally based civil liberties concerns.[134] Nevertheless, the important point is to see jurisdictional overlap in the state and supranational spheres as a hybrid legal space where alternative norms are proposed and contested.

Sometimes, instead of one jurisdiction's ultimately adopting the other's norms, we may see the existence of jurisdictional redundancy open up space for the creation of hybrid substantive norms. For example, as discussed in more detail in the next chapter, Graeme Dinwoodie has argued that national courts should decide international copyright cases not by choosing an applicable *law*, but by devising an applicable *solution*, reflecting the values of all interested systems, national and international, that may have a prescriptive claim on the outcome.[135] Similarly, where once courts simply adjudicated bankruptcies independently, on the basis of the presence of assets in their territorial jurisdiction, global insolvencies are now often dealt with by courts working cooperatively.[136]

Finally, it is important to note that jurisdictional redundancy can also work "bottom-up," with nonstate norms being appropriated into state (or international) law. Indeed, as discussed previously, the common law often

[134] *See* Kim Scheppele, The International State of Emergency: Challenges to Constitutionalism After September 11th, at 3–4, *available at* http://www.law.yale.edu/documents/pdf/Intellectual_Life/scheppele_ltw.pdf.

[135] *See* Graeme B. Dinwoodie, A New Copyright Order: Why National Courts Should Create Global Norms, 149 *U. Pa. L. Rev.* 469 (2000).

[136] *See generally* Jay Lawrence Westbrook, Theory and Pragmatism in Global Insolvencies: Choice of Law and Choice of Forum, 65 *Am. Bankr. L.J.* 457 (1991); *see also* Lore Unt, International Relations and International Insolvency Cooperation: Liberalism, Institutionalism, and Transnational Dialogue, 28 *Law & Pol'y Int'l Bus.* 1037 (1997); Anne-Marie Slaughter, A Global Community of Courts, 44 *Harv. Int'l. L.J.* 191, 214 (2003).

incorporates social custom and practice, regulatory regimes often reference nonstate accreditation standards,[137] statutes are frequently interpreted (or even supplanted) by reference to industry custom,[138] and rules promulgated in small nonstate communities can be explicitly adopted in formal legal regimes.[139] All of these can be seen as part of the ongoing jurisgenerative practice of jurisdictional redundancy.

Of course, all of these jurisdictional redundancies might be seen as perhaps necessary, but regrettable concessions to the realities of a world of normative disagreement. Such a view would focus on concerns about forum shopping, uncertainty about applicable rules, litigation costs, and so forth. In order to minimize such difficulties, we might seek international harmonization or more strict territorialist rules to cut off some of the overlap. But, as discussed previously, such efforts are unlikely ever to be fully practical. Thus, jurisdictional overlap is likely to continue to be a reality. Moreover, the cosmopolitan pluralist framework allows us to see ways in which jurisdictional redundancy might be a necessary (and perhaps sometimes a generative) feature of a hybrid legal world, and not simply a problem to be eliminated.

[137] *See, e.g.*, Jody Freeman, The Private Role in Public Governance, 75 *N.Y.U. L. Rev.* 543, 618–19 (2000) (describing government incorporation of accreditation standards on Health Maintenance Organizations first promulgated by a not-for-profit entity); *see also* Laura A. Dickinson, *Outsourcing War and Peace: Preserving Public Values in a World of Foreign Affairs Privatization* (2011) (proposing such an accreditation scheme for disciplining private military contractors).

[138] *See, e.g.*, Fuller, *supra* note 83, at 57–9 (arguing that the act of interpretation permits courts to adjust official legal norms to match custom or usage); Hurst, *supra* note 83, at 289–94 (1964) (describing the ways in which local norms in the Wisconsin lumber industry played a significant role in the way contract law was applied).

[139] Levit, *supra* note 85, at 165 (describing the incorporation of an informal "Gentleman's Agreement" on export credits as a safe harbor in the WTO's Agreement on Subsidies and Countervailing Measures).

8 A Cosmopolitan Pluralist Approach to Choice of Law

As noted previously, choice-of-law anaysis involves the decision regarding whose legal norms to apply to a dispute involving two or more different communities. In order to construct a cosmopolitan pluralist approach to choice-of-law problems, we can borrow elements from each of the dominant twentieth-century American choice-of-law approaches: the "vested rights" approach associated with Joseph Beale,[1] the "governmental interests" theory associated with Brainerd Currie,[2] and the substantive law method championed (in various forms) by Arthur von Mehren,[3] Friedrich Juenger,[4] Luther

[1] *See generally Restatement (First) of Conflict of Laws* (1934) (featuring Beale as Reporter for the volume); Joseph Beale, *A Treatise on the Conflict of Laws* (1935) [hereinafter Beale, *Treatise*].

[2] *See generally* Brainerd Currie, *Selected Essays on the Conflict of Laws* (1963).

[3] *See, e.g.*, Arthur Taylor von Mehren, Special Substantive Rules for Multistate Problems: Their Role and Significance in Contemporary Choice of Law Methodology, 88 *Harv. L. Rev.* 347, 371 (1974) [hereinafter von Mehren, Special Substantive Rules for Multistate Problems] (arguing that by adopting a substantive approach, "choice of law theory and practice could ... take a large step toward resolving the ancient conflict between the objectives of aptness and of decisional harmony"); *see also* Arthur Taylor von Mehren, Choice of Law and the Problem of Justice, *Law & Contemp. Probs.* (Spring 1977), at 27, 43 [hereinafter von Mehren, Choice of Law] (suggesting that "functional approaches" to choice of law issues achieve "a higher quality of... justice" than more traditional choice-of-law methods).

[4] *See, e.g.*, Friedrich K. Juenger, *Choice of Law and Multistate Justice* (1993) (calling for the adoption of a substantive approach based on qualitatively evaluating conflicting laws to give predictability and uniformity to conflicts thinking); Friedrich K. Juenger, Mass Disasters and the Conflict of Laws, 1989 *U. Ill. L. Rev.* 105, 126 (suggesting that

McDougal,[5] and others. The strengths and weaknesses of each of these approaches have been much rehearsed in the conflicts literature, and it is far beyond the scope of this book to attempt a full description of any of these theories. Therefore, this chapter simply highlights those aspects of each theory that contribute to (or contrast with) the articulation of a cosmopolitan pluralist vision of choice of law, before applying the resulting cosmopolitan pluralist vision to two illustrative transnational domain name trademark cases. Then, I turn to two relatively well-known disputes between the nation-state and a religious community in order to explore the possible benefits of thinking of even such debates as choice-of-law problems.

Territorialism

Beale's vested rights theory – which dominated U.S. conflicts thinking in the first part of the twentieth century and was embodied in the Restatement (First) of Conflict of Laws – derived from a strictly territorial notion of sovereign power.[6] Accordingly, vested rights focused only on

in a mass disaster case, the court look to "the place of the tortfeasor's conduct; ... the place of injury; ... [and] the home state of each party" and "select from the laws of these jurisdictions the most suitable rule of decision"); Friedrich K. Juenger, The Need for a Comparative Approach to Choice-of-Law Problems, 73 *Tul. L. Rev.* 1309, 1317 (1999) ("Instead of determining whether a contract is French or New York in nature or whether the New York rule on consideration applies, the substantive law approach asks whether there is an interstate or international rule on point."); *see also* Friedrich K. Juenger, American Conflicts Scholarship and the New Law Merchant, 28 *Vand. J. Transnat'l L.* 487, 496 (1995) (identifying other scholars who support a substantive law approach).

5 *See, e.g.*, Luther L. McDougal III, "Private" International Law: Ius Gentium Versus Choice of Law Rules or Approaches, 38 *Am. J. Comp. L.* 521, 536–7 (1990) ("[T]he best way to take appropriate account of substantive policies is to do so directly through the development and application of transnational laws.").

6 *See* 1 Beale, *Treatise*, *supra* note 1, at 311–12 (Because "the power of a state is supreme within its own territory, no other state can exercise power there," and thus "[i]t follows generally that no statute has force to affect any person, thing, or act ... outside the territory of the state that passed it."). To be sure, Beale's vested rights approach had a highly "privatist" cast, for Beale was as concerned with the universal right of a party to

the physical location of the essential act that, at least to Beale, constituted the cause of action. Beale looked to the place of the tort,[7] or the place of contracting,[8] or the location of the property at issue.[9] Having "localized" the cause of action, he concluded that only the state where the cause of action "vested" could apply its law to the dispute.[10]

These attempts to localize a cause of action were problematic from the outset. Some of the difficulties were practical. First, Beale was forced to create many exceptions to his general rules. For example, although contracts were generally governed by the law of the place where the offer was accepted, if the issue in the case concerned the legality, validity, or scope of the performance of the contract (rather than the fact of the contract itself), then the proper forum was the place of performance, not the place of contracting.[11] Second, it was difficult to determine whether a particular case fell within the scope of the general rule or the exception. For example, it is often far from obvious whether a contract issue actually concerns formation or performance. Likewise, "[h]ow is a judge deciding a tort case to know whether the issue is one of standard of care – governed by the law of the place of injury – or of duty or privilege – governed by the law of the place where the injurious conduct occurred?"[12] Third,

a certain law as he was with state sovereignty. Nevertheless, the rights of parties were determined largely by reference to territorial location within a particular sovereignty.

[7] *See Restatement (First) of Conflict of Laws* §378 (1934) ("The law of the place of wrong determines whether a person has sustained a legal injury.").

[8] *See* 2 Beale, *Treatise*, *supra* note 1, at 1091 (arguing that questions of contract validity can generally be determined "by no other law than that which applies to the acts, that is, by the law of the place of contracting.... If... the law of the place where the agreement is made annexes no legal obligation to it, there is no other law which has power to do so.").

[9] *See id.* at 938 (finding that immovable property, "being unable to be taken away from the state in which [it is located], must always in the last analysis be governed by the laws of that state").

[10] *See* 1 Beale, *Treatise*, *supra* note 1, at 64 ("[T]he chief task of the Conflict of Laws [is] to determine the place where a right arose and the law that created it.").

[11] *See Restatement (First) of Conflict of Laws* §360 (1934) (outlining provisions in case of illegality of performance).

[12] Lea Brilmayer, *Conflict of Laws* 24 (1995).

Beale's system allowed judges to characterize issues as contracts or torts and therefore avoid applying unpalatable laws.[13]

But even apart from these pragmatic difficulties, there are several other more fundamental objections to the vested rights approach, and these objections turn out to be particularly important for generating a cosmopolitan pluralist understanding of choice of law. First, the single-minded focus on territoriality is problematic. This is partly because Beale had difficulty justifying why the territorial location of only one event in a complicated set of transactions should determine the law to be applied. For example, in the oft-discussed case of *Alabama Great Southern Railroad v. Carroll*,[14] an employee was injured when a train coupling failed. The vested rights theory held that the relevant law was that of the state where the injury occurred.[15] However, given that the negligence took place elsewhere, the choice of the place of accident seems arbitrary. Similarly, it may be difficult to determine when and where an injury takes place (for example, in a toxic tort case), and again the state where the person happens to be when the first symptoms appear seems relatively unimportant.[16] Yet, under Beale's approach such a determination is the *only* relevant factor in choice-of-law analysis. Thus, even if one agreed that territorialism should be the criterion for choice of law, it is not at all clear how best to choose the appropriate territorial nexus, and Beale's mechanical rules seem to lack substance.

[13] For a discussion of the problems inherent in "characterization," *see, for example*, Albert A. Ehrenzweig, *A Treatise on the Conflict of Laws* § 108 (1962) (noting that what is accomplished through characterization could be achieved more directly through other legal methods); Robert A. Leflar, *American Conflicts Law* §§ 87–8 (3d ed. 1977) (calling characterization a "gimmick" and a "result-selection device"); Joseph M. Cormack, Renvoi, Characterization, Localization and Preliminary Question in the Conflict of Laws, 14 *S. Cal. L. Rev.* 221, 223–40 (1941) (discussing both primary and secondary characterization); Ernest G. Lorenzen, The Qualification, Classification, or Characterization Problem in the Conflict of Laws, 50 *Yale L.J.* 743, 743–8 (1941) (providing a useful summary of both continental and Anglo-American criticisms of characterization in the conflict of laws).

[14] 11 So. 803 (Ala. 1892).

[15] *See Restatement (First) of Conflict of Laws* §§377–8 (1934) (explaining that the place of wrong is where the last act occurred, and the law of that forum governs the tort).

[16] *See, e.g.*, Brilmayer, *supra* note 12, at 25–6 (discussing such difficulties).

Moreover, as with jurisdiction the focus on territoriality by definition ignores important nonterritorial factors, such as community affiliation. For example, two parties who are domiciled in one state could avoid a local contract rule by crossing the border, entering into the contract, and returning.[17] This is not at all hypothetical in the modern world of off-shore regulatory havens, where corporations frequently attempt to avoid various forms of governmental control by changing their territorial location. Even the U.S. government has, in recent years, attempted to evade U.S. law by locating military detention facilities in Guantánamo Bay, Cuba.[18] A purely territorial approach to choice of law, therefore, will have difficulty coping with a modern world where transactions and transportation across borders are so frequent. Indeed, although Beale treated as transcendental truth the idea that the state has complete and unchallenged authority within its own sphere and that no state, therefore, may meddle in another state's "local" affairs, we live today in a far more fluid world of jurisdictional assertions across territorial borders and entities that cause significant impact in faraway locations. A purely territorial choice-of-law rule is unlikely to be satisfying in such a world. Accordingly, a cosmopolitan pluralist conception needs to acknowledge that people may have multiple community affiliations beyond simply their territorial location at a particular moment in time, and it might therefore be appropriate for nonlocal law to apply to their transactions, at least under some circumstances.

Second, Beale assumed that only one state's law could ever apply to any particular transaction, a strikingly uncosmopolitan pluralist view. To Beale, this idea was essentially a corollary to his territorialism. If states

[17] *See* Currie, *supra* note 2, at 87–8 (discussing this scenario).

[18] *See* Brief for the Respondents at 14, *Rasul v. Bush*, 124 S. Ct. 2686 (2004) (Nos. 03–334, 03–343) (arguing that because detainees "are being held by the U.S. military outside the sovereign territory of the United States [,] … U.S. courts lack jurisdiction to consider claims filed on [their] behalf"). The U.S. Supreme Court rejected this argument. *See Rasul v. Bush*, 542 U.S. 466, 484 (2004) (concluding that no Supreme Court precedent "categorically excludes aliens detained in military custody outside the United States from the 'privilege of litigation' in U.S. courts").

have complete and unfettered sovereign power within their borders and no power beyond those borders, then as long as a cause of action could be "located" somewhere, it necessarily followed that only one state's law could apply.[19] Even under Beale's scheme, however, courts often evaded this requirement because Beale accorded to the forum state the ability to apply its own procedural law even if the vested rights approach dictated that foreign substantive norms must govern.[20] Thus, any judge wishing to apply local law to at least part of the dispute needed only to characterize the legal issue as "procedural." Even more importantly, the single-state approach rigidly rejects the reality that, in a complex multistate transaction, the norms of multiple states are obviously implicated. Therefore, arbitrarily choosing one to the exclusion of the others seems inappropriate. And again, to the extent that pure territorialism was arbitrary in the early twentieth century, it seems even more problematic today to insist that only one state's norms should apply to the huge variety of multistate transactions possible in a globalized world. In order to avoid such limitations, a cosmopolitan pluralist approach can recognize the possibility that norms of multiple states might apply to different parts of the dispute or that rules might ultimately be blended to account for the variety of normative systems implicated in a given transaction.

A third common objection to vested rights—that it is an a priori methodology unmoored to the law of any particular state—may be misplaced, however. It is true that a vested rights analysis chooses the applicable law on the basis of principles that are not necessarily contained in state law. Accordingly, the choice-of-law decision is made completely independently of the substantive norms that might apply. But, as we will see, it may be impossible to develop any choice-of-law regime through purely positive law because in order to apply positive law one

[19] *See* Brilmayer, *supra* note 12, at 28–9 ("Beale wished to assign to a single state the right to regulate a controversy, on the theory that the rights vested in one state only. This provided the basis for choice that was needed to make his multilateral system work.").

[20] *See Restatement (First) of Conflict of Laws* §585 (1934) ("All matters of procedure are governed by the law of the forum.").

must choose which state's positive law should apply, and that choice by definition cannot be made pursuant to any single state's positive law.[21] Moreover, why is it necessarily problematic for a choice-of-law regime to be based on principles that operate independently from the substantive law that will result? After all, the choice-of-law decision turns on when it is "legitimate" (whatever that word might mean) for a community to apply its norms to a dispute. Such issues of legitimacy will necessarily revolve around community definition, affiliation, and disputes about conflicting claims to governing authority. And none of those questions needs to involve the content of the various legal rules at all.

Thus, a cosmopolitan pluralist approach to choice of law clearly rejects the territorialism of vested rights as well as the idea that only one state's law could ever apply to any particular transaction. But cosmopolitan pluralism borrows from vested rights a willingness to make choice of law an a priori inquiry. The only difference is that, instead of an a priori inquiry attempting to "localize" a transaction in territorial space, cosmopolitan pluralism would engage in an a priori debate about community affiliation, definition, and effects in order to determine whether a given community may appropriately (or legitimately) apply its norms to a dispute. Further, cosmopolitan pluralism shares with vested rights the idea that this a priori determination is necessarily based on issues that are conceptually distinct from the substantive norms that might be applied.

[21] Larry Kramer, while deriding both Beale and Currie for separating the decision regarding choice of law from the decision on the merits of the suit, maintains that, in multistate cases, as in domestic cases, there is no need to make a prior "choice" of law; rather, the relevant question is "whether some rule of positive law gives the plaintiff a right to recover." Larry Kramer, Interest Analysis and the Presumption of Forum Law, 56 *U. Chi. L. Rev.* 1301, 1310 (1989). Once such a rule is identified, however, the court will still need to decide whether the rule appropriately applies. And while Kramer sees that process as no different from a domestic case where plaintiff and defendant are relying on different lines of legal authority, he does acknowledge that both parochial governmental interests and broader conflicts interests are relevant in a multistate case. Thus, even in Kramer's framework it still seems as if the process of identifying such governmental or conflicts interests will require application of some a priori principles about how best to identify those interests.

Parochialism

Brainerd Currie, building on legal realism, argued that choice of law must focus on specific policy aims, and not on the transcendent formal categories that Beale espoused.[22] In addition, Currie echoed positivist concerns that choice-of-law rules should not be divined from "general principles" unmoored to a particular state.[23] Rather, Currie argued that courts should look only to the rules of actual state-sanctioned law.[24] Thus, instead of starting from the idea that legal rights could "vest" on the basis of formal definitions even before a particular law was deemed to apply, Currie based his theory on the premise that a court granted power by the legislature of a particular state generally applies that state's law.[25] Indeed, Currie argued that so long as the forum government is deemed to have an "interest" in the dispute, its law should always govern, regardless of the multistate character of the events at issue in the case.[26] And although Currie subsequently softened this position somewhat in response to critics,[27] his governmental interest approach remains suffused with a parochial bias in favor of forum law.

[22] *See* Currie, *supra* note 2, at 181 ("The courts simply will not remain always oblivious to the true operation of a system that, though speaking the language of metaphysics, strikes down the legitimate application of the policy of a state.").

[23] *See id.* at 434 (criticizing the idea that choice of law is "a thing apart, a detached science of how laws operate in space; so conceived, it is an international science, transcending local concerns for the most part").

[24] *See id.* at 627 ("[T]he method I advocate is the method of statutory construction, and of interpretation of common-law rules, to determine their applicability to mixed cases.").

[25] *See id.* at 75 (stating his presumption in favor of forum law).

[26] For example, Currie wrote that "[j]ustice between the parties requires a decision on the merits. And where should the New York court look for a rule of decision that will do justice between the parties but to the body of principle and experience which has served that purpose, as well as the ends of governmental policy, for the people of New York in their domestic affairs?" *Id.* at 65.

[27] *See* Brainerd Currie, The Disinterested Third State, 28 *Law & Contemp. Probs.* 754, 757 (1963) (suggesting that, if a true conflict is found, a court might take a second look at the local policy it had uncovered to see whether a more "restrained" view might be possible).

Moreover, at least in the pure form in which Currie first articulated interest analysis, he made it clear that if the forum state has an interest in applying its own law to the dispute, the existence of that interest always means that forum law will apply, even if the competing state also has an interest.[28] Thus, the only time that forum law does not apply, under Currie's scheme, is when the forum state has no interest in applying its legal rules to the events at hand. Currie called such cases "false conflicts" and therefore did not really treat them as conflict-of-laws cases at all.[29]

Of course, Currie's approach ultimately turns on how one defines a governmental "interest." Currie argued that the judge must first ascertain the domestic policy that the legislature seeks to promote. Then, the inquiry turns to whether those policies would be advanced by applying the law to the particular facts under consideration.[30] Only then can one determine whether a state has an "interest" in having its law applied.

In practice, however, Currie defined governmental "interests" quite narrowly. Indeed, if one parses Currie's application of his choice-of-law theory, it becomes clear that the sole determinant of a governmental interest is whether application of a particular law will help a citizen of the state under consideration actually to win the lawsuit at hand. A state is therefore deemed to have an interest only in helping its citizens win. If, on the other hand, application of a state law would not help the citizen of that state to win, Currie concluded that the state has no interest, and the court is free to apply foreign law.

One can see this narrow focus by studying Currie's most famous example,[31] a hypothetical set of variations on the case of *Milliken v. Pratt*.[32]

[28] Currie, *supra* note 2, at 184.

[29] *See* Brainerd Currie et al., Comments on *Babcock v. Jackson*, a Recent Development in Conflict of Laws, 63 *Colum. L. Rev.* 1212, 1242 (1963) ("If the court finds that one state has an interest in the application of its policy in the circumstances of the case and the other has none, it should apply the law of the only interested state.").

[30] Currie, *supra* note 2, at 183–4.

[31] *Id.* at ch. 2.

[32] 125 Mass. 374 (1878).

Milliken involved a contract between a buyer and a seller of goods, under which the buyer's obligation had been guaranteed by his wife. At the time, Massachusetts had a law that invalidated such guarantees given by married women. The policy behind such a rule, supposedly, was to protect married women from being coerced by their husbands. But even assuming that a court has accurately identified the paternalistic Massachusetts policy, the question becomes how to translate the existence of such a policy into the existence of an interest in a particular case involving a contracting party from a state such as Maine, which does not have this rule.[33] Analyzing Currie's various permutations on the *Milliken* fact pattern, it is clear that, so long as the married woman is from Massachusetts (and applying Massachusetts law would help her to win), Currie would find a Massachusetts interest.[34]

Thus, in Currie's view, a government's interests for choice-of-law purposes extend only to helping its citizens win in the short term. Moreover, in a "true" conflict case, where the laws of each state help its respective citizens, Currie breaks the "tie" by again choosing forum law.[35] As a result, a parochial analysis of interests joins with a parochial set of default rules to produce a narrow focus on simply the domicile of the parties and whether the relevant legal rules will help the domiciliary to win. This parochialism echoes the sovereigntist emphasis on state interest discussed in Chapter 3. Indeed, governmental interest analysis, like sovereigntism, rejects the idea of a transcendent set of multistate legal norms in favor of a single-minded focus on the parochial interests of states. Moreover, both

[33] *Cf.* Herma Hill Kay, Theory into Practice: Choice of Law in the Courts, 34 *Mercer L. Rev.* 521, 540 (1983) (stressing the important difference between determining the relevant domestic policy that a legislature sought to promote, and finding that the state actually has sufficient connection to the dispute such that it has an interest in having its law applied).

[34] Currie, *supra* note 2, at ch. 2. Currie isolated four factors that might be relevant to the choice-of-law decision: the creditor's residence, the married woman's residence, the place of contracting, and the forum state. By varying these four factors, Currie developed sixteen hypothetical permutations and provided his choice-of-law conclusions for each. *Id.* at 82–3.

[35] *Id.* at 119.

of these approaches usually define state interests narrowly to include only those that serve short-term goals.

Yet, even if one is concerned only with purely power-driven state interest, one might easily imagine a state to have interests beyond simply allowing its citizen to win a particular case. Indeed, from a long-term geopolitical perspective, whether or not an individual citizen wins a lawsuit is actually of very little interest to a state. Instead, states may have an interest in being seen to comply with an agreed-upon international order. States benefit from a shared world system, with its interlocking set of reciprocal benefits and burdens. If a state is too parochial in pursuit of its short-term interests, it may damage its longer-term goals by creating a lack of trust in other states.[36] As economists have long recognized, repeat players tend to benefit from cooperative rather than parochial behavior.[37] Accordingly, a state that refuses to defer to foreign norms will

[36] As Larry Kramer has pointed out, even if we assume that states are interested only in advancing the domestic policies underlying their particular laws, "[e]nforcing foreign law in some cases only may do this better than always enforcing forum law because it invites reciprocal action that advances forum policies in cases brought elsewhere." Larry Kramer, Return of the Renvoi, 66 *N.Y.U. L. Rev.* 979, 1016 (1991). Kramer argues that "[i]f every state adopts the 'law of the forum' solution and enforces its law in true conflict cases, each state's policies will be advanced only in true conflicts litigated in that state's courts. But there is no guarantee that this will include even half the cases." *Id.* Likewise, Laurence Helfer and Graeme Dinwoodie observe that, though a country might pursue its objectives simply by mandating application of its law to all disputes, "a political unit might more rationally conclude that the best route to making its own internal policy values effective in the greatest possible number of multistate situations is to take into account more than proceedings before its own tribunals." Laurence R. Helfer & Graeme B. Dinwoodie, Designing Non-National Systems: The Case of the Uniform Domain Name Dispute Resolution Policy, 43 *Wm. & Mary L. Rev.* 141, 261 (2001). Accordingly, they observe, as does Kramer, that "the courts of State A may apply, or at least consider, the internal policies of State B in the hope (and expectation) that the courts of State B will consider the internal policy values of State A in cases where State A would have a strong interest in seeing its internal values applied." *Id.*

[37] *See, e.g.*, Robert Axelrod, *The Evolution of Cooperation* 19–20 (1984) (describing "tit for tat" strategy as an example of repeat play that can produce cooperation even among self-interested individuals); *see also* David M. Kreps et al., Rational Cooperation in the Finitely Repeated Prisoners' Dilemma, 27 *J. Econ. Theory* 245 (1982) (discussing the effect of repeat play on prisoner's dilemma games).

likely find that its norms receive less deference from others in the future. Currie, therefore, ignores the possibility that states might benefit from establishing a system of multilateral choice-of-law rules that each state would obey rather than asking whether a state has a short-term interest in each particular case.[38]

To be sure, some might say that there is no "agreed-upon international order." Moreover, though resistance to such an international order might seem provincial and selfish when it is a U.S. tribunal doing the resisting, it may look somewhat different when it is the tribunal of a smaller or more unorthodox community clinging to a distinctive practice that differs from international norms.[39] Yet, the point is not that deference to some international or transnational norm is always appropriate, just that courts need not assume that a parochial analytical framework based on short-term state interest is necessarily the only approach.

In addition, as we have discussed, international law norms that limit unfettered nation-state sovereignty do not necessarily lose their normative power just because they are not themselves issued by entities that wield coercive power. Indeed, while Currie rejected Beale's vested rights approach in part because it derived its authority from legal principles unmoored to a particular state's law, many such unmoored legal principles end up having real effect in the world. Thus, Currie assumes that only state interests are relevant and further assumes that those interests are unaffected by the very fact that the state is part of an international system. But, as we have seen, neither assumption is necessarily

[38] Indeed, Currie's understanding of a governmental interest suffers from flaws that behavioral economists have identified in many forms of "intertemporal decision making." The idea is that decision makers systematically mispredict their own future preferences because they fail to appreciate the ways in which their long-term preferences may differ from their current ones. For a discussion of this phenomenon, *see* Shane Frederick et al., Time Discounting and Time Preference: A Critical Review, 40 *J. Econ. Lit.* 351, 367–8 (2002). Interestingly, William Baxter's "comparative impairment" gloss on Currie's approach does deploy these important concepts of cooperation and long-term strategic behavior. *See* William Baxter, Choice of Law and the Federal System, 16 *Stan. L. Rev.* 1 (1963).

[39] I am grateful to Clyde Spillinger for this observation.

true. We could adopt a choice-of-law rule that takes the perspective not of an individual state but of the entire global legal system and then try to resolve the choice-of-law question. Moreover, even from the perspective of an individual state, the very fact that it is part of an international system and subject to diplomatic and other pressures means that courts cannot effectively further state interests by parochially making sure that the law applied to any given multistate case will always benefit its own citizens.

Currie cannot, in any event, avoid the problem of creating a priori choice-of-law norms unmoored to a state legal regime. This is because his governmental interest analysis necessarily looks to the domicile of the parties to determine whether a state has an interest in the dispute. But, we might ask, why is the domicile of the parties the most important connecting factor? Why not territory (as in vested rights) or some other potentially relevant rubric? The answer requires Currie to rely on some sort of normative judgment that precedes the choice-of-law decision itself. Thus, Currie's framework is as much an a priori philosophical position as Beale's is and cannot claim authority on the basis of being more connected to positive law.[40]

Finally, Currie's conception of a governmental interest tends to presuppose that the interest itself is a legitimate one for the government to pursue. For example, imagine that a given state took the position that its environmental protection statutes should apply to all citizens of the world because all citizens have a stake in a sustainable planet. Currie's interest analysis, by its terms, would need to give effect to this stated governmental interest. Yet in a case brought in that state involving two parties, neither of whom is a citizen of the state, one suspects that Currie would not insist on the application of forum law. Thus, whatever else one can say about governmental interest analysis, its scope seems to be

[40] *See* Kramer, *supra* note 21, at 1308 ("Currie... made the same conceptual mistake he correctly accused traditional choice of law scholars of making: he treated 'choosing' the applicable law as a threshold inquiry distinct from 'applying' the chosen law.").

derived from more general principles of legitimacy; it is not derived from legislative policy alone.

Nevertheless, despite these shortcomings, governmental interest analysis at least frees us from the rigid territorialism of vested rights and allows us to consider what the interests of states might be in a globalized multilateral system. We can therefore accept that a focus on interests is appropriate, without also accepting Currie's peculiarly narrow and parochial conception of such interests. Instead, a cosmopolitan pluralist vision can consider a broader set of governmental interests in being part of an interlocking world system of transnational regulation and multiple community affiliation.

Substantivism

Over the past few decades, several conflicts scholars have articulated (without fully developing) a distinct choice-of-law methodology that emphasizes the ability of judges to create special substantive rules in multistate cases. In 1974 Arthur von Mehren noted "the advantages, in certain multistate or multiple contact situations, of applying special rules that are not necessarily chosen from among provisions in the domestic law of any of the jurisdictions viewed as legitimately concerned with the resolution of the issues presented."[41] Such special multijurisdictional rules, von Mehren suggested, would involve some sort of compromise among the values of the various states involved.[42] Subsequently, Friedrich Juenger[43] and Luther McDougal[44] also argued for the development and application of transnational laws fashioned by judges in multistate cases.

[41] von Mehren, Special Substantive Rules for Multistate Problems, *supra* note 3, at 348; *see also* von Mehren, Choice of Law, *supra* note 3, at 27, 38–40 (suggesting circumstances in which conflict of laws might best be resolved by a compromise among the values of the states involved).

[42] *See* von Mehren, Special Substantive Rules for Multistate Problems, *supra* note 3, at 359 (discussing states' willingness to deal in foreign courts).

[43] For a sample of Juenger's work, *see* sources cited *supra* note 4.

[44] *See, e.g.*, McDougal, *supra* note 5.

And both have noted that this sort of substantive transnational law has historical antecedents dating back to the Roman Empire.[45] Yet, although the substantive law method helps avoid binary either/or choice-of-law questions, the rise of nation-states – and the accompanying positivist idea that law must be clearly identified with a sovereign entity – pushed substantive approaches to the background.

Most recently, Graeme Dinwoodie has argued for a substantive law approach to international copyright disputes.[46] Dinwoodie notes that courts in ordinary domestic disputes often must generate common law rules or glosses on legislative enactments.[47] Indeed, any time a court adjudicates a dispute that does not involve a single governing rule the judge must select among possible models. For example, a court asked for the first time to consider the validity of a contract formed via telephone might look for guidance both to prior rules concerning face-to-face negotiations and to prior rules concerning negotiations by mail. As Dinwoodie points out, a court may consider both rules but is not required to choose either; instead the court is likely to blend principles from both sets of rules.[48] Likewise, Dinwoodie argues, a court in a multistate dispute should not consider itself bound to choose one state's law over the other in toto; it should instead be free to craft a hybrid rule that reflects the interests of the multiple states and parties involved.[49]

Such substantive lawmaking is particularly important in the international context. First, as Dinwoodie points out, "statutory rules enacted by a national legislature are rarely enacted with an eye to international disputes or conduct."[50] And even when legislators actually consider

[45] *See, e.g.*, Juenger, *Choice of Law and Multistate Justice, supra* note 4, at 8–10 (discussing the development of the *ius gentium* by the *praetor peregrinus*, starting around 242 B.C., to deal with cases involving non-Romans).

[46] Graeme B. Dinwoodie, A New Copyright Order: Why National Courts Should Create Global Norms, 149 *U. Pa. L. Rev.* 469, 542–80 (2000).

[47] *See id.* at 548 ("Courts... often... generate rules, rather than merely apply them....").

[48] *Id.*

[49] *Id.*

[50] *Id.* at 548–9.

activities abroad, they do so to pursue domestic policy priorities, with little consideration for multistate implications.[51] Second, Dinwoodie argues that "a method that draws its applicable rule in international cases from an amalgam of national and international norms reflects the complex and interwoven forces that govern citizens' conduct in a global society."[52] Thus, a choice-of-law regime that forces binary choices requires citizens to be judged according to a single state norm in a world where those citizens affiliate with multiple states. Indeed, the mere fact that a dispute is multinational necessarily means that it implicates interests that are different from those in a purely domestic dispute. Accordingly, the substantive law method asks judges to consider these added factors and craft rules based on a variety of national and international legal norms.

The substantive method has much to recommend it. More than the other two approaches, it takes seriously the multistate nature of the dispute and seeks to find a way to reconcile the multiple communities potentially implicated. And, though it asks judges to engage in creative common law interpretation, which could result in a degree of unpredictability, such difficulties are likely to subside over time, as judges develop a series of international law norms that become relatively settled. Moreover, this method of creating international norms is likely to happen more rapidly than, for example, through the international treaty process. Thus, the substantive law method may allow legal rules to evolve more rapidly in the face of technological innovation.[53]

Nevertheless, I see at least two problems with the substantive approach. First, it may be more helpful, at least as a rhetorical matter, to think of the crafting of hybrid norms through the prism of governmental interests. This is because the hybrid norms that would result would at least be viewed as part of the long-term interests of the state in which

[51] *Id.* at 549.

[52] *Id.* at 550.

[53] *See id.* at 569 ("Using the substantive choice of law method as part of international lawmaking can supply the dynamism appropriately missing from classical public international lawmaking.").

the court sits, rather than as an unmoored exercise in judicial lawmaking. Dinwoodie himself acknowledges that governmental interest analysis, if expanded, could in fact be used to justify an approach like his substantive law method: "[I]f a legislature were consciously to address the policies by which it would seek to regulate international disputes before its courts, it might articulate a different policy that took into account the competing interests of other states as well as its own interest."[54] Thus, expanding the idea of governmental interests may raise fewer hackles from sovereigntists yet reach the same results.

Second, the substantive method, true to its name, focuses on the substance of the law to be applied rather than any external criteria that might be relevant to choosing the appropriate norms. Accordingly, although both vested rights and governmental interest analysis choose the applicable law on the basis of a priori considerations – the "location" of the cause of action or the domicile of the parties – the substantive method emphasizes the need to choose governing norms rather than a governing jurisdiction. But while proponents of the substantive law method tout this feature as an advantage,[55] something is lost by not conducting a separate inquiry concerning prescriptive jurisdiction. After all, it seems reasonable to expect that the extent of the parties' relationships to the various states whose law might apply should have some independent bearing on the choice-of-law inquiry. Moreover, such an inquiry need not be either the formalist exercise envisioned by Beale or the parochial one advocated by Currie. Rather, choice of law could become the locus for debates about the varieties of community definition and affiliation present in the case and the degree to which issues of physical geographical location should remain salient as a guide to choice of law. If courts focus too much on the substance of the possible governing norms without conducting a separate choice-of-law inquiry, this important discussion could be elided or deemphasized.

[54] *Id.* at 549.

[55] *See, e.g.*, *id.* at 547–8 (discussing the advantages of choosing rules or solutions rather than jurisdictions).

To be fair, Dinwoodie himself seeks to avoid this problem. Indeed, in resolving a hypothetical transnational copyright dispute using the substantive law method, he asks courts to consider "all relevant interests – national, international, and postnational,"[56] an inquiry that presumably could include a discussion of community affiliation. Moreover, he masterfully dissects the various governmental interests, the trends in the law that courts might consider, and the hybrid solutions that could be devised.[57] But even this admirable treatment of transnational choice of law still suffers from the substantive law method's insistence on combining the substantive analysis with the choice-of-law inquiry. Because of Dinwoodie's substantive focus, his discussion is almost completely confined to the various legal rules that might apply, their strengths and weaknesses, and the interests of the states involved. He does not, however, explicitly discuss the parties; nor does he engage in a discussion about the extent of the parties' affiliation with various normative communities or consider whether it is appropriate to see those parties as more connected to one of those communities in particular. Accordingly, while Dinwoodie's substantivism usefully employs a cosmopolitan pluralist framework when analyzing the norms in play, the substantive method tends (even in his version) to focus too little on the various possible definitions of community that might be available and the particular affiliations of the parties themselves.

Thus, although the substantive method appropriately asks judges to consider the distinctively transnational aspects of a dispute and to fashion creative hybrid solutions to multistate problems, it does so in a way that unnecessarily invites criticism from sovereigntists worried about state interests, and it short-circuits important discussion about the appropriate scope of prescriptive jurisdiction. To prevent such problems, a cosmopolitan pluralist approach is grounded in an expanded conception of governmental interests and allows debate about the scope of a community's

[56] *Id.* at 561.

[57] *See id.* at 561–9.

legal norms before addressing the norms themselves. Only through such debate can there be common law development of principles concerning the appropriate understanding of a legal community in a world of increasingly overlapping norm-generating groups.

Cosmopolitan Pluralism

A choice-of-law regime built on cosmopolitan pluralist principles asks courts to consider the variety of normative communities with possible ties to a particular dispute. In doing so judges must see themselves as part of an interlocking network of domestic, transnational, and international norms. Recognizing the "complex and interwoven forces that govern citizens' conduct in a global society,"[58] courts can develop a jurisprudence that reflects this cosmopolitan pluralist reality.

Such a jurisprudence looks to a variety of possible legal sources. First, courts can consider the multiple domestic norms of nation-states affected by the dispute. In considering which national norms to give greatest salience, courts must analyze the community affiliations of the parties and the effect of various rules on the polities of the affected states. Moreover, whereas most traditional choice-of-law regimes require a choice of one national norm, a cosmopolitan pluralist approach permits judges to develop a hybrid rule that may not correspond to any particular national regime. Second, international treaties, agreements, or other statements of evolving international or transnational norms may provide relevant guidance. Third, courts should consider community affiliations that are not associated with nation-states, such as industry standards, norms of behavior promulgated by nongovernmental organizations, community custom, and rules associated with particular activities, such as Internet usage. Fourth, courts should not develop rules that encourage a regulatory "race to the bottom" by making it easy to evade legal regimes.

[58] *Id.*

At first glance, this approach might seem similar to the one taken by the Restatement (Second) of Conflict of Laws, which permits courts to consult a "grab bag"[59] of factors to reach a choice-of-law decision, including "the needs of the interstate and international system."[60] Indeed, the Second Restatement's emphasis on finding the place with the "most significant relationship" to the dispute[61] does at least turn the focus from pure territorial contacts to relationships. It is unclear, however, whether such "relationships" include affiliations that are neither citizenship-based nor territory-based. In contrast, cosmopolitan pluralism would acknowledge such additional affiliations. The Second Restatement also maintains a series of Beale-like presumptions about the proper choice-of-law default rules for specific types of cases.[62] These presumptions tend to be based on territoriality and may actually trump the more general (and more cosmopolitan) guidance about the needs of the interstate and international systems.[63] Thus, though one could perhaps interpret the Second Restatement in a cosmopolitan pluralist way, the emphasis of the restatement is distinctly different.

A cosmopolitan pluralist approach does, however, share some basic tenets with the Restatement (Third) of Foreign Relations Law. Section 403 of this Restatement sets forth a series of principles intended to combat judicial (or legislative) parochialism. These principles include many of the factors a cosmopolitan pluralist approach privileges. For example, Section 403(2)(b) asks judges to consider "the connections, such as nationality, residence, or economic activity, between the regulating state and the person principally responsible for the activity to be regulated."[64]

[59] Brilmayer, *supra* note 12, at 74.

[60] *Restatement (Second) of Conflict of Laws* § 6 (1971).

[61] *See, e.g., id.* § 145(1).

[62] *Compare, e.g., id.* § 145 (listing general principles for tort cases), with *id.* § 188 (contract cases), and *id.* § 193 (insurance cases).

[63] *See, e.g., Wood Bros. Homes, Inc. v. Walker Adjustment Bureau,* 601 P.2d 1369, 1372–3 (Colo.1979) (ruling that, because the presumptions in section 196 had not been rebutted, the general principles in *section* 6 would not be considered).

[64] *Restatement (Third) of the Foreign Relations Law of the United States* § 403(2)(b) (1987).

Likewise, Section 403(2)(f) cites "the extent to which the regulation is consistent with the traditions of the international system."[65] These and the other nonexclusive "reasonableness" factors of Section 403 would certainly be among the criteria for making a choice-of-law decision using a cosmopolitan pluralist framework. Thus, to some extent the cosmopolitan pluralist vision I sketch here draws upon the Third Restatement, and judges employing the Third Restatement approach could comfortably fit the principles I describe into their customary analyses. Indeed, cosmopolitan pluralism could even be seen to provide an additional justification for the Restatement's emphasis on "connections" between the regulating state and the relevant actor.

On the other hand, a cosmopolitan pluralist conception asks judges explicitly to focus on community affiliation, which may prompt a different sort of inquiry from the Third Restatement's more generalized call to reasonableness. Indeed, among the benefits of a cosmopolitan pluralist framework is that it makes conflict of laws the site for ongoing legal discussions about the changing nature of community, personal identification, and social conceptions of space, distance, and borders. Such discussions may be less likely if judges are purporting to apply simply a multifactor reasonableness standard. Thus, even if many cases would ultimately be decided the same way under either a cosmopolitan pluralist test or one derived from the Third Restatement of Foreign Relations, the inquiry may be (though of course need not be) significantly different.

Perhaps most importantly, because a focus on community affiliation may lead us to consider nonstate communities, a cosmopolitan pluralist framework is far more likely to allow consideration of how norms generated outside formal governmental channels may bind sub-, supra-, and transnational communities. In contrast, the Third Restatement of Foreign Relations, though it takes a significant step forward by asking judges to consider norms of antiparochialism when making choice-of-law decisions, may ultimately be too state-centered to

[65] *Id.* at § 403(2)(f).

provide the theoretical underpinnings for conflict of laws in an era of diffused sovereignty.[66]

As mentioned previously, a cosmopolitan pluralist approach to choice of law borrows elements not only from the Third Restatement of Foreign Relations, but from each of the three major choice-of-law methods already discussed. While eschewing both Beale's rigid formalism and his reification of territorial location as the basis for choice-of-law decisions, cosmopolitan pluralism does recognize the importance of thinking about choice of law separately from the substantive norm to be applied. Thus, courts employing a cosmopolitan pluralist approach should discuss the possibly relevant community affiliations and consider their relative importance before turning to an application of substantive law. In this way, choice of law becomes the terrain for debate about the proper scope of community dominion in an era when territorial borders no longer adequately delimit community boundaries.

Likewise, while rejecting Currie's parochial application of governmental interest analysis, a cosmopolitan pluralist approach is firmly grounded in an expanded notion of governmental interests. Indeed, as courts consider multiple community affiliations and develop hybrid rules for resolving multistate disputes, they do so not because they are ignoring the policy choices of their home state, but because they are effectuating their state's broader interest in taking part in a global community. Thus, a cosmopolitan pluralist approach is ultimately moored to an expanded conception of how governments must operate in an interconnected world.

Finally, because it is based on this broader conception of governmental interests, a cosmopolitan pluralist approach avoids some of the concerns about democratic legitimacy raised by the substantive law method. Moreover, by treating choice of law as an a priori discussion

[66] *Cf.* Adeno Addis, The Thin State in Thick Globalism: Sovereignty in the Information Age, 37 *Vand. J. Transnat'l L.* 1, 85–104 (2004) (articulating a theory of state sovereignty that he calls "thin statism"); Anne-Marie Slaughter, The Real New World Order, *Foreign Aff.* (Sept./ Oct. 1997), at 184–6 (arguing that "[t]he state is not disappearing, it is disaggregating").

of community definition and affiliation, cosmopolitan pluralism rejects the undue emphasis on substantive rules that is the hallmark of the substantive law method. Yet cosmopolitan pluralism, like the substantive law method, asks courts resolving multistate disputes to see themselves as international and transnational actors who are engaging in an international dialogue about legal norms. Accordingly, they must consider how best to construct a world system of law (and not just pursue parochial interests), and they may develop hybrid norms for resolving multistate disputes.

A cosmopolitan pluralist approach to international adjudication, therefore, allows courts to engage in a dialogue with each other concerning the appropriate definition of community affiliation and the appropriate scope of prescriptive jurisdiction. In addition, the approach asks courts to develop international norms, thereby harnessing the generative potential of international litigation. Treaties and other formal instruments of international lawmaking are cumbersome and slow to adjust to changing technologies or social conditions; international common law adjudication is far more dynamic. As a result, international private law litigation can serve public values by creating a forum for debates both about community affiliation and about new common law international norms.[67]

Of course, such dynamism also raises important concerns.[68] For example, one might fear that common law norm development will diminish the predictability of legal rules. Accordingly, we might think a more cosmopolitan pluralist approach will increase the likelihood that disputes will be decided using norms of which the parties have little or no advance knowledge. If so, we might be reluctant to let go of the basic due process notion that parties should not be subjected to legal consequences

[67] *See, e.g.*, Jenny S. Martinez, Towards an International Judicial System, 56 *Stan. L. Rev.* 429, 444–8 (2003) (describing the importance of judge-made common law procedural doctrines in international and transnational litigation).

[68] The substantive law method also implicates these same concerns, and my discussion here largely tracks a similar discussion in Dinwoodie, *supra* note 46, at 571–5.

that they could not reasonably have foreseen when taking their actions.[69] Certainly, many actors would sacrifice some dynamism in exchange for the ability to predict judicial outcomes more effectively.

These concerns may, however, be overstated for several reasons. First, as with all common law rules, the amount of uncertainty diminishes over time as areas of doctrine become more settled. Thus, as courts develop norms for determining that certain activities establish community ties sufficient to justify the exercise of prescriptive jurisdiction, the uncertainty will be reduced. Second, current choice-of-law analysis is already quite unpredictable and often arbitrary.[70] Third, concerns about certainty in the commercial context are undermined by the fact that international commercial arbitration, which has few if any fixed substantive principles, has nevertheless been an extraordinarily popular means of resolving disputes. Fourth, in a world of rippling effects across multiple jurisdictions, it is not intrinsically unfair (or contrary to due process) to subject someone who conducts affairs that have multicommunity impact to the norms of those communities, even if there are many of them. Finally, we must remember that it is not unprecedented for courts to introduce some uncertainty during the transition from one choice-of-law regime to another. For example, in the classic conflicts case of *Neumeier v. Kuehner*,[71] the New York State Court of Appeals explicitly acknowledged that its rejection of a vested rights approach several years earlier had created uncertainty:

> When ... we rejected the mechanical place of injury rule in personal injury cases because it failed to take account of underlying policy considerations, we were willing to sacrifice the certainty provided by the old rule for the more just, fair and practical result that may best be achieved by giving controlling effect to the law of the jurisdiction

[69] I am grateful to Clyde Spillenger for suggesting this point.

[70] *Cf.* Kermit Roosevelt III, The Myth of Choice of Law: Rethinking Conflicts, 97 *Mich. L. Rev.* 2448, 2449 (1999) ("Choice of law is a mess. That much has become a truism."). For example, strict territorialism may encourage forum-shopping, with its concomitant lack of certainty.

[71] 286 N.E.2d 454 (1972).

> which has the greatest concern with, or interest in, the specific issue raised in the litigation. In consequence of the change effected – and this was to be anticipated – our decisions ... have, it must be acknowledged, lacked consistency.[72]

Nevertheless, the court went out of its way to embrace the ad hoc, case-by-case approach it had used to construct the new choice-of-law regime.[73] Significantly, the court emphasized that such common law development helps to uncover over time the appropriate values and policies to be weighed by courts, leading eventually to the formulation of new "rules of general applicability, promising a fair level of predictability."[74] The ultimate outcome, according to the court, is worth the short-term cost.

Another concern, discussed previously, is that a court taking a cosmopolitan pluralist approach is behaving illegitimately because it is not applying forum law. It must be remembered, however, that vested rights also often required courts to apply other states' laws; only the parochial understanding of governmental interests insists that forum law trumps. Moreover, with an expanded understanding of governmental interests, there is no reason to fear that a court applying a cosmopolitan pluralist vision is necessarily unmoored from the long-term interest of the government to which the court owes its legal authority. Finally, it is important to remember that this cosmopolitan pluralist lawmaking is being engaged in not by unelected international regulators or bureaucrats but by national or state judges. Such judges go to the bench through domestic political or bureaucratic processes, and they are local citizens presumably influenced by local culture and concerns. By definition, then, even when a court incorporates a cosmopolitan pluralist conception in its framework, it is doing so as a local actor articulating a new (cosmopolitan pluralist) domestic norm in a multinational dispute.

[72] *Id.* at 457 (citations omitted).

[73] *See id.* (noting that the prior cases "enable us to formulate a set of basic principles that may be profitably utilized, for they have helped us uncover the underlying values and policies which are operative in this area of the law").

[74] *Id.* (citing *Tooker v. Lopez,* 249 N.E.2d 394, 403 [N.Y. 1969] [Fuld, C.J., concurring]).

Cosmopolitan pluralism thus offers courts an opportunity to craft choice-of-law rules that reflect the realities of a world where people form multiple community affiliations that are not necessarily linked to physical geography. By considering these multiple affiliations, courts provide a forum for debate about the changing scope of prescriptive jurisdiction. Such debate can actually promote long-term international cooperation by providing incentives for other branches of government to negotiate international regulatory compromises.[75] And by recognizing the long-term interests that states have in being part of an interlocking world order, courts can engage in dynamic, transnational lawmaking, developing and applying international, transnational, or hybrid norms to govern multistate disputes. How might this approach work in practice? Let us see.

State-Sanctioned Courts

GlobalSantaFe Corp. v. Globalsantafe.com

Historically, the boundaries of trademark law have been delineated in part by reference to physical geography.[76] Thus, if I own a store in New York City called "Berman's," I will not, as a general matter, be able to prevent a person in Australia from opening a store that is also called "Berman's," even if I have previously established a trademark in my name. The idea is

[75] William Dodge sees this incentive as a reason to prefer interest analysis to vested rights. *See* William S. Dodge, Extraterritoriality and Conflict-of-Laws Theory: An Argument for Judicial Unilateralism, 39 *Harv. Int'l L.J.* 101, 105–6 (1998). He argues that in a world of concurrent jurisdiction, there will be conflicts arising from parochial application of forum law and that these conflicts provide useful incentives to negotiate. *Id.* at 106. A cosmopolitan approach offers similar benefits both because it permits (and promotes) concurrent jurisdiction and because it raises the conflict-of-laws questions to the surface rather than simply assuming a forum law default.

[76] *See* Graeme B. Dinwoodie, Trademarks and Territory: Detaching Trademark Law from the Nation-State, 41 *Hous. L. Rev.* 885, 887 (2004) ("[I]t is an axiomatic principle of domestic and international trademark law that trademarks and trademark law are territorial.").

that customers would be unlikely to confuse the two stores because they are in markets that are spatially distinct.[77] In the online world such clear spatial boundaries are collapsed because, as the domain name system is currently organized, there can be only one bermans.com domain name, and it can only point to one "location."[78]

In the early to mid-1990s, as corporations and entrepreneurs began to understand the potential value of a recognizable domain name, pressure increased to create trademark rights in such names. In response, Congress first passed the Federal Trademark Dilution Act[79] and then the Anticybersquatting Consumer Protection Act (ACPA), which provides an explicit federal remedy to combat so-called cybersquatting.[80] According to the congressional reports, the ACPA is meant to address cases where people who are not trademark holders register well-known trademarks as domain names and then try to "ransom" the names back to the trademark owners.[81]

[77] *See Hanover Milling Co. v. Metcalf,* 240 U.S. 403, 415 (1916) ("[W]here two parties independently are employing the same mark upon goods of the same class, but in separate markets wholly remote the one from the other, the question of prior appropriation is legally insignificant... [except in cases of bad faith]."). This is not an absolute rule, of course, because "famous or well-known marks may well leap oceans and rivers, cross national borders, and span language barriers to achieve international recognition." Dan L. Burk, Trademark Doctrines for Global Electronic Commerce, 49 *S.C. L. Rev.* 695, 720 (1998); *see also Vaudable v. Montmartre, Inc.,* 193 N.Y.S.2d 332, 332 (Sup. Ct. 1959) (enjoining the use by a restaurant in New York of the name and decor of Maxim's Restaurant in Paris). Nevertheless, the likelihood-of-confusion standard historically has tended to embed a geographical limitation.

[78] Of course, users going to www.bermans.com could be shown an introductory screen that provides a choice of which Berman site they wish to access.

[79] Federal Trademark Dilution Act of 1995, *Pub. L. No.* 104–98, 109 *Stat.* 985 (codified at 15 U.S.C.§§1125, 1127 [*Supp.* 1996]).

[80] Anticybersquatting Consumer Protection Act, *Pub. L. No.* 106–113, §3002, 113 *Stat.* 1501A-545, 1501A-545 (1999) (codified at 15 U.S.C.§1125(*d*) [2000]); *see H.R. Rep. No.* 106–412 (1999) (detailing the Act).

[81] *See H.R. Rep. No.* 106–412, at 5–7 (1999) (noting that "[s]ometimes these pirates put pornographic materials on theses sights [*sic*] in an effort to increase the likelihood of collecting ransom by damaging the integrity of a [trade]mark"); *S. Rep. No.* 106–140, at 4–7 (1999) (highlighting testimony regarding attempts to ransom domain names to the highest bidder).

The application of trademark law to domain names has meant that trademark law has become unmoored to physical geography and is now more likely to operate extraterritorially. Potentially, even those who are legitimately using a Website that happens to bear the name of a famous mark held by an entity across the globe could be forced to relinquish the name.[82] In addition, this unmooring of trademarks from territory creates the possibility that individual countries will interpret their trademark laws expansively, thereby reducing trademark rights "to their most destructive form": the mutual ability to block (or at least interfere with) the online use of marks recognized in other countries.[83] Moreover,

[82] In response to this problem, the World Intellectual Property Organization and the Assembly of the Paris Union for the Protection of Industrial Property adopted, in fall 2001, a Joint Recommendation calling for a definition of "use" for purposes of trademark law that would protect legitimate users of marks who disclaimed any intent to engage in commerce in a particular country. Joint Recommendation Concerning Provisions on the Protection of Marks, and Other Industrial Property Rights in Signs on the Internet art. 2 (2001), *available at* http://www.wipo.int/about-ip/en/development_iplaw/doc/pub845.doc. The ACPA at first glance seems to limit its extraterritorial scope in a similar way because it extends *in rem* jurisdiction only if the domain name violates rights protected by the Lanham Act, 15 U.S.C. §1125(d)(1)(a), which in turn requires that a mark be used "in commerce." *See* Dinwoodie, *supra* note 76, at 909; *see also id.* at 909 n. 85 (explaining that this requirement has been widely accepted by judges despite the lack of an explicit statutory basis). Presumably this "use in commerce" requirement means that the mark must actually be used in the U.S. market to give rise to a cause of action. However, because a Website located abroad may render services to customers in the United States, it is unclear whether the "use in commerce" requirement will in practice provide much of a limitation on the potentially extraterritorial application of the *in rem* provisions. *See, e.g., International Bancorp, LLC v. Société des Bains de Mer,* 329 F.3d 359, 364 (4th Cir. 2003) (ruling that providing services abroad to U.S. customers can constitute "use in commerce" for purposes of the Act). For a discussion of this case, *see* Dinwoodie, *supra* note 76, at 914–19.

[83] *See* Graeme B. Dinwoodie, Private International Aspects of the Protection of Trademarks 27, Presented at the WIPO Forum on Private International Law and Intellectual Property (Jan. 30–1, 2001) (WIPO Doc. No. WIPO/PIL/01/4 2001) (noting that "[t]his 'mutual blocking' capacity is neither efficient nor a positive contribution to the globalization of markets or the development of ecommerce"), *available at* http://works.bepress.com/cgi/viewcontent.cgi?article=1037&context=graeme_dinwoodie. Catherine T. Struve and R. Polk Wagner have also raised the specter that realspace sovereigns may increasingly attempt to segment the domain system itself, to ensure that any trademark action involving domain names will have the requisite territorial

the parties claiming ownership in a trademark could sue in different countries, and, because of differences in substantive law, both parties could win.[84]

This is the backdrop for *GlobalSantaFe Corp. v. Globalsantafe.com*.[85] On September 3, 2001, Global Marine, Inc., and Santa Fe International Corporation announced their agreement to merge into an entity to be known as GlobalSantaFe Corporation. Less than a day later, Jongsun Park, a citizen of South Korea, registered the domain name globalsantafe.com with the Korean domain name registrar Hangang. In response, Global Marine and Santa Fe filed an in rem action in the Eastern District of Virginia under the ACPA. The ACPA provides in rem jurisdiction over a domain name wherever that name is registered.[86] Thus, for example, if people register domain names online via a Website owned by Network Solutions, a domain name registrar[87] corporation located in Virginia, they potentially can be forced, under the ACPA, to defend a trademark action in Virginia whether or not they have ever set foot in Virginia or knew Network Solutions was a Virginia corporation.

In this case, however, jurisdiction was further complicated by the fact that Park had not even registered the domain name with a U.S.

nexus to support the assertion of jurisdiction. Catherine T. Struve & R. Polk Wagner, Realspace Sovereigns in Cyberspace: Problems with the Anticybersquatting Consumer Protection Act, 17 *Berkeley Tech. L.J.* 989, 1031–4 (2002). As Struve and Wagner point out, such territorially based segmentation of the domain name system would result in "the dramatic reduction in utility provided by the system itself." *Id.* at 1031.

84 *See, e.g., Mecklermedia Corp. v. D.C. Cong.* GmbH, 1998 Ch. 40, 53 (Eng.) (noting that the cause of action for using trademarked language is different in Germany and England, and, thus, simultaneous proceedings could continue).

85 250 F. Supp. 2d 610 (E.D. Va. 2003).

86 15 U.S.C. § 1125(d)(2)(C) (2000) ("In an in rem action... a domain name shall be deemed to have its situs in the judicial district in which... the domain name registrar, registry, or other domain name authority that registered or assigned the domain name is located....").

87 A registrar is one of several entities for a given top-level domain (such as .com, .edu, .gov, .uk) that is authorized by the Internet Corporation for Assigned Names and Numbers to grant registration of domain names. David Bender, *Computer Law* § 3D.05[3], at 3D-104 (2002).

registrar, but with a South Korean one. Nevertheless, the ACPA also authorizes in rem jurisdiction in the judicial district where the overall domain name *registry* is located.[88] On the basis of this provision, the district court determined that it could exercise jurisdiction because VeriSign, which administers the entire ".com" registry, is located in Virginia. And, having determined that the substantive provisions of the ACPA had been met, the court therefore ordered both Hangang and VeriSign to "take all appropriate steps to transfer the domain name" to GlobalSantaFe.[89]

Approximately a week later, Park filed an application for an injunction in the District Court of Seoul, South Korea, seeking an order preventing Hangang from transferring the domain name. Ruling that the Virginia court did not have proper jurisdiction, the Korean court provisionally granted the injunction, and Hangang, presumably responding to the Korean court's injunction, subsequently refused to transfer the domain name. In an effort to resolve this transnational stalemate, GlobalSantaFe returned to the court in Virginia seeking an additional order directing VeriSign to cancel the infringing domain name from the ".com" registry.

The district court reaffirmed that it had proper in rem jurisdiction over the case pursuant to the ACPA because VeriSign is located in Virginia. The court also reiterated that Park had violated the substantive provisions of the ACPA. And, after a lengthy discussion of the mechanics concerning how a registry company would effectively cancel or transfer a domain name, the court concluded that such a remedy was both available under the ACPA and appropriate given the unwillingness of Hangang to act in violation of the Korean court's order.

[88] *See supra* note 86. For each top-level domain (such as .com, .gov, . edu, .uk), a single registry company is responsible for keeping the records and a directory of all the domain names within that domain. When an individual or corporation company wants the rights to a new domain name, it contacts a registrar. The registrar submits the domain name to the registry, which enters the assigned domain name into a database. Currently, VeriSign Global Registry Services is the sole registry for ".com" domain names.

[89] *Id.* at 614.

From a conflicts perspective, what is most striking about the decision is that the court focuses almost exclusively on its jurisdiction to hear the case but never questions that the ACPA is the only possibly relevant legal regime. Indeed, the court seems to assume that the ACPA's legal reach is limited solely by the scope of the court's jurisdiction, not by any choice-of-law considerations. Thus, in the court's view, the only significant gap in the ACPA's trademark enforcement regime is for domain names registered under top-level domains whose registry is located outside the United States. Never does it seem to occur to the judge that, even if the court had jurisdiction over the action, it might nevertheless choose South Korean (or some other) law as providing the operative legal norms for resolving the dispute.

This single-minded focus on jurisdiction (and therefore the physical location of registry companies) poses potential problems for ACPA enforcement in the future. As the court recognizes, if jurisdiction is all, then the ACPA can only provide a broad-based remedy in domain name trademark cases so long as the registries of the most popular top-level domains remain in the United States.[90] Thus, if country-code top-level domains were to become more popular, or if the registries for generic domains such as ".com" and ".net" were relocated outside the physical territory of the United States, then U.S. trademark rights in domain names would face serious enforcement challenges.[91] Such difficulties are a natural consequence of laws that are deemed to apply to the full extent of their territorially based jurisdictional reach. But, of course, as choice-of-law scholars have long recognized, laws need not be applied to the full extent of their jurisdictional reach, and concerns about the establishment of competing or conflicting trademark systems on the Internet are precisely the sorts of concerns that might animate a more restrained application of forum law.

[90] *Id.*

[91] *See* Struve & Wagner, *supra* note 83, at 1019–41 (warning that aggressive assertion of U.S. jurisdiction over the domain name system may ultimately lead to the system's segmentation because other countries could establish competing systems for registries maintained outside the United States).

Indeed, it is not at all clear why the Eastern District of Virginia should exercise jurisdiction here, given that such jurisdiction is based principally on the arbitrary location of the registry company.

In any event, having concluded that the case was within its jurisdiction and that, therefore, U.S. law necessarily applied, the court only at the very end of its opinion asked whether "concerns of international comity" might dictate deference to the injunction issued by the Korean court.[92] Even here, however, the court did not ask about the content of South Korean trademark law; it only asked whether deference was owed to the court decision granting the actual injunction. Having framed the issue in this way, the court resolved it by reference to a principle that in rem cases should generally be decided by the first court to exercise jurisdiction over the property in question. And, since the original Virginia court order preceded the Korean court injunction, the Virginia court found deference inappropriate.

The vision of choice of law that emerges from the decision, therefore, is founded solely on jurisdictional power and a race to the courthouse. A state can enact legal norms with extremely broad extraterritorial reach, and courts within that state are bound to apply those norms to a multinational dispute so long as the case was commenced there first. Needless to say, this is not a particularly thoughtful or nuanced choice-of-law regime; nor does it take into account the possible long-term benefits that might accrue from adopting a more restrained application of forum law or from considering the forum's own interest in harmonious international adjudicatory processes.

Rather than simply insisting on applying U.S. law, a court with a cosmopolitan pluralist vision of choice of law would ask whether the community affiliations of the parties in GlobalSantaFe[93] made it more appropriate to apply the law of South Korea or the law of the United States (or some combination of the two). At first glance, such an analysis

[92] *GlobalSantaFe*, 250 F. Supp. 2d at 624.

[93] 250 F. Supp. 2d 610 (E.D. Va. 2003).

might seem to produce a draw. GlobalSantaFe is a U.S. corporation, but Park is a South Korean citizen who did not even register the domain name in dispute with a U.S. registrar.[94] Thus, even a tenuous, Internet-based contact with the United States is lacking.

Yet, relying on such literal "contacts" is a relic of territorialism (even when the contact in question is simply "visiting" a U.S.-based Web server). Instead, a cosmopolitan pluralist vision looks to affiliation. Here, Park purposely registered the domain name of a newly formed U.S. corporation, GlobalSantaFe, precisely because it was a newly formed corporation.[95] Accordingly, this is not a case where someone registers a domain name for independent reasons, and the name just happens to be the same as that of some distant entity that was likely unknown to the registrant. Instead, Park was fully aware of the U.S. corporation and deliberately picked the name to take advantage of the confusion and then sell the name back to the corporation. Thus, Park's actions were wholly aimed at a U.S. corporation based in the United States. On that basis, it seems that even a court using a cosmopolitan pluralist perspective would apply U.S. trademark law to the dispute. Moreover, had the South Korean court adopted such a view, it would have enforced the original U.S. court judgment rather than set up a parochial battle of dueling injunctions. Indeed, if one viewed this as a judgment recognition case, under a cosmopolitan pluralist vision the South Korean court should first have acknowledged Park's voluntary affiliation with the United States and then enforced the U.S. court's judgment in order to avoid precisely the sort of judicial impasse that occurred here. Such is the importance of conflicts values.

Does that mean that the citizenship of the alleged trademark holder should always govern the choice-of-law decision? Not necessarily. First, as noted previously, if Park had registered the name without any knowledge of, or intent to profit from, the U.S.-based corporate name, there would be

[94] *See id.* at 613 n.4 (noting that the domain name was registered in Korea).

[95] *See id.* at 616 (finding that the registrant "clearly" registered the domain name "after, and in response to" the merger announcement).

no voluntary affiliation with the United States. Second, if GlobalSantaFe, even if incorporated in the United States, were based in South Korea or conducted substantial activities there, then South Korean trademark law might well apply since both parties would have meaningful affiliations with South Korea.

Moreover, even though a cosmopolitan pluralist choice-of-law vision reaches the same result as the district court in this particular case, it would not support the district court's notion that the location of the registry company has any bearing at all on the choice-of-law decision.[96] Such a focus territorializes Internet transactions in a particularly arbitrary way, given that very few people know the whereabouts of, or interact with, the registry for a top-level domain. And as a practical matter, emphasizing the physical location of the registry company means that, for the foreseeable future, all domain name disputes (at least those in the most popular ".com" or ".net" or ".edu" domains) would be resolved under U.S. law. Such a system, while creating a certain degree of uniformity, is unacceptably parochial. Indeed, if in the future we were to see the emergence of a popular top-level domain whose registries were located outside the United States, there would likely be substantial objection from U.S. trademark holders. Thus, a system that privileges the arbitrary location of registry companies is an invitation to long-term segmentation of the domain name system, with different legal rules governing different top-level domains. A cosmopolitan pluralist vision, in contrast, though it may at times be less predictable, at least holds the promise of developing long-term common law consensus about which nation's laws should apply to which types of disputes.

A final potential jurisdictional actor in this dispute must be recognized. The Internet Corporation for Assigned Names and Numbers (ICANN) is not a governmental body at all, but a private corporation that administers the technological standards of the domain system.

[96] *See GlobalSantaFe*, 250 F. Supp. 2d at 617 (relying on the fact that the registry company was located within the district).

ICANN might be thought of as an Internet-based governing body,[97] and arguably it is therefore better positioned than a U.S. court to be undertaking the conflicts analysis. Indeed, because it is established as a global body, with elaborate consultative and representational arrangements, ICANN may be more likely to take account of the various interests involved, including the consuming public (global, not just American) and domain-name holders (global, not just American). ICANN can also account for the interest of states in protecting their citizens. There is, after all, no reason to think ICANN would find Korea to have any more legitimate interest in protecting its citizen cybersquatters than did the U.S. court. Of course, one might think that ICANN lacks the democratic accountability necessary to be a legitimate governing body[98] and that any

[97] *See* A. Michael Froomkin, Wrong Turn in Cyberspace: Using ICANN to Route Around the APA and the Constitution, 50 *Duke L.J.* 17, 20 (2000) ("For almost two years, the Internet Corporation for Assigned Names and Numbers (ICANN) has been making domain name policy under contract with the Department of Commerce...."); David G. Post, Governing Cyberspace, or Where Is James Madison When We Need Him? (June 1999), *available at* http:// www.temple.edu/lawschool/dpost/icann/comment1.html ("[N]otwithstanding the [U.S.] government's (and ICANN's) protestations to the contrary, this is about nothing less than Internet governance writ large."). Indeed, at the press conference convened in 1998 to unveil the Department of Commerce White Paper that led to the creation of ICANN, Becky Burr, Department of Commerce spokeswoman, stated: "We are looking for a globally and functionally representative organization, operated on the basis of sound and transparent processes that protect against capture by self-interested factions, and that provides robust, professional management. The new entity's processes need to be fair, open, and pro-competitive. And the new entity needs to have a mechanism for evolving to reflect changes in the constituency of Internet stakeholders." Press Release, Becky Burr, Associate Administrator, National Telecommunications and Information Administration's Office of International Affairs, Commerce Department Releases Policy Statement on the Internet Domain Name System (June 5, 1998), *available at* http://www.ntia.doc.gov/ntiahome/press/dnsburr.htm.

[98] For criticisms of ICANN from the perspective of democratic legitimacy and administrative transparency, *see, for example,* Froomkin, *supra* note 97, at 18; Jonathan Weinberg, ICANN and the Problem of Legitimacy, 50 *Duke L.J.* 187, 188 (2000); Post, *supra* note 97. *See generally* Centre for Global Studies, Univ. of Vict., Enhancing Legitimacy in the Internet Corporation for Assigning Names and Numbers: Accountable and Transparent Governance Structures (Sept. 18, 2002), *available at* http://www.markle.org/downloadable_assets/icann_enhancelegitemacy.pdf. For similar criticisms of WIPO,

tie between a Website operator and ICANN is largely involuntary[99] and therefore not a cognizable community affiliation. Nevertheless, ICANN might be a more inclusive governing body than a multistate intergovernmental process, where nonstate communities tend to be underrepresented. Indeed, the states that control such intergovernmental processes always have an incentive to protect state prerogatives, and so a nonstate entity such as ICANN may open up alternative space for voices that otherwise tend to be unheard.

Barcelona.com, Inc. v. Excelentisimo Ayuntamiento de Barcelona

Whereas the choice-of-law issues in *GlobalSantaFe* were made more complicated by the fact that the parties were from different countries, in *Barcelona.com* all of the principal actors in the dispute were from

see, for example, A. Michael Froomkin, Of Governments and Governance, 14 *Berkeley Tech. L.J.* 617, 618 (1999): "As an international body all too willing to take up the reins of global governance, WIPO attempted to create global e-commerce friendly rules by a process that, left to itself, seemed likely to consist predominantly of meeting with commercial interest groups and giving little more than lip service to privacy and freedom of expression concerns."

For criticism of the UDRP system on the ground that the arbitration system is fundamentally biased in favor of trademark holders, *see* Michael Geist, Fair.com?: An Examination of the Allegations of Systemic Unfairness in the ICANN UDRP, 27 *Brook. J. Int'l L.* 903, 903–13 (2002) (noting that the system is biased in favor of trademark holders); Michael Geist, Fundamentally Fair.Com? An Update on Bias Allegations and the ICANN UDRP 8 (2002), at http:// aix1.uottawa.ca/~geist/fairupdate.pdf (updating study, responding to methodological criticisms, and stating that bias continues). All of these criticisms might be relevant in determining whether a court should consider or defer to norms articulated through the UDRP process.

[99] As Michael Froomkin describes:

> Anyone who wishes to have a domain name visible to the Internet at large must acquire it from a registrar who has the right to inscribe names in an ICANN-approved domain name registry. ICANN determines which registries are authoritative. This power to make and break registries allows ICANN to require registries (and also registrars) to promise to subject all registrants to a mandatory third-party beneficiary clause in which every registrant agrees to submit to ICANN's UDRP upon the request of aggrieved third parties who believe they have a superior claim to the registrant's domain name.

A. Michael Froomkin, ICANN's "Uniform Dispute Resolution Policy" – Causes and (Partial) Cures, 67 *Brook. L. Rev.* 605, 612 (2002).

Spain.[100] Yet even here the Fourth Circuit, reversing a contrary ruling of the district court,[101] eschewed Spanish law and insisted on applying the ACPA.[102] Moreover, this decision was again reached without significant consideration of choice-of-law issues.

The case involved the right to the domain name barcelona.com. In 1996 Mr. Joan Nogueras Cobo ("Nogueras"), a Spanish citizen, registered barcelona.com with the Virginia-based domain name registrar, Network Solutions. Subsequently, Nogueras formed a corporation under U.S. law, called Bcom, Inc. Despite the U.S. incorporation, however, the company had no offices, employees, or even a telephone listing in the United States. Nogueras (and the Bcom servers) remained in Spain.

The Barcelona City Council asserted that Nogueras had no right to use barcelona.com under Spanish trademark law and demanded that he transfer the domain name registration to the city council. When Nogueras refused, the city council filed a complaint with the World Intellectual Property Organization (WIPO).[103] Several months later, the WIPO

[100] *Barcelona.com, Inc. v. Excelentisimo Ayuntamiento de Barcelona*, 330 F.3d 617 (4th Cir. 2003).

[101] *Barcelona.com, Inc. v. Excelentisimo Ayuntamiento de Barcelona*, 189 F. Supp. 2d 367 (E.D. Va. 2002).

[102] *Barcelona.com*, 330 F.3d at 630. To be sure, because the claim at issue sought only a declaratory judgment as to the plaintiff's rights under the Lanham Act, it is possible to construe the Fourth Circuit decision as merely clarifying U.S. law without requiring that this law be the ultimate rule of decision in the case. However, nowhere does the court state that it is rendering such a limited ruling and instead explicitly reverses the district court's application of Spanish law and remands so that the district court can "grant the appropriate relief under [the Lanham Act]." *Id.* at 630. In addition, the appellate opinion states that the ACPA can be used specifically to reverse arbitration decisions "grounded on principles foreign or hostile to American law." *Id.* at 626. Both of these statements strongly imply that the Fourth Circuit considered its application of U.S. law to be dispositive.

[103] *Id.* at 621. Every domain name issued by Network Solutions is issued under a contract, the terms of which include a provision requiring resolution of disputes through the Uniform Dispute Resolution Policy (UDRP) promulgated by the Internet Corporation for Assigned Names and Numbers. *Id.* The WIPO complaint was filed in accordance with the terms of the UDRP. *Id.*

panelist ruled in favor of the city council.[104] Instead of transferring the domain name, however, Bcom filed suit in federal court, again in Virginia, seeking a declaratory judgment that the registration of barcelona.com was not unlawful.

The district court, after deciding that the WIPO administrative proceedings would be given "no weight,"[105] turned to the elements of the ACPA, first considering whether either party possessed a valid trademark for the name "Barcelona." Significantly, the district court sought to answer this question by reference to both U.S. and Spanish law. And, although the court concluded that neither party possessed a U.S. trademark in the name "Barcelona," it did find that the city council possessed multiple Spanish trademarks containing the term "Barcelona," such as "Barcelona Teatre," "Barcelona Canal," and "Barcelona Television." The court also noted that, under Spanish law, if a trademark consists of two or more words, the operative issue is which word creates the dominant impression in the mind of the consumer. Here, that word is obviously "Barcelona." Finally, the court determined that, under Spanish law, the names of communities, municipalities, and provinces cannot be registered as trademarks without authorization by municipal officials, and neither Nogueras nor Bcom had received such authorization. Thus, the court ruled that the city council possessed a "legally valid Spanish trademark" for the word "Barcelona."[106] The district court then turned to the other elements of the ACPA, finding both the likelihood of consumer confusion and the requisite bad faith intent to profit from the domain name registration. Accordingly, the district court ruled in favor of the city council and refused to issue the declaratory judgment Bcom had sought.[107]

[104] *Id.*

[105] *Barcelona.com,* 189 F. Supp. 2d at 371.

[106] *Id.*

[107] *Id.* at 373. The court also ruled in favor of the City Council on an ACPA counterclaim against Nogueras, finding that Nogueras had engaged in bad faith intent to profit from the City Council's valid trademark. *Id.* at 372–7.

The Fourth Circuit reversed.[108] Significantly, the major issue on which the appellate court disagreed with the trial court was the use of Spanish law to determine whether the city council had a valid trademark. Citing Section 1114(2)(D)(v) of the ACPA, the Fourth Circuit emphasized that the principal issue to be decided is whether "plaintiff's registration or use of the domain name is not unlawful under the Lanham Act."[109] According to the appellate panel, this language makes clear that only U.S. law may be used to determine the existence of a valid trademark or its possible infringement. Having decided to apply U.S. trademark law, the court then concluded that "Barcelona" is "a purely descriptive geographical term entitled to no trademark protection" under the ACPA.[110] Accordingly, the court found nothing unlawful in Nogueras's registration of barcelona.com and therefore reversed the district court's ruling.[111]

Thus, the Fourth Circuit, like the court in *GlobalSantaFe*, applied U.S. law to an international trademark dispute, invoking principles of territoriality. Despite the fact that the principal actors in the dispute were all in Spain, the appellate court opined that the ACPA, "[b]y requiring application of United States trademark law to this action brought in a United States court by a United States corporation involving a domain name administered by a United States registrar," was consistent with "the fundamental doctrine of territoriality upon which our trademark law is presently based."[112]

This doctrine of territoriality likely derives from the 1883 Paris Convention for the Protection of Industrial Property[113] (upon which the

[108] *Barcelona.com, Inc. v. Excelentisimo Ayuntamiento de Barcelona*, 330 F.3d 617, 619–20, 629 (4th Cir. 2003).

[109] *Id.* at 626 (emphasis added).

[110] *Id.* at 629–30.

[111] *Id.* at 630. The Fourth Circuit also vacated the district court's decision concerning the City Council's counterclaim (without reaching the merits) because the appellate panel concluded that no counterclaim had actually been filed. *Id.*

[112] *Id.* at 628.

[113] Paris Convention for the Protection of Industrial Property, Mar. 20 1883, art. 10bis, as last revised at *Stockholm, Jul.* 14, 1967, 21 U.S.T. 1583, 828 U.N.T.S. 305.

Fourth Circuit relied). Indeed, the concern animating the convention was that absent a doctrine of territoriality, a country could create a "world mark" simply by granting a trademark under its local law, thereby preventing anyone, anywhere in the world, from using that name.[114] Such an extraterritorial encroachment was unacceptable in an era when it was presumed that trademarks could easily operate locally because the use of a trade name in one country would have no significant impact on the use of the same name by a different entity in another country.

When considering trademarks in domain names, however, a single-minded emphasis on territoriality may itself create law with substantial extraterritorial effects. For example, by applying the ACPA in *GlobalSantaFe*, the U.S. district court necessarily imposed U.S. trademark law on a South Korean domain name registrant and a South Korean domain name registrar, even though neither had any significant contact with the United States. Likewise, in *Barcelona.com*, the Fourth Circuit applied U.S. trademark law to a dispute where all the principal actors were Spanish and where the issue concerned a domain name associated with the name of a major city in Spain. Both of these cases demonstrate that, by applying a rigid conception of territoriality to international trademark disputes (at least in the context of domain names), courts run the risk of imposing U.S. law extraterritorially and creating precisely the sort of world mark that the principle of territoriality was originally designed to prevent.

Indeed, as Graeme Dinwoodie has made clear, courts have used the territoriality principle to preclude the need either to reconcile conflicting trademark claims or to articulate standards for determining the appropriate prescriptive law to apply.[115] Instead, courts "simply recognize forum-

[114] *See, e.g.*, Tortsten Bettinger & Dorothee Thum, Territorial Trademark Rights in the Global Village – International Jurisdiction, Choice of Law and Substantive Law for Trademark Disputes on the Internet (Part Two), 31 *Int'l Rev. of Intell. Prop. & Competition L.* 285, 286 (2000) (explaining the basis of the doctrine of territoriality with regard to trademarks).

[115] *See* Dinwoodie, *supra* note 83, at 30.

determined rights and apply forum law or, alternatively, dismiss the case if it does not implicate such rights or laws."[116] But in an era of global commercial activity, "where consumer understanding, product markets, and producer marketing[] disdain territorialism, the value of such a rule as the lodestar for international trademark law becomes questionable."[117] And, of course, the Internet renders such territorialism both impractical (because of the difficulty of locating a relevant transaction)[118] and unwise (because, as discussed previously, strict territorialism will actually result in extraterritorial encroachment on the trademark laws of other countries). In addition, "fictionally localizing an activity that is inherently non-local ... detaches the applicable law from social reality, which undermines its legitimacy."[119]

Accordingly, we need to reconsider the traditional assumption that trademark disputes must always be resolved by applying the law of the forum country. Instead, cases involving international actors require courts to use choice-of-law principles in order to determine the appropriate legal norms. Moreover, such cases may help suggest choice-of-law frameworks that take proper account of the actual community affiliations of the parties, as well as the interests nation-states have in being a functioning part of an interlocking international network of domestic trademark regimes.

In contrast to *GlobalSantaFe*, the domain name dispute in *Barcelona.com* has far less connection to the United States. Here we have a Spanish citizen registering a domain name using the name of a Spanish city to create a tourist portal for people visiting Spain. While it is true that Nogueras, the registrant, subsequently transferred the domain name to a

[116] *Id.*

[117] *Id.*

[118] *See, e.g.*, Am. Bar Ass'n, Cyberspace Jurisdiction Project, Achieving Legal and Business Order in Cyberspace: A Report on Global Jurisdiction Issues Created by the Internet, reprinted in 55 *Bus. Law.* 1801, 1826 (2000) ("[I]f an activity occurs in Cyberspace, it is impossible to ascribe it to any specific physical space."). Although somewhat exaggerated as a general matter, this statement is relatively accurate when considering the "location" of a domain name.

[119] Dinwoodie, *supra* note 83, at 32.

nominally American corporation, the corporation appears to have been created solely to hold the registration and had no actual presence in the United States beyond a domain name registration and a post office box.

A cosmopolitan pluralist vision of choice of law need not countenance legal formalisms such as the place of incorporation. Rather, the inquiry is focused on substantive community affiliations. Here, all the true principals in the case are in Spain, and the dispute concerns a Web portal for tourists intending to visit Barcelona. These are indeed strong affiliations with Spain.

Therefore, a cosmopolitan pluralist vision would embrace the approach of the district court and at least use Spanish law to determine whether the City of Barcelona held a valid trademark in names containing the word "Barcelona." In contrast, the Fourth Circuit panel applied U.S. trademark law, on the theory that the Spanish law should not be applied extraterritorially. When dealing with a globally interconnected communications system, however, the appellate court's conception of extraterritoriality is problematic because there is no way to avoid a ruling that will have some extraterritorial effect. The Fourth Circuit focused on the specter of Spanish trademark law's being applied in a case involving a U.S. corporation (never mind the fact that the corporation was only formally a U.S. entity). But the Fourth Circuit's approach is equally extraterritorial, because it applies U.S. trademark law in a case involving a Spanish trademark holder, various Spanish parties, and a Web portal for tourists to Spain.

Accordingly, the mere fact that some country's trademark law will be applied extraterritorially does not provide an answer to the choice-of-law problem. Indeed, it is precisely the existence of a reciprocal extraterritoriality problem that makes it a choice-of-law question in the first place. Thus, relying on territoriality is no solution. Instead, the court should have delved deeper, using choice-of-law principles to analyze the substantive community affiliations of the parties.[120]

[120] It is also worth noting that, at least in cases where both parties have a good-faith connection to a name, the domain name could be "shared," so that users typing in the

Finally, from a pluralist perspective it is worth noting that there is a third set of community norms in this case: not just those of the United States and Spain, but also the norms articulated by the WIPO arbitrator in the first place. These norms are a product of the Uniform Dispute Resolution Policy (UDRP) promulgated by ICANN, discussed previously.[121] The existence of the WIPO arbitration in this case reminds us that nonstate entities may be an important source of norms and must at least be considered in any conflicts analysis.

It is not that the outcomes in either of these cases are necessarily so egregious. What is particularly troubling, however, is the failure of these courts even to think of the cases before them as true choice-of-laws cases. As a result, nearly all of the conceptual and practical considerations that tend to arise in conflicts cases (as well as the voluminous scholarship on the subject) are ignored, and the truly transnational dimension of these cases is given short shrift. A cosmopolitan pluralist approach to choice of law yields a significantly different framework for analyzing these cases. Although the ultimate result may or may not shift, a cosmopolitan pluralist framework would affect the way in which judges view their task in considering cases with multinational dimensions.

Religious Communities

Turning from state-to-state conflicts to the assertions of nonstate normative communities, we can consider religious communities as a paradigm set of cases because such communities have historically provided some of the strongest challenges to state-based lawmaking. Indeed, the Treaty of Westphalia – widely viewed as the document that ushered in the era

domain name would be shown an introductory screen giving them the choice of which site they are seeking.

121 *See Barcelona.com,* 330 F.3d at 621 ("Every domain name issued by Network Solutions, Inc. is issued under a contract, the terms of which include a provision requiring resolution of disputes through the UDRP. In accordance with that policy, the City Council filed an administrative complaint with... WIPO, an ICANN-authorized dispute-resolution provider located in Switzerland.").

of the modern nation-state – was designed in large part to limit the influence of religious communities and their leaders. To this day, the ways in which state governments either accommodate or resist religious practices are among the most contentious issues such governments encounter in the negotiation between self and other, familiar and strange.

Here, I explore two well-known cases in which the U.S. Supreme Court was forced to determine how state-based lawmaking would interact with the norms of a religious community. First, in *Bob Jones Univ. v. United States*, the Court addressed an IRS decision to deny tax-exempt status to a religious school that interpreted Christian scriptures to forbid "interracial dating and marriage."[122] Second, in *Employment Div., Dept. of Human Resources of Oregon v. Smith*, the question was whether a general state statute forbidding certain narcotics should be applied to an Indian tribe's religious practice that included the use of peyote.[123] To my mind, viewing these conflicts as choice-of-law questions makes the analytical framework more coherent (though, it should be noted, no less difficult).

Bob Jones Univ. v. United States

Turning to *Bob Jones*, the Internal Revenue Service (IRS) had interpreted Section 501(c)(3) of the Internal Revenue Code, which gives tax-exempt status to qualifying charitable institutions, to apply to schools only if such schools have a "racially nondiscriminatory policy as to students." Accordingly, the service denied tax exemption to Bob Jones University, which had not admitted blacks at all until 1971 and had admitted them thereafter but had forbidden interracial dating, interracial marriage, the espousal of violation of these prohibitions, and membership in groups that advocated interracial marriage. Crucial to the case was the fact that the university grounded its rule not on racial attitudes, but on biblical

[122] 461 U.S. 574 (1983).
[123] 494 U.S. 872 (1990).

scripture. The school therefore considered the exclusion of interracial dating to be a principal tenet of its religious community. Nevertheless, although the text of Section 501(c)(3) did not speak to racial discrimination at all, the Supreme Court upheld the IRS determination, finding the service's interpretation of the code provision to be permissible.

Robert Cover, in his article "Nomos and Narrative," has famously criticized the reasoning of the *Bob Jones* decision, even while agreeing with the Court's result. According to Cover, the Court assumed "a position that places nothing at risk and from which the Court makes no interpretive gesture at all, save the quintessential gesture to the jurisdictional canons: the statement that an exercise of political authority was not unconstitutional."[124] In particular, Cover argued that, by grounding its decision on an interpretation of the Internal Revenue Code, the Court had sidestepped the crucial constitutional question of whether Congress could grant tax exemptions to schools that discriminated on the basis of race. This was a problem for Cover because he believed that if a state legal authority were going to "kill off" the competing normative commitment of an alternative community, it should do so on the basis of a profound normative commitment of its own.[125] By avoiding the constitutional question, Cover complained, the Court had disserved both the religious community – whose normative commitments would be placed at the mercy of mere public policy judgments – and racial minorities – who "deserved a constitutional commitment to avoiding public subsidization of racism."[126]

In contrast, had the Court viewed the clash between the university's religious rule and federal law as a choice-of-law decision, two aspects of the case would have been clarified. First, the Court would have analyzed and defined the relevant community affiliations at stake. Second, the Court would have been forced to grapple with the strength of its commitment to the principle of nondiscrimination, just as Cover urged.

[124] Robert M. Cover, The Supreme Court, 1982 Term – Foreword: Nomos and Narrative, 97 *Harv. L. Rev.* 4, 66 (1983).

[125] *See id.* at 52–60.

[126] *Id.* at 67.

As a result, instead of simply asserting federal law, a conflicts analysis encourages negotiation among the different norms advanced by different communities.

A cosmopolitan pluralist vision of conflict of laws recognizes that people and groups hold multiple community affiliations and takes those affiliations seriously. Thus, when a nonstate legal practice is largely internal and primarily reflects individuals' affiliation with the nonstate community, the practice should be given more leeway than when the state itself is part of the relevant affiliation. In this case, the issue at stake was a tax exemption, a quintessentially state matter. Indeed, Bob Jones University was asking for a particular benefit for charitable organizations that was contained in the U.S. tax code. Therefore, for these purposes the place of the university within the nation-state was the most salient tie, making application of the federal law more justifiable. In contrast, as we shall see, other nonstate normative commitments do not implicate the nation-state so directly.

Moreover, even if the relevant community tie were largely with the religious community itself, certain norms might be held so strongly by the nation-state community that such norms would be applied *regardless* of the community affiliation. In choice-of-law analysis, this is usually called the public policy exception, and it allows courts to refuse to apply foreign law that would otherwise apply, if those legal norms are sufficiently repugnant.[127] But application of the public policy exception is rare. Thus, if a court asserts such an exception, it must justify the use of public policy grounds by reference to precisely the sorts of deeply held commitments that Cover envisioned. In the *Bob Jones* case, for example, it might be that the nation-state's deep commitment to eradicating racial discrimination would independently justify overriding the religious norms, regardless of the community affiliation analysis.

[127] *Baker v. General Motors Corp.*, 522 U.S. 222, 223 (1998) ("A court may be guided by the forum State's 'public policy' in determining the *law* applicable to a controversy." [citing *Nevada v. Hall*, 440 U.S. 410, 421–4 (1979)]).

Accordingly, a cosmopolitan pluralist approach would not simply throw the claim of protected religious insularity to the mercy of political or bureaucratic judgments. Taking the ban on interracial dating seriously as law and performing a choice-of-law analysis would create the obligation to engage in crucial line drawing. And while the community affiliation and public policy exception analyses *in this case* might justify application of state law, that will not always be the case.

Employment Div., Dept. of Human Resources of Oregon v. Smith

Consider, by way of contrast, *Employment Div., Dept. of Human Resources of Oregon v. Smith*, in which the Supreme Court refused to extend First Amendment protection to the religious use of peyote.[128] Here, unlike the religious university at issue in *Bob Jones*, the Indian tribe was not negotiating its relationship with the state; rather, the use of peyote was part of a purely internal religious practice open primarily (or exclusively) to members of that community. Thus, a choice-of-law analysis based on community affiliation might well result in deference to the nonstate norm. Moreover, the normative commitment to drug enforcement is perhaps better characterized as a governance choice than as an inexorable normative command. As such, the public policy exception is arguably less appropriate in this context than when addressing racial discrimination. Applying these principles, a cosmopolitan pluralist choice-of-law analysis might well have permitted the religious practice in *Smith*.

IN THE END, HOWEVER, I AM LESS CONCERNED WITH THE PARTICULAR outcome than with the analytical framework. Conceiving of these clashes between religious and state-based norms in conflicts terms reorients the inquiry in a way that takes more seriously the nonstate community assertion. As a result, courts must wrestle both with the nature of the multiple community affiliations potentially at issue and with the need to

[128] 494 U.S. 872 (1990).

articulate truly strong normative justifications for not deferring to the nonstate norm. Both consequences make the choice-of-law decision a constructive terrain of engagement among multiple normative systems, rather than an arm of state government imposing its normative vision on all within its coercive power.

Of course, this vision is not unproblematic. Two related objections immediately present themselves. First, a choice-of-law rule that tends to defer to nonstate norms when they implicate only internal community affiliation might be seen to rest on the often-criticized distinction between public and private action. Indeed, the idea of deference in this context might come to look like the classic state deference to family privacy or autonomy.[129] And just as family privacy was often invoked to shield domestic violence and gender hierarchy, so too may deference to "internal" community norms become deference to fundamentally illiberal norms.

Second, as in the family context, we may make a mistake by assuming that the nonstate community at issue is monolithic. Indeed, it may be that some members of the relevant community would prefer to have the *state* norm applied to their situation. As Judith Resnik has noted, Cover's vision of multiple norm-generating communities did not address the problem of conflict "*within* [such] communities about their own practices and authoritative interpretations."[130] Yet, such "contestation from within"[131] (which is likely to occur along the fault lines of power hierarchies within the community) is an almost inevitable part of community norm creation. Thus, the choice-of-law question becomes, in part, a question of whose voices within a community are heard by which speakers of nation-state power.

As to the concern that too much deference to "private" norms within a community will overly empower illiberal communities, it is important

[129] *See, e.g.*, Frances E. Olsen, The Myth of State Intervention in the Family, 18 *U. Mich. J.L. Reform* 835, 836–7 (1985).

[130] Judith Resnik, Living Their Legal Commitments: Paideic Communities, Courts, and Robert Cover, 17 *Yale J. L. & Human.* 17, 27 (2005).

[131] *Id.*

to remember that, because of the public policy exception, these norms, if sufficiently abhorrent, need not be applied by the state authority. After all, a lynch mob may also be a statement of community norms, but it need not for that reason necessarily be embraced. The object of a choice-of-law analysis is not to follow nonstate community norms blindly, but to ensure that if a state asserts its own norms it does so self-consciously. Indeed, simply identifying the state's jurispathic power does not necessarily mean that we must reject all exercises of that power.[132] Even Cover recognized the utility of a state court's speaking in "imperial mode."[133] He noted that when judges kill off competing law by asserting that "*this one* is the law," they may do violence to the competing visions, but they also make peace possible both because too much law is too chaotic to sustain and because some laws are simply too noxious to be applied.[134] The point then is simply to make sure that the imposition of imperial, jurispathic law is not done blindly or arrogantly, but with intentionality and a respect for the other sources of lawmaking that are being displaced.[135] A conflicts analysis at least opens space for such self-consciousness and care.

More difficult is the problem of how to respond to Resnik's arguments about inevitable conflicts within a nonstate community concerning the content of that community's norms. Certainly the existence of substantial disagreement within the community might be factored into the decision of whether or not to apply the state norm. Thus, if some substantial portion of the nonstate community were clamoring for the application of *state* law, such clamoring might blunt somewhat the need to defer to the nonstate norm.

More importantly, in thinking about how to address disputes within a nonstate community, we must distinguish between two types of challenges.

[132] *See id.* at 25.

[133] Cover, Nomos and Narrative, *supra* note 124, at 13–14.

[134] *Id.* at 53.

[135] *See* Resnik, *supra* note 130, at 25 ("[Cover] wanted the state's actors … to be uncomfortable in their knowledge of their own power, respectful of the legitimacy of competing legal systems, and aware of the possibility that multiple meanings and divergent practices ought sometimes to be tolerated, even if painfully so.").

One concerns the proper understanding of what the content of the community's law *actually is*, and the other concerns what that law *ought to be*. For example, in *Santa Clara Pueblo v. Martinez*, a woman who was a member of an Indian tribe challenged her tribe's refusal to consider her children to be tribal members.[136] She did so, however, not on the basis of an argument that the tribe had improperly interpreted its own community law (which based tribal membership on the father's tribal membership not the mother's). Instead, she argued that the tribe's law was inconsistent with a federal equal protection statute. Thus, the case did not present a contestation about the content of the community's norms; it merely raised a choice-of-law issue about whether the tribal law or the federal statute should govern. And however difficult the resolution of that choice-of-law question might be, it does not raise the conundrum of how to determine the appropriate content of the nonstate norms in the first place.

Finally, in those relatively infrequent situations when the actual content of the nonstate norm *is* at issue, courts can seek evidence to determine that community's governing norm. Historical documentation, anthropological testimony, and evidence of ongoing practice might all be relevant. And again, to the extent that there are concerns that the nonstate norm is the product of hierarchy, those concerns can be factored into the choice-of-law inquiry itself; they do not render it impossible to determine the content of the norm.

In any event, we can see that for both state-to-state disputes and disputes among state and nonstate communities, a cosmopolitan pluralist approach permits a more direct engagement with the issues of jurisdictional overlap and a far more nuanced and explicit effort to negotiate among normative communities. Thus, the choice-of-law inquiry can itself become a mechanism for managing, without eliminating, hybridity.

[136] 436 U.S. 49 (1978).

9 Recognition of Judgments and the Legal Negotiation of Difference

AS NOTED PREVIOUSLY, JUDGMENT RECOGNITION INVOLVES the circumstances under which one community enforces another community's prior judgment regardless of how the enforcing community might have ruled on the issue originally. And, just as with choice of law, a cosmopolitan pluralist vision of judgment recognition requires decision makers to see themselves as part of an international network of decision makers and to see the parties before them as potentially affiliated with multiple communities. Those various communities might legitimately seek to impose their norms on such affiliated parties. Thus, when faced with an enforcement decision regarding a foreign judgment, decision makers should not necessarily assume that their own local public policies block such enforcement. Instead, they must undertake a nuanced inquiry concerning whether the affiliations of the parties render the original judgment legitimate. Although the local policies of the forum community are not irrelevant, those policies should be weighed against the overall systemic interest in creating an interlocking system of adjudication.

This is not so different from what U.S. courts already do in domestic cases raising judgment recognition issues. Indeed, the U.S. Supreme Court has long held that states cannot invoke public policy to refuse to enforce sister-state judgments.[1] This is true even

[1] *See, e.g.*, *Baker v. Gen. Motors Corp.*, 522 U.S. 222, 233 (1998) (clarifying that there is no public policy exception to the full faith and credit due judgments).

when the judgment being enforced would be illegal if issued by the rendering state.[2]

Of course, in the domestic context, the recognition of judgments has a constitutional dimension because of the full faith and credit clause.[3] Moreover, within a single, relatively homogeneous country, the idea of one state's enforcing another state's judgment does not seem quite so controversial because the legal variations among states are likely to be relatively minor. On the other hand, the full faith and credit clause derives from the Articles of Confederation,[4] which were drafted when the colonies were less homogeneous and more akin to separate nation-states than they are today.

In any event, while the decision to enforce a foreign judgment will surely be less automatic, many of the same principles are still relevant. Most importantly, what we might call the "conflicts values" that underlie the full faith and credit command should be part of the judgment recognition calculus. Thus, decision makers should acknowledge the importance of participating in an interlocking international legal system, where litigants cannot simply avoid unpleasant judgments by relocating. Indeed, in a cosmopolitan world, there is no need for inherent suspicion of foreign judgments. As in the choice-of-law context, deference to other decision

[2] *See, e.g.*, *Estin v. Estin*, 334 U.S. 541, 546 (1948) (finding that the full faith and credit clause "ordered submission ... even to hostile policies reflected in the judgment of another State, because the practical operation of the federal system, which the Constitution designed, demanded it"); *Milwaukee County v. M.E. White Co.*, 296 U.S. 268, 277 (1935) ("In numerous cases this Court has held that credit must be given to the judgment of another state, although the forum would not be required to entertain the suit on which the judgment was founded.... "); *Fauntleroy v. Lum*, 210 U.S. 230, 237 (1908) (holding that the judgment of a Missouri court was entitled to full faith and credit in Mississippi even if the Missouri judgment rested on a misapprehension of Mississippi law).

[3] U.S. Const. art. IV, § 1.

[4] The Articles of Confederation contained a provision similar to article IV, section 1: "Full faith and credit shall be given in each of these States to the records, acts, and judicial proceedings of the courts and magistrates of every other State." U.S. Articles of Confederation, art. IV. For a concise history of full faith and credit, *see* Robert H. Jackson, Full Faith and Credit – the Lawyer's Clause of the Constitution, 45 *Colum. L. Rev.* 1 (1945).

makers may have long-term reciprocal benefits. And, particularly when the parties have no significant affiliation with the forum state, there is little reason for a court to insist on following domestic public policies in the face of such competing conflicts values. As Benjamin Cardozo has observed: "We are not so provincial as to say that every solution of a problem is wrong because we deal with it otherwise at home."[5]

This is not to say that foreign judgments should always be enforced. Even in a cosmopolitan pluralist system, one would expect that decision makers might sometimes interpose local public policies where they would not in the domestic state-to-state setting. But if we acknowledge the importance of the conflicts values effectuated by strong judgment recognition, we will necessarily reject the idea that, because a judgment could not have been issued by a decision maker in the first instance, that decision maker is simply unable to enforce the judgment. Instead, we will appreciate that enforcing a foreign judgment is fundamentally different from issuing an original judgment. Indeed, judgment recognition implicates an entirely distinct set of concerns about the role of law in a multistate world.

Recognizing the Judgments of Foreign States

In most areas of law, U.S. courts have generally invoked these conflicts values and enforced foreign judgments as a matter of comity.[6] As far back as 1895, in *Hilton v. Guyot*,[7] the U.S. Supreme Court made clear that comity "is the recognition which one nation allows within its territory to the legislative, executive, or judicial acts of another nation, having due regard both to international duty and convenience, and to the rights of its own citizens, or of other persons who are under the protection of its

[5] *Loucks v. Standard Oil Co.*, 120 N.E. 198, 201 (N.Y. 1918).

[6] *See* Mark D. Rosen, Exporting the Constitution, 53 *Emory L.J.* 171, 176 (2004) (noting that, since the nineteenth century, "the United States has been at the vanguard of enforcing foreign judgments").

[7] 159 U.S. 113 (1895).

laws."[8] The Second Restatement of Conflict of Laws codified this idea, noting that a "judgment rendered in a foreign nation ... will, if valid, usually be given the same effect as a sister State judgment."[9] Moreover, validity is based only on whether the court that rendered judgment had proper personal jurisdiction over the parties and utilized procedures that were not inherently unfair.[10]

In addition, while courts enforcing foreign judgments (as opposed to domestic ones) have applied a public policy exception to avoid enforcing particularly egregious rulings, the exception has been construed very narrowly.[11] Accordingly, courts only refuse to enforce "where the original claim is repugnant to fundamental notions of what is decent and just in the State where enforcement is sought."[12] Likewise, the United Nations Convention on the Recognition and Enforcement of Foreign Arbitral Awards and the Uniform Foreign Money-Judgments Recognition Act require that a U.S. court enforce a judgment or arbitral award unless there is fraud or if doing so would be repugnant to the public policy of the enforcing forum.[13] Thus, in most recognition of judgments cases, "[c]ourts consistently have enforced foreign judgments even if they would have refused to entertain suit on the original claim on grounds of public policy."[14]

In stark contrast to this general policy of respecting foreign judgments, however, U.S. courts generally have assumed, at least where U.S. constitutional values seem to be at stake, that enforcing an "unconstitutional"

[8] *Id.* at 164.

[9] *Restatement (Second) of Conflict of Laws*, § 117 cmt. c (1971).

[10] *Id.* § 92.

[11] *See* Rosen, *supra* note 6, at 177–9 (surveying U.S. case law on enforcement of foreign judgments).

[12] *Restatement (Second) of Conflict of Laws*, § 117 cmt. c (1971).

[13] *See, e.g.*, Convention on the Recognition and Enforcement of Foreign Arbitral Awards, June 10, 1958, 330 U.N.T.S. 38 (requiring courts to enforce the judgment or arbitral award unless there is fraud or if doing so would be repugnant to the public policy of the enforcing forum); Unif. Foreign Money-Judgments Recognition Act §4, 13 pt. II U.L.A. 58–59 (2002) (discussing situations where foreign judgments need not be recognized).

[14] Rosen, *supra* note 6, at 178–9.

judgment of a foreign state community is itself a violation of the U.S. Constitution. As a result, courts have effectively imposed U.S. constitutional norms on foreign disputes, even in circumstances where the dispute has little connection with the United States.[15]

Consider, for example, the case of *Telnikoff v. Matusevitch*.[16] This was a libel case between two British citizens concerning writings that appeared in a British newspaper. After a complicated sequence of proceedings in the United Kingdom, a jury ruled for Telnikoff and ordered damages, but Matusevitch moved to the state of Maryland and subsequently sought a declaration that the British libel judgment could not be enforced in the United States, pursuant to the First Amendment, and he therefore could not be required to pay the British judgment. The Maryland Supreme Court ultimately ruled that, because British libel law violates the speech-protective First Amendment standards laid out by the U.S. Supreme Court in *New York Times Co. v. Sullivan*[17] and its progeny, the British judgment violated Maryland public policy and could not be enforced.

But there is no reason to think that the U.S. Constitution is necessarily implicated in such an enforcement action. First, it is debatable whether the simple enforcement of a judgment creates the requisite state action to implicate constitutional concerns.[18] Second, with regard to

[15] For an insightful critique of this practice, *see id.*, at 227–32.

[16] 702 A.2d 230 (Md. 1997).

[17] 376 U.S. 254 (1964); *see id.* at 280 (holding that the First Amendment limits recovery for libel to false statements made with "actual malice – that is, with knowledge that it was false or with reckless disregard of whether it was false or not").

[18] In *Shelley v. Kraemer*, 334 U.S. 1 (1948), the U.S. Supreme Court ruled that the equal protection clause precluded a court from enforcing a private racially restrictive covenant. In so doing, the Court determined that, although the covenant itself was entered into by private actors who were not subject to the commands of the Fourteenth Amendment, the action by the courts in enforcing the covenant was sufficient state action to trigger constitutional scrutiny. *Id.* at 18–19. *Shelley*, therefore, appears to block judicial enforcement of a private agreement (or a foreign order) that would be unconstitutional. Indeed, courts, in refusing to enforce foreign "unconstitutional" judgments, have explicitly relied on *Shelley*. *See, e.g.*, *Yahoo!, Inc. v. La Ligue Contre Le Racisme Et L'Antisémitisme*, 169 F. Supp. 2d 1181, 1189 (N.D. Ca. 2001) (citing *Shelley*), rev'd on other grounds, 433 F.3d 1199 (9th Cir. 2006) (en banc). Since the time *Shelley* was issued,

interstate harmony, a refusal to enforce the British libel judgment effectively imposes U.S. First Amendment norms on the United Kingdom. Such parochialism in judgment recognition, as in choice of law, is cause for concern. Third, while it is true that constitutional considerations could conceivably generate sufficient public policy reasons to refuse to enforce a judgment, the libel dispute in *Telnikoff* did not in any way implicate U.S. public policy because neither party had any particular affiliation with the United States at the time of the events at issue.

Thus, even if U.S. constitutional values or public policy considerations might sometimes require a court to refuse to enforce a judgment, there is no basis for a categorical rule preventing enforcement, and little reason to refuse to enforce an otherwise valid foreign judgment absent significant ties between the dispute and the United States. Instead, courts should take seriously the conflicts values that would be effectuated by enforcing the foreign judgment, weigh the importance of such values against the relative importance of the local public policy or constitutional norm, and then consider the degree to which the parties have affiliated themselves

however, courts and commentators have backed away from its sweeping ramifications. This is because, under *Shelley*'s reasoning, any private contract that is being enforced by a police officer or court would be transformed into state action. *See* Laurence H. Tribe, *American Constitutional Law* 1697 (2d ed. 1988) (arguing that *Shelley*'s approach, "consistently applied, would require individuals to conform their private agreements to constitutional standards whenever, as almost always, the individuals might later seek the security of potential judicial enforcement"). Although generations of legal realists and critical legal studies scholars have articulated similarly sweeping conceptions of state action (*see* Paul Schiff Berman, Cyberspace and the State Action Debate: The Cultural Value of Applying Constitutional Norms to "Private" Regulation, 71 *U. Colo. L. Rev.* 1263, 1279–81 (2000) (surveying these critiques)), courts have largely resisted *Shelley* and have limited its holding only to the context of racially restrictive covenants. Even in cases implicating the First Amendment, "with virtually no exceptions, courts have concluded that the judicial enforcement of private agreements inhibiting speech does not trigger constitutional review, despite the fact that identical legislative limitations on speech would have." Rosen, *supra* note 6, at 193; *see also id.* at 192–5 (discussing cases that have addressed the judicial enforcement of private contracts). Thus, it is not clear how robust *Shelley* still is and whether it would truly pose a constitutional bar in an action to enforce a foreign judgment. For further discussion of *Shelley* and its implications for judgment recognition, *see* Rosen, *supra* note 6, at 186–209.

with the forum. Only then can courts take into account the multistate character of the dispute and the flexible nature of community affiliation in a cosmopolitan world.

Returning once more to the *Yahoo!* case, after the French court ordered Yahoo! to block access to French users of the disputed Holocaust denial and Nazi memorabilia material, Yahoo! chose a two-pronged strategy. First, it decided to remove the auction sites from its servers altogether, but it claimed that such a decision was "voluntary" and unrelated to the French court ruling.[19] Second, it filed suit in U.S. District Court in the Northern District of California, seeking a declaratory judgment that the French court's orders were not enforceable in the United States pursuant to the First Amendment.[20]

Faced with the question of whether or not to enforce the French court's order, the district court started from the assumption that U.S. law (and U.S. constitutional norms) must apply. Thus, the court framed the issue for decision solely in U.S. constitutional terms: "What is at issue here is whether it is consistent with the Constitution and laws of the United States for another nation to regulate speech by a United States resident within the United States on the basis that such speech can be accessed by Internet users in that nation."[21]

Conceptualized in this way, the district court had little difficulty determining that enforcement of the French court order would violate the First Amendment, concluding both that the French judgment

[19] *See* Press Release, Yahoo!, Yahoo! Enhances Commerce Sites for Higher Quality Online Experience (Jan. 2, 2001) (announcing new product guidelines for its auction sites that prohibit "items that are associated with groups which promote or glorify hatred and violence"), *available at* http:// docs.yahoo.com/docs/pr/release675.html. *But cf.* Troy Wolverton & Jeff Pelline, Yahoo to Charge Auction Fees, Ban Hate Materials, CNET News.com, Jan. 2, 2001, at http://news.cnet.com/news/0–1007–200–4352889.html (noting that Yahoo!'s new policy regarding hate-related materials followed action by the French court).

[20] *Yahoo!, Inc. v. La Ligue Contre Le Racisme Et L'Antisémitisme,* 169 F. Supp. 2d 1181, 1186 (N.D. Ca. 2001), rev'd on other grounds, 433 F.3d 1199 (9th Cir. 2006) (en banc).

[21] *Id.* at 1186 (emphasis omitted).

constituted impermissible viewpoint discrimination and that it was unconstitutionally vague. The court therefore concluded that a U.S. court could not have issued such an order in the first instance without violating constitutional free speech norms.[22] But of course, in a judgment recognition case, that is not the appropriate inquiry. Indeed, as discussed previously, the full faith and credit clause requires recognition even of judgments that might actually be illegal in the state where recognition is sought. Thus, the real question is whether this is the type of judgment that should be *recognized*, not whether the court could have issued the ruling *as an original matter*.

To its credit, the district court did include a brief discussion of the judgment recognition issue in a section titled "Comity."[23] And the court acknowledged that "United States courts generally recognize foreign judgments and decrees unless enforcement would be prejudicial or contrary to the country's interests."[24] Yet, after reiterating that the French judgment "clearly would be inconsistent with the First Amendment if mandated by a court in the United States,"[25] the district court judge concluded that, because the foreign order would unconstitutionally chill speech occurring within U.S. borders, "the principle of comity is outweighed by the Court's obligation to uphold the First Amendment."[26]

Thus, while ostensibly addressing principles of judgment recognition, the court ultimately returned to the idea that if a judgment would be unconstitutional if issued in the United States, enforcing that judgment also would be unconstitutional, or at least sufficiently contrary to state interests as to overwhelm any principles of comity. By eliding the difference between issuing a judgment and enforcing a judgment, however, the court neglected to apply in more detail the various principles of

[22] *Id.* at 1189–90.
[23] *Id.* at 1192–3.
[24] *Id.* at 1192.
[25] *Id.*
[26] *Id.* at 1193.

judgment recognition or to consider more carefully those circumstances in which U.S. interests might not truly be threatened by the application of a foreign norm.[27]

So, how does a court adopting a cosmopolitan pluralist framework approach the question of whether to recognize the French judgment? To begin, we must acknowledge that this is a difficult case. To the extent that local public policies should have any valence in an international judgment recognition decision, here the U.S. public policy is particularly strong. Not only is the First Amendment a constitutional command, but it goes to the heart of American self-identity and arguably helps to define American democracy. Moreover, unlike in *Telnikoff*, Yahoo! is a U.S. corporation based in the United States. Thus, Yahoo!'s entitlement to First Amendment protection is far stronger than was Matusevitch's.

On the other hand, in weighing the relevant conflicts values, it becomes clear that this case is not a matter of France's simply imposing its norms on an entity with no affiliation in France. Rather, as has been discussed, Yahoo! is a sophisticated, multinational operator, with a business plan aimed at reaching Web users worldwide,[28] a marketing strategy touting its "global footprint,"[29] and a French subsidiary in which it has a 70 percent ownership stake.[30] Indeed, Yahoo! exerted substantial

[27] The Ninth Circuit ultimately reversed, sitting en banc, but it did so without reaching the judgment recognition issue. *Yahoo!, Inc. v. La Ligue Contre Le Racisme Et L'Antisémitisme*, 433 F.3d 1199 (9th Cir. 2006). The appellate court decided instead that until the French plaintiffs actually seek enforcement of the order in the United States, courts cannot address the recognition question.

[28] *See* Yahoo! Inc., 1999 Annual Report 2 (2000) [hereinafter Yahoo! 1999 Annual Report] ("Yahoo! Inc.... is a global Internet communications, commerce and media company that offers a comprehensive branded network of services to more than 120 million users each month worldwide."), *available at* http://www.sec.gov/Archives/edgar/data/1011006/0000912057-00-014598-d1.html.

[29] *See* Press Release, Yahoo! Inc., Yahoo! Reports Fourth Quarter, Year End 2000 Financial Results (Jan. 10, 2001) ("Yahoo! remained committed to broadening its global footprint and maintaining a leadership position worldwide."), *available at* http://docs.yahoo.com/docs/pr/4q00pr.html.

[30] Yahoo! 1999 Annual Report, *supra* note 28, at 5.

control over this subsidiary, dictating some of the links and content of the French site and requiring the subsidiary to maintain links to its U.S.-based site.[31] Moreover, Yahoo! routinely profiled French users in order to target them with advertisements written in French.[32] Given these efforts to take advantage of the French market and affiliate itself with France, Yahoo! has less cause for complaint concerning France's "extraterritorial" judgment.

Thus, the *Yahoo!* case falls between two extremes. At one pole is *Telnikoff*, in which the relevant community affiliations of both the parties and the dispute were exclusively British, and therefore enforcing the British libel judgment would be appropriate. At the other pole is a hypothetical case in which a small local Website based in the United States is prosecuted in France solely because of material available on the site. The company's utter lack of community affiliation with France would likely mean that the French judgment should not be enforced in the United States. In that instance, the strong First Amendment values would outweigh the need to enforce the judgment in order for the recognition court to remain a cooperative member of an international judicial community. In *Yahoo!,* there are both significant affiliation with the United States and significant affiliation with France. In the end, under a cosmopolitan pluralist approach, I think that the extent of Yahoo!'s business activities abroad justifies the French judgment and should make it enforceable in the United States. But regardless of the final outcome, it is clear that courts could not simply cite the First Amendment and refuse to enforce a foreign judgment without actually considering the conflicts values implicated by the enforcement decision.

[31] *See* Yahoo! France License Agreement, art. 3 (1996), in Yahoo! Inc., 1996 Annual Report exhibit 10.33, at 141–61 (1997) (setting forth the terms of the licensing agreement between Yahoo! Inc. and Yahoo! France), *available at* http://www.sec.gov/Archives/edgar/data/1011006/0000912057-97-011353.txt.

[32] *See* T.G.I. Paris, May 22, 2000, *available at* http:// www.juriscom.net/txt/jurisfr/cti/tgiparis20000522.htm (describing Yahoo!'s practice of profiling and targeting French users).

Recognizing the Judgments of International and Substate Communities

As discussed previously, a conflicts perspective encourages negotiation between self and other, local and distant, familiar and strange. Sometimes the distant and unfamiliar other will be embodied in the norms asserted by international bodies. Adopting a cosmopolitan pluralist framework allows scholars to consider the impact of such international norms without endless debates about whether in fact such norms should count as "law." Because legal pluralism turns the gaze to an analysis of how such norms actually affect behavior on the ground, we can focus not on abstract questions of legitimacy, but on empirical questions of efficacy. The important point for legal pluralism, after all, is what people come to believe and with what commitment.

Accordingly, there is nothing inherently illegitimate, from a cosmopolitan pluralist point of view, about a state-sanctioned court's considering norms articulated in an international forum. To the contrary, one can think of the potential conflict between a state norm and an international one as raising a conflict-of-laws question. And, even when a court does actually decide to defer to an international norm, the court might be seen not as thwarting the democratic will of the local polity, but as effectuating a broader domestic governmental interest in being part of an interlocking and smoothly functioning global legal order.

In the domestic federalism context, as in the international arena, we see jurisdictional overlap open space for competing views of regulatory issues. Indeed, the multiple authorities inherent in a federal system provide opportunities for contestation. For example, with regard to climate change, states and localities have been pursuing initiatives (sometimes in direct dialogue with international treaty regimes) that contrast with those preferred by federal authorities.[33] Such activities have even involved

[33] *See* Daniel C. Esty, Revitalizing Environmental Federalism, 95 *Mich. L. Rev.* 570 (1996); Bradley C. Karkkainen, Collaborative Ecosystem Governance: Scale, Complexity, and Dynamism, 21 *Va. Envtl. L.J.* 189, 214–16 (2002); Hari M. Osofsky & Janet Koven Levit,

states' suing the federal government regarding regulatory enforcement.[34] Similarly, localities have, in recent years, sought to create alternative immigration regimes,[35] gay marriage procedures,[36] securities regulation,[37] and foreign policy strategies.[38] To be sure, some of these initiatives have been beaten back by federal action, either judicial or otherwise. Yet, as with international legal pronouncements, state action has often resulted in changes in popular opinion that have altered the regulatory landscape and played a key role in pushing federal authorities to act differently than they otherwise would have.

Nevertheless, just as international law is often discussed as an epiphenomenon of nation-state sovereignty, federalism in the United States is often discussed only in terms of state sovereignty. Thus, we are told that the colonies were originally completely separate sovereign entities and that though they ceded some authority to the federal government, they retained their sovereign prerogatives. Accordingly, so the story goes, we live in a system of fifty-one sovereignties, and discussions of federalism are about how best to negotiate the relative power of these different sovereign entities.[39]

The Scale of Networks?: Local Climate Change Coalitions, 8 *Chi. J. Int'l L.* 409 (2008) [hereinafter Osofsky & Levit, The Scale of Networks?]. The dual system of bank regulation in the United States is another example. *See* Kenneth E. Scott, The Dual Banking System: A Model of Competition in Regulation, 30 *Stan. L. Rev.* 1 (1977).

[34] *See, e.g.*, *Massachusetts v. EPA*, 549 U.S. 497 (2007).

[35] *See, e.g.*, Federation for American Immigration Reform, Non-Cooperation Policies: "Sanctuary" for Illegal Immigration, *available at* http://www.fairus.org/site/PageServer?pagename=iic_immigrationissuecenters0173.

[36] *See, e.g.*, Richard C. Schragger, Cities as Constitutional Actors: The Case of Same-Sex Marriage, 21 *J.L. & Pol.* 147 (2005).

[37] For example, as Robert Ahdieh has recounted, then–New York attorney general Eliot Spitzer's broad assertions of authority to regulate the New York financial industry "repeatedly forced the SEC to follow his lead, or at least to join in his regulatory endeavors." Robert B. Ahdieh, Dialectical Regulation, 38 *Conn. L. Rev.* 863, 865–6 (2006).

[38] *See, e.g.*, *Crosby v. Nat'l Foreign Trade Council*, 530 U.S. 363 (2000).

[39] *See New York v. United States*, 505 U.S. 144 (1992), for an example of this conceptual framework.

This, however, is not the only way of thinking about federalism. Indeed, there is a different story we could tell, perhaps best captured in the oft-quoted idea of the states as "laboratories" of democracy.[40] Here the federal system is important not so much because such a system maintains the autonomy of different sovereign entities, but because it provides the opportunity for multiple decision makers to try out different solutions to similar problems. Moreover, the dialogue among the multiple decision makers may cause better solutions to spread through the system or may cause decision makers to recognize that varying solutions may be appropriate given varying local conditions. From this perspective, the overlapping jurisdiction of federal and state entities is seen as opening the possibility for creative innovation. This is what might be called a pluralist justification for federalism.

Scholars, many influenced by the seminal work of Robert Cover,[41] have recently come to embrace a more pluralist approach to both American federalism and international law.[42] They have touted the

[40] *See, e.g.*, *New State Ice Co. v. Liebmann,* 285 U.S. 262, 311 (1932) (Brandeis, J., dissenting) ("It is one of the happy incidents of the federal system that a single courageous State may, if its citizens choose, serve as a laboratory; and try novel social and economic experiments without risk to the rest of the country."); *see also*, e.g., *Truax v. Corrigan,* 257 U.S. 312, 344 (1921) (Holmes, J., dissenting) ("There is nothing that I more deprecate than the use of the Fourteenth Amendment beyond the absolute compulsion of its words to prevent the making of social experiments that an important part of the community desires even though the experiments may seem futile or even noxious to me...."). This narrative about federalism has been less prominent since the New Deal. *See, e.g.*, Richard C. Schragger, The Anti–Chain Store Movement, Localist Ideology, and the Remnants of the Progressive Constitution, 1920–1940, 90 *Iowa L. Rev.* 1011 (2005) (discussing decline of localism following the New Deal).

[41] *See* Robert M. Cover, The Uses of Jurisdictional Redundancy: Interest, Ideology, and Innovation, 22 *Wm. & Mary L. Rev.* 639 (1981).

[42] *See, e.g.*, Robert B. Ahdieh, Between Dialogue and Decree: International Review of National Courts, 79 *N.Y.U. L. Rev.* 2029 (2004); Ahdieh, Dialectical Regulation, *supra* note 37; Paul Schiff Berman, Global Legal Pluralism, 80 *S. Cal. L. Rev.* 1155 (2007); Daniel C. Esty, Revitalizing Environmental Federalism, 95 *Mich. L. Rev.* 570 (1996); Osofsky & Levit, The Scale of Networks?, *supra* note 33; Judith Resnik, Afterword: Federalism's Options, 14 *Yale L. & Pol'y Rev.* 465, 473 (1996); Judith Resnik, Foreign as Domestic Affairs: Rethinking Horizontal Federalism and Foreign Affairs Preemption in Light of Translocal Internationalism, 57 *Emory L.J.* 31 (2007) [hereinafter

important virtues of jurisdictional redundancy and intersystemic governance models in which multiple legal and regulatory authorities weigh in regarding the same acts and actors. And, like Cover, they argue that such jurisdictional redundancies are not just a necessary accommodation to the reality of a world of multiple authority; they may actually be beneficial. In short, we can view legal pluralism (to use the parlance of computer science) as a feature and not a bug. What would such a hybrid jurisprudence look like? To explore this question, I turn to *Medellin v. Texas*,[43] in which the U.S. Supreme Court intervened in a dispute among the International Court of Justice, the George W. Bush administration, and the State of Texas regarding the appropriate role of the Vienna Convention on Consular Relations[44] in a state capital murder case. Although the Supreme Court majority emphasized the need to delineate clear, nonoverlapping spheres of international, national, and state authority, I draw on the insights of cosmopolitan pluralism to proffer a more flexible approach to the interaction of multiple sources of law implicated by the case.

Disputes about the role of the Vienna Convention on Consular Relations[45] in state capital cases arose in several different forms during the period from 1998–2008, a period during which the U.S. Supreme Court addressed the issue on at least four different occasions,[46] and the questions presented have generated a large scholarly debate. Essentially, this contentious line of cases arose because for years various state authorities

Resnik, Foreign as Domestic Affairs]; Judith Resnik, Law's Migration: American Exceptionalism, Silent Dialogues, and Federalism's Multiple Ports of Entry, 115 *Yale L.J.* 1564 (2006); Robert A. Schapiro, Toward a Theory of Interactive Federalism, 91 *Iowa L. Rev.* 243 (2005).

43 552 U.S. 491 (2008).

44 Vienna Convention on Consular Relations and Optional Protocol on Disputes, Apr. 24, 1963, 21 U.S.T. 77, 596 U.N.T.S. 261 [hereinafter Vienna Convention on Consular Relations].

45 Vienna Convention on Consular Relations, *supra* note 44.

46 *Medellin v. Texas*, 552 U.S. 491 (2008); *Sanchez-Llamas v. Oregon*, 548 U.S. 331 (2006); *Fed. Republic of Germany v. United States*, 526 U.S. 111 (1999); *Breard v. Greene*, 523 U.S. 371 (1998).

around the United States, in processing suspects in their respective criminal justice systems, ignored (or were unaware of) their obligations under the Vienna Convention on Consular Relations, which the federal government had signed in 1963.[47] The convention, among other things, requires that foreign nationals arrested in a signatory country be able to contact their consulate in order to coordinate their defense or otherwise help in negotiating a foreign legal system.[48] In each of the cases, a foreign national was arrested in the United States, the relevant consulate was not notified, and the suspect was subsequently found guilty at trial and sentenced to death.

Under the terms of the Vienna Convention, the International Court of Justice (ICJ) is the legal entity given jurisdiction to adjudicate claims concerning alleged violations of the convention.[49] In early 2003 Mexico initiated proceedings against the United States in the ICJ, claiming that among those sentenced to death in violation of their Vienna Convention rights were fifty-two Mexican nationals.[50] The United States participated in the proceedings before the ICJ, which ultimately ruled, in the *Avena* case, that the United States had breached Article 36(1)(b) of the Vienna Convention in the cases of fifty-one of the Mexican nationals by failing "to inform detained Mexican nationals of their rights under that paragraph" and "to notify the Mexican consular post of the[ir] detention."[51] The ICJ held further that in forty-nine of the cases, the United States had also violated its obligations under Article 36(1)(a) "to enable Mexican consular officers to communicate with and have access to their nationals, as well as its obligation under paragraph 1(c) of that Article regarding

[47] Vienna Convention on Consular Relations, *supra* note 44.

[48] *Id.* art. 36.

[49] Optional Protocol Concerning the Compulsory Settlement of Disputes, Vienna Convention on Consular Relations, *supra* note 44.

[50] Case Concerning Avena and Other Mexican Nationals (*Mex. v. U.S.*), 2004 *I.C.J.* 12, 17, 23 (Mar. 31).

[51] *Id.* at 53–4, 71–2.

the right of consular officers to visit their detained nationals."[52] Finally, the ICJ held that in thirty-four cases, the United States had also violated its obligation under Article 36(1)(c) "to enable Mexican consular officers to arrange for legal representation of their nationals."[53]

Significantly, however, the ICJ denied Mexico's request for annulment of the convictions and sentences.[54] Instead, the ICJ required only that U.S. courts provide review and reconsideration of the convictions and sentences of the fifty-one Mexican nationals to determine whether the violations of the Vienna Convention prejudiced the various defendants' ability to obtain a fair trial.[55] All that was necessary, according to the ICJ, was that this review be conducted as part of a "judicial process" and could not be barred by any procedural default doctrines that might otherwise thwart such review.[56]

At the time the ICJ decision was issued, Jose Ernesto Medellin's application for a certificate of appealability from the denial of federal habeas relief was pending before the Fifth Circuit. Medellin, having been convicted in Texas state court, was one of the Mexican nationals whose case was addressed in the ICJ's judgment. Nevertheless, the Fifth Circuit, following its own precedent, ruled that Article 36 of the Vienna Convention was not judicially enforceable.[57] Medellin petitioned for certiorari, which the U.S. Supreme Court granted.[58]

While the appeal in the U.S. Supreme Court was pending, then President George W. Bush issued a signed, written determination that state courts must provide the required review and reconsideration to the fifty-one Mexican nationals named in the ICJ judgment, including

[52] *Id.* at 54, 71–2.
[53] *Id.* at 54–5, 71, 72.
[54] *Id.* at 60–1.
[55] *Id.* at 72.
[56] *Id.* at 65–6.
[57] *Medellin v. Dretke,* 371 F.3d 270, 280 (5th Cir. 2004).
[58] *Medellin v. Dretke*, 543 U.S. 1032 (2004).

Medellin, notwithstanding any state procedural rules that might otherwise bar review of their claims.[59] The president declared:

> I have determined, pursuant to the authority vested in me as President by the Constitution and laws of the United States, that the United States will discharge its international obligation[s] under the decision of the International Court of Justice in [*Avena*], by having State courts give effect to the decision in accordance with general principles of comity in cases filed by the 51 Mexican nationals addressed in that decision.[60]

That same day, the United States filed an amicus brief in Medellin's case stating that the United States had a "paramount interest in prompt compliance" with the ICJ judgment.[61] Specifically, the president had determined that compliance would "serve [] to protect the interests of United States citizens abroad, promote[] the effective conduct of foreign relations, and underscore[] the United States' commitment in the international community to the rule of law."[62] The United States stressed that "[c]onsular assistance is a vital safeguard for Americans abroad, and the government has determined that, unless the United States fulfills its international obligation to achieve compliance with the ICJ *Avena* decision, its ability to secure such assistance could be adversely affected."[63]

Moreover, the U.S. brief stated that pursuant to the president's determination, an individual Mexican national named in the judgment "may file a petition in state court seeking [the] review and reconsideration [ordered by the ICJ], and the state courts are to recognize" the ICJ decision.[64] In such a case, "a state court would not be free to reexamine

[59] Memorandum from George W. Bush to the Attorney General (Feb. 28, 2005), app. 2 to Brief for the United States as Amicus Curiae Supporting Respondent, *Medellin v. Dretke*, 544 U.S. 660 (2005)(*No.* 04–5928), 2005WL 504490.

[60] *Id.*

[61] Brief for United States as Amicus Curiae Supporting Respondent, *supra* note 59, at 41.

[62] *Id.*

[63] *Id.*

[64] *Id.* at 42.

whether the ICJ correctly determined the facts or correctly interpreted the Vienna Convention."[65] Finally, state procedural rules that might otherwise prevent a state court from giving effect to the ICJ judgment "must give way."[66]

The U.S. Supreme Court dismissed certiorari as improvidently granted, "[i]n light of the possibility that the Texas courts [would] provide Medellin with the review he seeks pursuant to the *Avena* judgment and the President's memorandum."[67] The Court did, however, note that it could once again review the case if further proceedings did not provide Medellin with the relief he sought.[68]

Back before the Texas Court of Criminal Appeals, the issue became whether Medellin's habeas petition was barred by Texas Criminal Procedure law regulating applications by petitioners who have previously sought postconviction relief. Medellin argued that the ICJ judgment and the president's determination to comply with it constituted binding federal law that, by virtue of the supremacy clause of the U.S. Constitution, preempted any inconsistent provisions of Texas law.[69] Meanwhile, the United States, as amicus curiae, urged the Texas court to grant Medellin the review and reconsideration he sought, on the ground that the president's determination constituted preemptive federal law.[70]

Nevertheless, on November 15, 2006, the Texas court dismissed Medellin's application, holding that Texas law barred the petition and that neither the ICJ decision nor the president's determination preempted or superseded local law.[71] The U.S. Supreme Court ultimately agreed.[72]

[65] *Id.* at 46.

[66] *Id.* at 43.

[67] *Medellin v. Dretke,* 544 U.S. 660, 666 (2005) (per curiam).

[68] *Id.* at 664 n.1.

[69] He also argued that, in any case, he satisfied the requirements of the Texas law. *Ex parte Medellin,* 223S.W.3d 315, 324 (Tex. Crim. App. 2006).

[70] Brief for United States as Amicus Curiae at 49–50, *Ex parte Medellin,* 223 S.W.3d 315 (No. AP-75, 207), 2005 WL 3142648.

[71] *Ex parte Medellin,* 223 S.W.3d at 351–2.

[72] *See Medellin v. Texas,* 552 U.S. 491 (2008).

The six-member majority sought to draw clear lines between the spheres of authority at issue in the case. In this vein, the Court first held that while an international treaty may create an international commitment of sorts, it is not binding domestic law unless the treaty is explicitly implemented through domestic regulation or ratified by Congress as a "self-executing" treaty. Second, with regard to the presidential order, the Court similarly sought to define clear lines of authority, ruling that neither the president's power under the treaty itself, nor his power to conduct foreign affairs, nor his power to "take care" that laws are faithfully executed authorized the president to turn a non-self-executing treaty into a self-executing treaty, absent congressional action. Thus, given the lack of international or presidential authority in the matter, the Court held that Texas was free to ignore both the ICJ ruling and the presidential directive. The Court's approach envisions no interaction among multiple sources of law, no interplay among multiple pronouncers of law, and no accommodation to the multiple interests at stake.

In contrast, a cosmopolitan pluralist approach would, first of all, seek to preserve spaces for interaction among the various communities involved. Such an approach would eschew the position put forth by hardline international law triumphalists that the violations of the Vienna Convention necessarily invalidate all the various convictions, regardless of Texas law on the matter. But a pluralist would also reject the hardline sovereigntist idea that Texas should focus only on its own law and pay no attention to the Vienna Convention or the pronouncements of the ICJ. And finally, the Bush administration's efforts simply to take the issue away from the state by ordering adherence to the ICJ decision also would be rejected.

So, what would we be left with? Let us start with the ICJ. In a cosmopolitan pluralist account, the ICJ does not necessarily trump all other decision makers simply because it is an international body enforcing universalist treaty-based norms. Instead, the ICJ should take seriously the prerogatives and interests of other relevant communities and only squelch those other communities if it justifies why it needs to act jurispathically by attempting to kill off competing views.

This is precisely what the ICJ in *Medellin* did, discussing at length the need for an interlocking and reciprocal system of consular rights. In addition, the tribunal took seriously the competing claims to a limited sphere of local autonomy. As with the margin of appreciation doctrine of the European Court of Human Rights, the ICJ attempted to be restrained in imposing its international norm, thereby trying to leave as much space as possible for local variation. Accordingly, the ICJ denied Mexico's request to invalidate the convictions altogether. Instead, the ICJ decision asks only for a serious judicial consideration of possible prejudice. Finally, using a cosmopolitan pluralist analysis, the ICJ decision is more justifiable if it is giving voice to the norms of communities that are not necessarily represented adequately in other fora, because they either are not parties to the suit or have no centralized voice. Here, for example, the communities who might care about reciprocal consular rights (U.S. citizens who travel abroad, potential immigrants who may be more reluctant to enter the country for fear of becoming trapped in the criminal justice system, and so on) are dispersed and have no real ability to advance their interests. Similarly, there were significant voices within Texas itself who may have wanted these consular rights to be protected. Indeed, in 2006 Texas attorney general Greg Abbott implemented a comprehensive set of reforms at the local level to try to make sure Vienna Convention rights are protected in the future.[73] The ICJ decision can, therefore, be seen as representing the interests of these alternative epistemic communities.

Turning to Texas, from a cosmopolitan pluralist point of view, a decision of the ICJ is not necessarily binding absent a local decision to be bound. That does not mean, however, that the ICJ decision should be ignored altogether. Rather, the Texas Court of Criminal Appeals should

[73] *See* Greg Abbott, Attorney Gen. of Tex., Magistrate's Guide to Consular Notification under the Vienna Convention (2006), *available at* http:// www.oag.state.tx.us/AG_Publications/pdfs/vienna_guidebook.pdf. For further discussion of local governmental and nongovernmental initiatives to increase compliance with the Vienna Convention, *see* Janet Koven Levit, Sanchez-Llamas v. Oregon: The Glass Is Half Full, 11 *Lewis & Clark L. Rev.* 29, 40–6 (2007).

treat the ICJ decision similarly to the way it might think about recognizing any other foreign judgment. And, as previously discussed, foreign judgments are often recognized and routinely enforced.[74]

Thus, if we acknowledge the importance of the values effectuated by strong judgment recognition, we will necessarily reject the idea that Texas is simply unable to enforce the ICJ judgment just because the local procedural default rule would have barred the Texas court from hearing the appeal had it gone directly to the court. Instead, there will always need to be engagement with the foreign statement of norms; one could not simply reject the foreign as alien and therefore place it automatically beyond consideration.

In order to see an example of how this sort of engagement might work, consider the 2004 decision of the Oklahoma Court of Criminal Appeals in a similar Vienna Convention case, *Torres v. Oklahoma*.[75] Responding to an identical ICJ order, the court stayed a pending execution and remanded the case for an evidentiary hearing to determine, in part, whether Torres was "prejudiced by the State's violation of his Vienna Convention rights."[76] The governor commuted Torres's sentence to life in prison without parole later that day.

Although a hardline sovereigntist might see the Oklahoma court's deference to the ICJ decision as inappropriate and an abdication of the autonomy of the Oklahoma courts, looking at the decision from a cosmopolitan pluralist perspective helps to clarify the issues at stake. Indeed,

[74] In most areas of law, U.S. courts have generally enforced foreign judgments as a matter of comity. *See* Mark D. Rosen, Exporting the Constitution, 53 *Emory L.J.* 171, 176 (2004) (noting that, since the nineteenth century, "the United States has been at the vanguard of enforcing foreign judgments"). The Second Restatement codifies this idea, noting that a "judgment rendered in a foreign nation will, if valid, usually be given the same effect as a sister State judgment." *Restatement (Second) of Conflicts of Law* §117, cmt. c (1971). Moreover, validity is based only on whether the court that rendered judgment had proper personal jurisdiction over the parties and utilized procedures that were not inherently unfair. *Id.* § 92.

[75] *Torres v. State* (*Torres II*), No. PCD-04–442, 2004 WL 3711623 (Okla. Crim. App. May 13, 2004).

[76] *Id.* at *1.

thinking of *Medellin* and *Torres* using a judgment recognition frame encourages courts to consider the normative community that the ICJ decision represents. This normative community, significantly, includes the United States. Indeed, the Optional Protocol to the Vienna Convention, which makes the ICJ the venue to consider all "[d]isputes arising out of the interpretation or application" of the Convention,[77] was not only ratified but also drafted (and championed) by the United States in the first place.

Thus, as Judge Chapel wrote in a special unpublished concurrence to the Oklahoma Court of Criminal Appeals decision,[78] the United States freely and consensually signed and ratified the Vienna Convention, including the Optional Protocol, creating binding, contractlike legal obligations between the United States and other state parties. The Court of Criminal Appeals was therefore "bound by the Vienna Convention and Optional Protocol" and was obligated "to give effect" to both.[79] And the ICJ decision, because it was a "product of the process set forth in the Optional Protocol," deserved, according to Judge Chapel, the "full faith and credit" of the Court of Criminal Appeals.[80] By conceiving of the ICJ decision's force in terms of judgment recognition, Judge Chapel was able to stave off concerns about encroachments on local state sovereignty.

In contrast, the concept of sovereignty is unhelpful to resolve the Texas (or Oklahoma) case because there is no monolithic set of "state interests" to be effectuated; there are myriad voices within Texas. Texas must interact with the world, its citizens go abroad and might well want their consular notification rights honored, the Texas attorney general has actively attempted to educate local law enforcement concerning Vienna

[77] Optional Protocol Concerning the Compulsory Settlement of Disputes, Vienna Convention on Consular Relations, *supra* note 44.

[78] *See Torres v. State* (*Torres II*), No. PCD-04–442, 2004 WL 3711623, at *2 (Okla. Crim. App. May 13, 2004) (Chapel, J., concurring).

[79] *Id.*

[80] *Id.* at *3.

Convention rights, and so on. In addition, the procedural default rule at issue here was most likely not enacted specifically with foreign defendants in mind. As previously discussed, legislatures are rarely focused on international or transnational disputes when they enact such statutory rules. And even when legislators actually consider activities abroad, they do so to pursue domestic policy priorities, with little consideration of multistate implications.[81] Thus, a choice-of-law regime that only offers two options (the home state or the foreign one) improperly insists on judging citizens according to a single state norm in a world where those citizens affiliate with multiple states or nations. Indeed, the mere fact that a dispute is multinational necessarily means that it implicates interests that are different from those of a purely domestic dispute. Accordingly, judges should consider these added factors and craft rules on the basis of a variety of national and international legal norms. Here, there are obviously many additional interests at play to distinguish the case from a purely domestic one, including concerns about diplomacy, foreign relations, citizens abroad, the federal government's stated interest in compliance with the ICJ order, and so on.

Finally, as noted previously, the ICJ did satisfy the two requirements for the sort of intersystemic jurisdictional assertions that should command deference. First, it provided a detailed justification for its decision to intervene in an otherwise seemingly "local" criminal case. Second, it issued a very limited order, not attempting to overturn the convictions in toto, but instead simply asking for a further evidentiary hearing. Thus, the ICJ attempted a nuanced balance of international and local interests, and the decision therefore deserves a similar kind of deference and accommodation from the Texas court. Indeed, once the distorting filter of Texas's purported sovereign power is put aside, this seems to be a relatively easy call.

And what about the federal government? From a cosmopolitan pluralist perspective, the Bush administration was wrong on both parts of

[81] *See* Graeme B. Dinwoodie, A New Copyright Order: Why National Courts Should Create Global Norms, 149 *U. Pa. L. Rev.* 469, 548–9(2000).

its argument. First, contrary to the solicitor general's contention before the U.S. Supreme Court, the ICJ decision should be deemed applicable to the states (at least in the judgment recognition sense described previously), regardless of the position of the executive branch. Second, to the extent that the administration relied on a preemption or supremacy rationale to justify trumping the Texas procedural bar, such a rationale would not be sufficient from a cosmopolitan pluralist perspective, unless it were accompanied by a strong normative statement as to why the federal interest must trump state interests. Such a justification was not a part of the executive statement at issue in *Medellin*. In addition, a pluralist would not allow any automatic supremacy argument to win the day. This is in contrast to a strand of U.S. Supreme Court doctrine, discussed previously, that has interpreted the U.S. Constitution to contain an implicit foreign affairs preemption doctrine that cuts off the interplay of federal and local authority.[82] In these cases, the Court has refused to allow localities to take actions that were deemed to encroach on the exclusive national prerogative to conduct foreign affairs. Yet, as Judith Resnik has argued, lost in this approach is the idea that "[n]on-uniformity is a predicate of federalist systems, which can impose a national norm but which ought to be dedicated to local divergence whenever tolerable."[83] From a cosmopolitan pluralist perspective, simply asserting foreign affairs pre-emption should not allow the federal voice automatically to drown out the voice of states (at least without further justification).

The *Medellin* case has now been decided by the U.S. Supreme Court, and although positivists view such a decision as the "final" word on this

[82] *See Am. Ins. Ass'n v. Garamendi*, 539 U.S. 396 (2003) (striking down California law requiring insurance companies doing business in California to disclose any business activities in Europe during the Nazi Holocaust); *Crosby v. Nat'l Foreign Trade Council*, 530 U.S. 363 (2000) (prohibiting Massachusetts from banning state expenditures on imports made with forced labor); *Zschernig v. Miller*, 389 U.S. 429 (1968) (striking down Oregon statute that had the effect of preventing a resident of East Germany from inheriting property probated in the state). For a discussion of these cases, *see* Resnik, Foreign as Domestic Affairs, *supra* note 42.

[83] Resnik, Foreign as Domestic Affairs, *supra* note 42, at 86.

dispute, pluralists know that no statement of law, no matter how seemingly authoritative, is ever really final. Thus, the conversation will go on. Moreover, the Vienna Convention and the ICJ decision will continue to have an impact, regardless of the Supreme Court, because local law enforcement authorities around the country are now cognizant of their obligations in a way that they were not fifteen years ago.[84] Indeed, the U.S. State Department maintains a Consular Notification and Outreach Division specifically to help educate local prosecutors and police officers of their obligations under the Vienna Convention.[85] Thus, cosmopolitan pluralism recognizes the tangible, day-to-day ways in which international law is "brought home,"[86] sometimes regardless of official legal pronouncements.

Recognizing the Judgments of Ethnic Communities

A cosmopolitan pluralist perspective on conflict of laws would take seriously the fact that even citizens of a nation-state may have strong ethnic ties with a "homeland" that are sufficiently significant to warrant application of the ethnic group norm rather than the state-based one. The relevant question in such cases would be whether the applicable community affiliation is more appropriately deemed to be the community of current residence or the ethnic identity.

For example, Anupam Chander has written about the fact that many members of the Indian-American diaspora purchase bonds issued by their home country of India.[87] The purchase of these bonds obviously reflects the ongoing tie these members of the Indian diaspora feel for their "homeland." Thus, using a cosmopolitan pluralist framework, one might argue that, even when these bonds are purchased in the United

[84] Levit, *supra* note 73, at 41–6.

[85] *See id.* at 42–3 (describing the work of the division).

[86] *See, e.g.*, Harold Hongju Koh, Address, The 1998 Frankel Lecture: Bringing International Law Home, 35 *Hous. L. Rev.* 623, 641–2 (1998).

[87] *See* Anupam Chander, Diaspora Bonds, 76 *N.Y.U. L. Rev.* 1005 (2001).

States, the purchases should be governed by Indian, rather than U.S., securities laws because the bond sale reflects a substantive (and voluntary) tie between the purchasers and the Indian government.

Of course sometimes, particularly in multiethnic states with uncertain or unstable political sovereignty, we may see dueling legal systems operating among different ethnic populations within the same territorial space. Indeed, as previously discussed, some of the classic pluralist literature focused on the interaction of colonial and indigenous legal systems in the African colonies. More recently, Elena Baylis has written about the two parallel court systems currently operating in Kosovo, one Serbian and the other largely Kosovar Albanian and controlled by the United Nations Administration Mission in Kosovo (UNMIK).[88] Baylis notes that "for the people of Kosovo these parallel systems create legal uncertainty and conflict on a basic, day to day level."[89] Because the systems do not recognize each other's judgments and do not share court files, records of land titles, births, deaths, marriages, or divorces, even run-of-the-mill civil matters must be pursued in both courts, leading to conflicting judgments, speculation, and arbitrage. Meanwhile criminal suspects may face trial in both courts.

Moreover, as Baylis observes, Kosovo's parallel courts present in an acute form a problem facing many divided societies:

> How, for example, should Mexico treat decisions from Zapatista courts? What about the judgments of religious and indigenous authorities in Iraq, Afghanistan, Nigeria, or France? How can long-divided societies like the Greek and Turkish administrations in Cyprus incorporate each other's judicial determinations if they are eventually unified?[90]

Significantly, while bringing to justice those accused of the worst human rights abuses has long been the focus of international law scholars and

[88] Elena Baylis, Parallel Courts in Post-Conflict Kosovo, 32 *Yale J. Int'l L.* 1 (2007).
[89] *Id.* at 3.
[90] *Id.*

activists, the day-to-day operation of these plural legal systems and their resolution of more ordinary disputes may be just as important to the local population and may be an even more crucial element in the rebuilding of postconflict societies.

Although Baylis does not identify the problem she describes as one involving conflict of laws, she offers a solution grounded in a cosmopolitan pluralist conception of judgment recognition. While acknowledging that the competing claims to sovereignty in Kosovo are fundamentally political (or military) problems, she points out that, in real practical terms, the parallel courts have issued legal decisions for years now and will continue to do so. Thus, "for so long as people in Kosovo continue to rely on these decisions, past or present, questions of whether and how those judgments should be recognized and enforced is a legal question that must be addressed."[91] And significantly, in a world of plural norm creation, it is not necessary for courts to recognize each other's actual *legitimacy* or claims to *sovereignty* to recognize each other's legal *judgments*, at least in most day-to-day cases. Indeed, as Baylis argues, such negotiation of difference could actually provide a foundation for political compromise on the broader question of sovereignty.

Of course, in a land of intense ethnic rivalry and contest, some judgments may so reek of ethnic favoritism that enforcing the judgment will be anathema. But that is simply another form of the line-drawing problems discussed throughout the book. The crucial points to consider are, first, that many judgments do not implicate fundamental political or normative differences and can therefore be enforced easily, and, second, that the dialogue involved in considering recognition can help bridge gaps between communities and lead to broader political dialogue. In any event, such recognition regimes are essential in hybrid legal spaces simply to solve practical problems people encounter in their day-to-day lives. Accordingly, a cosmopolitan pluralist vision of judgment recognition, as discussed previously, will take seriously the systemic value of having a

[91] *Id.*

functioning, interlocking judicial system and therefore deny recognition only in those rare cases where the judgments are so tainted by bias or so contrary to local policy that they cannot be followed. And even then, the general norm of recognition would require explanation of, and justification for, any deviations from this norm. Such a mutual recognition regime poses one way of moderating the effects of political gulfs in these complex spheres of overlapping legal and quasi-legal authority.

AGAIN IT MUST BE EMPHASIZED THAT VIEWING THESE VARIOUS DISPUTES through a cosmopolitan pluralist conflicts lens will not solve the intractable problem of plural communities with plural norms. Indeed, in a plural world, eradicating normative conflict is not only impossible, it is undesirable. In the interaction between self and other, I follow Arendt and Young in accepting that we are strangers forever, living in a space of unassimilated otherness. Thus, I believe that conflict-of-laws doctrines are best understood not as seeking harmonization and convergence among the world's legal regimes. Rather, I view conflicts as both a celebration and negotiation of difference. Accordingly, even if, as some have suggested, the nation-state legal regimes of the world are increasingly converging and developing a world law, we would still need conflicts thinking so as to acknowledge and accommodate nonstate norms that may operate outside this harmonization process. Moreover, we would need conflicts as a way of emphasizing important normative differences that remain among the peoples of the world, rather than seeking homogenization. Of course, reaching *individual* resolutions to conflicts is what law does and has to do. But the point is that such individual resolutions must be reached with an understanding of and sensitivity to the cosmopolitan pluralist reality of which that decision is a part.

Adopting a conflicts framework, we can turn the gaze to the discursive interaction among a wide variety of norm-generating communities that are based on the entire panoply of multiple overlapping affiliations and attachments people actually experience in their daily lives, from the local to the global (including some affiliations not based on territory at all). In this vision, a jurisdictional assertion is part of an international and transnational process of community definition and norm creation. Moreover, the state need not only be seen as a jurispathic force that imposes its law and eradicates all others. Instead, the state, through a broader commitment to the governmental interest in being part of a functioning and interlocking global legal order, might actually be jurisgenerative, enabling recognition of, discussion about, and even deference to nonstate norms, at least some of the time.[92] And even when deference is impossible (because substantive agreement about norms is impossible), we may at least be able to develop a legal language in which the negotiation of difference can take place. As Stuart Hampshire has written, although we inevitably disagree about values, we might sometimes reach provisional compromises about procedures.[93] Therefore, we may find ways to "bear with" each other, as Arendt hoped, without needing to assume away normative difference. In any event, given a reality of hybrid legal spaces, where communities cannot avoid encounters with strangers both within and without, law's potential role as a site for communication across difference grows ever more important.

[92] In this sense, my argument may expand on Cover, who arguably did not see a jurisgenerative role for the state. *See* Robert C. Post, Who's Afraid of Jurispathic Courts?: Violence and Public Reason in *Nomos and Narrative,* 17 *Yale J. L. & Human.* 9, 14 (2005) ("Ultimately *Nomos and Narrative* denies the state a role in jurisgenesis because it is skeptical of the possibility of a jurisgenerative politics."). *But see* Judith Resnik, Living Their Legal Commitments: Paideic Communities, Courts, and Robert Cover, 17 *Yale J. L. & Human.* 17, 26 (2005) ("[U]nlike Robert Post, who reads Robert Cover as turning 'quite palpably away from the state' when he focused on the violence done in the name of court orders, I read Cover as endlessly fascinated with the interactions between the state and paideic communities – and with the potential for such interactions themselves to be jurisgenerative moments.") (footnotes omitted).

[93] *See generally* Stuart Hampshire, *Justice Is Conflict* (2000).

10 Conclusion

TRY AS SOME MIGHT TO AVOID IT, WE LIVE IN A HYBRID world. We cannot seal ourselves off from outside influence (and indeed any "we" we might conceptualize already contains outside influence within it). We cannot simply assert a normative position and expect it to triumph in a world of conflicting normative positions. And we cannot expect that a single universal normative position is likely to prevail either, except in limited spheres and for limited times.

The world is simply messier than many hope it will be. And that poses a particular challenge for law because law often seeks certainty and tends to assume fixed boundaries between those who are within and those who are without. Of course sometimes – perhaps often – such line drawing works out well enough to operate on a day-to-day basis. Thus, if I leave my house to go for a walk and get hit by a car, it makes some sense that local laws and local courts might apply to my suit against the driver. But even in that case, as soon as the driver alleges that she was out of control because of a defect in the design or manufacture of the car, then we are suddenly out of the local and addressing relationships between that accident and a global assembly line of component part manufacturers, multinational corporations, and multiple legal regimes. The unfamiliar other cannot be kept at bay.

Meanwhile, ideas seep across boundaries too. So if we want to trace the impact of legal norms, we cannot simply look at formal processes. We also need to trace influences that "foreign" legal ideas have in shaping legal consciousness or in providing leverage to local actors.

And finally, we need a more capacious definition of law so that we do not miss the hugely important influence of normative communities that, even without state sanction, can and do assert alternative normative universes, enforce order in certain spheres, and exert a strong hold on those who deem themselves bound by their judgments. Without such a broader conception, we will miss the way law actually operates in everyday life and retreat into a formalist, positivist conception of law that imposes exclusively from above, shedding nuance along the way.

Yet our discourse and our legal frameworks are too often trapped in a language of sovereignty with its purportedly clear lines of demarcation, its assumed allocation of authority, and its formalistic conceptions of legitimacy. Such a language cannot hope to guide us in a world of interdependence, inevitably permeable borders, multiple communities, and overlapping jurisdictions. Indeed, regardless of the positions one might adopt as a matter of political theory, the most important point to remember is that a total rejection of foreign, international, or nonstate influence and authority is unlikely to be fully successful in a world of global interaction and cross-border activity. Likewise, a model of universal harmonization ignores important and enduring normative differences across communities and is therefore unlikely ever to be either fully satisfying or fully successful.

Thus, in the face of hybridity, we can retreat and insist on a set of pure theoretical models hopelessly divorced from reality, or we can accept (and perhaps even celebrate) the potentially jurisgenerative and creative role law might play in a plural world order. Accordingly, instead of bemoaning either the "fragmentation" of law[1] or the messiness of jurisdictional overlaps, we should accept them as a necessary consequence of

[1] *See, e.g.*, U.N. Int'l Law Comm'n, Study Group on Fragmentation of Int'l Law, Fragmentation of International Law: Difficulties Arising from the Diversification and Expansion of International Law, U.N. Doc. A/CN.4/L.682 (2006) (finalized by Martti Koskenniemi).

the fact that communities cannot be hermetically sealed off from each other. Moreover, we can go further and consider the possibility that this jurisdictional messiness might, in the end, provide important systemic benefits by fostering dialogue among multiple constituencies, authorities, levels of government, and nonstate communities. In addition, jurisdictional redundancy allows alternative ports of entry for strategic actors who might otherwise be silenced.

A cosmopolitan pluralist perspective does not privilege one set of norms as somehow hierarchically superior and therefore able to dictate compliance. Instead, it recognizes the role of all legal pronouncements as fundamentally rhetorical, and it views the question of legitimacy not through formalisms such as sovereignty but rather on the basis of what statements come to be accepted as true over time. Thus, legitimacy becomes a sociological question about changes of legal consciousness, and a cosmopolitan pluralist legal system seeks to keep those multiple voices in dialogue with each other to the extent possible.

As noted at the outset, a cosmopolitan pluralist approach to mechanisms, institutions, and practices for managing hybridity is unlikely to satisfy anyone fully. Human rights advocates will prefer a stronger emphasis on universal norms. Those craving certainty in business transactions will prefer more focus on transnational and international harmonization. Those troubled that international agreements may override local environmental, labor, and consumer protection standards will resist giving any play to nonlocal norms. Indeed, the multiple ports of entry that can be used by those silenced elsewhere can also, of course, be used by the powerful to shop for norms.[2] And sovereigntists concerned about the primacy of the territorially based nation-state will reject giving nonstate

[2] *See, e.g.*, Lisa Conant, Individuals, Courts, and the Development of European Social Rights, 39 *Comparative Political Studies* 76 (2006) (describing advantages enjoyed by repeat players in navigating the European system); Daniel W. Drezner, The Power and Peril of International Regime Complexity, 7 *Perspectives on Politics*, 65–70 (2009) (arguing that powerful states can use the proliferation of regimes strategically to advance their interests).

norms a place at the table. Finally, some will see in my invocation of pluralism either an undue romanticization of local communities given the fact that such communities can sometimes be profoundly illiberal and repressive, or an undue romanticization of the international, which likewise can sometimes be profoundly illiberal and repressive.

My answer, I suppose, is that pluralism is messy, but it is the necessary condition of a deterritorialized world where multiple overlapping communities seek to apply their norms to a single act or actor. In such a world, universal harmonization is unlikely to be fully achievable even if it were normatively desirable. Likewise, insisting on local or state prerogatives against all incursions is impractical and takes no account of multiple community affiliations apart from the state. Hybridity is therefore a reality, and it is the task of scholars and policymakers to develop, evaluate, and improve the mechanisms, institutions, and practices for managing pluralism. Doing so emphatically does not commit one to embracing the norms of all normative communities in all circumstances. Indeed, each of us has political and normative commitments of our own, which will cash out differently depending on context.

The messiness of hybridity also means that it is impossible to provide answers ex ante regarding occasions when pluralism should be honored and occasions when it should be trumped. For example, we might ask, How do we know when a nonstate community has been constituted? Who is a member of a community and when will he or she be able to invoke that community's norms as part of a legal process? And which community norms are sufficient to rise to the level of law? This strikes me as the wrong set of questions to be asking because the whole point of a pluralist perspective is that there is no single answer to such a question. And one cannot find an external location where one can say "should" without trepidation. Thus, as noted throughout, such line-drawing questions can be exceedingly difficult, and every person or community will draw the line a bit differently depending on political interests and normative commitments. Moreover, any answer is inevitably both "local" and transient, because it will immediately be contested by other communities.

Indeed, part of the reality of pluralism is that no answer is ever final or followed by all. In a world of permeable borders, multiple affiliations, and overlapping interests, law is diffused in myriad ways, and the construction of legal communities is always contested, uncertain, and open to debate.

Here, my hope is only to orient thinking about all of these problems in terms of managing pluralism and to provide a set of examples in order to suggest the degree to which a wide variety of transnational and international regulatory problems can be conceptualized in this way. In addition, the processes, institutions, and practices surveyed provide a menu of options for communities seeking to manage hybrid legal spaces in the future. The advantage of this cosmopolitan pluralist approach is that, rather than seeking ways to solve problems of hybrid legal spaces quickly by, for example, arbitrarily localizing a transaction and then applying a territorially based norm, we will ask ourselves about other possible norm-generating communities that might have an interest in the question at issue and seek ways of effectuating various competing norms if possible. Moreover, when such accommodation is not possible, we will at least articulate the reasons why we cannot accommodate. Finally, in many instances the very existence of jurisdictional overlap and redundancy will create multiple ports of entry and therefore also provide the possibility of forging alternatives through an iterative and jurisgenerative process of dialectical interaction.

In the end, procedures, institutions, and practices for managing pluralism may at least sometimes be preferable because they can instantiate a social space in which enemies can be turned into adversaries. Of course, some may not seek shared social space and may instead wish simply to annihilate those with whom they differ. If enough people feel that way, war is the likely result, and the analysis here has little to say about communities that are in the midst of war. But for those willing to countenance the idea that multiple communities have norms that at the very least deserve a respectful hearing, mechanisms, institutions, and practices for managing pluralism hold out the possibility of forging provisional compromises. Moreover, by seeking to manage pluralism rather than eliminate it, we are more likely to preserve spaces for contestation, creative adaptation, and innovation and to inculcate ideals of tolerance, dialogue, and mutual accommodation into our adjudicatory and regulatory institutions. And as we address the reality of law beyond borders, preserving such hybrid spaces and inculcating such tolerant ideals may often be the best that law can do to create the possibility of peaceful coexistence in a diverse and contentious world.

Index

CPSIA information can be obtained at www.ICGtesting.com
Printed in the USA
LVOW100118210912

299540LV00002B/1/P

9 780521 769822